Crisis, Collapse, Militarism and Civil War

Crisis, Collapse, Militarism and Civil War: The History and Historiography of 18th Century Iran

EDITED BY MICHAEL AXWORTHY

OXFORD
UNIVERSITY PRESS

OXFORD
UNIVERSITY PRESS

Oxford University Press is a department of the University of Oxford. It furthers the University's objective of excellence in research, scholarship, and education by publishing worldwide. Oxford is a registered trade mark of Oxford University Press in the UK and certain other countries.

Published in the United States of America by Oxford University Press
198 Madison Avenue, New York, NY 10016, United States of America.

© Oxford University Press 2018

Library of Congress Cataloging-in-Publication Data
Names: Axworthy, Michael, editor, author.
Title: Crisis, collapse, militarism and civil war: The History and Historiography
of 18th Century Iran / [edited by] Michael Axworthy.
Other titles: History of eighteenth century Iran
Description: New York, NY : Oxford University Press, 2018. |
Includes bibliographical references and index.
Identifiers: LCCN 2017033642 | ISBN 9780190250324 (bb : alk. paper)
Subjects: LCSH: Iran—History—16th–18th centuries. | Civil war—Iran.
Classification: LCC DS292 .H55 2018 | DDC 955/.03—dc23
LC record available at https://lccn.loc.gov/2017033642

1 3 5 7 9 8 6 4 2

Printed by Sheridan Books, Inc., United States of America

CONTENTS

PREFACE

DAVID MORGAN

In the early 1980s, the late Professor Peter Holt invited me to contribute a volume to his projected series, 'A History of the Near East' in the Islamic period. There was to be a volume on the first period, from the origins of Islam until the mid-11th century. Holt would himself write a volume on the Arab lands from the 11th century till the Ottoman conquest. There would be another on the Ottoman Empire until the end of the 18th century (this was in fact never published), and then a volume on the whole of the Near East up to 1923. Other volumes were later added. This left Iran, or as we both preferred to call it, Persia, from the arrival of the Seljuks until the accession of the Qajar dynasty; and such was my assignment. It appeared in 1988, entitled *Medieval Persia 1040–1797*, with an updated edition being published in 2016.[1] It had long seemed to me that European periodization fitted very uneasily on to the history of the Middle East, and that the notion that 'modern' or perhaps 'early modern' history began with the 'Rise of the West', c.1450–1500, bore very little relation to what had happened, and had not happened, in Persia. Hence my deliberately provocative title, which was intended to suggest that there was a certain 'medieval' unity in the history of Persia between the mid-11th and the late 18th centuries, and that the country's 'modern' history in reality began with the impact of the West in the 19th century. I have tended to feel confirmed in this view by the persuasive argument of John Darwin, in a very remarkable book, that the 'Rise of the West' should in fact be dated somewhere in the 18th century, not as early as the 15th or 16th.[2]

My assignment did of course mean that my final chapter would need to be a treatment of Persia in the 18th century. Gene Garthwaite confessed, in his conference paper, that when he came to write his admirable one-volume survey, *The Persians*,[3] he proceeded straight from a chapter on the Safavids to one on the Qajars: in effect, he dealt with the 18th century in just a few pages at the end of his Safavid chapter. Such an expedient was not available to me. So I searched for what historians had written on the period. What I found was not very encouraging, as the 'Bibliographical Survey' at the end of my book demonstrates. I could manage a short paragraph on the published primary sources, but when it came to secondary literature, there was very little to which I could point, apart from some discussion of the significant developments in Twelver Shi'ism which had occurred at that time. The relevant and (so far) final volume of the *Cambridge History of Iran* had not yet been published.[4] Readers who wished to take their knowledge of 18th-century Persia further still had to be referred to two books by Laurence Lockhart: his biography of Nader Shah of 1938 and his study of the fall of the Safavid dynasty, published in 1958. The latter book seemed to be remembered chiefly because it had provoked a savage review article by Martin Dickson.[5] I have remarked elsewhere that that article 'as a whole stands as something of an object lesson in how not to review a book'.[6] That was in the context of a review of Rudi Matthee's excellent study, *Persia in Crisis: Safavid Decline and the Fall of Isfahan*,[7] the appearance of which means that no one need bother any longer, except for historiographical purposes, with Lockhart's book—or, I would suggest, with Dickson's intemperate denunciation of it.

If one discounted Lockhart's books, I was able to list only one outstanding recent book on the entire period: John Perry's *Karim Khan Zand: A History of Iran, 1747–1779*.[8] Karim Khan has generally been thought of as Persia's 'good ruler' (not that the competition for this title is especially strong); and Perry's book tended to confirm this positive impression, though it would still seem that even Karim Khan could be dangerous to be near at times. I concluded by mentioning Ann Lambton's celebrated article, almost the only recent study of substance on the non-religious history of the period, on 'The tribal resurgence and the decline of the bureaucracy in eighteenth century Persia', in the Naff and Owen collection.[9] I found this a persuasive discussion, which may have had something to do with the fact that Professor Lambton had been both my Persian teacher and my PhD supervisor, but I think her conclusions were generally accepted as valid at the time, and for long after. It may, however, be worth mentioning that historians especially of Inner Asia—but this would apply also to Persia—have tended to become a little nervous—perhaps more so than they need be—about explanation in terms of tribal organization since the appearance of the anthropologist David Sneath's book on the subject.[10] I do not, however, think that Professor Lambton would have been in any way affronted by Willem Floor's critical examination of her ideas in this volume. I am confident that— whether or not she agreed with Floor's criticisms—she would have been pleased to find that historical study of the period has made some progress, and indeed that her article, after forty years, was still considered worthy of assessment by a scholar of high standing in the field.

So when Michael Axworthy invited me to attend his conference on the 18th century, to participate, to chair a session, but not to have to present a paper, I agreed with alacrity and enthusiasm. And I was far from disappointed with the results, many of which are presented here to a wider audience. It was refreshing to discover that study of the period has indeed made considerable progress in the thirty years since I wrote my brief account of it.

In his introduction, Michael Axworthy quotes Sir Roger Stevens's dismissal of the period, in his generally splendid introduction to Persia, *The Land of the Great Sophy*, as 'horrible' and to be discussed 'with the greatest possible brevity'. I spent some time with Sir Roger, near the end of his life, in Shiraz in 1977. He had been British ambassador to Iran in the 1950s, and after retirement from the diplomatic service was vice-chancellor of Leeds University. It was very evident from conversation with him that he had a deep love of the country, and—as indeed his book demonstrates—that he knew a great deal about it, which he was able to present in a way that was both accessible and scholarly. So if that was his view of the 18th century, it should be taken seriously as an opinion that was, in its day, very widespread even among Iranophiles.

For Stevens, Nader Shah was 'a brilliant soldier but a hopeless ruler', who after his sack of Delhi 'seems to have continued a career of conquest for lack of anything better to do'.[11] Here, at least, perceptions have changed since Lockhart wrote his biography long ago. This is principally because two serious studies in English have appeared: Michael Axworthy's *The Sword of Persia: Nader Shah, from Tribal Warrior to Conquering Tyrant*[12] and Ernest Tucker's *Nadir Shah's Quest for Legitimacy in Post-Safavid Iran*.[13] Horrible as Nader Shah may have been—and he was not assassinated for no reason—it seems, in the light of what Axworthy suggests, that he should be given credit in at least two respects: that he inaugurated a kind of parallel to the European 'military revolution'; though this was not followed up after his death and that but for his rule, his military career, and his extensive if ephemeral conquests, it is very possible that Persia would have vanished from the map, its territories swallowed up by its predatory neighbours—Russians, Ottomans, and so forth. As Axworthy recognizes, this is 'What if?' history; though that seems to be an historical genre that has become more respectable in recent years than it used to be. But this particular specula-tion is at the very least plausible, as the disappearance, for more than a century, of Poland during the same period demonstrates.

So the reader will find, in these pages, convincing evidence that 18th-century Persia is in need of reappraisal and that that process has indeed begun, though there is still a long way to go. That does not, however, mean that, contrary to what was previously supposed, the century was one of sweetness and light. The impression given by the collection of papers is far from being a parallel to recent reassessments of Mongol rule in the 13th and 14th centuries, in which a much

more positive spin—far too positive at times, in my opinion—is put on the character and effects of Mongol hegemony in Persia and elsewhere. The economy, as
Willem Floor argues in his other paper, was reduced to dire straits. The population fell drastically. There were long periods of civil war. But as 15th-century
Italy showed, political stability is not necessarily a condition for cultural efflo-
rescence; and Sussan Babaie's paper provides convincing evidence that there
could, in 18th-century Persia, be significant developments in artistic culture.
The results of Nader Shah's conquest of Delhi were not all negative. And, as has
long been clear, religious change since the fall of the Safavids was of great and
lasting significance, not least because the state was no longer able to exercise the
degree of control over the religious establishment that the Safavids had sometimes been able to do; and even if such an attempt at control had been made, the
fact that several of the principal Shi'i centres of learning were in Ottoman Iraq,
not—except briefly during Nader Shah's conquest—under Persian sovereignty,
enabled Shi'i thought and practice to evolve independently. The results of the
struggle between Akhbari and Usuli Shi'is, with the Usuli school emerging tri-
umphant, were of immense long-term significance, and that remains the case in
today's Islamic Republic of Iran. So the 18th century deserves a great deal more
scholarly attention than it has usually received. This collection, and the conference that gave rise to it, show that most persuasively.

Notes

1. *Medieval Persia 1040–1797* (London & New York, 1988); 2nd edition (London &
   New York, 2016).
2. John Darwin, *After Tamerlane: The Global History of Empire since 1405* (London, 2007).
3. Malden, MA & Oxford, 2005.
4. Peter Avery, Gavin Hambly, and Charles Melville (eds), *The Cambridge History of Iran, Volume
   7: From Nadir Shah to the Islamic Republic* (Cambridge, 1991).
5. 'The Fall of the Safavi Dynasty', *Journal of the American Oriental Society* 82 (1962), pp. 503–517.
6. *Times Literary Supplement*, 7 December 2012, p. 9.
7. London & New York, 2012.
8. Chicago & London, 1979. Perry has since published another book, rather shorter than the
   first, on his subject: *Karim Khan Zand* (Oxford, 2006).
9. Thomas Naff and Roger Owen (eds), *Studies in Eighteenth Century Islamic History* (Carbondale
   & Edwardsville, 1977), pp. 108–129 and 377–382.
10. *The Headless State: Aristocratic Orders, Kinship Society, and Misrepresentations of Nomadic Inner
    Asia* (New York, 2007).
11. *The Land of the Great Sophy*, 3rd edition, 1979, p. 30.
12. London & New York, 2006.
13. Gainesville, 2006.

CONTRIBUTORS

Michael Axworthy
University of Exeter

Sussan Babaie
Courtauld Institute of Art,
   University of London

Willem Floor
Independent Scholar

Gene R. Garthwaite
Dartmouth College

Rudi Matthee
University of Delaware

David Morgan
University of Wisconsin

Andrew Newman
University of Edinburgh

Goodarz Rashtiani
University of Tehran

Sajjad Rizvi
University of Exeter

Giorgio Rota
Institute of Iranian Studies, Austrian
   Academy of Sciences

Ernest Tucker
US Naval Academy, Annapolis

NOTE ON TRANSLITERATION

For this book we have transliterated Persian words and names according to a simplified version (avoiding diacritic marks, and omitting the mark signifying *hamza*) of the scheme used by the journal *Iranian Studies*. Although some might have preferred another arrangement, we have done so in the belief that it is better to follow a single usage (as far as possible), that will sound familiar rather than alien to Iranians.

That said, there are bound to be some inconsistencies. Some are deliberate—notably the transliteration of names that have had a life of their own in western writing: Isfahan, mullah, Ali (rather than 'Ali) for example. Beyond that, there may be some unintended inconsistencies, and for those we can only apologize to the attentive reader.

Crisis, Collapse, Militarism
and Civil War

1

Introduction

MICHAEL AXWORTHY

In March 2013, when I welcomed participants to the small conference in Exeter that was the origin of most of the papers in this volume, I said that when I first set about organizing it, I had hoped to persuade perhaps one or two of the most distinguished names in this field to attend—but that instead I seemed to have got almost all of them. It was a good conference, and I believe it has led to an excellent collection of work on what has previously been a neglected area of study, contributing, I believe, to the emergence of the study of 18th-century Iran to a higher level of academic attention and understanding (a further conference, on Nader Shah, hosted by Giorgio Rota and Florian Schwarz at the Institute of Iranian Studies of the Austrian Academy of Sciences in Vienna in December 2016, took the process forward by another major step). The March 2013 event could only be held thanks to the generous grant support provided by the British Institute of Persian Studies (BIPS); so we have them to thank in turn for this volume also.

The events of the 18th century are of central significance to the modern history of Iran. There are various possible reasons for the previous neglect of the period, but here is one put forward by Roger Stevens in his book *The Land of the Great Sophy* in 1971:

> The eighteenth century is a horrible period in Iranian History—horrible to read about, horrible to disentangle, horrible to have tried to live in. . . . I propose to treat this grisly epoch with the greatest possible brevity.

After a time studying 18th-century Iran, one might be inclined to sympathize with Stevens's view—that it is better to look away, and to think of another Iran—a country of poetry and gardens, blue-glazed ceramic tiles, music, and carpets. That is a tendency—sometimes in turn as a reaction to those who caricature Iran today as a place of fanatics, terrorists, and warmongers. But for serious historians, it's not good enough. Many short histories of Iran (or books that in passing give an overview of Iranian history) skip over the 18th century, often jumping from a chapter on the Safavids to a chapter on the Qajars; sometimes with a cursory mention for Nader Shah and Karim Khan Zand.[1]

Although some writing in this volume rightly encourage us to look beyond these stark facts, it was a century of revolt, war, political disorder, anarchy, and lawlessness, disruption of trade, economic collapse, famine, emigration, and general misery. It has been estimated that the population of the country fell from around 9 million at the beginning of the century to perhaps 6 million at the end.[2] In the 1720s it seemed, after the collapse of Safavid rule in 1722, that Iran might disappear altogether, partitioned between her neighbours.[3] Within a few years the country surged back to make a bid for regional dominance under Nader Shah, but lapsed again into civil war after his untimely death in 1747. Nader's demise led to the founding of new states in Afghanistan and Georgia, formerly Persian territory, by two of his former officers. The civil wars lasted almost until the end of the century, albeit with an interlude of relative calm and good governance under another of Nader Shah's officers, Karim Khan Zand, who ruled the central territories of Persia from the mid-1750s until his death in 1779. In 1796, after more civil wars, Agha Mohammad Shah had himself crowned as the first monarch of the Qajar dynasty, which lasted until 1925.

Periods of crisis, turmoil, and trauma are often formative and decisive—they create opportunities as well as misery. They may reveal what previously have been hidden tendencies or underlying phenomena. They may serve as a terrible warning or as part of a founding myth for subsequent generations. It may also be that, because of the apparently overwhelming nature of negative political and economic phenomena, that other contrary considerations, perhaps minor in relative terms but nonetheless significant, go neglected. There are many aspects to this formative period of Iranian history that are disputed, controversial, or at least undefined—from the causes of the fall of the Safavid dynasty to the nature and significance of Nader Shah's period of rule, the significance of Karim Khan Zand, the nature of the civil wars in the latter part of the century after Karim Khan Zand's death (an episode, within this generally neglected period, which has received hardly any attention at all), and finally, the rise to dominance of Agha Mohammad Khan Qajar. In terms of the historiography, figures of the past like Marshall G. Hodgson and Ann Lambton cast a long shadow—particularly the latter, with her characterization of the period as one of tribal resurgence and bureaucratic decline. More recently, some have begun to question or at least qualify both Hodgson's Gunpowder Empire characterization of Safavid Iran,[4] and Lambton's analysis of tribal resurgence in the 18th century (on the latter, see Willem Floor's piece in this volume, and the comments in my own chapter). As Rudi Matthee says in the concluding remarks of his piece in this volume, it is important to look at Iranian history in its own terms, not as an adjunct or response to Europe, nor indeed necessarily as a backdrop to the Iranian present.

Beyond those, I raised two further points at the outset of the 2013 conference, involving the effects of the events of the 18th century on political and religious phenomena in the Qajar and later periods. In the Qajar period, Iran had, firstly, a relatively devolved governmental system, and, secondly, a clerical establishment that tended to stress the quietist tradition in Shi'ism. These were both important features of 19th-century Iran (with significant further consequences later), and both could be seen as developing out of the trauma of the 18th century. Is that correct, and can thinking of that kind be found in the contemporary sources? Is devolved government in some way a response to the perceived failure of Nader Shah's centralizing militarism (and that of Agha Mohammad Shah after him)? Was the quietism of the ulema in this period a response to the collapse of the Safavids and a perception of the complicity of the clergy in that collapse? Is there evidence for that? An aspect of the neglect of this period is that the roots of later phenomena in the period are unclear—something our conference set about beginning to change.

After the conference almost all the participants agreed to contribute papers to the edited volume of proceedings, based on the papers they delivered, and those contributions now form the chapters of this book. **David Morgan**, who participated in the conference and chaired a session, has contributed a penetrating and characteristically erudite preface.

With the writings of Ibn Khaldun, Marshall G. Hodgson, and Ann Lambton in the background (but also those of Anne Porter, Daniel Potts, and Pamela Crossley), **Gene Garthwaite's** chapter ' "What's in a Name?": Periodization and "18th-Century Iran" ' considers the justification for categorizing the 18th century as a distinct period in Iranian history, and in so doing presents and highlights some of the central features of the period. Is it to be viewed primarily as a phase in the post-Mongol history of Iran, or as the early modern baseline for European-influenced developments later? Either way, four phenomena are central to the period: relations between nomadic and sedentary populations, the development of clerical roles and thinking, the importance of rulership (with Nader Shah as an archetype), and the enduring vitality of the Persian language despite pressure from the Turkish spoken by tribal leaders and the Arabic of the clerics.

Rudi Matthee's chapter 'Historiographical Notes on the Eighteenth Century in Iranian History: Decline and Insularity, Imperial Dreams, or Regional Specificity?' seeks to bring some historiographical coherence to the rather chaotic 18th century in Iranian history. It suggests that rather than looking at the period in dynastic terms, as a tale of 'great men', or as a mere tribal interlude between the 17th-century Safavid and the 19th-century Qajar dynasties, it is more productive to view it in its own right. It puts forward three interpretive models for future research on this transitional period: a 'supranational' or regional approach, situating Iran in a broader Eurasian framework; a more narrow purview which perceives the country as a singular political and cultural entity, although not necessarily through a nationalist lens; and a regional perspective, in recognition of the fact that Iran at the time was not yet a nation-state but rather a conglomerate of poorly connected and relatively autonomous regional centers.

In my own chapter, 'The Awkwardness of Nader Shah', I consider some of the various ways in which Nader Shah's reign seems to be problematic; still often sidelined, ignored, or dismissed as eccentric (or described inaccurately). In his lifetime and for sixty years afterwards Nader was a well-known figure in Europe, and both Napoleon and Wellington studied his campaigns. But later in the 19th century memory of his exploits faded, and there is still in Western historiography today an impression that he just does not fit—whether because the violence and brutality of his period is distasteful, or because his military and political skill (and achievements) do not accord with an analysis that stresses the weakness and backwardness of Iran (and the Middle East region as a whole) in the 18th century, or for other reasons. This chapter considers the arguments for Nader Shah as an innovative, forward-looking figure, developing arguments I have presented elsewhere that his period of rule initiated developments that in Europe have been identified with the state-building phenomenon known as the Military Revolution. Iran did not eventually follow this path, because of the failure of Nader's reign and his dynasty. Instead Iran remained weak and succumbed to the domination of European powers in the 19th century. But Nader's period of rule suggests that other outcomes were possible.

Sajjad Rizvi's chapter 'Whatever Happened to the School of Isfahan? Philosophy in 18th-Century Iran' begins with the observation that since much of the literature on the history of 18th-century Iran is animated by a notion of decline, including in the cultural and intellectual fields, it is not surprising that philosophical trends are also seen in such terms: philosophy was supposedly killed off by the chauvinism and hostility of the late Safavid milieu, and the Afghan sack and occupation of Isfahan. However, this article argues that, in the midst of these challenges, philosophy grew, prospered, and became widely disseminated, taking advantage of the new patronage of the emerging regional centres of Qom, Mashhad, and the Iraqi shrine cities. After a consideration of the sources and contexts that we have in the period, the chapter takes a biographical approach analysing the contributions of five philosophers and Sufis in the course of philosophy in 18th-century Iran.

Andrew Newman's chapter, 'Of Mullas, Migration, and Manuscripts: Aspects of Twelver Shi'i Community Life in the 18th Century', considers the general historiographical position and questions the traditional take on it by assessing whether the picture of decline and collapse can be consistent with the significance of different trends of thought among the clerical community in Iran in the 18th century, as indicated by the relative popularity of significant texts, demonstrated by the numbers of those texts in manuscript collections.

Willem Floor has two chapters in this volume. The first, 'The Persian Economy in the Eighteenth Century: A Dismal Record', describes the economic situation of Persia around 1700, focusing on its human resources, the structure of the economy, and international trade, followed by a discussion of individual economic sectors. Thereafter, the changes in the economy after 1722 are discussed, when Persia was conquered and occupied by the Afghans, the Russians, and the Ottomans, followed by an almost perpetual state of war until the 1790s.

Willem's second chapter, 'Tribal Resurgence in the Eighteenth Century: A Useful Label?', addresses the tribal resurgence theory of Ann Lambton, first proposed in the 1970s. To gauge the usefulness of the term tribal resurgence and to better understand its alleged symptoms—decline of the bureaucracy and breakdown of central government—it is necessary to understand the context in which the term is used, i.e. within the structure of Iran's political system. Only then can we better understand these alleged symptoms, if these actually occurred. Therefore, this chapter briefly outlines the main characteristics of that political system, and then discusses whether the terms 'tribal resurgence' and 'decline of the bureaucracy' really enlighten us as to the functioning of the political system of 18th-century Iran.

Goodarz Rashtiani could not secure a UK visa to attend the 2013 conference, but his paper was read in his absence and appears here as a chapter: 'Iran-Russian Relations in the Eighteenth Century'. Its purpose is to analyse the features governing the relations between Iran and Russia in political, economic, and social spheres in the period from the fall of Isfahan (1722) to the rise of the Qajar dynasty (1796), and to examine the reasons for the difference in these relations compared to previous periods and Russia's actions in Iran's territory (the Caspian Sea and the Caucasus), with an emphasis on developments in both countries, the role of ethnic minorities and local khanates, and the effect of regional and international conditions on the relations between the two countries.

Giorgio Rota's chapter 'Persia 1700–1750: Some Views From Central Europe' offers brief descriptions and analyses of five virtually unknown 18th-century European sources on Persia written in different languages and spanning a period from the reign of Shah Soltan Hosein Safavi to the very first years of the reign of Fath-Ali Shah Qajar. It also presents the text of a sixth source, with commentary, from an unknown author, entitled 'Varij ragionamenti sopra lo stato presente, e la Crisi, in cui la Persia si trova', and advances the hypothesis that it could have been written by the famous Ragusan diplomat in Russian service,

Florio Beneveni. Taken together, the six sources not only provide interesting information on what has often been thought of as an obscure phase of Persian history, but also show that although interest in Persia at European courts may have decreased by comparison to the Safavid period, it was still considerable.

Ernest Tucker's chapter 'Iran and the Ottomans after Nader Shah: The Dorrani-Ottoman Exchange of Letters in Their Eighteenth-Century Iranian Context' discusses correspondence in early 1761 between Ahmad Shah Dorrani and Ottoman Sultan Mustafa III. Just after Ahmad Shah secured control over northern India, he sent Mustafa a letter proposing that they divide Iran between them, since Ahmad had also recently conquered Khorasan. Ahmad also asked the Ottomans to give him land in Medina on which to build a mosque.

Mustafa's response was measured. It called on Ahmad to give charity to the poor if he wanted to show piety, but did not offer to provide him any land in Medina for building a mosque. The letter also asked Ahmad to honour the 1746 Kordan Treaty, which had created the basis for peace between the Ottomans and Nader Shah.

The initial letter and its response are analysed in the 18th-century context of the rapidly changing political circumstances of Iran as well as the Dorrani and Ottoman Empires.

Sussan Babaie did not attend the 2013 conference in Exeter, but delivered a lecture on visual and aesthetic culture in the 18th century, and the effect on it of Nader Shah's Indian expedition, at the Annual General Meeting of BIPS in London in November 2015. I felt that paper could be the basis of a useful and appropriate addition to this volume, and so, since thankfully she agreed, a chapter from her appears here too, with the title 'Nader Shah, the Delhi Loot, and the 18th-Century Exotics of Empire'. The famous plunder of Delhi that followed the 1739 defeat of the Mughals at the Battle of Karnal by Nader Shah (r. 1736–1747) represents, in retrospect, the last world-conquering design to have risen from the Islamicate world before the 20th century. This article argues that Nader Shah's building projects, initiated after the Indian campaign, introduced a self-consciously historicized articulation of an Indo-Persian empire in the 18th century. His venture, echoing those of Timur in his post-Indian conquest, included looting of building materials and technologies that were made available by hundreds of Indian craftsmen and artists taken as booty and assigned to work with locals to make a spectacularly hybrid monument as the centerpiece of an urban retreat within a natural fortress—Kalat-e Naderi in northeastern Iran. Nader Shah's patronage represents an unexpectedly un-European visualization of the exotics of empire on the eve of colonial expansion.

These chapters constitute a wide-ranging, diverse, and innovative range of material, in a hitherto under-studied field. Unsurprisingly, there are some tensions and points of disagreement between the different chapters (one inconsistency is the use by some contributors of the term 'Naderi', where others prefer 'Afsharid' for Nader Shah's government and his dynasty[5]). At the conference in 2013, I said ruefully at the end of my own presentation that I believed I had managed to disagree with just about everybody present. As editor, I have seen it as my job sometimes to question points of disagreement with the authors and to draw their arguments out more fully, but not to try to conceal the disagreements, to remove them, or to try to paper over the cracks. History is, or should be, a dynamic and continuing activity. In my view disagreement, especially in an emerging field, is a sign of creative tension and vigour, rather than something to be disguised by false consensus.

Peterhouse, Cambridge
Palazzo Pallavicini-Rospigliosi, Rome
April 2017

Notes

1. Other, sometimes quite distinguished authors, perhaps betraying a similar lack of interest, make quite basic errors. So for example, Bernard Lewis in his book *What Went Wrong* (London, 2002) wrote (pp. 20–21) of the 'wars between Turkey and Iran that ended in 1730 with a victory for the even less modernised Persians'. The wars did not end then (they continued until 1745), and the phrase 'less modernised' is sloppy, to say the least. See also this volume pp. 51–53; Cronin and other examples.
2. Willem Floor, *The Economy of Safavid Persia*, Wiesbaden, 2000, p. 3; Charles Issawi, *The Economic History of Iran*, 1971, p. 20.
3. See Jeremy Black *Warfare in the Eighteenth Century* (London 1999), p. 38.
4. Rudi Matthee, 'Unwalled Cities and Restless Nomads: Firearms and Artillery in Safavid Iran', in *Safavid Persia: The History and Politics of an Islamic Society*, ed. Charles Melville (London, 1996).
5. Personally, I prefer 'Naderi' or 'Naderid' (in his 1973 article on the battle of Mehmandust, Chahryar Adle used the term 'époque naderie'—Chahryar Adle, *La bataille de Mehmandust (1142/1729)*, in *Studia Iranica* 2, Fascicle 2, 1973, pp. 234–241, p. 236). As I wrote in my book *Empire of the Mind* (p. 162), Nader was not in any simple sense a tribal leader, and in many ways remained an outsider throughout his life. He was not born into the leadership of the tribe from which he sprang (unlike Agha Mohammad Shah, who founded the Qajar dynasty, for example), and some of his most determined enemies throughout his career were fellow Afshars, who resented him as an upstart. From the beginning his followers were diverse, including especially Kurds and Jalayir tribesmen. Later he repudiated his (Afshar, Qezelbash) Shi'a heritage, turned Sunni (at least for public consumption), and depended most heavily on his Afghan troops. Like other Persian leaders (as well as Napoleon), he was close to his immediate family and promoted them politically, but in his wider connections he was an opportunist, and the term 'Afsharid', often applied to him and his dynasty, is misleading. The name Nader means 'rarity' or 'prodigy', and both are appropriate. He was *sui generis*. In his own time his officials described his regime in diplomatic documents as '*dowlat-e naderiyya*', and when this matter was discussed at the Nader Shah Revisited conference in Vienna in December 2016, where there seemed to be an emerging consensus in favour of the term 'Naderi' or 'Naderid', none of the experts present could recall a contemporary use of the term 'Afsharid'. But as in other respects, I have not tried to impose uniformity in this volume.

2

"What's in a Name?": Periodization and "18th-Century Iran"

GENE R. GARTHWAITE

> For on the surface history is no more than information about political events, dynasties, and occurrences of the remote past . . . It shows how changing conditions affected (human affairs), how certain dynasties came to occupy an even wider space in the world, and how they settled the earth until they heard the call and their time was up.[1]

> History refers to events that are peculiar to a particular age or race [people]. Discussion of the general conditions of regions, races, and periods constitutes the historian's foundations.[2]

Eighteenth-century Iran poses basic questions for historians. And the questions include: Why a century; then, how do you define that century? Is it just the century itself? Or is it a "short" century or a "long" one, any of which must be justified? Or, is the eighteenth century something of an interlude between the Safavids and the Qajars?

Most important, was there something unique to the eighteenth century that sets it apart from how Iran's history is conceived and organized—other than that there was no dominant dynasty? In other words, what were the continuities, the changes, and what brought those changes about: all questions that are central to history.

Eighteenth-century Iran easily divides along three fault lines: the collapse of the Safavids, the emergence and rule of Nader Shah Afshar, and post-Afsharid fragmentation with the rise of the Qajars. In comparison with the Safavid and Qajar periods, the eighteenth century is neglected in recent scholarship, except for a focus on Nader Shah. Michael Axworthy's *The Sword of Persia*, Ernest Tucker's *Nadir Shah's Quest for Legitimacy in Post-Safavid Iran*, and Willem Floor's use and translations from the Dutch East India Company have made recent, important contributions to our understanding of that pivotal leader in the eighteenth century.[3] But, how does Nader Shah fit into Iranian history? His extraordinary conquests and brutality hearken back to Timur; however, aspects of his rule and policies have been described by Axworthy and Tucker as modern; in other words, how may the eighteenth century, but especially Nader Shah and his impact, be conceptualized?

History, as noted in the first Ibn Khaldun quotation, his attempt to uncover past events, was about change and the factors that brought it about, and then about interpretation and analysis. The second quotation suggests the unique factors that defined a period of time and the general categories that brought about change. There is the period itself and how it relates to both the preceding and succeeding ones, especially how that period of time is both similar and different: the central historical problem of continuity and change—or, the short versus long term, the necessary versus the essential, the superficial versus that which is deeper—and again, what is change? What are its catalysts? Consequently, this chapter then is less about history, although that is a critical factor, but more about underlying concepts and organization.

Probably the most commonplace, and for many even the unconscious and broadest, division of history in the West is into grand epochs: ancient/classical, medieval, and modern. There is something of a consensus on the end of the ancient and beginning of the medieval period with the fifth-century fall of Rome, and then the start of the modern period at the fifteenth century with the age of exploration and the consequent changes that resulted. Agreement on the subdivisions in each of these periods is more variable, as is how these divisions relate to the constituent parts that make up essentially the European world and to the causes that brought about change—such as military defeat or imperial domination or economic factors. The assumptions that underlay such divisions include time/chronology, geography (physical, social, and economic), politics, and culture. Moreover, in the Western tradition, history is seen not only as a linear process but a progressive one as well. In the nineteenth century, when the economic factor looms large, the essential tripartite historical chronology was challenged by Marx, who argued for a process of distinct stages through which societies progress in sequence. Ibn Khaldun, on the other hand, also viewed history as stages, but he did not view history as linear but cyclical and with an emphasis on ethnicity, based on his knowledge of, and sources from, Arab and Maghreb history, all of which were framed within repeated generational spans. Famously, it is 'asabiyya, the social glue, that waxes and wanes within a group that brought it to power; the exception, of course, was in the instance of divine intervention through prophets. Explicit then in Ibn Khaldun's explanation of history is a concern for the causes of change that were essentially social, political, and cultural—only implicitly economic. Implicit, too, in Ibn Khaldun was history as process—a concern of anthropology and even the *longue durée* of the Annales School.

Marshall Hodgson, in his magisterial *The Venture of Islam* (Chicago, 1974) thought globally—beyond simply the West, for the tripartite division was seen by many as Eurocentric—to argue for a civilizational approach, where language and culture play key roles along with economic and political ones, but with the division of time into two Oikoumene–ecumene: the "Agrarian Age" (from Sumer through the seventeenth–eighteenth centuries) and the "Modern Technical Age" (post-eighteenth century).[4] In addition, in these macro-divisions of history, there were important comparative elements. Significantly within Islamic historiography, interest in comparisons can be found to a degree in Ibn Khaldun, but also in Rashid al-Din's great *Compendium*.[5] Within the Iranian tradition of writing history, and like Rashid al-Din, historians not only wrote history but recorded it. In this instance, they were not chroniclers so much as attempting to set the record straight so as to justify and embellish their patrons' roles. Here, in addition, is consciousness and a kind of morality at play.

Consequently, historians, and probably even chroniclers were/are concerned about their sources, contexts, and comparisons, conscious or not; for "setting the record straight," or interpretation; how their story fits in the larger narrative; accuracy; audience; and their own reputations, in terms of their patrons, be it the ruler, or in the case of more contemporary historians, their peers, university, or press.

Let's turn to another big-picture development that might prove useful for placing eighteenth-century Iran, and that is global history. Global historians utilize geographic space as much as time, but also in comparative terms, to move beyond exceptionalism and national history and to discern themes that cut across the borders of space and time. Interestingly, both Ibn Khaldun and Marshall Hodgson prefigure global history's development. Global historians critique and use other historical classifications including the tripartite division that characterizes "European" history, but move beyond it to the larger globe; here I am indebted to my colleague Pamela Crossley's "The Early Modern Paradox."[6]

First, Crossley, along with many others, argues not for European or East Asian history, but for Eurasian history—also, including North Africa and the African India Ocean littoral—where the supposed differences in material, cultural, and political history between Europe and China, in fact, can be strikingly parallel. Take for example the break between medieval and modern, or better still between medieval and early modern, and that the great division between east and west Eurasia may not be 1500, but possibly even 1800. The Mongol conquest across the thirteenth century and then the subsequent post-Mongol period, Crossley argues, sets the basis for the early modern period across Eurasia; here Iran, including the eighteenth century comes into play.

The Mongol legacy is described briefly in general terms in David Morgan's *The Mongols*,[7] and then in its second edition,[8] and in far greater detail in Reuven Amitai-Preiss and David Morgan's *The Mongol Empire & Its Legacy*.[9] In both of these admirable and invaluable studies, emphasis—quite correctly—falls on sources and direct historical causation; consequently, the Mongol, or post-Mongol legacy in Iran ends with the Ilkhans in the fourteenth century with no carry-over into Iran's subsequent fragmentation and possibly only into the early fifteenth century with the Timurids, but certainly not into the sixteenth century. (In Morgan and Amitai-Preiss, interestingly, there is carry-over into the possibility of a Mongol impact on the early Ottomans.) Morgan, however, observes: "The Mongols of Persia, probably always fairly small in number, were in due course absorbed into the Turkish tribal population which, apart from a brief interlude in the eighteenth century, provided Persia with its rulers until 1925."[10] Could this not make the Qajars Mongol successors? (This also brings up the issue of the number of Turks in, say, the classical Mongol period.[11]) The impact of the Mongols in Iran far exceeded their actual numbers.

I would like to generalize and broaden the notion of the Mongol legacy in a global context and then relate those generalizations to Iranian history, particularly the eighteenth century. The Mongol impact launched broad, common changes across Eurasia that resulted in what can be called "early modern," a distinct break with the medieval period. This break would include economic and material changes such as technology, industry, trade, and population movement that, in turn, resulted in cultural and political formations, including the rise of the state. Crossley continues:

> I would argue that cultural and political change can be explored in ways analogous to the studies done and ongoing respecting trade, economy, technology and industrialization. We are still in some ways dealing with the ideas that rationalism, secularism, neo-classicism/humanism, and other trends marked Europe off from the rest of the world in the later early modern period, ushering in modernity.[12]

And, Crossley contends that these changes can be observed across Eurasia as the result of the Mongol domination of much of the continent during the thirteenth and fourteenth centuries. "All the areas that felt the Mongol impact, whether controlled, dominated or threatened, experienced similar cultural changes that clearly presaged the early modern era."[13] Crossley continues on to identify six key cultural post-Mongol trends, among others, across Eurasia: (1) traditional elites gave way to new ones in government and education; (2) languages of the elites gave way to vernacular ones; (3) religious orthodoxies gave way to populist ones; (4) merchant and military elites challenged religious and government ones for high status; (5) regional political geographies were reshaped; and (6) the emergence of "simultaneous rulership."

In short, the Mongols precipitated profound change in at least the six categories noted above through interaction with Eurasian cultures; hence, the variations that one finds among them in what can be called "the early modern" period that brings to end the medieval one. These same developments are explored in Iran's near neighbor, the Ottoman Empire, by Cemal Kafadar[14] and Karen Barkey.[15] Elements of "early modern Iran" can be seen in certainly in the case of Shah 'Abbas I (1588–1629), and I would argue that the early modern "period" continues until the first quarter of the twentieth century, when the modern period of Iran's history begins under the Pahlavis—to make Morgan's point even more explicit.[16]

Here, I can feel Professor Lambton's presence and her assertion that such attempts of categorization are not history; I would answer that it better helps to understand history and historical processes. Continuity, or its modification through these changes precipitated by the Mongols is what I would like to turn to now, especially in eighteenth-century Iran. First, I shall leave economic factors such as trade and, to a degree, demographics to others. Second, I shall combine several of Crossley's six factors, for they are interrelated, under specific headings and will assume the vernacular language one as a given, when, and as a result of Mongol administration, Persian became dominant.

The movement of peoples (Crossley's #1, 4, and 5) typified Iran's eighteenth century and is emphasized by the Ghilzai Afghans' conquest and deposition of the last Safavid ruler, Shah Sultan Hosein (1694–1722). Nader Qoli Khan Afshar, from another Turkic tribal base and from a non-elite family, consolidated his power to emerge as shah (1736–1747), and yet another Turkic tribal confederation, the Qajars, would bring the century to its close under Agha Mohammad Khan, then shah (1779/1796–1797). In addition to the Afshars and the Qajars, there would be the short-lived diarchy of two other tribal leaders Karim Khan Zand and Ali Mardan Khan Bakhtiyari. Moreover, throughout the eighteenth century there was forced movement of peoples such as Nader Shah's often-cited transfer of Bakhtiyari and others from the Zagros to Khorasan, who after his death returned to their own territory. This too brief synopsis again brings to mind Ibn Khaldun, but with greatly compressed generations of domination from rise to stasis to fall.

For my argument regarding the post-Mongol impact on Iran, the role of the great tribal confederations and the movement of peoples, however, Daniel Potts' *Nomadism in Iran: From Antiquity to the Modern Era*[17] suggests another explanation. Potts' essential argument is that tribal pastoral nomadism came to Iran in two different and separate historical periods. The first marked the arrival of the Iranians themselves during the first millennium BC. It was the second movement in the eleventh century, with first the Turks and then the Mongols and Turks, that resulted in the pastoral nomadism that became associated with Iran. Potts notes that before the Turkic-Mongol impact, Iran was character-ized by an agrarian economy. (See also, Jean Aubin, *Deux Sayyids de Bam au XVe siècle* [Wiesbaden, 1956].) And Potts continues on to make the follow-ing arguments: nomads/tribes are both political and ideational; they describe complex relationships that are flexible and situational, hierarchical and egali-tarian, etc. (Similar arguments are to be found in Anne Porter's recent *Mobile Pastoralism and the Formation of Near Eastern Civilizations: Weaving Together Society* [Cambridge, 2012].) Essentially, Potts asserts that Iran's economy was agrarian and that agriculturalists also practiced animal husbandry with varia-tions depending upon geography, and that the two forms cannot be separated out one from the other and that they shared the same social and political spaces. Pastoral nomadism that we commonly associate with the Iranian plateau, and its tribal manifestation, such as the Bakhtiyari and the Qashqa'i, is a post-eleventh-century, essentially a post-Mongol, phenomenon.

Basically such confederations were sociopolitical composites with an empha-sis on animal husbandry. While the Qashqai and the Qajars were Turkic in ori-gin, sound references to their origins date only from the end of the fifteenth century. There are relatively few references to the Bakhtiyari before the Safavid period, and only in the eighteenth century do they seem to play much of a politi-cal role. And there are three central problems—and not just for the Bakhtiyari—here: sources, pastoral nomadism, and tribe as a political category, with the essential question as to whether or not named leaders in the latter sources were pastoral nomads themselves, or local large landowners or magnates or, even possibly, officials who exercised political or military skills—for example, Nader Shah, himself.

Or, were the references in sources to regions and their administration? Tribal confederations, moreover, were composites of various groups that did not necessarily share the same ethnicities and languages. Tribe–state relations are another topic that I won't develop here, but some tribal confederations were state created. In the nineteenth century, Naser al-Din Shah in effect created con-federations through his awards of titles, land grants, and tax exemptions. Potts and Porter effectively challenge archeologists, anthropologists, and historians to rethink their analyses of nomadism, and especially challenge them on projecting what is known in one time period back on an earlier one, which is Potts' starting point. Potts' essential postulation on the arrival of pastoral nomadism in Iran, however, serves to re-enforce the Mongol impact on Iran's economy and society.

Let us return to the issue of periodization. In the aftermath of the Mongols and Ilkhans, Iran would be politically fragmented until the emergence of the Safavids, and its economy and society dramatically affected. Even before the

Mongols, however, Iran had experienced vast movements of peoples from Central Asia, especially the Seljuqs with the arrival of Turks with their families and flocks. Here there seems to have been something of a "pull" effect—the attraction of pasturelands across northern Iran, especially in Azerbaijan and on to the northwest into Anatolia. The pull effect was probably a factor, too, in the Mongol expansion into Iran for pastures to support their cavalry as they moved further west. The "push" effect in the movement of populations could be seen in the disruption of fleeing and forced population movements during and after the Mongol conquests. Population push and pull effects, too, characterized post-Mongol Iran, notably, the transfer of populations from Safavid Caucasia, and then the flight of the Muslim populations into Iran during the Safavid period as the result of Russian expansion into that region.

These same phenomena continued to occur throughout the eighteenth century; moreover, there may have been a resurgence of pastoral nomadism in Iran in the absence of the state and with regional fragmentation. Tribalism was an important political manifestation of pastoral nomadism and under dynamic leaders reshaped Iran's political, even social geography.[18] This relates, of course, to the factor of shifting elites and can be seen in the Afghans crushing the Safavids, Nader Shah, Bakhtiyari-Zands, and Qajars in the eighteenth century.

Changing elites enter into Crossley's third characteristic of early modern Eurasia in the tension between "orthodoxies" or official religion and religious populism. Mongol leaders had not only played one religion against another, but within Islam favored sufis, for example, over and against the 'ulema and this same factor is seen dramatically in the rise of the Safavids to power, and the continuing challenge to the Shi'i 'ulema, especially by extreme Shi'i populism.[19] Safavid shahs themselves were caught between the two and derived legitimacy from both. Throughout the Safavid period, the 'ulema's official power increased despite competing factions within it[20] and to the extent that royal authority itself was being challenged.[21]

Moreover, the emergence of increased 'ulema authority also meant greater political, economic, and social power for them within and outside Iran. For example, after the loss to the Ottomans of the Shia shrine cities, the *atabat,* of Iraq, notably, Najaf and Karbala, they became vital centers of Shia learning and authority independent of Iranian governments. In addition, the collection of *khoms*, the fifth, by the 'ulema helped to make them economically independent of government as well.

The 'ulema, aside perhaps from the great tribal confederations such as the Qajars, were the institution that continued into the nineteenth century. And in the nineteenth century, 'ulema power and reach even increased in theory and practice when mujtahid domination—the Usulis—surmounted all challenges, notably from the Akhbaris, in the Iraq shrine cities. This process, however, began in the eighteenth century under the leadership of the great mujtahid, Agha Mohammad Baqer Whahid Behbahani (c.1705–1791). At this same time, popular Shi'ism found expression in the taz'iya and other forms that focused on the observances of the martyrdom of the early Imams. Religious dissent, including populist forms, would play out throughout the nineteenth and twentieth centuries.

Just as these religious tensions had roots in the Safavid era,[22] so did the issue of merchant and military elites challenge religious and government ones for high status—Crossley's fourth category. Lambton argued:

> The old social structure was modified during the eighteenth century . . . apart from the changed position of the tribes and the temporary decline in the influence and bureaucracy, the religious classes no longer enjoyed the power and influence which they held under the Safavids. . . . Whereas in earlier times it was frequently the *qazis* [sic] (judges) and other members of the religious classes who came forward as local leaders in times of crisis, in the eighteenth century it seems rather to have been the local officials, such as the *kalantars* [sic] and the *kadkhodas* [sic] of the cities and towns who emerged as such when the central administration broke down.[23]

What is especially important in examining simultaneous rulership in Iranian history is that many of the other of Crossley's five categories come together with it—her #6—to challenge age-old notions of government in which the ruler's authority combined religion and "secular" ideas—justice and the sword. This monism gave way to rivalry between these ideas and roles and the emergence of not just competing ideas but the very basis for new institutions was laid. Simultaneous rulership is, according to Crossley, ". . . a hallmark of Eurasian early modernity. I contrast this to the phenomenon of 'medieval' patterns of dual governance."[24] For example in the Middle East, Crossley finds: "A fundamentally similar pattern is also easily seen in the Islamic model of legitimacy prescribed for the *khalif* and *sultân* [imamate and sultanate] during the devolution of military authority in the later Abbasid period and in the Ottoman period before the middle 1400s."[25] Gustave E. von Grunebaum had reached that same conclusion regarding the collapse of the 'Abbasid caliphate in his *Medieval Islam*, when he wrote, "The *civitas Dei* had failed, and the Muslim community had accepted its failure."[26]

Crossley's simultaneous ruler narrated identities, often parallel ones. Such rulership expressed itself within Iran's political culture through interactions of the ruler, his government, and institutions, with ascribed constituent identities within a framework of shared values, culture, and economy. Here representation of the ruler to the ruled was a matter of legitimacy, or multiple legitimacies, or what Crossley calls simultaneous rulership. Most successful rulers of Iran have also sought to legitimize their rule to preceding rulers and have seen themselves as the rightful heir of a tradition of rulership even in the face of—or especially because of—the discontinuity that has so characterized Iranian history. Legitimacy is not just the representation of the ruler to the ruled, or the interaction between them, but between the ruler and the tradition, to history.

Iranian rulership represented a form of imperial expression in which the ruler transcended the realm's, or more typically, the empire's parts, to create a historical reality, and congruent images and symbols not to mention actual institutions—in Nader Shah's case, with his military and in religion. Clearly, precedents are found earlier in Iranian history as well as in such rulers as Timur (1336–1405), Shah 'Abbas I, and others. Moreover, the ruler created, or could destroy, constituencies, that existed as expressions of his rulership. Simultaneous rulership—or, in our instance, Iranian rulership—describes multiple ruling personae within one political individual, and functioned in the context of a hierarchical cosmology and political culture. Moreover, the ruler ruled over an ethnically and geographically complex society. Such rulership represents a form of imperial expression in which the ruler transcends the realm's, or more typically, the empire's parts and peoples, to create a historical reality, with congruent images and symbols.

Gustave von Grunebaum's first important book, *Medieval Islam: A Study in Cultural Orientation*[27]—whose subtitle is mostly ignored if not forgotten altogether—was followed later by his *Modern Islam: The Search for Cultural Identity*.[28] The former examined Islamic culture from the seventh century through the thirteenth century, with several forays back to the classical world of the Mediterranean and with comparisons with Christendom. The latter analyzed the period of the Western impact on the Middle East, basically the twentieth century, under such topics of self-image and identity, nationalism, and acculturation and adaptation, but its first chapter goes back to the first Islamic centuries. These studies were "medieval" and "modern" to what? European history as a model for other parts of the world was assumed by von Grunebaum and many others, along with the essentialism inherent in these comparisons. This is neither Crossley's nor my point in raising the question of periodization, but to look at history more broadly across Eurasia and not just from a Eurocentric view. From Crossley's vantage point of Chinese and East Asian history, she emphasized striking parallels not with individual European states but with the whole of Europe—a geographic entity comparable with China—within the greater context of Eurasia.

My point springs from both Crossley and Marshall Hodgson, and attempts to understand the long-term trends that began as a consequence of the Mongol impact on a broader history rather than a narrower view of history limited by chronology or dynasty, and to fit Iran's eighteenth century into Eurasian history. Apt comparisons with Ottoman history, in particular, could easily be made.

As Hodgson observed: "The three centuries after about 1500 are most obviously important for us because they form the immediate background of our own age. The Islamdom that entered into Modern times was that which took shape in these centuries [in other words, the early modern period] . . . and it is the Islamdom of just these recent centuries which, historically, has been most relevant to their present posture." And Hodgson continues: "At the start of the sixteenth century, a general realignment of political forces among all Muslim peoples afforded an opportunity for extensive political and then cultural renewal."[29] Crossley argues that such realization was the result of the Mongol impact.

In conclusion, I concur and would emphasize three major themes and then a fourth that I have only mentioned. First, pastoral nomadic confederations and their leaders shaped Iran's eighteenth-century political map at every level, with consequences that persisted until after World War I. Second—and this relates especially to Hodgson's Islamic renewal themes—was the conflict within the 'ulema among the Usulis and Akhbaris, and possibly the philosopher-mystics among them (and not to mention religious populism) and the victory of the Usulis in the nineteenth century that continues to affect Iran down to the present day.

The Islamic Republic of Iran is clearly a modern phenomenon. This conflict related very much to rulership—my third theme—in which the crises of legitimacy, separated further the ruler's "sultanate" from "imamate." This is clearly seen in the various titles eighteenth-century rulers appropriated for themselves; most significantly, Karim Khan Zand's use of both *Vakil al-Daulah-i Iran* (regent/deputy of the Government of Iran) and *Vakil al-Ra'ya* (regent/deputy of the people). Consequently, there was a *de facto* separation of authority that laid another basis for how the ruler represented himself to his subjects—and not always to the ruler's advantage in the nineteenth century. While such representation was within the Shia framework of rituals and belief, national ones linked to Iran's pre-Islamic past assumed new importance and ultimately in the twentieth century led to nationalism, even a kind of secularism. Lastly, the Persian language continued its domination in culture and administration—Arabic was relegated to the religious classes—despite the political success of the Turkic-speaking Qajars at the century's turn. Nader Shah dominated the eighteenth century to stand as the archetypal early modern ruler. Here there is both continuity, with earlier roots going back to the Mongols—reinforced by Timur—and profound changes that have reached into the twentieth century.

Notes

1. Ibn Khaldun, *The Muqaddimah: An Introduction to History*, translated by Franz Rosenthal, ed. and abridged by N. J. Dawood (Princeton, 1967), p. 5.
2. Ibid., p. 29.
3. Michael Axworthy, *The Sword of Persia: Nader Shah, from Tribal Warrior to Conquering Tyrant* (London, 2006). Willem Floor, *The Rise and Fall of Nader Shah: Dutch East India Company Reports, 1730–1747* (Washington, DC, 2009). Ernest S. Tucker, *Nadir Shah's Quest for Legitimacy in Post-Safavid Iran* (Gainesville, 2006).
4. Marshall Hodgson, *The Venture of Islam*, vol. I, (Chicago, 1974), p. 110.
5. Rashid al-Din Fazullah, *Jami' al-Tavarikh*, 3 vols. (Cambridge, MA, 1998–1999).
6. Pamela Kyle Crossley, "The Early Modern Paradox," for the panel "Rethinking World History: A Roundtable," annual meeting of the American Historical Association, San Diego, January 7, 2010.
7. David Morgan, *The Mongols* (Oxford, 1986).
8. David Morgan, *The Mongols* (Oxford, 2007).
9. Reuven Amitai-Preiss and David Morgan, *The Mongol Empire & Its Legacy* (Leiden, 1999).
10. Morgan (1986), p. 199.
11. Joseph Fletcher, "The Mongols: Ecological and Social Perspectives," *Harvard Journal of Asiatic Studies*, vol. 46 (1986), pp. 11–50. Beatrice Forbes Manz, *The Rise and Rule of Tammerlane* (Cambridge, 1989).
12. Crossley (2010), p. 4.
13. Ibid., p. 5.
14. Cemal Kafadar, *Between Two Worlds: The Construction of the Ottoman State* (Berkeley, 1995).
15. Karen Barkey, *Empire of Difference: The Ottomans in Comparative Perspective* (Cambridge, 2008).
16. Morgan (1986), p. 199.
17. Daniel Potts, *Nomadism in Iran: From Antiquity to the Modern Era* (Oxford, 2014).
18. Gene. R. Garthwaite, "Transition: The End of the Old Order—Iran in the Eighteenth Century," in *The Cambridge History of Islam*, ed. by Michael Cook and David Morgan (Cambridge, 2010), pp. 504–525.
19. Kathryn Babayan, *Mystics, Monarchs, and Messiahs: Cultural Landscapes of Early Modern Iran* (Cambridge, MA, 2002).
20. Andrew J. Newman, *Safavid Iran: Rebirth of a Persian Empire* (London, 2006).
21. Zackery M. Heern, "Usuli Shi'ism: The Emergence of an Islamic Reform Movement in Early Modern Iraq and Iran," (University of Utah, Ph.D. dissertation, 2011).
22. Sussan Babaie et al., *Slaves of the Shah: New Elites of Safavid Iran* (London, 2004).
23. A. K. S. Lambton, "The Tribal Resurgence and the Decline of the Bureaucracy in the Eighteenth Century," *Studies in Eighteenth Century Islamic History*, ed. by Thomas Naff and Roger Owen (Carbondale and Edwardsville, IL, 1977), pp. 120–121.
24. Ibid., p. 6.
25. Ibid.
26. Gustave E. von Grunebaum, *Medieval Islam: A Study in Cultural Orientation* (Chicago, 1961).
27. Ibid.
28. Gustave von Grunebaum, *Modern Islam: The Search for Cultural Identity* (Berkeley, 1962).
29. Marshall Hodgson, *The Venture of Islam; Conscience and History in a World Civilization*, vol. III (Chicago, 1974), pp. 3–4.

3

Historiographical Reflections on the Eighteenth Century in Iranian History: Decline and Insularity, Imperial Dreams, or Regional Specificity?

RUDI MATTHEE

Introduction

Unlike the situation in Mughal India and, to a lesser extent, the Ottoman Empire, the study of the eighteenth century in Iranian history remains woefully underdeveloped and severely limited in the repertoire of themes and topics that have been addressed. We have shelves filled with scholarly studies about the dissolution and collapse of the Mughals in the eighteenth century and the incorporation of parts of the Indian Subcontinent into various new state structures, the most important and consequential of which was, of course, the expanding British Empire. We have far less on the same period for the Ottoman Empire, just as we had, until quite recently, very little on the period between 1600 and 1800 in Ottoman history—all the focus being on the sixteenth century, the 'Golden Age' of Süleyman the Lawgiver (or the Magnificent), and the nineteenth century, the era of the Tanzimat reforms followed by the empire's manifest weakening preceding its disintegration. Yet the number of studies on this period in Ottoman history still exceeds the handful of works on Iran between the Safavids and the Qajars, and it is growing rapidly.

The 'Ottoman' eighteenth century is different from the same period in Iranian and Mughal history, to be sure. The Ottoman state suffered nothing as radical as the total collapse of the Safavids or the atrophy of the Mughals; its ability to fight decreased, leading to recurrent losses on the battlefield, but it continued to interact in accelerating ways with the world around it, especially with European nations. The Ottoman 'eighteenth century' thus is far less of a caesura or a vacuum than that of Iran and India—it is, in traditional parlance, mostly a phase in the protracted and continuous decline of the Ottomans or, in a more contemporary reassessment, a period of 'temporary' as opposed to 'definitive' decline.[1]

Iran's eighteenth-century experience is different from what befell the Mughal state as well. Both the Safavid and the Mughal states disintegrated, but the dissolution of the Mughals was a slow process that involved the creeping incorporation of much of their territory into a new, colonial dispensation. The Safavids, by contrast, fell hard and precipitously, causing parts of the Iranian plateau to slide into protracted chaos. P. J. Marshall wrote of the eighteenth century in Indian history that 'for most historians of the past and for some now, the hundred years in Indian history between 1700 and 1800 have no overall coherence. They are years marked by great disruption and discontinuity: the fall of the Mughals, the transitory life of the successor states, and the rise of the British.'[2] Much of this is valid for Iran in the same period, including the 'rise of the British' (and, more consequentially, the 'rise of the Russians') as of the late eighteenth century. The difference is, of course, that in the case of Iran the inchoate character of the country's state and society did not immediately end with the emergence of a new regime and the intrusion of newly aggressive outside powers at the turn of the nineteenth century.

Bracketed by the Safavids and the Qajars, the century following the fall of Isfahan continues to be mainly seen—and summarily treated—as a chaotic and a largely self-contained interregnum. The Ottomans did not just continue to interact with the world but, indisputably, over time became even more enmeshed with it. They started losing their wars with some regularity but increasingly, although perhaps reluctantly, extended relations, even permanent ones, with the courts of Europe. The early eighteenth-century Tulip Period reflects a keen awareness of and a fascination with, things European among the Ottoman upper classes. India post-Plassey was brought into the British orbit, causing its elite gradually to become familiar with the ways of the new colonizers. Iran, by contrast, in this period rapidly 'retreated' from the global scene as its ties with the outside world diminished in frequency and intensity. Iran's eighteenth century thus runs contrary to the perceived 'global eighteenth century', exemplifying a new level of (elite) connectivity.[3]

This image is enhanced by modern perceptions. Among modern Iranians the Safavids are known as the glorious dynasty that 'reconquered' the country, unified it, and helped it regain its 'natural' stature as a great power, in the process creating the contours of the modern Iranian nation-state. The Safavids, moreover, enjoy the reputation of being the last ruling house presiding over a proud and independent Iran. The Qajars, by contrast, the dynasty that would bring the country to the threshold of the modern age, generally count as weak and decadent, even though attempts at rehabilitation have recently been undertaken.[4]

They suffered a series of humiliating defeats against the Russians, losing large swathes of territory as a result. The Qajars also oversaw Iran's creeping incorporation into a Western-dominated imperialist network, so that the principal blame for the loss of land and sovereignty the country suffered under their watch can, and often is, laid on the imperial powers, the British in first place, who ceaselessly meddled in the country's affairs, preventing it from regaining its 'natural' greatness. The period in between is not so easily classified, for it seems neither a glorious moment in national history nor a century of potential splendour snatched away by foreign powers. Dark, seemingly directionless, and relatively short on written sources, the eighteenth century in Iranian history remains a poorly examined historiographical problem.

Of the many problems presented by the period one of the more serious ones is indeed the lack of source material relative to what exists for the two hundred years preceding the collapse of the Safavid dynasty, or the wealth of information available for the nineteenth century. In a trend that precedes the actual fall of Isfahan, we have relatively few indigenous, Persian-language sources for especially the mid to late eighteenth century. For the period immediately after the collapse of Safavid rule there are various important writings by the well-known man of letters, Hazin Lahiji, the recently published *Bada'eh al-akhbar* by Mirza 'Abd al-Nabi Sheykh al-Eslam Behbehani, which recounts events in and around Behbehan, and Mohammad Shafi' Tehrani's *Mer'at-e varedat*, which reports on the otherwise poorly covered region of Sistan.[5] The reign of Nader Shah generated various chronicles, too, most of them written in his orbit and for his greater glory, such as the *Tarikh-e 'alam-ara-ye Naderi* and the *Tarikh-e jahangosha-ye Naderi*.[6] These are substantial and offer a great deal of useful information, even if this is often hard to extract amid the floweriness and bombast. Other informative chronicles, covering the period following Nader's assassination and the subsequent ascent and rule of the Zands, include the *Mojmal al-tavarikh*, the *Tarikh-e geyti-gosha*, and the *Tarikh-e Mohammadi*.[7] We also have some very interesting narrative sources, such as the diary of Mirza Mohammad Kalantar-e Fars, and, more retrospectively, the amusing mix of fact and fiction proffered by the nineteenth-century man of letters, Rostam al-Hokama, known as the *Rostam al-tavarikh*.[8]

Unevenly distributed are the foreign accounts, which are so useful in complementing Persian-language sources in the seventeenth century, and sometimes indispensable for illuminating what domestic sources do not—agriculture, commercial life, urban society, daily life, ordinary people, peasants, workers, and women. The accounts of two Armenian chroniclers, Abraham of Erevan and Abraham of Crete, are important for the period until 1738.[9] Until the 1750s and the 1760s, the Dutch and the English, respectively, continued to be active in the Persian Gulf, albeit at a reduced level; and their reporting remains essential for the Gulf littoral, especially during the reign of Nader Shah. Some Russian sources exist for the northern parts.[10] The works of the nineteenth-century French orientalist M. F. Brosset are invaluable for Georgia and its relations with Iran.[11] Since foreign visitors tended to avoid Iran, now considered dangerous, European travelogues fall off considerably after 1722 and precipitously after the reign of Nader Shah, both in quantity and quality. For the first decades following the fall we still have the important eyewitness account of the Polish missionary Thaddeus Krusinski, the writings of the Italian Carmelite Cecilia di Leandro, and the reporting of the English merchant-traveller Jonas Hanway.[12] The subsequent period is covered by the Armenian-Iranian Joseph Emin, a protagonist of Armenian unity, by the Greek Basile Vatatzes, who met Nader; by Jacob Lerch, who accompanied a mission sent by Nader Shah to the Russians; by Samuel Gmelin who in the 1770s visited northern Iran representing the newly formed Russian Imperial Academy of Sciences; by William Francklin, an East India Company officer who in 1786–1787 visited Iran from Bengal; and by the Danish cartographer-explorer Carsten Niebuhr, an accidental visitor who ended up in southern Iran after being the sole survivor of a Danish scientific expedition to Arabia.[13] With the exception of Francklin and Niebuhr, all just spent time in the north, and none is nearly as insightful and informative as even the travellers of the second echelon who visited Iran in the seventeenth century. Among the few French travellers who made it to Iran after 1722, only Jean Otter, an originally Swedish academician who made it to the court of Nader Shah in 1738, Père Louis Bazin, the French Jesuit who served as Nader's physician, the secret agent Comte de Ferrières Sauveboeuf, who witnessed the turmoil that befell Iran following the death of Karim Khan Zand in 1779, the botanist André Michaux who, accidentally stranded in Iran in 1782, collected valuable information on the country's flora, and Guillaume-Antoine Olivier, visiting Iran in 1796 as a member of a Revolutionary French scientific and commercial mission, wrote eyewitness accounts of any significance.[14]

As in the case with the Safavids, only more so, both the indigenous and the foreign sources disproportionately coalesce around great men, and, of course, the 'greatest' of these are Nader Shah and Karim Khan Zand. Both stand out as military commanders who managed to create identifiable, functioning albeit short-lived states and thus give a semblance of coherence and direction to Iranian history in an otherwise tumultuous and rather bewildering period. It is therefore little surprising that modern scholars have followed the focus in the sources on these two towering figures in their efforts to piece together the history of eighteenth-century Iran. Volume 7 of the *Cambridge History of Iran*, for instance, covers the period with two essays that centre on Nader Shah and Karim Khan Zand, respectively.[15] Western scholars especially have written informative biographies of both. After the pioneering work of Laurence Lockhart and the Russian-language study by Arunova and Ashrafiyan, published twenty years later, we now have studies of Nader Shah's life and career from the hand of Ernest Tucker and Michael Axworthy, a digest of sources by Willem Floor, and, most recently, even a psychohistorical analysis of his widely presumed madness.[16] Karim Khan Zand has received less attention, European-language biographies of him and his dynasty being limited to studies by Mehdi Roschan-Zamir and, of course, the classic and comprehensive treatment by John Perry.[17] Iranian scholars, handicapped by limited access to material such as exists and mostly dependent on the Persian-language chronicles from the period, have nonetheless made some notable contributions as well. Mention should be made of Reza Sha'bani and Nur Allah Larudi for the Afsharid period, and of Parviz Rajabi, Gholamreza Varahram, and Abdol Hosein Navai for Zand history, in addition to a popular author, Semnan Panahi, who has written several potted histories of major Iranian rulers in the period between 1600 and 1900.[18]

Different Interpretations

The tendency among modern Iranians to see and treat any period in their country's history as a meaningful episode in a national, unbroken, and teleological civilizational narrative that stretches from the Achaemenids to the Islamic Republic has complicated a proper assessment of Iran's 'short' eighteenth century, the roughly seventy-five years that separate the fall of the Safavids from the rise of the Qajars. Whereas the regional ruler Karim Khan Zand has never stirred the imagination of Western observers, the reception of Nader Shah in eighteenth-century Europe was as swift and dramatic as it was complex. The publication of the anonymous *Histoire de Thamas Koulikan* in 1740–1741, six years before his assassination, and Jacob Fraser's *The History of Nader Shah*, which came out in London in 1742, set the tone for this fascination. The literate Western public came to perceive Nader following his attack on the Ottomans as a relentless tyrant, the antithesis of the cultured (and useful because anti-Ottoman) Safavids, but also as the saviour of his nation against the 'barbarian' Turks, ready to restore Iran's greatness. Shortly after the publication of the two above works Nader became the subject of various plays, in France as well as in Holland, which portrayed him as a complex ruler, not just as a bloodthirsty tyrant but as a despot who paired cruelty to magnanimity.[19] More importantly, his blood-soaked career came to be seen as a latter-day instalment of the Asian hordes threatening European civilization, following in the footsteps of the Huns, the Mongols under Ghengiz Khan and Timur Lang (Tamerlane). Ruling over the ruins of what was once a magnificent civilization, Nader and his story also became a morality tale, the personification of the fickleness of fate, and thus a projection of contemporary European Enlightenment anxieties.[20] In the early nineteenth century, Europeans came to see him as the 'Iranian Napoleon' and the last of the great Central Asian conquerors. To the extent that Nader Shah and eighteenth-century Iran figure at all in the modern Western mind, he continues to be portrayed as such.

Iranians, on the other hand, scholars as much as the general public, tend to have a take on the only two personalities who seem to rise above the quarreling tribal mêlée as identifiable leaders that is similar as well as more closely aligned with an overall, teleologically marked interpretation of their history. Particularly prone to a Carlylean 'great man' view of history, they have tended to celebrate Nader Shah and Karim Khan Zand not just as the only two rulers who defied the period's centrifugal forces, but, following the initial reception in Europe, as national heroes who revived Iran's genius. The first, representing military vigour, did so by reconquering much of the territory traditionally associated with the Iranian plateau—and went beyond this by next taking on Hindustan. The historians writing in the orbit of his direct successors naturally disregarded him so as to legitimize their own employers, and especially Agha Mohammad Shah, the founder of the Qajar dynasty that came to prevail in Iran at the turn of the nineteenth century, had to distance himself from Nader for having devi-ated from the Shi'i foundations laid by the Safavids and that Agha Mohammad Shah invoked to buttress his own legitimacy.[21] As of the late nineteenth century, historians espousing a new nationalist agenda would re-evaluate Nader—in part on the basis of the rather positive image John Malcolm presents of him in his *A History of Persia*—which was translated into Persian and published in the 1870s (in India).[22] In the Iranian collective memory he thus emerged as the forceful leader who restored the national honour that had been lost during the assault by the presumably foreign Afghan warriors who had brought down Isfahan. This process culminated in the reign of Reza Shah (1921–1941), who liked to see his own martial qualities and aspirations reflected in the disciplinarian that Nader was.[23] Nader's fate, in short, has been similar to what John Malcolm said of the memory of Lotf Ali Khan, a latter-day scion of the Zand dynasty, whose 'faults, which were numerous, have been forgotten by his countrymen, who speak only of his manly beauty, the elevated courage, and the cruel destiny of the last prince of the family of Kurreem Khan.'[24]

The second giant of the eighteenth century, Karim Khan, clearly falls short of Nader Shah as a military commander. He was, in the words of a modern scholar, 'unable to reunite the land of Iran.'[25] But he made up for this flaw by project-ing kindness and benevolence, and he thus constitutes a counterpoint to the indisputably ruthless Nader. If Nader Shah stands for military power, Karim Khan Zand represents the quintessentially important Iranian notion of justice.

Bridging the classic division between *dowlat* and *mellat*, state and people, Karim Khan, too, embodies the nation, and not just because of his presumed humanity. Karim Khan, after all, is often presented as the ruler who, by brushing off a British envoy, most likely Major George Skipp (who was actually a representative of the English East India Company), resisted the country's creeping incorporation into a colonial dispensation that had begun with the Portuguese entry into the Persian Gulf in the early sixteenth century and that saw its first English manifestation with the visit of Anthony Jenkinson to the court of Shah Tahmasp in 1562.[26]

The fact, finally, that Nader Shah and Karim Khan Zand are, in some ways, each other's antipodes, at least in the modern imagination—the one forceful, the other (relatively) benevolent—does not alter that role, and may in fact reinforce it. Just as in the case of India, there is an imperialist and a nationalist interpretation of eighteenth-century Iran.[27] In the Iranian case the two are not necessarily mutually exclusive; indeed, they often go together, especially in the hands of modern Iranian historians.

Suggestions for Future Research

What to do with Iran in the eighteenth century, a country whose relative insularity seems radically to defy the modern trend of the 'global eighteenth century'? Are we stuck with an eighteenth-century Iran of 'big men', either illustrious leaders who sought to revive the nation and restore its pride, or brutal warlords who extorted what was left of the country's wealth among a hapless, depleted population? Does the eighteenth century in Iranian history present us with an 'unusable' past? Not necessarily, I would argue. While the nature of the written source material for the period makes it difficult to break out of dynastic history with its focus on rulers and their entourage and, concomitantly, its seemingly preordained periodization, it nevertheless offers various alternative possibilities. Here I suggest that there are more productive ways of viewing the eighteenth century in Iranian history than as a mere interlude, either a period of utter chaos and misery, or an ill-fitting phase in a teleological national narrative.

Three approaches present themselves as holding promise in this regard: a 'supranational' or regional way of looking at eighteenth-century Iran, situating it in a broader Eurasian framework; a more narrow purview which perceives the country in this period as a singular political and cultural entity, although not necessarily through a nationalist lens; and a regional perspective, in recognition of the fact that Iran at the time was not yet a nation-state but rather a conglomerate of poorly connected and relatively autonomous regional centers.

I. The Transnational Approach

The fact that Iran interacted with the West in less significant ways between 1722 and 1800 than it had done under the Safavids naturally does not mean that it existed in total isolation. One way of approaching the country—or rather the territory encompassing the Iranian plateau—in this period is through the lens of global or at least hemispheric history, in recognition of the fact that at any point in its long history Iran was part of a wider universe and interacted with the surrounding world. C. A. Bayly in 1988 published an essay in which he situated eighteenth-century Muslim India, the northern part of the Subcontinent, the Deccan, and even the Carnatic in a larger framework, connecting it with West and Central Asia. His justification for his attempt to 'dissolve' the regional divisions into more complex patterns was direct links in military, economic, and religious organization between the subcontinent, Iran, Afghanistan, and Turanistan, and the profound effect the modification of these links in the eighteenth century had on the nature of colonial India and the conditions of nineteenth-century West Asia.[28] In his subsequent *Imperial Meridian*, the same author further developed this line by categorizing Nader Shah's career as one of the so-called 'tribal break-outs' in the early eighteenth century that threatened and in some cases brought down the various sedentary regimes that had ruled West and South Asia for a considerable period of time.[29]

The most expansive elaboration of this type of analysis is the recent study by Gagan D. S. Sood, *India and the Islamic Heartlands: An Eighteenth-Century World of Circulations and Exchange*. Taking a self-avowed supraregional approach, Sood looks at the vast area of 'India and the Islamic heartlands', the world encompassing South, West, and Central Asia in the mid-eighteenth century, as a universe 'characterised by an absence of great hegemons and a plethora of successor regimes', and considers this very absence the reason why this period 'brimmed with unscripted possibilities'. His focus is on circulation and exchange, which he sees as unfolding in a 'coherent, self-regulating arena of activities', thus following in the tradition of those who equate the breakdown of quasi-centralized early modern regimes with the flowering of regional energy and creativity, if not stability.[30]

Sood's approaches hovers over the political and the religious as constitutive forces of the societies he examines. But both are inarguably pivotal elements in any analysis that wants to be more than generic and abstract. The most obvious subject in an approach that goes beyond Iran is that of cross-border religious connections and networks. The fall of the Safavids led to a great scattering of people beyond the borders of Iran, and part of this centrifugal movement involved the dispersal and outward migration of clerics and mystics. The networks these created and maintained, from Najaf in Iraq to Lucknow in India, have been studied individually, by Cole and, most recently by Heern, but surely more work needs to be done in this area.[31]

Nader Shah himself fits into a transnational scheme with a religious focus in various ways. One could start with his bold attempt to make Iran less particularistic and more palatable to the surrounding world by suggesting the recognition of Twelver Shi'ism as a legitimate fifth, Ja'fari *madhhab*, 'school' of Islam.[32] Whether or not this initiative was a preliminary move in a 'design of creating a new Khilafat or pan-Islamic state',[33] it preceded his brazen campaign that took him and his army far beyond the Iranian plateau, across the Hindu Kush and into the plains of northern India all the way to the gates of Delhi.[34] It appears that this expedition was preplanned, and it seems quite obvious that Nader's endeavour was mainly motivated by the legendary wealth of the subcontinent, which he is said to have referred to as the 'Banyan caravanserai'.[35] Yet it is clear that its projected subjugation, as that of the Ottoman Empire and Central Asia, was also part of an imperial agenda of a ruler who, given his lack of royal lineage, had few other options than raw conquest to establish his fame and reputation—hence his association with the memory of Timur Lang.[36]

Sanjay Subrahmanyam has taken the notion of situating post-Safavid Iran, a larger context encompassing West Asia and South Asia by way of using Nader Shah one step further. Ostensibly seeking to demolish a narrow Indian national interpretation of history whereby even without British colonialism the subcontinent would have evolved into a unified nation state, but actually dreaming of a West and South Asian history without (British) colonial domination, Subrahmanyam engages in a counterfactual scenario. This views Nader's reign as a break with traditional dynastic rule and a blend of personal charisma and institutional innovation, opening the possibility of a radical configuration of the entire area stretching from Tabriz to Bengal in the form of a tributary Perso-Indian administration underpinned by Iran's military prowess and Indian fiscal-bureaucratic capacity—generating a newly invigorated state that might have deterred the British in their colonial adventurism while preserving Persianate culture as a globally significant force.[37] Nader in this scenario is not so much Timur Lang revived as Napoleon foretold—the way modern Iranians tend to see him.[38]

Regardless of our interpretation of it and even if we regard it as a unique event or even an aberration, Nader's Indian campaign does invite one to look at eighteenth-century Iran as part of a larger Eurasian canvas. The way in which the mystique of Nader Shah resonated and left a legacy, not unlike Timur Lang three centuries earlier, throughout West and Central Asia, has recently been investigated by James Pickett, but otherwise remains largely unexamined.[39] Especially the reverberations of Nader's rule and legacy in Central Asia, most notably in the form of the Manghit Dynasty that ruled Bokhara from the year of his death in 1747 until the Soviet takeover of 1920, awaits further exploration. Post-Safavid

Iran may not have been in the forefront of foreign entanglement, but it continued to interact with adjacent states, and it still played a role in the global struggle
for power between the French, the British, and the Russians.

The level of entanglement of the Iranian-Ottoman-Russian relationship
comes out in Ernest Tucker's suggestion that the Ottoman-Iranian truce of 1736
allowed the Ottomans to turn their attention to the Russian threat, and that the
subsequent Russo-Ottoman wars in turn allowed Nader Shah to direct his attention to India.[40] The Ottomans and the Russians indeed were by far the greatest
concern to Iran's post-Safavid successor states. An acute awareness of the growing turmoil in Iran prompted the former in 1720 to send an envoy to Isfahan
with the task of gathering intelligence on political and military conditions in
the Safavid realm.[41] Even before the fall of Isfahan, Istanbul had taken the decision to attack the severely weakened country, even if the Ottoman armies waited
until after the Afghan occupation of the capital before moving toward Yerevan,
Tabriz, and Hamadan.[42] They subsequently seized a large swathe of the country's northwestern region in a process that remains relatively unknown and that
awaits further investigation.[43] The *Fathnameh-ye Iravan*, recently translated into
Persian, which describes the Ottoman conquest of parts of the Caucasus including Yerevan in 1724, suggests the existence of Turkish-language sources for this
period and region. Nader's campaigns into the Caucasus, too, are still to be to
examined on the basis of Ottoman and Georgian sources as well as possibly
Armenian ones beyond the above-mentioned ones.[44]

Russian pressure on Iran's northern territories goes back to the sixteenth
century. Yet it was Peter I's attack on Shirvan, Talesh, and Gilan in the waning
days of the Safavid state which set the tone for St Petersburg's policy vis-à-vis
Russia's southern neighbour for the next two centuries.[45] Tsar Peter's invasion
of northern Iran in 1720, too, came on the heels of a Russian mission to Isfahan
that, while claiming to have regular political and commercial goals, in reality
sought to gather intelligence about the state of Iran's army. P. P. Bushev's study
of Artemiia Volynski mission remains poorly known among Safavid scholars.[46]
Russia's simultaneous expansionism via the eastern littoral Caspian Sea, inaugurated with the 1716 Bekovich-Cherkasskii mission to Khiva and the expedition
the Italian Florio Beneveni undertook two years later on behalf of the tsar, too,
remains to be explored for its effect on Iran by way of a growing and enduring
Russian naval and territorial presence in the area around Astarabad (modern
Gorgan).[47] We now have a thorough study of the aftermath, the expedition that
took the Russian army to the Iranian shores of the Caspian Sea, but this, too, is
only accessible to scholars with a reading knowledge of Russian.[48]

Iran's contacts with the Indian subcontinent in the eighteenth century went
far beyond the military confrontation between Nader Shah and the Mughals.
The continued level of cultural exchange between the two is most striking. As

is well known, the migration of Iranians to the subcontinent long preceded the Safavid period. India, so much larger and richer, had long beckoned talented and ambitious Iranians looking for career opportunity and fortune at one of its courts. This influx and the attendant Persian influence on India accelerated and culminated in the eighteenth century, creating a culture in the subcontinent with resonance until modern times. Awareness of this exchange has grown with the emergence of the relatively new and now burgeoning field of 'Persianate studies', which has already yielded some valuable studies of its various aspects and is sure to produce more in the future.[49]

According to Ernest Tucker, 'By mid-century it was no longer sufficient [for Iranian rulers] to emulate Timur—new forces were now intruding, the Europeans.'[50] The surviving sources suggest that Iranians, even the elites, at the time were hardly aware of the changing world this portended—and if they were, this hardly comes through in the Persian-language sources. It is indeed far more difficult to identify Iranian agency with regard to contacts with the European powers in the eighteenth century than during much of the Safavid period. Iranian scholars (and Iranians in general) tend to see an unbroken English presence in their country from the moment Anthony Jenkinson, a representative of the English Muscovy Company, visited the court of Shah Tahmasp in the mid-sixteenth century, and to consider this a teleological tale of preordained (semi) colonial subjugation.

In reality, the role of the English in eighteenth-century Iran never much exceeded a commercial interest and was minimal (and decreasing) at best. The English (and the Dutch) had been active in Iran since the early 1600s, but, owing to logistical difficulties and long distances they had never woven the same web that reached into the production areas of the commodities they traded in and that involved revenue farmers and collectors as much as producers as they did, say, on the Coromandel region or the Bengal Coast of India. Roiled by falling profits, they began to despair about doing business in the Persian Gulf region as soon as Isfahan succumbed to the Afghans and the Safavids fell. Centralized political power was vital to their operation, as is evidenced in the good relations the English enjoyed with Nader Shah in the mid-1740s. When it crumbled and the two companies threatened to fall under the sway of warlords, they packed up and left a country of limited resources and profitability. As a result, the Persian Gulf (and the Western Indian Ocean at large, encompassing Basra and al-Mukha/Mocha) never knew the equivalent of Anglo-French rivalry that was to characterize their encounter, especially in North America and to a lesser extent in India as well.[51]

The early part of the century is rather marked by a—rarely noticed and little-studied—French attempt to gain not just commercial leverage but a political foothold in Iran as part of a larger scheme designed to extend France's influence in Asia from the eastern Mediterranean to the Indian Ocean. This went back to the establishment of the Compagnie Française des Indes Orientales in the 1660s, which was intended by foreign minister Colbert as the French counterpart and rival to the English and Dutch East India companies. This Company's organizational capacities soon proved to fall far short of its aspirations, but a lack of commercial success did not prevent Louis XIV from pursuing a greater political role in Iran, going back to a long-standing French desire to gain commercial and political traction in Iran vis-à-vis other European powers. France and Iran exchanged various missions on the eve of the fall of the Safavids. Officially these aimed at the conclusion of a commercial treaty between France and Iran. But their secret objective, initiated by Paris, was a Franco-Iranian alliance designed to take over Masqat. It envisaged French—as opposed to Portuguese— assistance to Iran in conquering the port town, in return for which the French would receive a free port and a share in the pearl fishing proceeds of the Persian Gulf. This grandiose dream was really designed to dominate West and South Asia, encompassing Iran, the Ottoman Empire, and the Mughal state from the chokepoint of the Persian Gulf.[52]

This French project sounds strikingly modern yet was ultimately a sideshow to Iranian history—desultory in its immediate as well as long-term consequences, and particularly irrelevant to the more pressing concerns of the disintegrating Safavid state. There was no follow-up; the French were not really vested and invested in Iran.

Only the turn of the next century witnessed the beginnings of serious British political interest in Iran and Persian Gulf, increasingly with the protection of India as the main and ultimate rationale. Malcolm's three missions to Iran as envoy, officially representing the East India Company but really an expanding British India, demonstrated this interest. It is clear that, like Karim Khan before him, 'Abbas Mirza was fully aware of the intent. According to Gaspar Drouville, the Qajar crown prince looked at Malcolm's visit askance, suspecting that the money the British diplomat spent so liberally was designed to 'buy' the Iranians. 'Abbas Mirza was especially aware of the British treatment of the Indians, how they had taken advantage of the weakness of the Mughals to increase their power in India, and feared that they might have the same intentions in Iran. Malcolm's request to reopen the factory of Bushehr and to be allowed to station troops in that port town only strengthened him in this suspicion.[53]

II. The 'National' Approach

National history need not be dismissed and discarded as incongruent with a modern, critical scholarly approach for being maudlin and celebratory. Without the teleology of the regenerative spirit embodied by the two major leaders discussed here, one still detects strains of a nascent national consciousness in the way some Iranian leaders at the time of looking at the world and Iran's place in it.[54] The uniquely Iranian blend of superior aloofness and admiring fascination vis-à-vis especially Westerners, which is already visible in Safavid times, in the century following the fall of the Safavids gradually turned into admiration tinged with unease and, ultimately, anxiety and outright fear. As becomes clear from his conversation with George Skipp in Basra in 1767, Karim Khan did show an awareness of British operations in neighbouring India.[55] The same is true of other Iranian officials. In the words of Abbas Amanat, a 'concern for preserving the precarious tranquility of the country at the uncertain start of the new [Qajar] regime' is what prompted Fath 'Ali Shah's grand vizier, Mirza Ebrahim Kalantar-e Fars, to resist the offer by the British to have Iran assist them in organizing a campaign against Zaman Shah, the ruler of Kabul.[56]

One detects the same impulse in the *Rostam al-tavarikh*, the complex, idiosyncratic, and somewhat enigmatic account presumably penned by Mohammad Asef. Birgitt Hoffmann has recently advanced the notion that this work should be read less as the narrative of a detached chronicler than as a series of messages by an observer deeply concerned about Iran's weakening political and territorial integrity. Mohammad Asef, she argues, advocates a strong state led by a responsible capable ruler. Disturbed by the loss of land, he also aimed his arrows at the British.[57]

Another avenue to be pursued is that of domestic continuity, evolution, or gradual transformation. Indian historians have recently argued that even the massive disruption caused by the incorporation of large swathes of India into the British Empire in the eighteenth century should not occlude the multiple continuities that exist—which, according to some, may actually be more striking than the rupture embodied by the fall of the Mughals.[58]

Iran experienced a cataclysmic break with the fall of the Safavids, but many things continued as well, as they always do. For one, there is continuity in much of Iran's economic orientation. International, now rapidly globalizing, trade began to run on different tracks, especially after the European maritime companies cut their losses and retreated from the Iranian side of the Persian Gulf. But regional and supraregional, land-based commercial circuits remained in place in ways that have yet fully to be investigated. The monetary system, too, by and large continued to operate along patterns inherited from the Safavid period, including the outflow of large amounts of specie to the Indian subcontinent via the Persian Gulf ports, which reflected Iran's relative weakness as an economic power.[59] Numismatic studies, rudimentary for the Safavid period, are almost non-existent for eighteenth-century Iran, leaving a rich field to be explored by future generations of scholars.[60]

The study of coins is intimately related to the question of legitimacy and administrative order, especially for times when written evidence is scarce or absent. For much of the eighteenth century, the legend of the Safavids lingered to the point where various successor regimes invoked them as avatars in order to bolster their own legitimacy, either as sovereigns over the land of Iran or as the defenders of the Shi'i faith that the Safavids had proclaimed their 'national' creed.[61] Thus Agha Mohammad Khan, consenting to being crowned after sub-duing Georgia, 'refused to wear the gorgeous crown of Nadir Shah, the rich plumes of which denoted the kingdoms he had subdued: but he consented to gird on the royal sabre, which was consecrated at the tomb of the holy founder of the Safavean family. . . .'[62] The Qajars, who originated in the Safavid period and rose to prominence in the period after their fall, are a rich object of study here. With *Pouvoir et succession en Iran: Les premiers Qajars*, Hormuz Ebrahimnejad made a pioneering contribution to the question of the roots of the legitimacy of the Qajars in the period before they rose to political power.[63] Assef Ashraf has followed the same line of inquiry with his recent dissertation on the formation of the Qajar state.[64] Yet much more work needs to be done on patterns and symbols of legitimacy in this transitional period.

Gradual change, alongside continuity, can be detected in the administrative order as expressed in the nature of offices and how they evolved over time.[65] Both are visible in the way Iranians wrote about their past and present circum-stances. Ernest Tucker discusses the historiography of the eighteenth century and the early Qajar period, which is in several ways a transitional period, during which a nostalgic perspective prevailed and historians serving unstable rulers grappled with questions of legitimacy. Tucker detects in this period several fea-tures that foreshadow the Qajar era, such as a steady decrease in the emphasis on sacral kingship, a growing focus on justice, and an incipient positivism as legiti-mizing devices.[66]

Given the large and growing amount of available source material, a most promising avenue is that of religious movements and developments. The emerg-ing preeminence of the 'olama, surviving the turmoil that befell Iran in the wake of the fall of the Safavids as the only protectors and spokesmen of a suffering, exhausted population, remains poorly known and understood. The same holds for the—related—fate of the Sufis, and the fascinating story of Sheykhism and its influence on what ultimately would erupt in the form of the Babi faith. Abbas Amanat and Denis McEoin have done valuable preparatory work for a compre-hensive picture of this religious landscape.[67] It might be useful to investigate the religious environment in the orbit of Nader Shah to understand how and why the rather hardline religious milieu of the late Safavids gave way to the latitu-dinarian worldview of Nader. Similarly, the growing suppression of organized Sufism, especially of the Sunni variant, in late Safavid Iran, and the subsequent privatization of mysticism into a gnostic form called 'erfan, requires more research. For such continuities between the Safavid period and the eighteenth century we now have a Ata Anzali's study on the fate of Sufism in the wake of the fall of the Safavids.[68]

III. The Regional Approach

The Afsharid and Zand period undeniably had a centrifugal effect on Iranian history, not just in the sense that any cohesiveness known in Safavid times was fractured, but, historiographically, inasmuch as separate regions rather than 'Iran' at large call our attention after the fall of Isfahan. In the absence of at least a geographical center of gravity other than the plateau itself, and *pace* the 'primordial' cultural nationalism commonplace among Iranians as well as many scholars, Iranian history arguably has always been a matter of multiple oasis cities interacting with their hinterlands as largely autonomous entities. Not only that, but much of the country's history is a matter of people moving from the periphery into the centre, so much so that 'periphery' and 'centre' are often hard to distinguish in Iranian history. Despite Shah 'Abbas's thrust toward the Persian Gulf, the Safavids themselves were and remained mostly focused on the northern half of the country: Azerbaijan, the Caucasus, and the Caspian provinces, their ancestral lands and the country's most productive parts both in terms of revenue and as a source of military manpower. The reign of Nader Shah represents a pull to the northeast, to Khorasan, albeit a short-lived and tenuous one in light of his inability to consolidate his dominion followed by his untimely death.[69] With the Zands, Iran's centre of gravity moved south for the first time since the Buyid period. A distinctly southern orientation is also embodied by Agha Mohammad Khan as well as by the aforementioned Mirza Ebrahim kalantar-e Fars, Fath 'Ali Khan's grand vizier until he was discarded and cruelly executed by the latter. When, still operating in Fars, Mirza Ebrahim broke with the Zands to side with the Qajars in 1205/1791, he initially seems to have had the formation of a 'federative government', a southern league of semi-autonomous cities and tribal regions as his objective.[70]

The most promising of these, it seems to me, is microhistory, an approach that is based on the recognition and realization that, in spite of its unifying elements, the Iranian plateau was not (yet) a nation state but a conglomerate of autonomous 'city-states', archipelagos of urban centers and their hinterlands overseen by regional families operating as extended households, connected in tight webs of marriage and service arrangements. Thomas Ricks set the tone for an approach along these lines with his 1975 dissertation on 'southern Iran and the Gulf' between 1745 and 1765.[71] More recently, Christoph Werner enriched the field with his insightful monograph about eighteenth-century Tabriz, *An Iranian Town in Transition*.[72] In her recent study on Herat, Christine Noelle Karimi follows a similar path by examining the town and its surroundings over a long span of time between the Timurids and the Qajar period.[73] And Willem Floor has contributed to this in his uniquely prolific way by publishing multiple studies on various Persian Gulf port cities and their fate over the centuries.[74]

It should also be possible to research other parts of the country, especially on the fringes, for which either newly discovered sources might be used, or material other than Persian-language sources. As for the first, mention should be made of the recently edited *Mer'at-e varedat*, and the anonymous work that has been titled *Tajdar-e nafarjam*, chronicles that cover the rulers of Sistan during and immediately following the fall of the Safavids.[75] Examples of the second are Ardalan and other parts of Iranian and Iraqi Kurdistan, for which Ottoman source material is likely to be available—and the study of which would overlap with the 'supraregional' approach; and parts of the Caucasus, where the Russians were represented by consuls who wrote reports in the eighteenth century and for which we have Georgian and Russian-language writings on administrative matters and trade relations.[76] Recent studies on Kurdistan and Talesh show what can be done by assiduously using available source material.[77]

A new balance between the forces of disruption and the elements of continuity might emerge from an analysis of Iran in this period in its continued, albeit reduced interaction with the wider, regional, and transregional world, in conjunction with a more concentrated focus on the mostly autonomous regions that made up the Iranian plateau at this time and well into the nineteenth century. Regardless of the approach or combined approaches, we should 'reconstruct' the eighteenth century on Iran's terms. In all this we neither have to argue that the country was different from the surrounding lands in being predisposed to backwardness, nor to maintain that indigenous initiatives and actions appear forlorn and futile without the helping hand of Western agents and actors.[78]

Notes

1. See for the difference, Sanjay Subrahmanyam, 'The Fate of Empires: Rethinking Mughals, Ottomans and Habsburgs', in Huri Islamoğlu and Peter C. Perdue, eds., *Shared Histories of Modernity: China, India and the Ottoman Empire* (London, New York, New Delhi, 2008), 82. For comparative notes on the fate of the Ottoman, Safavid, and Mughal empires in the eighteenth century, see Rudi Matthee, 'The Decline of the Safavids in Comparative Perspective', *Journal of Persianate Studies* 8 (2015): 276–308.
2. P. J. Marshall, ed., *The Eighteenth Century in India History*, introd., 35.
3. See Felicity Nussbaum, *The Global Eighteenth Century* (Baltimore 2005), and for the French perspective and role, Thierry Sarmant, *1715: La France et le monde* (Paris 2014).

4. See, for example, most of the essays in Roxane Farmanfarmaian, ed., *War & Peace in Qajar Persia: Implications Past and Present* (London and New York, 2008); and, generally, the contributions to the journal *Qajar Studies*, the publication of an organization that seeks, among other things, to rehabilitate the Qajars.

5. Mohammad Ali ben Abi Taleb Hazin Laheji, *Tarikh va safarnameh*, ed. ʿAli Davani (Tehran 1375/1996); idem, *Rasael-e Hazin-e Lahiji*, ed. Ali Owjabi et al., (Tehran, 1377/1998); Mohammad Shafiʿ Tehrani, *Merʾat-e Varedat: Tarikh-e soqut-e Esfahan, pey-amadha-ye an va farmanravaʾi-ye Malek Mahmud Sistani*, ed. Mansur Sefatgol (Tehran, 1383/2004).

6. Mohammad Kazem Marvi, *ʿAlam-ara-ye Naderi*, ed. Mohammad Amin Riyahi, 3 vols (Tehran, 2nd edn., 1369/1990); and Mirza Mehdi Khan Astarabadi, *Tarikh-e Jahan-gosha-ye Naderi* (Tehran, 1368/1989).

7. Abdoʾl Hasan b. Mohammad Amin Golestaneh, *Mojmal al-tavarikh*, ed. Sayyed Mohammad Taqi Modarres Razavi (Tehran, 1356/1977); Mirza Mohammad Sadeq Musavi Nami Esfahani, *Tarikh-e geyti-gosha* (Tehran, 2nd edn., 1363/1984); and Mohammad Fath Allah b. Mohammad Taqi Savari, *Tarikh-e Mohammadi (Ahsan al-tavarikh)*, ed. Gholamreza Tabatabai (Tehran, 1371/1992).

8. Mirza Mohammad Kalantar-e Fars, *Ruznameh-ye Mirza Mohammad Kalantar-e Fars*, ed. ʿAbbas Eqbal Ashtiyani (Tehran, 1362/1983); and Mohammad Hashem Asef (Rostam al-Hokama), *Rostam al-Tavarikh*, ed. Mohammad Moshiri (Tehran, 2nd edn., 1352/1973). A new theory, proposed by Jalil Nowzari, holds that Rostam al-Hokama was a pseudonym and that the real author of his work was Reza Qoli Khan Hedayat, who was active as court historiographer under Naser al-Din Shah. See http://www.ibna.ir/fa/doc/report/225187.

9. Abraham of Crete, *The Chronicle of Abraham of Crete*, tr. and ed. George A. Bournoutian (Costa Mesa, 1999); and Abraham of Erevan, *History of the Wars 1721–1738*, tr. and ed. George A. Bournoutian (Costa Mesa, 1999).

10. See G. V. Abullaev, *Iz istorii Severno-vostochnogo Azerbaidzhana v 60-80 gg. XVIII veka* (Baku, 1958); T. Mamedova, *Russkie konsuly ob Azerbaidzhane 20-60-e gody XVIII veka* (Baku, 1989); Dzh. M. Mustafaev, *Severnye khanstva Azerbaidzhana i Rossiia (konets XVIII nachalo XIX v)* (Baku, 1989); and A. I. Yukht, *Torgovliia s vostochnymi stranami i vnutrennii rynok Rossii (20-60-e XVIII veka)* (Moscow, 1994).

11. See, most notably, M.-F Brosset, *Histoire de la Géorgie depuis l'Antiquité jusqu'au XIXe siècle*, 7 vols. (St Petersburg, 1858).

12. Tadeusz Juda Krusinski, *The History of the revolutions of Persia* (London, 1728), Leandro di Sicilia, *Persia ovvero secondo viaggio di F. Leandro di Sicilia* (Rome, 1757); Jonas Hanway, *An Historical Account of the British Trade over the Caspian Sea, with a Journal of Travels through Russia into Persia*, 4 vols. (London, 1753).

13. Joseph Emin, *The Life and Adventures of Joseph Emin*, ed. Amy Apcar (Calcutta, 1918); Michael Axworthy, 'Basile Vatatzes and His History of Nader Šah', *Oriente Moderno*, new ser. 25 (2006): 331–343; Samuel Gottlieb Gmelin, *Travels through Northern Persia 1770–1774*, trans. and annotated Willem Floor (Washington, DC, 2007); William Francklin, *Observations Made on a Tour from Bengal to Persia in the Years 1786-7* (London, 1790); Carsten Niebuhr, *Reisebeschreibung nach Arabien und andren umliegenden Ländern*, 2 vols. (Copenhagen, 1774–1778); and Lawrence J. Braack, *Undying Curiosity: Carsten Niebuhr and the Royal Danish Expedition to Arabia (1761–1767)* (Wiesbaden, 2014), 215–235.

14. See Jean Otter, *Voyage en Turquie et en Perse: Avec une relation des expéditions de Tahmas Kouli-Khan* (Paris: Guérin frères, 1748; new edn., *Journal de voyages en Turquie et en Perse 1734–1744*, Paris, 2010); Jean-Louis Bazin, 'Mémoires sur les derrières années du règne de Tahmas Kouli-Kan et sa mort tragique', in *Lettres édifiantes et curieuses* (Paris, 1780): 277–321; L.-F. Comte de Ferriéres-Sauveboeuf, *Mémoires historiques, politiques et géographiques des voyages faits en Turquie, en Perse et en Arabie depuis 1782 jusqu'en 1789*, 2 vols. (Paris: Buisson, 1790); André Michaux, *L'extraordinaire voyage d'un botaniste en Perse*, ed. Régis Pluchet (Toulouse, 2014); and G.-A. Olivier, *Voyage dans l'empire Othoman, l'Égypte et la Perse*, 3 vols. (Paris, 1801–1807).

15. Peter Avery, 'Nader Shah and the Afsharid Legacy', *The Cambridge History of Islam*, vol. 7, *From Nadir Shah to the Islamic Republic* (Cambridge, 1999), 3–62; and John Perry, 'The Zand Dynasty', in ibid., 64–103.

16. M. R. Arunova and K. Z. Ashrafiyan, *Gosudarstvo Nadir-Shakha Afahara* (Moscow, 1958); Michael Axworthy, *The Sword of Persia: Nader Shah, from Tribal Warrior to Conquering Tyrant* (London, 2006); Ernest S. Tucker, *Nadir Shah's Quest for Legitimacy in Post-Safavid Iran* (Gainesville, 2006); Willem Floor, *The Rise and Fall of Nader Shah: Dutch East India Company Reports 1730–1747* (Washington, DC, 2009); and Fouad Saberan, *Nader Chah ou la folie au pouvoir dans l'Iran du XVIIIe siècle* (Paris, 2013).

17. Mehdi Roschanzamir, *Die Zand Dynastie* (Hamburg, 1970); P. Rajabi, *Iran unter Karim Han* (Göttingen, 1970); and John R. Perry, *Karim Khan Zand* (Chicago, 1979). Also see John R. Perry, *Karim Khan Zand* (Oxford, 2006).

18. Reza Sha'bani, *Tarikh-e ejtema'i-ye Iran dar 'asr-e Afshariyeh*, 2 vols. (Tehran, 1369/1990); Nur Allah Larudi, *Nader: Pesar-e shamshir* (Tehran, 1387/2008); Parviz Rajabi, *Karim Khan Zand va zaman-e u* (Tehran, 2nd edn., 1355/1976); Gholamreza Varahram, *Tarikh-e siyasi va ejtema'i-ye Iran dat 'asr-e Zand* (Tehran, 1366/1987); Mahbubeh Tehrani, *Karim Khan Zand. Tarikh-e siyasi ejtema'i-ye Iran dar dawreh-ye Zandiyeh* (Tehran, 1386/2007); Abdol Hosein Navai, *Karim Khan Zand* (Tehran, 1391/2012); Ahmad Panahi Semnani, *Nader Shah: Baztab-e hamaseh va faje'eh-ye melli* (Tehran, 1373/1994); idem, *Lotf Ali Khan Zand: Az shahi ta tabahi* (Tehran, 2nd edn., 1373/1994).

19. Oliver H. Bonnerot, *La Perse dans la littérature et la pensée françaises au XVIIIe siècle: De l'image au mythe* (Paris, 1988), 257–258; C. G. Brouwer, ed., *Achmet & Thamas Koelikan: Turkse en perzische tragedies van Droste en van Steenwijk* (Amsterdam, 1993).

20. For the image of Nader Shah in contemporary Europe, see Jürgen Osterhammel, *Die Entzauberung Asiens: Europa und die asiatische Reiche im 18. Jahrhundert* (Munich, 2010), 224. Also see Rudi Matthee, 'The Imaginary Realm: Europe's Enlightenment Image of Early Modern Iran', *Comparative Studies of South Asia, Africa and the Middle East* 30:3 (2010): 449–462.

21. Abbas Amanat, 'The Kayanid Crown and Qajar Reclaiming of Royal Authority', *Iranian Studies* 34:1–4 (2001): 23.

22. Jan Malkom, *Tarikh-e Iran*, trans., Mirza Isma'il Heyrat (Bombay, 1876).

23. For this process, see Farzin Vejdani, *Making History in Iran: Education, Nationalism and Print Culture* (Stanford, 2014), 92–93.

24. John Malcolm, *A History of Persia*, 2 vols. (London, 1815), 2: 201.

25. Sayyed Javad Tabatabai, *Dibacheh-i bar nazariyeh-ye enhetat-e Iran* (Tehran, 1380/2001), 108.

26. For this perspective, see 'Abd al-Hadi Ha'iri, *Nakhostin ruyaru-iha-ye andisheh-geran-e Iran ba du-ru'i-ye tamaddon-e burzhvazi-ye gharb* (Tehran, 1367/1988); and, more recently, Hamid Hajiyan-Pur, 'Karim Khan Zand va Englis dar Khalij-e Fars', *Keyhan-e Andisheh* 79 (1377/1998): 51–60. For the encounter between Karim Khan Zand and, presumably, Skipp, see Rostam al-Hokama, *Rostam al-tavarikh*, 383; Ann Lambton, 'Some New Trends in Islamic Political Thought in Late 18th and Early 19th-Century Persia', *Studia Islamica* 39 (1977): 95–128; and Perry, *Karim Khan Zand*, 261–262, 267. In reality, Karim Khan's dismissive treatment of the English envoy may have been caused by irritation that the English had not succeeded in taming the Arab warlord Mir Muhanna, as the Carmelites surmised. See H. Chick, ed., *A Chronicle of the Carmelites in Persia* (London, 1939; new edn., 2012), 667–668.

27. For a discussion of these in the Indian case, see Burton Stein, 'Eighteenth-Century India: Another View', in P. J. Marshall, ed., *The Eighteenth Century in India History: Evolution or Revolution?* (Delhi, 2003), 62–89.

28. C. A. Bayly, 'India and West Asia, c. 1700–1830', *Asian Affairs. Journal of the Royal Society for Asian Affairs*, new ser. 19 (1988): 3–19.

29. C. A. Bayly, *Imperial Meridian: The British Empire and the World 1780–1830* (Harlow, UK, 1989), 35ff.

30. Gagan. D. S. Sood, *India and the Islamic Heartlands: An Eighteenth-Century World of Circulations and Exchange* (Cambridge, 2016), xii, 11–12.

31. See J. R. I. Cole, *Roots of North India Shi'ism in Iran and Iraq: Religion and State in Awadh, 1722–1859* (Berkeley, 1988); and Zackery M. Heern, *The Emergence of Modern Shi'ism: Islamic Reform in Iraq and Iran* (Oxford, 2015).

32. See Tucker, *Nadir Shah's Quest for Legitimacy.*

33. C. A. Bayly, *Imperial Meridian: The British Empire and the World 1780–1830* (Harlow, UK, 1989), 39. See also Axworthy, *Sword of Persia*, 168.

34. For the Indian campaign, see Lockhart, *Nadir Shah*, 122–162; Axworthy, *Sword of Persia*, 175–208; and Willem Floor, 'New Facts on Nadir Shah's Indian Campaign', in Kambiz Eslami, ed., *Iran and Iranian Studies: Essays in Honor of Iraj Afshar* (Princeton, 1998), 198–219.
35. Floor, 'New Facts on Nadir Shah's Indian Campaign', 199.
36. Ernest Tucker, 'Seeking a World Empire: Nadir Shah in Timur's Path', in Judith Pfeiffer and Sholeh A. Quinn, eds., *History and Historiography of Post-Mongol Central Asia and the Middle East: Studies in Honor of John E. Woods* (Wiesbaden, 2006), 332.
37. Sanjay Subrahmanyam, 'Un Grand Dérangement: Dreaming an Indo-Persian Empire in South Asia, 1740–1800', *Journal of Early Modern History* 4:3–4 (2000): 337–378. See also Axworthy, *Sword of Persia*, 212–213 and notes, and note 44, p. 290.
38. Ibid., 368.
39. See James Pickett, 'Nadir Shah's Peculiar Central Asian Legacy: Empire, Conversion Narratives, and the Rise of New Scholarly Dynasties', *International Journal of Middle East Studies* 48 (2016): 491–510. For underused sources, see 'Abd al-Karim Kashmiri, *Bayan-e vaqe'*, also called *Tarikh-e Naderi* or *Nadernameh*, ed. K. B. Nasīm (Lahore, 1970).
40. Ernest Tucker, 'The Peace Negotiations of 1736: A Conceptual Turning Point in Ottoman-Iranian Relations', *The Turkish Studies Association Bulletin* 20:1 (1996): 16–37; and Axworthy, *Sword of Persia*, 175–178.
41. This was the embassy of Ahmad Dourry Efendy as described in *Relation de Dourry Efendy, ambassadeur de la Porthe Otomane auprès du roy de Perse*, trans. by M. de Fiennes; edited by L. Langlès (Paris, 1810).
42. Mostafa Agha Salahshur Khasseh Kamani, *Fathnameh-ye Iravan: Ravabet-e Iran va 'Osmani dar astaneh-ye bar oftadan-e Safaviyan 1132–1137 h.q.*, ed. Mehmet Munir Aktepe, trans. Nasrollah Salehi and Safiya Khadiv (Tehran, 1394/2015).
43. To date, studies of this period are limited to Robert Olson, *The Siege of Mosul and Ottoman-Persian Relations 1718–1743: A Study of Rebellion in the Capital and War in the Provinces of the Ottoman Empire* (Bloomington, IN, 1975); Fariba Zarinebaf-Shahr, 'Tabriz under Ottoman Rule (1725–1731)' (PhD dissertation, University of Chicago, 1991); Clemens P. Sidorko, '"Kampf den kezerischen Qizilbash!": Die Revolte des Haggi Da'ud (1718–1728)', in Raoul Motika and Michael Ursinus, eds., *Caucasia between the Ottoman Empire and Iran, 1555–1914* (Wiesbaden, 2000), 133–145; and Nasrollah Salehi, *Tarikh-e ravabet-e iran va 'Osmani dar 'asr-e Safavi* (Tehran, 1394/2015), 251–276.
44. See Ali Sinan Bilgisi, 'Osmanli ve Safevi hakemiyetlerinde Tiflis (XVIII yuzyil)', *Türk Kültüru Incelem Eleri Dergisi* 21 (Istanbul, 2009): 23–62; Sirri Efendi, *Risaletu't tarikh-i Nadir Şah (Makale-i Vaki'a-i muhasara-i Kars)*, ed. Mehmet Yasar Ertas (Istanbul, 2012); and Helen Giunashvili and Tamr Abuladze, 'Researches on Persian and Georgian Historical Documents of Nader Shah's Times from Georgian Depositories', *Analytica Iranica* 4–5 (2013): 189–211.
45. The exception is the period of Nader Shah. Nader had an effective alliance with Russia against the Ottomans from the early 1730s until 1740–41, when it broke down because the Russians did not like Nader moving into the north Caucasus. See Axworthy, *Sword of Persia*, 71–72, 121, 124, 145–148, 236, 247–248.
46. See P. P. Bushev, *Posol'stvo Artemiia Volynskogo v Iran v 1715–18 gg.* (Moscow, 1978).
47. See V. G. Volovnikova, *Poslannik Petra I v vostoke: Posol'stvo Florii Beneveni v Persiiu i Bukharu v 1718–1725 godakh* (Moscow, 1986).
48. I. V. Kurukin, *Persidskii pokhod Petra Velikogo: Nizovoi korpus na beregakh Kaspiia (1722–1735)* (Moscow, 2010). For a new Russian study of Russo-Iranian relations in the eighteenth century, see I. V. Bazilenko, *Ocherki istorii rossisko-iranskikh otnoshenii (konets XVI-nachalo xx vv.)* (St. Petersburg, 2017), esp. 31–87.
49. See, for instance, Kumkum Chatterjee, *The Cultures of History in Early Modern India: Persianization and Mughal Culture in Bengal* (Oxford, 2009); and Mana Kia, 'Limning the Land: Social Encounters and Historical Meaning in Early Nineteenth-Century Travelogues between Iran and India', in Roberta Micallef and Sunil Sharma, eds., *On the Wonders of Land and Sea: Persianate Travel Writing* (Boston and Washington, DC, 2013), 44–67.
50. Tucker, *Nadir Shah's Quest for Legitimacy*, 73.
51. For the Franco-British rivalry in India between 1750 and 1850, see Maya Jasanoff, *Edge of Empire: Lives, Culture, and Conquest in the East 1750–1850* (New York, 2005).

52. Anne-Marie Touzard, *Le drogman Padery: Émissaire de France en Perse (1719–1725)* (Paris, 2005).
53. Gaspar Drouville, *Voyage en Perse fait en 1812 et 1813,* 2 vols (Paris, 1825), 1: 244.
54. As Abbas Amanat puts it: 'Through diaster and defeat, one can detect flickers of a new national awareness, one no longer tied to Safavid sovereignty but to the sorrowful memory of a glorious past, one that repeatedly would be invoked in the later Iranian experience.' See Abbas Amanat, *Iran. A Modern History* (New Haven and London, 2017), 173.
55. Perry, *Karim Khan Zand,* 267.
56. Abbas Amanat, 'Ebrahim Kalantar Shirazi', *Encyclopaedia Iranica* 8 (1998), 70.
57. Birgitt Hoffmann, 'The Rustam al-Tawarikh Revisited: An Early Qajar "Chronicle" Read as an Ego-Document', in Eva M. Jeremias, ed., *At the Gate of Modernism: Qajar Iran in the Nineteenth Century* (Piliscaba, 2012), 77–79.
58. Marshall, ed., *The Eighteenth Century in India History,* introd., 3ff.
59. For this, see Rudi Matthee, Willem Floor, and Patrick Clawson, *The Monetary System of Iran: From the Safavids to the Qajars* (London, 2013).
60. The one exception is the Caucasus. See, for instance, Irakli Paghava, 'The Currency of the Afsharid Dynasty in the Monetary Circulation of the Caucasus', *Studies in Modern and Contemporary History* 2/8 (2010): 391–408.
61. See John Perry, 'The last Safavids', *Iran: British Journal of Persian Studies* 9 (1971): 59–71.
62. Malcolm, *History of Persia,* 2: 193–194.
63. Hormoz Ebrahimnejad, *Pouvoir et succession en Iran: Les premiers Qajars 1762–1834* (Paris, 1999).
64. Assef Ashraf, 'From Khan to Shah: Social Ties and the Formation of the Qajar State in Iran, 1785–1848' (PhD dissertation, Yale University, 2015).
65. Christoph Werner, 'Ambiguity in Meaning: The "Vakil" in 18th and early 19th-century Iran', Proceedings of the Third European Conference of Iranian Studies: Held in Cambridge, 11th to 15th September 1995, ed. Nicholas Sims-Williams, *Mediaeval and Modern Persian Studies,* ed. Charles Melville (Wiesbaden, 1999), 317–325.
66. Ernest Tucker, 'Persian Historiography in the 18th and 19th Century', in Charles Melville, ed., *Persian Historiography* (London, 2012), 258–291.
67. Abbas Amanat, *Resurrection and Renewal: The Making of the Babi Movment in Iran, 1844–1850* (Ithaca and London, 1989); and Denis McEoin, *The Messiah of Shiraz: Studies in Early and Middle Babism* (Leiden, 2009).
68. Ata Anzali, *'Mysticism' in Iran: The Safavid Roots of a Modern Concept* (Columbia, SC, 2017).
69. Mansur Sefatgol, 'Bar oftadan-e farmanrava'i-ye Afshariyan az Khorasan va setizeh-ha-ye pay-ani-ye Afshariyan ba Qajariyan', *Fasnameh-ye 'elmi-ye pezhuhashi* 9/3 (1375/1996), 293–338.
70. Sir Harford Jones Brydges, *The Dynasty of the Kajars* (London, 1833), clxxxvii; and Amanat, 'Ebrahim Kalantar Shirazi', 68–69.
71. Thomas Ricks, 'Politics and Trade in Southern Iran and the Gulf, 1745–1765' (PhD dissertation, Indiana University, 1975), now available as *Notables, Merchants, and Shaykhs of Southern Iran and Its Ports: Politics and Trade of the Persian Gulf Region, AD 1728–1789* (Piscataway, NJ, 2013).
72. Christoph Werner, *Tabriz. An Iranian Town in Transition: A Social and Economic History of the Elites of Tabriz, 1747–1848* (Wiesbaden, 2000).
73. Christine Noelle-Karimi, *The Pearl in Its Midst: Herat and the Mapping of Khurasan (15th–19th Centuries)* (Vienna, 2014).
74. Willem Floor, *The Rise of the Gulf Arabs: The Politics of Trade on the Persian Littoral 1747–1792* (Washington, DC, 2007); *The Rise and Fall of Bandar-e Lengeh: The Distribution Center for the Arabian Coast, 1750–1930* (Washington, DC, 2010); *Bandar Abbas: The Natural Trade Gateway of Southeast Iran* (Washington, DC, 2011); *The Hula Arabs of the Shibkuh Coast of Iran* (Washington, DC, 2014); *Muscat: City, Society & Trade* (Washington, DC, 2015); with D. T. Potts, *Khark, The Island's Untold Story* (Washington, DC, 2017).
75. Tehrani, *Mer'at-e Varedat;* and 'Ali Reza Jannati Sarab, ed., *Tajdar-e nafarjam. Tajgozari-ye nafarjam-e Malek Mahmud Sistani dar Mashhad* (Mashhad, 1393/2014).

76. See the sources mentioned in n. 10, as well as Mostafa Agha, *Fathnameh-ye Iravan*; and Giunashvili and Abuladze, 'Researches on Persian and Georgian-Persian Historical Documents'.

77. Yamaguchi Akihiko, 'Urban-Rural Relations in Early Eighteenth-Century Iran: A Case Study of Settlement Patterns in the Province of Hamadan', in Kondo Nobuaki, ed., *Persian Documents: Social History of Iran and Turan in the Fifteenth-Nineteenth Centuries* (London, 2003), 147–185; and Soli Shahvar and Emile Abramoff, 'The Khan, the Shah and the Tsar: The Khanate of Talesh between Iran and Russia', in Rudi Matthee and Elena Andreeva, eds., *Russians in Iran. Diplomacy and Power in the Qajar Era and Beyond* (London, 2018), 24–48.

78. See Partha Chatterjee, *The Nation and Its Fragments: Colonial and Postcolonial Histories* (Princeton, 1993), 33.

4

The Awkwardness of Nader Shah: History, Military History, and Eighteenth-Century Iran

MICHAEL AXWORTHY

In December 2007 the journal *Iranian Studies* published an article from me with the title 'The Army of Nader Shah.'[1] Having given a description of Nader Shah's army, the article showed that Nader Shah's military successes had been due to a radical series of innovations in army structure, organization, and training, emphasizing in particular greatly increased firepower and a significant jump in army size. Developing from ideas in an earlier piece by Rudi Matthee,[2] and drawing on the research I had done toward my book *The Sword of Persia*,[3] the article drew a parallel with what has been called the Military Revolution in Europe, where similar developments—by demanding higher tax revenue, a greater degree of logistic and administrative sophistication, and, ultimately, higher education standards and a greater level of commitment to the State from all social classes—brought about the modern European nation state. It suggested that, but for Nader Shah's untimely demise, something similar could, with time, have happened in Iran. The force of these arguments relies on a train of logical steps taken to enhance the effectiveness of gunpowder weapons. The immediate utility of these measures (drill, regular pay, increase in numbers) would have been manifest at the time; the wider consequences (a greater need for bureaucratic support, administrative efficiency, and fiscal sophistication) initially probably not. It was not a question of Nader Shah having a blueprint for state building from the start, nor consciously (or even unconsciously) copying or following a Western model. Nor is it a question of Nader Shah being a great statesman or in any sense a Great Man. The Military Revolution theory says rather the opposite: that the pressure to maximize firepower and military efficiency had a logic of its own, and characteristic and logical consequences, if followed, independently of the personality or qualities of any individual.[4]

This piece is based on a presentation I made at the conference we held in Exeter in March 2013 to address some objections to my arguments that emerged in discussions of the 2007 article when it was presented as a lecture and at other times, some of which arose from misunderstandings about the military history, or the Military Revolution theory, or both. It also discusses some ways in which the Nader Shah episode still seems to be problematic in Iranian historiography more widely.

One objection (brought forward by Paul Luft), in a nutshell, has been that Persia in the eighteenth century was not Prussia. In other words, that eighteenth-century Persia was not in a position militarily or economically to develop in the way that Prussia, for example, developed from the mid-seventeenth century onwards.

But at the start of its trajectory toward power in Europe, Prussia was not Prussia either—neither literally nor metaphorically. The title of King in Prussia was only granted in 1701—prior to that the rulers of what became Prussia were known as the Electors of Brandenburg. That might seem a pedantic point, but it has a wider significance. Brandenburg was small and desperately weak in the seventeenth century, and did not look like a candidate for European hegemony. When Frederick William the Great Elector acceded in 1640, his territories were under Swedish occupation and were among the most severely devastated of the German lands ravaged in the terrible Thirty Years War. It has been estimated that the population of Brandenburg dropped by 50 per cent between 1618 and 1648.[5] The territory was in any case not rich, consisting for the most part of sandy and unproductive agricultural land. Brandenburg had never been one of the more economically advanced or politically significant German states, and in 1641 the Elector had an army of just 3,000 demoralized soldiers.[6] Brandenburg-Prussia was still weak later—in 1708 bubonic plague reduced the population by a third, and one historian has commented that as late as the 1730s and even during the reign of Frederick the Great 'a governmental infrastructure had scarcely begun to emerge.'[7] As with many early-modern states, Prussia's finances were shaky and dangerously highly geared, heavily dependent on loans and foreign subsidies. In the Seven Years War Prussia was almost annihilated altogether by an alliance of enemies—saved only by what Frederick the Great himself called the 'Miracle of the House of Brandenburg' after his defeat at the battle of Kunersdorf in August 1759.[8]

Persia in 1730 was also devastated by foreign invasions and occupation, and by the consequences of internal revolt in addition. Economic and political conditions were plainly very different, but it is not self-evident that Persia in 1730 was in a weaker position for political and military take-off than Brandenburg in 1640. It is true that Persia was not in Europe, and was in particular not subject to peculiarly intense European conditions of inter-state competition that prevailed in Europe. But competition is partly about a will to compete, which Nader certainly had. To insist on unique European conditions for Military Revolution risks a tautology that says it could only happen in Europe because it could only happen in Europe.[9]

Another doubt—springing perhaps from a similar background position, is about the figures. Some have been sceptical that Nader Shah's army could have been as big as I claimed; in particular, that the figure I quoted of 375,000 for the army at the beginning of the campaign of 1743 must be inflated.[10] But the overall assessment given in the *Iranian Studies* article does not depend on one piece of evidence or on a stream of evidence from one source. It depends on a triangulation from a diverse range of sources. They show that Nader's army grew from around 2,000–3,000 at the time he joined forces with the Safavid prince Tahmasp in 1726, to 25,000–30,000 in 1729, 80,000–100,000 in 1733, 120,000 or more in 1735–1736, and 150,000 in 1741. Sources for the figures include a Russian diplomat, a Greek traveller, the Dutch East India Company, an Armenian patriarch, an English merchant, and Ottoman sources, as well as Persian officials and historians.

The 375,000 figure comes from the account of a pay clerk recorded in the work of an official within Nader Shah's administration, Mohammad Kazem Marvi,[11] who was in a position to know whereof he wrote and was generally reliable. It represents the peak of Nader's power, when he was using the wealth of his Indian conquests to prepare for what he intended to be his decisive campaign against the Ottomans; he had apparently warned his commanders to expect three years of war. The total was broken down to show the numbers from different parts of the empire—25,000 from Hamadan and Kermanshah, 65,000 from Khorasan, 70,000 from Afghan and Indian territories, and so forth. Other sources for the climactic year of 1743 suggest a figure of 200,000 for the main field army that marched on Kirkuk and Mosul,[12] but that is not inconsistent with the larger figure of 375,000, which represents the total before detachments were separated off for garrisons and separate tasks, notably the pacification of smaller places in Iraq and a force sent to besiege Basra. One must allow for a degree of inaccuracy in these figures of course, but they are detailed and plausible, and I would suggest a margin of error of no more than 10–15 per cent.

Perhaps, given the scepticism, it would be worth including at this point a brief discussion, with examples, of some of the ways that troop numbers as given in sources may be misleading or ambiguous, and ways in which one may nevertheless attempt, despite the complications of conflicts between the sources, to reach a reasonable approximation.

There are two instances where the sources suggest directly that Nader attempted to deceive his enemies by giving the impression that his troops were more numerous than was the case in fact. One comes from early on in his career, when he joined forces with the Safavid pretender Tahmasp in September 1726. The Russian envoy Avramov in his account of this event wrote that Nader had 5,000 troops with him at this point,[13] but the Greek traveller Basile Vatatzes says that Nader had appointed four officers of the rank of *min-bashi*, who would normally command 1,000 men, with subordinate officers in proportion, in order that the structure of his forces would give the impression that there were more troops than the actual number, which was 2,000–3,000.[14] In this instance, as in most other cases, it seemed sensible to base an estimate on the lower end of the range. On another occasion, in 1733, Nader attempted to demoralize the besieged inhabitants of Baghdad by sending troops surreptitiously out of his camp by night, with orders to return the next day in full sight of the city walls, with colours flying and bands playing; thus giving the impression that his army was being augmented regularly by new arrivals of fresh troops.[15]

As at other times, there was uncertainty about the number of troops Nader had with him at the siege of Baghdad and at the battle that followed, in July 1733. The account of James Fraser, drawing on information from the English East India Company representative Cockell, suggested 120,000 troops at the time of the battle and gave a figure of 200,000 (albeit including servants) for the Ottoman army.[16] The Dutch East India Company gave a figure of 300,000 for the inhabitants of the Persian camp besieging Baghdad, of which 100,000 were fighting troops, and later reported that the Ottoman relief force was made up of 50,000 men from Istanbul and an equal number 'from Yerevan'. But at another point the Dutch reported that the Ottoman relief force was 250,000 strong and that on the day of battle Nader marched against them with 150,000 men.[17] Nader's own court historian, Mirza Mahdi Astarabadi, gave the Ottoman troop strength as 100,000 (the general scarcity of troop numbers for the Persian forces in Mirza Mahdi's account is probably another indicator of Nader's own preference for keeping potential enemies guessing).[18]

But none of these sources (with the possible exception of the last) were eyewitnesses; all were reporting at second or third hand. One of the few known eyewitness sources was Jean Nicodème, a Frenchman who had been physician to Topal Osman Paşa, the Ottoman commander. As presented by von Hammer-Purgstall, Nicodème's account suggests that Nader left 12,000 men in the siege lines round Baghdad (which is supported by other sources) and marched against the Ottomans with about 70,000. His account also suggests that the Ottomans had 60 cannon.[19] La Mamye-Clairac's *Histoire de Perse* appends a translated report from Topal Osman himself, giving an estimate of 80,000 troops for the Persian army.[20] I have preferred these lower figures, taken from eyewitnesses.

On another occasion, however, it seemed sensible not to go for the lower figure. After the battle of Murchakhor in November 1729, it appears that before a hurried departure from Isfahan one of the Afghans told the Dutch East India Company representative that an army of 40,000 Afghans had been defeated by 5,000–6,000 Persians.[21] Aside from the fact that this imbalance was improbable anyway, it does not fit with figures from other sources for the two armies in the campaign leading up to Murchakhor.[22] In this case it seems likely that the Afghan informant played down the number of Persians the better to express his indignation and chagrin that the Afghans had been defeated so dishonourably. The numbers for both armies were probably in the range 25,000–40,000.

An important source for troop numbers in the period 1743–1744 is the English merchant traveller Jonas Hanway,[23] who spent some time in Nader's camp in the spring of 1744, after the army had been wound down somewhat after the recent abortive campaign in Ottoman Iraq. J. R. Perry in his article on Nader Shah's army in the *Encyclopedia Iranica*[24] reports Hanway's comment to the effect that the numbers actually in camp when he arrived there were about 90,000, of whom 30,000 were actual soldiers.[25] But Hanway says at the same point that other large bodies of troops were dispersed in other parts of Nader's territories at that time (as would be normal when the army was not concentrated for operations against the enemy). A few pages later Hanway says that the army was 200,000 strong in total, but admits that the sum total of the different elements he goes on to enumerate in detail falls short of that figure ('the above computation falls short of 200,000 men; but they may be reckoned in this proportion'[26]). The total of different kinds of troops, and others (heralds, eunuchs, executioners, footmen) listed by Hanway comes to 168,160. Within this figure the combatant troops add up to 153,000 at least (more if some categories like camp guards and men serving the function of military police are counted as combatants). It seems likely that his interlocutors told him that the army was 200,000 strong because that was the expected, full-strength 'rule of thumb' figure for the size of the army at that time.

Beyond the question of troop numbers, there has been scepticism about the ability of industries in Persia to produce the firearms and particularly the cannon for this large army. But again, the evidence (both evidence for the production of the weapons, and for their existence and use thereafter) comes from a diversity of normally reliable sources, and includes pictorial evidence. Some of the best pictorial evidence comes from the illustrations included in the manuscript edition of Astarabadi's history from the 1750s, published in facsimile by Soroush and Negar in Tehran in 1991 with an introduction by Abdolali Adib Barumand. The image of Nader's victory over the Afghans at the battle of Mehmandust in 1729 is a particularly vivid depiction of his use of artillery *en masse* (the illustrations are in a naïve style, but there is no reason to doubt their accuracy; the images tend to reflect the descriptions in Astarabadi's text, as one would expect). The records of the Dutch East India Company report cannon-founding workshops in Isfahan being exhorted to produce more, and better, cannon (after Nader's defeat at Baghdad in 1733),[27] and young recruits being sent off to Afghanistan with new muskets so large they could barely lift them. An Ottoman source says Nader's army was furnished with a siege train of 116 heavy cannon and 230 mortars in 1743;[28] the sources confirm that the mortars virtually obliterated the interior of the city of Mosul during the siege of that year.[29]

Part of the scepticism about the figures springs perhaps from a historiographical position which tends to stress the weak and undeveloped nature of
the Iranian economy and the Iranian state, both in the Safavid period and later.
In those terms an Iran capable of producing a well-equipped, powerful army of
200,000 or more, especially in a period of economic dislocation, might appear
to be an anomaly. It's awkward. But it happened. Aside from the evidence of
the figures for the army in diverse and reputable historical sources, there is
the evidence of what the army *did* (and how). It conquered the capital of the
largest and economically most powerful Islamic state, Moghul India (albeit
briefly), and it repeatedly defeated the armies of the state strongest in military
terms, the Ottoman Empire (causing a series of major political upheavals within
the Ottoman state).[30] A quick count shows that Nader's troops defeated the
Ottomans in six major battles, and within that figure defeated the main field army
of the Ottoman state three times. Nader's armies were beaten by the Ottomans
just once, at Baghdad in 1733. The victories against opponents other than the
Ottomans were achieved largely by superior firepower; against the Ottomans
the Persians were more evenly matched, but their cavalry had an edge, and command and control were often better (and at least one source suggests that by the
end of Nader's reign his artillery was better than the Ottomans'[31]).

So this model of weakness and underdevelopment may be broadly correct,
but some further development of the argument is needed if the events of the
first part of the eighteenth century are going to fit, whether or not my arguments
for the beginnings of a Military Revolution are accepted. It is plain that Nader's
regime eventually placed unsupportable strain on the Iranian economy; it is also
plausible that the underlying conditions of poor infrastructure and poor communications; the wide separation of the cities of Iran and their forced depend-
ence on their own resources for subsistence, placed great strain on Nader and
his regime, contributing to the failure of his project (the way that the crisis of
1739–1742 unfolded, caused at root by Nader's absence in India and his son's
inexperience as viceroy at home, is a pointer to this). But I would nonetheless
argue that the extent of Nader's real achievements undermines a dismissive or
simplistic assertion of inevitability based on these factors.

Another view that disagrees with my analysis, from another angle though
not necessarily contradicting the previous one, has been put by Willem Floor.
Focussing especially on the reign of Abbas the Great in the late sixteenth/early
seventeenth century, Floor has pointed out that the Persian army at that time
was well armed with gunpowder weapons, and used them effectively, especially
against the Ottomans. His suggestion, therefore, is that my argument for a cat-
egorical shift during the reign of Nader Shah is exaggerated.

I do not dispute Shah Abbas's military achievement, but some of the progress
he made with military reforms was lost in the following generations, and even

at its peak, when he had around 40,000 men armed with gunpowder weapons (including a corps of around 12,000 artillerymen), his transformation of the Persian army did not match that of Nader Shah. Abbas's firearm troops were always outnumbered within his field armies by troops equipped with traditional weapons (typically, cavalry wielding lance, sword, and bow). By contrast, various independent eyewitnesses make clear that the overwhelming majority of Nader's troops were equipped with firearms.[32] More importantly, the nature of Shah Abbas's army was not transformed by the adoption of gunpowder weapons; the majority of his troops still thought of themselves and their tactical role in the traditional way. Nader Shah's troops were not just garnished with muskets and cannon—they were trained and constantly drilled to use them to maximum effect; their commander relied primarily for his battlefield successes on their firepower, and expanded the army well beyond the overall size Shah Abbas had achieved. The argument (made before me by Rudi Matthee[33]) does not say that the Safavids did not use gunpowder weapons—it is an argument of degree rather than absolutes. But Nader Shah's employment of firepower marked a significant change.

Another difference between Nader's more regularized army and those of his predecessors pertains to the relationship between him and his troops. They had to pay for much of their equipment and uniform themselves, though they were expected to buy them from specific suppliers of standard items, in the camp. But horses seem to have been an exception, as Abraham of Crete says, '. . . and if a man killed his horse by riding it too hard, he would immediately be given a replacement without quibble.'[34] In another context, when showing clemency to Moghul prisoners after the battle of Karnal and resisting pressure from his own men to take the prisoners' horses from them, Nader made a general statement that tells us why: 'the Bread of Soldiers depends on their Horses, most of them are in wretched and indigent Circumstances; should they lose their Horses, they and their Families would be reduced to Beggary and Starving.'[35] It was necessary for Nader to supply his troops with replacement horses (remounts) because otherwise they might hang back, delay, go slower, or avoid dangerous situations, for fear that their horses might be killed, injured, made sick or lame. Nader needed his troops to follow his orders boldly and aggressively at all times. Hence the commitment to supply them with remounts without quibble. Where previously, and in other regional armies, soldiers had been more in the position of independent contractors retained by payment only for a period, under Nader they were moving toward a new, more regular, and more dependent status, as was the case in Europe at the time.

Another objection, advanced by Edmund Herzig, while accepting the argument for a change in the nature of warfare under Nader Shah, has pointed to a lack of evidence for state-building under his rule; little evidence for military reforms

leading to fiscal or administrative development, as the Military Revolution theory would suggest. Rather the contrary—his style of rule tended to be rapacious
and destructive even before the mental disintegration of his last years.[36]

It is plain that Nader's rule did not last, and no modern state did in fact emerge.
But there *are* signs of the beginnings of this, despite the brevity of Nader's reign.
Some of these developments were explored (perhaps rather against the thrust
of her main argument) in Ann Lambton's important 1977 article.[37] It is worth
noting in this context that one of the first signs of Nader's likely eventual grab for
supreme power was his insistence on the right to raise taxes throughout Persia
in the settlement he made with Tahmasp II in 1729/1730. Similarly, a salient
feature of his religious policy was his expropriation of religious endowments[38]—
an action that has significant resonances with the expropriation of religious
endowments by state-building princes in Europe at the time of the Protestant
Reformation and after. Like many, if not most other early-modern military
entrepreneurs (one thinks of Wallenstein in particular), Nader always paid close
attention to the raising of money.

As Lambton's article explains, while in Isfahan in October–November 1736,
Nader set about far-reaching changes to the administration of the country that
would have produced a major modernization if they had been completed. Nader
had taken over the services of the old Safavid bureaucracy, but moulded his
administration to a new form. The functions of high officials were more limited, and some key offices, notably that of the chief vizir, were discontinued.
The nature and function of other offices changed. Nader eroded the distinction
between crown lands administered directly (*khassa*) and lands administered by
provincial governors or others (*mamalek*), towards a system whereby provincial governors collected taxes locally and remitted the proceeds to the centre
once they had made deductions for their own expenses. The openness of this
system to abuse by governors and other officials was corrected by Nader's fear-
some reputation and his use of spies. But while in Isfahan he also ordered a systematic assessment of all landed property, beginning with the provinces of Fars,
Isfahan, and Azerbaijan, making no distinction between crown lands, religious
properties, or the properties of other notables and previously protected groups.
It seems that Taqi Khan Shirazi, who was governor of Fars province, where the
assessment and reforms went ahead first, was the architect of this innovation; it
is significant that he was summoned to Isfahan for its inauguration. Governors
and officials were expected regularly to present detailed accounts of tax revenue
and expenditure, and they were harshly punished if the accounts were found
wanting. The purpose of all this was, of course, to maximize revenue for the
army. Later rulers (notably Karim Khan Zand) built on the tax records that
had been put together in Nader's time, which were admired for their accuracy
and thoroughness. It is reasonable to see in these reforms the first impulse of

his military revolution toward what could have been greater administrative and economic efficiency.[39]

Nader's relationship with his courtier and favourite Taqi Khan is suggestive in this context. Nader appointed him governor of Fars in 1734, but his activities went well beyond that office. The VOC records (in which there are many examples of his financial dealings on Nader's behalf) speak of him at one point as Nader's 'great mignon'[40] but although the two were obviously close, the suggestion of a sexual relationship is not otherwise attested—the term may simply have signified 'favourite'. His main value to Nader was as his financial adviser. Nader's peculiar trust in Taqi Khan Shirazi emerges in a number of ways—not least in the fact of his continued service after his rebellion (and terrible punishment) in 1744.[41]

This relationship, in some ways an unlikely one, between military innovator and financial conjuror, again has resonances with other states in the process of Military Revolution. There is a kind of inexorable logic to this alliance of skills, skills unlikely to be united within a single individual in any culture. Wallenstein had the Flemish Calvinist financier Hans de Witte.[42] One could say something similar of Louis XIV and Colbert (who characterized the conduct of tax policy as being like plucking a goose—the trick was to secure the maximum amount of feathers with the minimum of hissing). Frederick II of Prussia had two key financiers and moneyers, the Jews Veitel-Heine Ephraim and Daniel Itzig.[43]

It is worth noting also that all these cases, in which huge military expansion was facilitated by dubious financial juggling, were also marked eventually by acute economic trauma (often resulting at least in part from currency manipulation). The cumulative effects of the wars of Louis XIV on the economy of France, for example, were devastating. Military revolution was seldom a smooth ride, militarily, economically, or fiscally. It has been suggested that Nader lacked statesmanship because his rapacity resulted in economic exhaustion; the exhaustion is undeniable (though possibly exaggerated by some—and it seems Nader did not bring Persia to rock bottom: that was achieved by the civil wars that followed his death[44]). But in terms of the Military Revolution theory, these comparisons show that the economic trauma of Nader's Iran fits the thesis, rather than disproving it. It is also important (this is one of the central points of analysis in my book *The Sword of Persia*) to make a distinction between Nader's ruthless and intensely focussed conduct of policy in the years 1726–1739, and his brutal, obsessively avaricious, eventually deranged, and self-destructive conduct in the years 1742–1747.

Other indications of awkwardness appear in two recent publications from Cambridge University Press, namely Stephen F. Dale's book *The Muslim Empires of the Ottomans, Safavids and Mughals*,[45] and Gene Garthwaite's chapter on eighteenth-century Iran in volume 3 of the new *Cambridge History of Islam*.[46]

Both of these favour the overall argument developed by Ann Lambton—the idea that the eighteenth century in Iran was a period of tribal resurgence and bureaucratic decline.[47] Garthwaite in addition proposes that there was a kind of continuity of Safavid rule (a view advanced also by Andrew Newman[48]). Dale states that Nader Shah was the leader of the Afshar tribe, which was never really the case. Garthwaite says, 'While Nadir's military exploits and his political skill in forming an effective military force . . . are undoubted, yet his motives and purpose continue to elude us. Even less explicable is the purpose behind his religious proposals to bring Shi'ism more in accord with Sunnism.' Yet Ernest Tucker made a sophisticated and convincing reassessment of Nader Shah's religious policy in his 2006 book, and my own book on Nader Shah (published at almost the same time) also discussed these points at some length.[49] Both of us brought forward serious new analysis and conclusions, which these other authors appear to have set aside without comment. In fact, Nader stated explicitly in 1733 (at the coronation of the infant Abbas III) what his military and political objectives were—to 'throw reins around the necks of the rulers not only of Ottoman Turkey and Kandahar, but also Turkestan and India'.[50] In other words, his purpose was to bring all of the central Empires of Islam under his control, and he came close to achieving it. My view is that his religious policy was manifestly aligned with that overall purpose—it was necessary, if Nader was to achieve hegemony, for him to present himself and his regime as Sunni rather than Shi'a, given that Sunnism was the majority position of Islam as a whole.

Another surprising example comes from Stephanie Cronin's 2013 book *Armies and State-Building in the Modern Middle East*, which includes the following passage:

> In the eighteenth century Nadir Shah, having concluded that the Europeans' victories over the Ottomans were due to the discipline and order with which they fought, studied foreign methods, began to organise an artillery, and entrusted the direction and command of newly raised infantry to European, mostly French, officers. Nonetheless he too continued to depend principally on his cavalry, the new infantry regiments playing little part in fighting his wars.[51]

Unfortunately she substantiates none of these statements with a note. Nader Shah may have had some awareness of the Ottomans' wars with European powers, but to my knowledge no contemporary source reports his views on them, nor any study by him of 'foreign methods'. In fact, during the period of Nader's reign the Ottomans achieved a significant victory against the Austrians—at Grocka in 1739—leading to the Treaty of Belgrade by which the Habsburg monarchy ceded that city to the Ottomans. If Nader had known of that, he might have drawn opposite conclusions to those suggested by Cronin. As acknowledged in my book *The Sword of Persia* and in my *Iranian Studies* article of 2007, Nader's relations with Russia had a military dimension.[52] There is an intriguing reference in Astarabadi's account to *ferenghi* artillery specialists in Nader's army at the battle of Mehmandust in 1729; the term is ambiguous and could in isolation mean French, but could also mean generically 'foreign/European', and this is more likely, in that time and place, signifying Russian or Russian-supplied gunners (given the known contacts between Nader and Russian emissaries around this time, and the absence of any evidence for contacts with France).[53] There is evidence that Russian (not French) artillery engineers helped Nader with his siege of Ganja in the autumn of 1734–1735.[54] One source (French) suggests that he had 40 Russians and three Englishmen with him in India in 1738/1739, but that source is uncorroborated and doubtful.[55] There is no evidence that infantry units were directed or commanded by French, Russian, or other European officers. It is *possible* that he had more help from the Russians than appears from the sources available, including with infantry drill, but there is no evidence for it.[56] Nor is it true that Nader depended principally on his cavalry in his tactics and strategy. In most of his battles, infantry firearms and artillery played a major role, and often the decisive role, as is plain enough from contemporary accounts of the battles of Mehmandust in 1729 and Karnal a decade later, among other examples.[57] In my 2007 article I pointed up parallels between Nader's tactical system and that of Napoleon.[58] Nader Shah's successes in fact depended on the innovative use of gunpowder weapons and the integrated action of mutually supporting combined arms. Cronin's reference to 'new infantry regiments' is also misleading—seeming to anticipate the events of Fath Ali Shah's reign, or perhaps the Nezam-e Jadid reforms of Selim III in the Ottoman empire at the end of the eighteenth century, rather than the reforms of Nader Shah.

Lambton's 1977 article is thought-provoking and contains much that is important, and it should not be discarded merely because it has been around more than a couple of decades, but there are some flaws in the tribal resurgence argument, and I am not alone in discerning them (Willem Floor explores these matters elsewhere in this volume). For one thing, it describes more than it explains. We are left little the wiser as to why the tribes surged or the bureaucracy declined. It seems likely that in Iran at least the tribes surged simply because the collapse of the Safavid monarchy allowed them to, which places us back with the need for an explanation of Safavid collapse. And collapse is the right word. There were Safavid princes in positions of apparent power after 1722, but they were all puppets to a greater or lesser extent, and few of them lasted long. There is good evidence that, somewhat contrary to the continuity line, the Safavid dynasty were held in contempt by some by the mid-eighteenth century. One need only read the enjoyable writings of Rustam ol-Hukama to explore this, but there are others too, and I argue in *The Sword of Persia* that Nader Shah's conduct of government was in itself a critique of Safavid practice and a deliberate break with it, in a series of ways.[59] There plainly was a lingering loyalty to the old dynasty in some quarters, but it seems to have had little more practical resonance than the nostalgic Jacobitism among some in England in the latter part of the eighteenth century, for example. Descendants of Nader Shah ruled in Khorasan until the 1790s, and there was sentiment in their favour after that. When Agha Mohammad Shah was crowned in 1796 he chose to hold the ceremony in exactly the same place on the Moghan plain as Nader Shah's coronation in 1736, and he held it exactly 60 years later to the day, buckling on Nader Shah's sword. That sword, along with other elements of the crown jewels deriving from Nader, remained an important part of the regalia of the monarchy into the Pahlavi period. But few would seriously claim any substantial Naderi continuity. Similarly, forward claims for Safavid continuity seem to me to be misleading. The fundamental fact is that Safavid rule ended in 1722 and what followed was different (continuity of traditional forms in government, politics, and society more generally is another matter—a number of those forms predated the Safavids in any case).

I said earlier that Nader Shah was not the leader of the Afshar tribe—in important ways he was not a tribal leader at all. Unlike Agha Mohammad Shah later, he did not descend from any of the leading families of the tribe to which he belonged, and throughout his career important Afshars were his enemies (probably at least in part because they saw him as an insufferable upstart, but there seem also to have been feuds originating in violent incidents early in his career). Aside from his own immediate family, his most trusted companions were Jalayirs, Afghans, Kurds, and Persians from Shiraz and Astarabad, but there were few Afshars among them. His style of warfare was innovative rather than tribal or traditional.

Similarly his religion and politics. Somewhat against the standard characterization of dynastic and tribal politics that we have for this period, Nader exploited forces from below in his rise to power. There is evidence from Nader's coup against the puppet king Tahmasp II in 1732, and from his coronation in 1736 (both achieved without, or in the latter case, almost without bloodshed), that a response to popular opinion, and in particular a popular demand for strong leadership, was part of his calculations. Before the coup of 1732, Nader issued a manifesto against the humiliating peace treaty Tahmasp had just concluded with the Ottomans, condemning it, appealing to religious sentiment and to fellow-feeling for Shi'a Persians captured or enslaved by the Sunni Ottomans. At the same time he wrote letters to provincial governors that were also intended for wide circulation, declaring 'The peace . . . neither meets the approbation of the nobles nor [that of] the commonalty of the empire.'[60] With these documents

Nader was defying not just the treaty, but also the will and the traditions of the Safavid monarchy, and appealing to popular sentiment. According to the categories in which some think of early modern Iran (emphasizing tribal and communal loyalties, and denying the existence of wider political allegiances), such a thing is nigh-on inconceivable. But it happened. Similarly with Nader's coronation in 1736—coercion was implicit at least, but there was also a genuine canvassing for a popular demand for strong government to replace the discredited Safavids. This emerges from a variety of sources, but a notably valuable eyewitness one is the chronicle of the Armenian patriarch, Abraham of Crete.[61]

The term 'Afsharid' for Nader and his dynasty is misleading (as suggested in the introduction to this volume, 'Naderi' or 'Naderid' may be better). Like the idea that his conquests were somehow purposeless and random, the 'tribal leader' tag seems sometimes to be intended to diminish and marginalize Nader Shah, perhaps rather like the notion we already came across, that his religious and other policies were inexplicable or bizarre, when they were not. In the *Encyclopedia Iranica*, Ernest Tucker has referred to Nader's invasion of Daghestan in 1741–1742 as 'quixotic'—but it was not. The tribes he set out to punish there had defied Nader's authority and had killed his brother, Ebrahim. No autocratic leader like Nader could afford to allow a rebel to defy his authority or dent his prestige. Whatever Nader Shah's real faults, and they were many, his purposes and his place in Iranian history should be seen for what they were.

This is a strange situation. Why would anyone want to ignore or marginalize this period in Iranian history? I suggested in *The Sword of Persia* some reasons why Nader Shah might have been neglected in the nineteenth century—the crude Victorian view of Persia and the Orient generally was that they were incorrigibly passive, decadent, and corrupt—ripe for colonization and improvement from outside. A vigorous, ruthlessly efficient ruler like Nader did not fit in that picture, so he was sidelined. In addition, his military successes in India might have appeared to detract from the glory of Clive and the other colonizers, and could have brought some to question the supposedly inherent superiority of Western arms—all most important to the myth of Empire. So despite the respect he had inspired among his European contemporaries, in the nineteenth century he was regarded as little more than an anomaly in the history of India.

But there is an impression that he is still a problem, that people still leave him out of the contemporary historiography. Why?

One possible reason we have already explored—that Nader Shah appears not to fit into a particular view of Iran as economically and politically weak in the early modern period. Another reason to leave him out could be that he might appear superficially to lend force to those who foolishly claim that throughout history, and again in the present, Iran has been inherently, incorrigibly expansionist and imperialist. But there is perhaps another reason too—a tendency since 1979, understandably, to look to the history of the ulema as the central important question in this period. This says that the important thing in Iran is the clergy, and the rise of the clergy, and the trajectory towards 1979. Part of that is perhaps a tendency to ignore hard realities of power politics in favour of the self-projection of the Safavid regime, which of course favoured the ulema. Hence, perhaps, the Safavid continuity idea. In my view, part of the reason the Safavids fell was believing their own propaganda—or if you prefer, their own self-legitimation—is it to be a sign now of a certain kind of study that we have to be taken in by it too? The resurgence of the Shi'a ulema after their complicity in the fall of the Safavids is important—it may even be the most important historical phenomenon in eighteenth-century Iran. But it is not the *only* important phenomenon, and even if it were, an understanding of Nader Shah's religious policy has a significant part within that story also.

The rise of the ulema is not the only trajectory. There is also the trajectory towards 1921 and the coup that brought the military government of Reza Shah to power. Time, place, and circumstances were plainly different, and there is more to say on the subject, but one obvious point of comparison between Nader and Reza Shah was policy toward the tribes. Where Nader focussed on division, resettlement, and the exploitation of manpower for his army,[62] Reza Shah's policy was aimed more at sedenterization (though conscription was also part of it).[63] But both had the same end: breaking the independent power of the tribes and forcing them to accept central authority and control; in Weberian terms, the achievement of a State monopoly of military force. And the means was the same: coercion (brutal if necessary) by a strong army backed up by solid logistical and financial structures.

Technocratic military autocracy was an option in Iran, as in Egypt under Mehmet Ali, as in Prussia under the various Frederick Williams and Fredericks, and in Russia under Peter the Great, in France under Louis XIV, and a variety of other states. To compare these people and their activities is not to fall into approbation or hero worship of so-called 'Great Men', nor to overestimate their significance. Aside from the other comparisons, they showed a similar indifference to human life and the loss of it, seeing soldiers and noncombatants alike as means to an end. To recognize that and to take it seriously as a historical phenomenon is not to applaud or approve it.

The theory of Military Revolution is itself controversial.[64] But even some of its critics (and some have begun as critics only to become proponents, albeit with amendments[65]) accept the overall argument of long-term state development necessitated by military competition and military innovation. For a historian of the Middle East, there is a congruence between the ideas of Roberts[66] and Parker on the one hand, and those of Marshall G. Hodgson[67] about what

Hodgson calls technicalization and the differential development of Europe and the Middle East on the other. And those of John A. Hall[68] and Ernest Gellner.[69] In the theory of science, one of the tests of new theory is that it should be found to apply when new evidence appears. One might think of the example of Nader Shah in that light.

There is room at the table for different kinds of history, and insights from military history have their place too. Especially when the period of history in question is dominated by a militarist like Nader Shah. If our model of Iran in the early modern period cannot explain the tightly organized, centralized, militaristic state that battered its neighbours into submission, restored and then extended the country's previous borders, and conquered Delhi between 1730 and 1740, then it needs to be adjusted.

Notes

1. Michael Axworthy, 'The Army of Nader Shah', *Iranian Studies*, vol. 40, no. 5, December 2007.
2. Rudi Matthee, 'Unwalled Cities and Restless Nomads: Firearms and Artillery in Safavid Iran', in *Safavid Persia: The History and Politics of an Islamic Society*, ed. Charles Melville (London, 1996).
3. Michael Axworthy, *The Sword of Persia* (London, 2006).
4. That is not to gainsay the advantages long acknowledged by historians of unity of command, of a commander having under his own hand the direction of all military, political, and administrative matters, without the interference of administrative committees or other authorities. That is a separate matter.
5. Christopher Clark, *Iron Kingdom: The Rise and Downfall of Prussia, 1600–1947* (London, 2007), p. 35.
6. Clark, 2007, pp. 34 and 43.
7. Clark, 2007, p. 112.
8. See Tim Blanning, *Frederick the Great: King of Prussia* (London, 2015), pp. 239–241 and 278–280. The Miracle has sometimes been attributed to another event; the weakening of the anti-Prussian alliance after the death of Empress Elizabeth of Russia in January 1762 (including, it seems, *in extremis*, by Goebbels and Hitler; see Hugh Trevor-Roper, *The Last Days of Hitler*, London, 1947, pp. 106–110); but Blanning argues persuasively in his excellent biography that to do so is mistaken.
9. Paul Luft has also argued that Nader had no posterity, that his achievements ended with him. This is plainly more difficult to contest, but it is not my argument that Iran actually became a modern state; I accept that Nader's regime failed and the Military Revolution foundered with it. Nevertheless, Nader did have some posterity; aspects of Qajar royal iconography nodded to him as a predecessor (as discussed elsewhere here) and in many ways, both in spirit and in military terms, Ahmad Shah Dorrani's Afghanistan can be regarded as a Naderi successor state, as Gommans has argued (Jos Gommans, *Rise of the Indo-Afghan Empire 1710–1780*, Leiden, 1995, and Jos Gommans, 'Indian Warfare and Afghan Innovation During the Eighteenth Century', in *Warfare and Weaponry in South Asia 1000–1800*, ed. J. L. Gommans and D. H. A. Kolff, [OUP India, 2001]); see also Amin Tarzi, 'Tarikh-i Ahmad Shahi: The First History of "Afghanistan"', in Nile Green (ed.), *Afghan History Through Afghan Eyes* (London, 2015).
10. Perry in his *Encyclopedia Iranica* article (J. R. Perry, 'Army IV: Afshar and Zand', in *Encyclopaedia Iranica*, ed. Ehsan Yarshater [London and New York, 1987], vol. II, pp. 506–508) did not dispute the 375,000 figure from Mohammad Kazem Marvi.

11. Mohammad Kazem Marvi Yazdi, *Alam Ara-ye Naderi* (3 vols, 3rd edition) (AAN), ed. Mohammad Amin Riyahi (Tehran, 1374/1995), pp. 887–888.
12. Notably an Ottoman source quoted in J. von Hammer-Purgstall, *Geschichte des Osmanischen Reiches* (Pest, 1831), vol. 8, p. 47.
13. N. D. Miklukho-Maklai, 'Zapiski S Avramova ob Irane kak istoricheskii Istochnik', in *Uchenye Zapiski Leningradskogo gosudarstvennogo universiteta: Seriia vostokovedcheskikh nauk*, part 3 (128) (Leningrad, 1952), p. 93.
14. Basile Vatatzes (ed. N. Iorga), *Persica: Histoire de Chah-Nadir* (Bucharest, 1939), pp. 77–79.
15. Jonas Hanway, *An Historical Account of the British Trade over the Caspian Sea ... to which are added The Revolutions of Persia during the present Century, with the particular History of the great Usurper Nadir Kouli* (4 vols) (London, 1753), vol. 4, pp. 83–84; Hanway seems to have drawn on La Mamye-Clairac (see note below), among others, for his account, but does not name his sources.
16. James Fraser, *The History of Nadir Shah* (London, 1742), p. 109.
17. Willem Floor, *The Rise and Fall of Nader Shah: Dutch East India Company Reports 1730–1747* (Washington, DC, 2009), pp. 29–31.
18. Mirza Mohammad Mahdi Astarabadi, *Jahangusha-ye Naderi*, translated into French by Sir William Jones as the *Histoire de Nader Chah* (London, 1770), vol. 1, p. 167 (original Persian text ed. Abdollah Anvar [Tehran: Anjoman Asar va Mafakher-e Farhangi, 1377/1998]).
19. Von Hammer (French trans. by J. J. Hellert), *Histoire de l'Empire Ottoman* (Paris, 1835–1843), vol. XIV, pp. 290, 517.
20. Louis André de la Mamye Clairac, *Histoire de Perse* (Paris, 1750), vol. 3, p. 308.
21. Willem Floor, *The Afghan Occupation of Safavid Persia 1721–1729* (Paris, 1998), p. 262.
22. Adle (Chahryar Adle, *La bataille de Mehmandust (1142/1729)*, in *Studia Iranica* 2, Fascicle 2, 1973, pp. 234–241), following Otter and Mohammad Kazem Marvi, believed (p. 240) that 50,000 Afghans fought at Mehmandust in September 1729, and that Nader commanded about 44,000 there, though he accepted that the figures could have been exaggerated to some extent. In Axworthy, 2006, I suggested 25,000 for Nader's army at Mehmandust and 40,000 for the Afghans (pp. 90–91 and notes).
23. Jonas Hanway, *An Historical Account of the British Trade over the Caspian Sea ... to which are added The Revolutions of Persia during the present Century, with the particular History of the great Usurper Nadir Kouli* (4 vols) (London, 1753).
24. J. R. Perry, 'Army IV: Afshar and Zand', in *Encyclopaedia Iranica*. ed. Ehsan Yarshater (London and New York, 1987), vol. II, pp. 506–508.
25. Hanway, 1753, vol. 1, p. 242.
26. Hanway, 1753, vol. 1, pp. 251–253.
27. Floor, 2009, pp. 33–34.
28. Von Hammer, 1831, vol. VIII, p. 48—note that eighteenth-century mortars and modern mortars are quite different weapons (Axworthy, 2006, p. 252n).
29. Robert W. Olson, *The Siege of Mosul and Ottoman-Persian Relations 1718–1743*, (Bloomington, IN, 1975), pp. 174–175 and 186–187.
30. Including the Patrona Khalil revolt of 1730 in Istanbul and the deaths of two more Grand Viziers after that—see Olson, 1975, *passim*, and Axworthy, 2006, pp. 109–110, 151–152, and 268–269.
31. Vatatzes/Iorga, 1939, pp. 283–284; Axworthy, 2006, p. 268.
32. See particularly Abraham of Crete, p. 118, and Hanway, vol. 1, pp. 251–253.
33. Matthee, 1996.
34. Abraham of Crete, p. 118.
35. Fraser, 1742 (account of Mirza Zaman), p. 218.
36. Points made at the Exeter workshop, March 2013. Herzig's own paper presented some evidence for the period of Nader Shah's reign from Armenian sources, notably Joseph Emin, (evidence presented also in Axworthy, 2006, p. 270). Emin reported Nader's brutal treatment of people brought before him in Isfahan at the beginning of 1746. The purpose of my argument is not to suggest that Nader was an admirable human being or a role model, and the enumeration of sources favourable to Nader (Astarabadi, Vatatzes, Fraser) and unfavourable (VOC, Hanway, etc.) would not in itself be a fruitful exercise.

37. Ann K. S. Lambton, 'The Tribal Resurgence and the Decline of the Bureaucracy in the Eighteenth Century', in *Studies in 18th Century Islamic History*, ed. Thomas Naff and Roger Owen (Carbondale and Edwardsville: Southern Illinois University Press, 1977), pp. 108–129; see also Axworthy, 2006, pp. 167 and 180.

38. Axworthy, 2006, pp. 171–172; Fraser, 1742, pp. 121–122; Mansur Sefatgol, *The Question of Awqaf Under the Afsharids* in *Studia Iranica: Cahiers vol. 21 / Materiaux pour l'Histoire Economique du Monde Iranien*, eds Rika Gyselen and Maria Szuppe (Paris, 1999), pp. 209–229, p. 229.

39. Lambton, 1977, pp. 126–128; drawing on Rustam ol-Hukama and the *Fars-Nama* of Hajji Mirza Hasan Fasai.

40. Willem Floor, *The Rise and Fall of Nader Shah: Dutch East India Company Reports 1730–1747* (Washington, DC, 2009), p. 90.

41. Axworthy, 2006, pp. 264–265; at another point the VOC records call him Nader's joker (boufon)—Floor, 2009, p. 57.

42. Golo Mann, *Wallenstein* (London, 1976), pp. 175–178, 314–315, and *passim*.

43. Clark, 2007, pp. 257–258.

44. Rudi Matthee, Willem Floor, and Patrick Clawson, *The Monetary History of Iran: From the Safavids to the Qajars* (London, 2013), pp. 173–174.

45. Stephen F. Dale, *The Muslim Empires of the Ottomans, Safavids, and Mughals* (Cambridge, 2009).

46. 'Transition: The end of the old order—Iran in the eighteenth century', in *The New Cambridge History of Islam,* vol. 3 (Cambridge, 2010).

47. Lambton, 1977.

48. *In Our Time*, BBC Radio 4, January 12, 2012.

49. Ernest Tucker, *Nadir Shah's Quest for Legitimacy in Post-Safavid Iran* (Florida, 2006); Axworthy, 2006.

50. AAN, p. 234.

51. Stephanie Cronin, *Armies and State-Building in the Modern Middle East: Politics, Nationalism and Military Reform* (London, 2013), p. 46.

52. Axworthy, 2007, pp. 643–644.

53. Axworthy, 2006, p. 303 (note 44).

54. Axworthy, 2006, p. 147.

55. Axworthy, 2006, p. 198 and note p. 317.

56. Axworthy, 2007, pp. 643–644.

57. See Axworthy, 2006, pp. 93 and 200–203.

58. Axworthy, 2007, p. 644.

59. Axworthy, 2006, pp. 165–168 and elsewhere—a point that has been taken up by Rudi Matthee in his book *Persia in Crisis: Safavid Decline and the Fall of Isfahan* (London, 2011).

60. Axworthy, 2006, p. 118.

61. Abraham of Crete, *The Chronicle of Abraham of Crete*, ed. and trans. G. A. Bournoutian (Costa Mesa: Mazda Publishers, 1999), p. 92; Axworthy, 2006, p. 162.

62. See Axworthy, 2006, pp. 111–113; also J. R. Perry, 'Forced Migration in Iran during the Seventeenth and Eighteenth Centuries', in *Iranian Studies*, 1975, vol. 8, part 4, pp. 199–215.

63. See, for example, Kaveh Bayat, 'Riza Shah and the Tribes: An Overview', in *The Making of Modern Iran*, ed. S. Cronin (RoutledgeCurzon, 2003).

64. For a recent run around some of the issues, see Jeremy Black, *Beyond the Military Revolution: War in the Seventeenth-Century World* (Basingstoke, U.K., 2011).

65. Geoffrey Parker, *Military Revolution* (Cambridge, 1988).

66. Michael Roberts, *The Military Revolution 1560–1660*, (Belfast, 1956).

67. Marshall G. S. Hodgson *The Venture of Islam* (Chicago, 1974).

68. John A. Hall, *Powers and Liberties* (Harmondsworth, U.K.: Pelican, 1986).

69. Ernest Gellner, *Muslim Society* (Cambridge, 1981); also 'The Tribal Society and Its Enemies', in *The Conflict of Tribe and State in Iran and Afghanistan*, ed. R. Tapper (London, 1983).

5

Iran and the Ottomans after Nader Shah: The Dorrani-Ottoman Exchange of Letters in Their Eighteenth-Century Iranian Context

ERNEST TUCKER

Introduction

Much has been written about the terrible upheavals visited upon Iran and its neighbors by Nader Shah's reign of foreign adventure and domestic severity. His impact was undeniably felt long after his assassination, since ensuing succession struggles broke Iran up into several autonomous regions over the next few decades. Despite this domestic turbulence, Iranian relations with the Ottomans after Nader became gradually more stable over the next few decades, based on the framework created by the Kordan Treaty of 1746.[1]

This agreement, concluded between Nader and the Ottomans after many years of conflict, re-established conditions of relative peace that had characterized the Ottoman-Iranian relationship between the 1639 Treaty of Qasr-e Shirin (known in Iran as the "Treaty of Zohab") and the Afghan invasion of the 1720s. Building on the earlier treaty, the Kordan accord now included specific recognition of Persian visitors in Ottoman lands as enjoying equal status with all other Muslims there and openly acknowledged their rights to visit Shi'i tombs in Iraq. Despite Nader's demise soon after its signing, the new agreement's terms remained in force even during later episodes of renewed Ottoman-Iranian conflict, when relations were challenged by intermittent episodes of heightened religious tension as well as incessant border disputes. There were many inherent points of tension between Iran and the Ottomans, most notably the continual background friction produced by pilgrimage traffic between Iran and the shrine cities of Iraq. Although this required steady monitoring on both sides in times of peace and could be exploited by either in times of domestic and foreign conflict, it never really called into question the basic terms of the Kordan accord.

Continued adherence to the specific terms of this treaty and later agreements that built on it meant that unlike in Safavid times, Ottoman-Iranian relations gradually became construed more and more in "national" rather than "dynastic" terms. During the Safavid era, royal relations at the highest imperial level had often been quite familiar and personal, given that individual members of the Ottoman and Safavid dynasties developed close ties and became involved in each other's court intrigues. In the post-Nader period, the steady development of a more formal diplomatic relationship between the two sides as "states" that began at Kordan ultimately culminated in various twentieth-century agreements.

The period of Ottoman-Iranian relations between 1639 and the Ottoman-Iranian Treaty of Erzurum in 1848 has sometimes been depicted mostly as a background for the rise of Europe in the region and the growth of the European world-system as it extended its reach globally.[2] More recently, such Eurocentric approaches to globalization theory have been challenged by scholars suggesting that multiple centers of change in the world interacted more dynamically and less in one direction than has been supposed.[3] Whatever theoretical models might be adopted and regardless of which dynasty ruled, later agreements between Iran and the Ottoman Empire continued to build on the system created at Kordan.

Numerous challenges to this stable framework arose upon Nader's demise as Iran's successive eighteenth-century rulers tried to establish their legitimacy. Ottoman skill in preserving an established *longue durée* of relations with Iran despite the vagaries of Iranian dynastic politics through this period deserves further notice. Exploration of how this worked may shed some light on the elusive continuities of the Ottoman-Iranian system, which seemed able to find ways to preserve enduring ties even when international relations suddenly became strained, hostile, and completely rearranged.

One illustrative example can be found by exploring how the Ottomans managed diplomacy with Iran during the first two decades after Nader's fall. Their attempts to continue as before with his successors culminated in a diplomatic exchange in the early 1760s between Ottoman Sultan Mustafa III and Ahmad Shah Dorrani. Ahmad Shah, founder of the Dorrani dynasty and today most notably credited with the establishment of modern Afghanistan, did establish a measure of sovereignty over major portions of northern India and Iran for much of the last half of the eighteenth century. His activities bore resemblance to Nader's imperial projects, since Ahmad Shah enjoyed significant early successes against adversaries on all sides of his domains much as Nader had at first. Thus, it is revealing to examine how the Ottomans handled such a ruler with similar aspirations to change the basic parameters of the existing regional political order.

The Context of the Ottoman-Dorrani
Exchange of Letters

The Ottoman-Dorrani exchange was certainly not the first chapter in Ottoman-Iranian relations following Nader's demise. After his death at the hands of his own troops, his nephew Aliqoli had taken the throne briefly as " 'Adel Shah" after having killed all of Nader's progeny except Shahrokh, one of his grandsons. After 'Adel Shah sent his own brother Ebrahim to Isfahan, Ebrahim turned on him and raised his own army to claim the throne. When their forces clashed, Ebrahim captured 'Adel Shah and had him blinded. Ebrahim Shah then tried to secure control, but was soon deposed himself in another coup.

Despite this turmoil, both of these brothers dispatched letters to Istanbul during their short, turbulent tenures that reflected a persistent and common desire for continuity in Ottoman-Iranian relations. 'Adel Shah's chief religious official, Mollabashi Ali Akbar (who had also served as Nader's chief religious adviser) wrote a letter to his Ottoman counterpart, the sheikh ül-Islam, soon after 'Adel Shah took power. In it, he explained how Nader had suffered some illness that turned him into such a tyrant that his subjects rose up against him and killed him. The letter also included a message that the new Iranian ruler wanted to keep existing agreements between the Ottomans and Iran in place. Soon thereafter, the new Ebrahim Shah dispatched another letter to the Ottomans in January 1749 affirming that he too wanted to continue the stable and good relations established at the end of Nader's reign. His message specifically called for the restoration of the provisions of the 1639 Ottoman-Iranian treaty.[4]

At the same time that these nephews of Nader were battling to secure control of his domains, a third pretender, Nader's grandson Shahrokh, was raised to the throne by a coalition of his followers in Mashhad in October 1748. Although he quickly secured power and ended up remaining on the throne for over four decades, his long reign was to be defined by his being blinded in a failed counter-coup shortly after he became Iran's ruler. Despite this injury, Shahrokh was able to continue as ruler for many years because his subjects remained unaware of this defect, which his powerful supporters kept secret.

Shahrokh's status was also soon confirmed and supported by Ahmad Shah Dorrani, who made Shahrokh his vassal in January 1751 after himself taking control of Khorasan and northern Iran following his decisive victory over Afsharid forces in Herat.[5] This conquest provided Ahmad Shah the context for eventually negotiating with the Ottomans himself, since he could now truly claim to rule over Nader's only lineal descendant still on the throne. Ahmad Shah's chance to parlay with them finally arrived in the early 1760s. By then, the Dorrani ruler's career had reached a zenith. He had established his authority over large parts of the vast territories earlier conquered by Nader. Most recently, Ahmad Shah had trounced his biggest military rivals, the Maratha confederation, at the Battle of Panipat that took place just north of Delhi in January 1761.

Following this victory, Ahmad briefly secured control over much of northern India, eastern Iran, and Afghanistan, as well as parts of Central Asia. His empire, although relatively short-lived, was among the last attempts to create a domain whose strength lay in its ability to dominate Central and South Asia militarily in ways reminiscent of earlier generations of steppe conquerors. The Afghans, as mainstays of Nader's army, were quickly able to secure control over a good portion of his former domains using a well-established formula of fielding a powerful mobile military that had the power to collect rents over a sustained period from overland trade routes either through raids or taxation. Unlike in earlier times though, the rapidly expanding commercial and military scope of European empires in Asia now confronted such local rulers who harbored any dreams of imitating the successes of their steppe ancestors.

Nevertheless, successes that the Dorranis did enjoy relied on the dynasty's ability to draw on Central Asian ruling traditions and use them effectively. The Dorranis' considerable prosperity and longevity challenge theories about the decline of local rulers during this era.[6] Dorrani dynasty founder Ahmad Shah's claim to rule had its ultimate roots back in the 1709 *loya jirga*, at which Mir Veys Khan Ghilzai had been acclaimed leader of an Afghan movement to throw off Safavid Iranian rule. This in turn set the stage for the complete overthrow of the Safavid dynasty, soon followed by the rise of Nader Shah. Nader made himself Iran's monarch in a 1736 ceremony dubbed a *quriltai* in obeisance to Turco-Mongol tradition, but which also bore some resemblance to the earlier *loya jirga* as well. In 1747, Ahmad Shah was acclaimed ruler after another *loya jirga*, building on both of these earlier legitimating events. This assertion of authority and power, however, differed in important ways from both previous ritual gatherings. Not a supporter of Nader's pan-Islamic project, Ahmad took power as a staunch defender of Sunni Islam, although not so much against Iranian Shi'i Muslims as against Hindu Marathas. In this regard, his installation was also different from that of his Afghan predecessor Mir Veys, since Mir Veys had taken a distinctly anti-Shi'i approach that Ahmad Shah did not repeat.

The Dorrani Proposals

After his defeat of the Maratha forces at Panipat in January 1761, Ahmad Shah proposed in a letter to Ottoman Sultan Mustafa III that the Ottomans invade Iran and divide it up with him. His letter conveyed his achievements as a defender of Islamic rule, inviting the Ottomans to join him in securing Iran, and seeking their grant of a plot of land in the city of Medina on which he might be allowed to erect a mosque. In this letter and in other court documents, he portrayed himself as a "good" version of Nader: like that earlier ruler a victorious conqueror, but one who would now rule wisely and justly in contrast to Nader's tyranny.[7] One Dorrani court chronicle even had Nader predict that Ahmad would rule after him and portrayed Nader as imploring Ahmad to treat his descendants with kindness.[8] Ahmad's chroniclers also adapted and reconfigured various legitimating devices from Nader's ruling ideology. This included labeling the Afghans (and in particularly the Dorrani family) as the "il-e jalil-e Afghan" or "il-e jalil-e Dorrani" in imitation of the phrase "il-e jalil-e Torkman" used by Nader's court historians. These epithets also alluded to how Afghani Dorrani rulers had been established as monarchs for many generations before Timur, both recalling Nader's focus on his parallels with and ties to this earlier conqueror, as well as trying to best Nader's legitimating claims that such connections entailed.[9]

By the late 1750s, Ahmad's court historians also began to title him "shahanshah" while referring to Shahrokh Afshar and the current Mughal ruler Alamgir II, only as "shah" or "padishah." This signaled their status as subordinates in ways that paralleled how Nader's chroniclers had depicted Mughal and Uzbek rulers' vassal relationships with Nader. Ahmad also married his son Timur Shah to daughters of both Shahrokh and Alamgir, creating "son-in-law" relationships with the Afsharids and Mughals that recalled how Nader had tried to build his own lineage ties with the Safavids and Mughals.[10]

Ahmad, like Nader, sought to establish his piety by cultivating ties to Mecca and promoting the hajj pilgrimage. In Ahmad's case, this focused on showing how he possessed unimpeachable Sunni credentials, since unlike Nader, he had no need to seek approval for any innovative concepts to reconcile Sunni and Shi'i Islam as Nader had presented in his "Ja'fari *mazhab*" proposal.[11] In fact, accounts of Ahmad and documents produced by his court turned the idea of waging war to defend Islam and the Muslims away from attacking Shi'is, shifting focus to his campaigns against the Hindu Marathas and uprooting the political power of unbelievers.[12]

The Ottoman Response

Ottoman Sultan Mustafa III sent a very measured reply to Ahmad's suggestions. He congratulated Ahmad on his military success, but deferred from making any promises implying that the Ottomans might invade Iran or that he would provide any land in Medina to Ahmad or his representatives for any purpose. He invited Ahmad instead to make charitable gifts to the poor if he wished to demonstrate his piety and commitment to Islam. The Ottoman reply concluded with this summary of the situation from the Ottoman perspective:

> The reason for the lack of desire and wish on the part of our everlasting exalted State to send an army to Iran and to take territory [there] is that the sincere and friendly [treaty] provisions concluded and agreed upon before Nader Shah's death between our exalted [Ottoman] Sultanate and the Iranian state are not limited only to him and his time. This treaty between the two states should, as long as God wills, be fixed, enduring, and not interrupted during the reigns of the two sides' successors and descendants. Despite its maintenance having been a goal of [our] attention and care, for some time now conflicts have been taking place, begun by military commanders who are raising the flag of independence in Iran. Soldiers and peasants have been slaughtered, armies killed, and the population thrown into upheaval. By God's grace, however easy it would be for us with our resources, armies, and materiel to secure the country of Iran ... [it would ultimately be a bad idea for all concerned].[13]

Mustafa's letter to Ahmad stressed the Ottoman goal of maintaining the terms of the Kordan agreement at all costs. Even if it might have been possible or defensible for the Ottomans to get involved militarily in securing the unstable internal situation of Iran after Nader's demise, they were determined to avoid this entirely.

The Broader Historical Context of the Ottoman-Dorrani Exchange

The real reasons for this rejection can easily be found in surveying the course of Ottoman-Iranian relations over the previous few centuries. Despite occasional flare-ups and clashes, it would not be misleading to assert that on the whole, ordinary relations between the Ottoman and Iranian empires in the Ottoman "Classical Age" right up to the end of the Safavid era were mostly reflective of relative peace for long periods of time. An Iranian commercial representative functioned very effectively through the seventeenth century in Bursa as the *shahbandar-e 'Ajam*.[14] Overland and maritime trade, although subject to all the well-known turbulences of economic successes and failures, continued at a fairly steady pace throughout the Safavid era.

Even in the uncertain new situation of the 1720s after Safavid power had collapsed, although Ottoman diplomatic overtures to Iran reflected a certain degree of confusion, they generally tried to preserve the pragmatic essence of the previous relationship with Iran as far as possible. When Ottoman forces invaded Iran in the spring of 1723, for example, ostensibly to protect Sunnis in the Caucasus from the depredations of the Shi'i rulers (the time-honored justification for initiating conflict with the Safavids), their most obvious agenda at this point was in fact to forestall Russian advances southward. After both the Russians and Ottomans had secured some additional territory at Safavid expense, they signed an agreement whose most telling provision was that neither party would recognize a *non-Iranian* as the Iranian head of state, and that the Safavid pretender Tahmasp II, then driven into exile by the invading Afghans, should be assisted in reclaiming the Iranian throne.[15] The Ottomans, in realpolitik fashion, shifted from being prepared to wage war against Iran in order to uphold Sunni Islam to defending Safavid legitimacy against any foreign invaders, be they fellow Sunnis or others.

The initial establishment of Afghan control over Iran in the 1720s challenged long-standing Ottoman assumptions in other new ways. When an Afghan delegation presented the Ottoman sultan with a proposal that Iran, as a sovereign polity now controlled by fellow Sunnis, should now be considered an independent Afghan *dowleh,* the Ottoman response was to have a senior group of Ottoman clerics issue a fatwa denouncing this idea as "judicial independent reasoning not based on precedent" ["*ijtihad*"].[16] The Ottomans had never before confronted the possibility of an independent Sunni Muslim polity as an immediate neighbor that could not be considered a tributary or associate power like Crimea or various domains in the Maghreb. The greater issue with the Afghans, although cloaked in religious garb, was that the Ottomans remained skeptical about their ability to retain control over Iran.

Still a different sort of challenge to the stability of the Ottoman Empire's eastern frontiers was then offered by the rise of Nader Shah, who mixed offers of peace with waging combat in his dealings with the Ottomans to try to force them to consent to a peace on his terms that would have radically redefined the Ottoman-Iranian relationship. He either presented himself as trying to create, on the one hand, a political rapprochement between Sunni and Shi'i Islam, as well as inventing a tradition to link Uzbek, Mughal, Ottoman, and Afsharid Iranian rule as putative common inheritors of Chingizid/Turkman legitimacy, or on the other, to be seen as a world conqueror in the mold of Timur or Chingiz Khan. When the chaos of battle finally receded after the signing of the Kordan accord, the Ottomans were able to achieve peace on their terms. They ultimately neutralized Nader's military, political, and diplomatic efforts by remaining focused on reviving the past stability of Ottoman-Iranian relations.

Over the previous centuries, the Ottomans had displayed considerable skill in perpetuating the stability of their relationship with the Safavids and their successors by forging peace agreements to keep the parameters of the old relationship, but which also included further provisions to enhance continuity and stability even more, such as agreements to exchange ambassadors and facilitate the safe transit of pilgrims across borders. Although the inherent tensions which Shi'i pilgrims and communities in Ottoman Iraq always experienced often became very severe in crisis situations, such as during the intermittent Ottoman-Safavid wars, the Kordan accord helped define and build an underlying framework for stability that would endure long beyond the end of the Ottoman Empire, having an effect even as far as the Iran-Iraq War in the 1980s.

The rejection of Ahmad Shah Dorrani's diplomatic overtures and proposals in the early 1760s thus can be viewed as good evidence for the staying power of the Ottoman vision for how relations with Iran should be designed. Halil İnalcık, in his study of the Ottoman "classical age," describes a moment in the late sixteenth century when "the Ottoman state and Ottoman society appear to have achieved harmony and equilibrium within its own system and ideals. It was a society interested . . . in the preservation of the existing order."[17] Considerably after this zenith of classical Ottoman times, the Ottoman-Iranian relationship also combined flexibility with continuity to preserve a stable framework of relations even during prolonged periods of political upheaval. In the current era of internal and external turmoil now plaguing the old Ottoman-Iranian border zone, defined as an area that includes modern Turkey, Iran, Armenia, Azerbaijan, Iraq, Syria, and the Persian Gulf, it might be useful to view the Ottoman era there as a whole in order to distinguish more clearly between lasting and fleeting elements in how this border was defined. It is ironic to note that the Dorrani story after this point blends more particularly into the saga of how modern Afghanistan was created, with its own set of complexities. In this case, artificial borders such as the Durand Line drawn by Britain as the outside colonial power contributed to the numerous problems that confronted Afghanistan as it struggled to define its status as a nation, but questions of border delineation and definition have always remained central to the politics of the larger region.

Notes

1. Ernest Tucker, *Nadir Shah's Quest for Legitimacy in Post-Safavid Iran* (Gainesville, Florida: University Press of Florida, 2006), 99.
2. See Matthee's discussion of Emmanuel Wallerstein in Rudolph Matthee, *The Politics of Trade in Safavid Iran: Silk for Silver, 1600–1730* (Cambridge: Cambridge University Press, 1999), 2.
3. For such an approach, see Sanjay Subramanyam, *Explorations in Connected History* (New Delhi: Oxford University Press, 2005).
4. For texts of these letters, see Mohammad Reza Nasiri, *Asnad va mokatebat-e tarikhi-ye Iran: dowreh-ye Afshariyeh* (n.p.: Jehad-e Daneshgahi-ye Daneshgah-e Gilan, 1364/1985), 177–181, 189–193.
5. Mahmud ebn Ebrahim el-Hoseyni, *Tarikh-e Ahmad Shahi*, ed. Mohammad Sarvar Mowlai (Tehran: Mohammad Ebrahim Shari'ati Afghanistani, 1386/2007), 253. For

discussion of how Ahmad Shah secured Khorasan, see Pirouz Mojtahed-Zadeh, *Small Players of the Great Game: The Settlement of Iran's Eastern Borderlands and the Creation of Afghanistan* (London: Routledge, 2004).

6. See Jos J. L. Gommans, *The Rise of the Indo-Afghan Empire c. 1710–1780* (Leiden & New York: E. J. Brill, 1995).

7. For the Persian text of this letter, see Gholam Jeylani Jalali (ed.), *Nameh-ye Ahmad Shah Baba beh nameh-ye Soltan Mustafa Sales-e Osmani* (Kabul: Historical Society, 1346/1967). For its Turkish translation and commentary, see Y. Hikmet Bayur, "Nadir Şah Afşar'ın Ölümünden Sonra Osmanlı Devletini Iran'ı Istilaya Kışkırtmak için yapılan iki deneme," *Belleten* 1948 (12:46), 420–463.

8. Gommans, 55.

9. El-Hoseyni, 49, 51, 190, 253.

10. El-Hoseyni, 578. Louis Dupree, *Afghanistan* (Princeton, NJ: Princeton University Press, 2014), 337.

11. For discussion of the Ja'fari *mazhab* proposal, see Tucker, 11–12, 39–42.

12. For a good example of this, see the 1169/1756 Dorrani-Mughal accord. (Reproduced in el-Hoseyni, 329–331.)

13. Bayur, 468.

14. In that city at that time, the Safavids maintained a quasi-diplomatic representative known as the *shahbandar-e A'jam* to look after the interests of Iranian merchants there. See Haim Gerber, *Economy and Society in an Ottoman City: Bursa, 1600–1700* (Jerusalem: Hebrew University, 1988), 116.

15. For more discussion of this point, see Tucker, 24–25.

16. Tucker, 27.

17. Halil Inalcık, *The Ottoman Empire* (New York: Praeger, 1973), 45–46.

6

Whatever Happened to the School of Isfahan?: Philosophy in 18th-Century Iran

SAJJAD RIZVI

Writing about the late Safavid period and in particular the aftermath of the destruction of the Tekke-ye Fayz in Isfahan,[1] the literary historian Reza-Qoli Khan Hedayat (d. 1288/1871) characterized the attack upon philosophy and Sufism thus:

> As the foundation of the livelihood of the people of the path [i.e. the Sufis] came to an end, they [the detractors] labelled the ascetics as fools, and scholars (*'ulama*) as imitators, the philosophers (*hukama*) as innovators, the mystics (*'urafa*) as heretics. They prevented the contemplators from practicing the invocation of God and destroyed the books of the Sufi orders.[2]

I have argued in a recent piece about the conflation of Sufism and philosophy in the period and how the attack on one was often related to the other.[3] Nevertheless, a particular narrative of the history of philosophy—the word used was *hikmat*, which also denotes wisdom, and rarely the transliterated Greek term *falsafa*—in Iran, after its apogee in the Safavid renaissance in Isfahan, goes like this: First, after the flourishing of philosophy and mysticism in the Isfahan of Shah 'Abbas, in the later 17th century through the rise of shari'a-minded scholars at court including Mohammad Baqer Majlesi (d. 1100/1699) and Mulla Taher Qummi (d. 1096/1686), the attack on philosophical inquiry (and on Sufism) accelerated through the writing of works such as *Hikmat al-'arifin* (Wisdom of the mystics) by Qummi and the persecution and marginalization of philosophers and philosophical inquiry in the madrasas; the public discourse itself became more hostile to metaphysical speculation.[4] Second, the murder of Mulla Sadeq Ardestani during the sack of Isfahan in 1722 (along with the deaths of other philosophers) symbolized the death of philosophy in Safavid Iran. Third, philosophical inquiry—which had either died or gone into occultation— only returned to Isfahan as it was revived as a major cultural centre in the Qajar period with the figure of Mulla Ali Nuri (d. 1246/1831), whence the renewal of philosophy in Iran.[5]

Therefore, the 'death' of philosophy in Iran of the 18th century is associated with internal factors (the anathemization of the study of philosophy) and external ones (the Afghan sack and occupation of Isfahan from 1722 to 1729). However, the textual evidence that we increasingly have seems to bring such a narrative into question. The real problem has been the lack of texts from the period—but the situation is changing: back in the 1970s the late Seyyed Jalal al-Din Ashtiyani (d. 2005) edited a number of texts from the period, and since then work on the figures, as well as historical and biographical studies, have proliferated.

In this chapter, I will show some of the evidence for the continuity of philosophical inquiry in the period through the perpetuation of both the Avicennian tradition, as well as the newly emerging Sadrian tradition focusing upon some of the key figures such as Mulla Na'ima Taleqani (d. 1160/1747), Aqa Mohammad Bidabadi (d. 1198/1783), and Mohammad Mahdi Naraqi (d. 1209/1794), and the role of philosophy in the madrasa curriculum, and secondly, show how philosophical inquiry changed and intersected the emergence of a new discourse of 'irfan. Without a proper understanding of this dual process, it is difficult to ascertain what emerged in the Qajar period and what defines to a large extent, even today, philosophical and mystical inquiry in the Shi'i seminary in Qom. And as for the 'standard' account I mentioned above, it turns out to be based on a number of myths: the fact that Ardestani was not killed in the sack of the Isfahan symbolizes the mythology of the demise of philosophy itself. Any critical engagement with decline should not overcompensate—philosophy was not, after all, the primary concern of many of the successor rulers to the Safavids, and patronage and material resources were sparse. But a careful reading of the texts establishes enough evidence for the continuity of philosophical inquiry such that we cannot consider the Qajar revival to have been ex nihilo. I take a biographical approach considering the major figures of the 18th century, their locations, their texts, networks, patrons, and dissemination. In doing so, I include philosophers and Sufis— and the link with the latter was critical in a period of the revival of the formal Sufi orders in Zand and Qajar Iran.

Historiography of Decline and
the Nature of Philosophy

Nasr claims that philosophy was curtailed in Isfahan before the Afghan invasion and points to the case of Ardestani chased out into exile by the Majlesi circle under Shah Sultan Hosein, suffering and then dying in exile in 1133/1721.[6] Ashtiyani similarly laments the anathemization of philosophers and mystics in the late Safavid period (including the exile of Ardestani), while allowing for the continuity of the Avicennian tradition in the seats of learning in Isfahan.[7] Nasr tries to bridge the eclipse of philosophy with some sort of continuity:

> Yet, despite all the opposition to *ḥikmat* in Isfahan during the latter part of Safavid rule, and despite the devastation brought about by the Afghan invasion, *ḥikmat* continued to survive albeit precariously in Isfahan, and once the political situation settled down, it was in this city that philosophical activity and especially the teachings of Mullā Ṣadrā's *al-ḥikmat al-mutaʿāliyah* were revived.[8]

He also cites other philosophers like Esmaʿil Khwajui (d. 1173/1760) suffering losses in the sack of 1722. Philosophy then was absent from Isfahan until the more settled time of the Zand ascendency.[9] Nasr's other major claim is that philosophy was also better disseminated and that the revival of philosophy was due to the roots put down in the towns by thinkers in the later Safavid period. It began in Kashan with Fayz Kashani (d. 1090/1679), who settled there at the end of his life and later with Naraqi, and continued in Qom with figures like ʿAbd al-Razzaq Lahiji (d. 1070/1660), Qazi Saʿid Qummi (d. 1105/1696), and his students such as Hasan Lahiji (d. 1121/1709), the grandson of Mulla Sadra.

Corbin's assessment is somewhat different.[10] While acknowledging the 'difficult and chaotic' situation for philosophers including those who died in the siege of Isfahan such as Ardestani and his disciple Hamza Gilani, he mentions figures who remained active in Isfahan from the time to Ardestani to Bidabadi including ʿInayatullah Gilani (d. after 1134/1722 in Qazwin), Baha al-Din Isfahani, known as Fazel-e Hindi (d. 1137/1725), Mohammad Taqi Almasi (d. 1159/1746), and the Zahabi shaykh Qutb al-Din Nayrizi (d. 1173/1760), as well as Esmaʿil Khwajuʾi (d. 1173/1760); the last three were all active in Isfahan and teachers of Bidabadi. Corbin's argument for the neglect of these thinkers is that the political chaos meant that their works were destroyed and scattered and hence have not attracted the attention of historians. However, that would surely also be the case of others from previous generations whose works were in Isfahan? Similarly, Anzali has recently questioned the significance of the expulsion of Ardestani from Isfahan and suggested that it was neither related to his attachment to Sufism nor to his philosophy.[11] Ashtiyani had also indicated that the 18th century was not a period of decline or absence but one of the creativity of philosophy.[12]

The study of philosophy was common in the madrasas of Isfahan right up to 1722—for example, in the Jami'-ye Sultani and Madrasa-ye Chahar Bagh, where figures like the mulla-bashi Seyyed Mohammad Baqer Khatunabadi (d. 1127/1715) taught the works of Avicenna such as al-Isharat and al-Shifa', and the Madrasa-ye Hoseiniyeh (completed in 1133/1722) had a number of philosophy texts endowed for it.[13] However, some other madrasas such as Maryam Begum built in 1115/1703 forbade the study of philosophy; the vaqfnama stipulates that:

> Books of conjectural 'sciences', which are dubious and objectionable the likes of the rational sciences and the philosophy that is famous, such as the Shifa', Isharat, Hikmat al-'ayn and their ilk should not enter into the preliminary training of the religious sciences.[14]

Opponents of philosophy in the late Safavid period complained that the study of the discipline in the seminaries of the city was dominant.[15] Even in the Zand period that did not boast much by way of patronage of philosophy, there was a residual and proverbial bombast relating to the philosophical past: Mirza Mohammad Hosein Farahani who led the forces entering Basra in April 1776 was praised in the official chronicle Tarikh-i Giti-gusha of Mirza Mohammad Sadeq Musavi Nami (d. 1204/1789–1790) as one 'well versed in hikmat possessing the nature of Plato and the very rank of Aristotle'—it also reflects the role, perhaps, of philosophy in the training of the administrative class (the mirzas).[16] Slightly later, we find the philosopher Ali Nuri was the recipient of the patronage of Ja'far Khan Zand (r. 1785–1789) who bestowed, through the mediation of Mirza Mohammad Baqer Navvab, the tax revenues of a number of villages upon him including Aliabad and Habibabad near Isfahan.[17] Since Ja'far Khan took Isfahan in 1785 and died four years later, the grant of the villages was probably made in that period.[18]

Contexts, Figures, Texts

In what follows I begin with a consideration of the sources that provide us with the historical, cultural, and intellectual context of philosophy in this period, followed by a consideration of some case studies of philosophers engaging with their texts to discern the trends and philosophical inclinations of the period.

Apart from the actual works of philosophers, the 18th century was rich in sources on the social, cultural, and intellectual history of Iran from the late Safavid period until the consolidation of the Qajar monarchy. For the sketch in this work, I have drawn upon the following works that can be categorized into various genres.

The first genre is the poetic *tazkira*, the notices of poets, their compositions, and lives, an informative source since philosophers were often poets as well. At the beginning of the period, we have *Tazkira-yi Nasrabadi* of Mohammad Tahir Nasrabadi (d. *c.*1099/1688) which commenced in 1083/1672–1673—although this does not cover the later period under Shah Sultan Hosein when philosophers and Sufis were under greater pressure. In his discussion of poets and also of 'ulama, a number of philosophers and Sufis are cited, as he frequented coffeehouses and shrines.[19] His son later became the poet laureate of Shah Sultan Hosein. His account begins with the major figures of the period of Shah 'Abbas such as Shaykh Baha al-Din al-'Amili (d. 1030/1621) and Mir Damad (d. 1040/1631), and moves onto Mulla Mohammad Baqer Sabzavari (d. 1090/1679) and Aqa Hosein Khwansari (d. 1099/1688), important figures of the time of Shah Suleiman and teachers of Avicenna. While there is a brief mention of the anti-Sufi Mulla Mohammad Taher Qummi, there is no entry for Mohammad Baqer Majlesi (d. 1100/1699).[20] These were all critical figures who were the teachers and critics of the first generation of thinkers in the 18th century.

An Indo-Persian example of the genre provides a useful insight into the late Safavid and Afsharid period, being the *Tazkira-yi Riyaz al-shu'ara* of Valih-e Daghestani (d. 1169/1756), penned around 1160/1747.[21] Valih was born in 1124/1712 in Isfahan into the family of the hereditary rulers of Daghestan. After the sack of Isfahan, he fled to Delhi, arriving in 1734, and became the recipient of Mughal patronage. He includes a number of classical philosophers in his account as well as Safavid ones such as Mir Abol-Qasem Fendereski, Hakim Abol-Fath Gilani, Mir Damad, Afzal al-Din Turka Isfahani, Hosein Khwansari (about whom the author says that he heard directly from his family), Rafi' Naini, Mohsen Fayz Kashani, and Fayyaz Lahiji.[22] Most of the entries are short, and as one would expect, focused on the poetry.

A similar work is the *Atashkada* of Lutf Ali Begdeli 'Azar' (d. 1195/1781), who produced his work during the reign of Karim Khan in 1174/1760, comprising notices of literary figures.[23] He was born in Isfahan into a prominent family and at the Afghan invasion, he fled with them to Qom. He joined the retinue of Nader Shah after the latter made his father governor of Lar, being based in Shiraz, and spent some time in the shrine cities of Iraq after the death of his father in 1738. After the sack of Isfahan by Ali-Mardan Khan, he gained the patronage of Karim Khan Zand, and later retired to Qom, where he died. His work is unusual in that it arranges the notices of poets based on their region and hometown—the main section is divided therefore into three: poets of Persia (Iraq is included in the section entitled 'Iraq-i 'arab), of Central Asia, and of North India. He includes notices on a number of major Safavid figures. An example is that on Mohsen Fayz Kashani of whom he says, approvingly, that he perfectly epitomized both 'philosophy and Sufism' and the 'scriptural and rational' disciplines.[24]

Related, but towards the end of our period, is the *Tajribat al-ahrar wa-tasli-yat al-abrar* of 'Abd al-Razzaq Beg 'Maftun' Donboli (d. 1243/1827–1828), who grew up in Shiraz and included a number of notices on 'ulama.[25] Written in a mixture of Arabic and Persian—a common feature of the period—alongside notices of the famous jurists such as Seyyed Mahdi Bahr al-'ulum (d. 1212/1797) and the heads of the *usuli* and *akhbari* factions Mohammad Baqer Behbahani (d. 1205/1791) and Yusuf Bahrani (d. 1186/1772), he also discusses a few major philosophers and teachers of philosophy: Esma'il Khwajui, described as an expert in law and philosophy in Isfahan, and an eminent scholar who died in the early years of the reign of Karim Khan;[26] a much longer notice is dedicated to Mohammad Isfahani (better known as Bidabadi), the master 'of the East and the West', 'pole of the mystics' (*qutb al-'arifin*), 'the lordly spiritual master' (*al-mur-shid al-samadani*), whose very presence illuminated Isfahan, and whose company of Sufis (*fuqara*) and expertise in the occult was famed—Donbuli claims to have been a direct disciple of his;[27] Mirza Abol-Qasem Modarres Khatunabadi (d. 1212/1797), a student of Bidabadi and well-known teacher of the glosses of Aqa Hosein Khwansari on *al-Shifa'* and *al-Isharat* of Avicenna 'to which he paid more attention than the teaching of law';[28] Mirza Mohammad Mahdi Mashhadi, described as a mystic of noble character and teacher of the rational and scriptural arts who died from the wounds he received at the conquest of Mashhad by the Qajars; Seyyed Hosein Qazwini (d. 1208/1793–1794), a teacher of philosopher and a saintly figure who was a judge in Qazwin much sought out by students for the elegance of his style and the eloquence of his speech;[29] and finally, perhaps the shortest entry is on the most important philosopher of the 18th century, Mahdi Naraqi, who taught in Naraq, although Donbuli does mention that he was very prolific and had very many students.[30] Given his interest in poetry and inclination to mystical language, it seems that Donbuli's preference was for philosophers who were more mystically inclined than Avicennian, which is true of many of the sources that we have in this period linked to the revival of Sufism in Iran.

The second genre is the biographical dictionary of 'ulama. The famous biographical dictionary of al-Hurr al-'Amili (d. 1104/1693) that originally focused (in two parts) on his fellow countrymen in the Levant and its diaspora in Iran and elsewhere, *Amal al-amil*, enjoyed two continuations in the 18th century.[31] The first, a *ta'liqa*, was written by Mulla 'Abdullah Afandi (d. 1130/1718), a tradent and figure of the Majlesi circle who was involved in the collation and completion of *Bihar al-anwar* and who penned his own biographical dictionary *Riyad al-'ulama' wa-hiyad al-fudala'*.[32] Although Afandi was better known as a tradent, he had studied philosophy with Hosein Khwansari and his son Jamal (d. 1121/1709) as well as with Fazel-e Hindi; his own students in Isfahan included teachers of philosophy such as Seyyed Mohammad Hosein Khatunabadi (d. 1151/1739 in Mashhad) and Mohammad Ali 'Hazin Lahiji.[33] He includes many entries, most of them little more than a name, with a focus on jurists and tradents but still remains a useful source for the scholarly culture of Isfahan in the late Safavid period. Among them he includes his teachers in philosophy.[34] The second part on non-'Amili thinkers includes a number of interesting notices. Seyyed Ibrahim b. Mirza Hamadani (d. 1026/1616) is mentioned as a teacher of the works of Avicenna and the Avicennian tradition as well as a gloss on the *Sharh Hikmat al-ishraq*; he is credited with writing primarily in rebuttal of Mirza-jan Shirazi.[35] No teachers or students of his are mentioned. Another intriguing entry is on Mulla Hosein b. Musa Ardebili (d. 1098/1686–1687), said to be a student of Mulla Sadra who later died in Astarabad and is credited with Persian commentaries on various scriptural works and about whom Afandi says that 'he inclined towards Sufism, which he probably got from his teacher'.[36] A brief entry is given over to Mirza Rafi' al-Din Naini, who died before Afandi and whose Persian works in philosophy are extant.[37] Surprisingly, while he has an entry on the leading anti-Sufi jurist Taher Qummi, he fails to mention his particular works against Sufism and philosophy.[38]

More significant for the study of philosophy was the *Tatmim Amal al-amil*, produced by 'Abd al-Nabi Qazwini (d. *c*.1197/1783).[39] He had himself studied philosophy in Mashhad and Isfahan, and his biographical dictionary contains a number of philosophers. Of the 137 notices, almost 40 per cent mention philosophy as one of the disciplines of the scholars discussed. His teachers included those known for their skill in philosophy including Mir Mohammad Ibrahim Hoseini (d. 1145/1732–1733), famed for his extensive library of 1,500 codices, Ibrahim Mashhadi (d. 1148/1735–1736), author of a large work on philosophical theology entitled *al-Fawa'id* with whom he studied in the shrine city of Mashhad, Seyyed Ibrahim Razavi Qummi (d. *c*.1168/1755), whom he frequented in Hamadan, and Mirza Ibrahim Khuzani (d. 1160/1747), who was a judge in Isfahan and later became the military judge in Nader Shah's camp.[40] Qazwini also spent some time in Karbala with the circle of Vahid Behbahani.[41] He has a long entry on Esma'il Khwajui, about whom he says that it was reported that he had read the *Shifa'* of Avicenna thirty times and knew it by heart; in particular he cites his refutation of Khwansari on the unreality of time.[42] An Isfahani philosopher, in the late Safavid period, with glosses on *al-Isharat* of Avicenna and a number of treatises on philosophy, was Seyyed Esma'il Khatunabadi (d. 1116/1704).[43] His son Mohammad Baqer was close to Sultan Hosein, and he taught Avicenna in the royal seminary, although it seems that he was not very accomplished at that.[44] Philosophy remained a concern of the clerical elite in Isfahan; Mohammad Taqi Almasi (d. 1159/1746), a descendant of Majlesi and the Friday prayer leader of Isfahan under Nader Shah, taught it.[45] An example of an itinerant philosopher was Mohammad Baqer Mazandarani, who taught Avicenna and Avicennian theology in Isfahan in the period of Nader Shah, then in Najaf, and finally in Mecca later in the 18th century. As with other entries, it shows that while philosophy was taught in other centres such as Mashhad, Qom, and Hamadan, it returned to Isfahan soon after the Afghan occupation. Sometimes, we are acquainted with those considered to be minor figures now but who were leading teachers of the time; an example is Mir Mohammad Taqi Shahi (d. 1150/1738), a polymath and renowned teacher in Mashhad whom Qazwini, in a long notice, describes as 'a great mystic' and an 'accomplished philosopher' of the Mulla Sadra tradition.[46] Of the first generation to teach the work of this tradition in Hamadan was Mohammad Taqi Hamadani in the middle of the 18th century, whom the author had met.[47] Another major centre for philosophy was Qom, where Mirza Hasan Lahiji, the grandson of Mulla Sadra, although not of his school, taught.[48] Sufis were another interest; a major figure of the late Safavid period was Hasan Lonbani (d. 1094/1683), on whom there is a short notice.[49] Even the margins of the empire were not devoid of philosophy; a notice is made of Mohammad Hosein Qatifi, who taught in Najaf in the Nader Shah period before returning to eastern Arabia where he died some time before the 1780s.[50] Qazwini was associated with Hamza Gilani (d. 1134/1722), on whose transcripts of Sadeq Ardestani's classes entitled *Hikmat-i Sadiqiyya* he wrote a set of glosses.[51] He also provides some useful insights into the situation during the siege of Isfahan in 1722: in his notice on Mir Asaf Qazwini (d. 1136/1723) he mentions that hunger and shortages meant that members of the scholarly elite resorted to eating donkey meat.[52] Another anecdote—drawing on the famous trope of Diogenes and Alexander—finds the Afghan leader Ashraf Ghilzai, after the sack of Isfahan, visiting Ibrahim Khatunabadi, the famous jurist of the city who taught at the Madrasa-ye Sultani; Khatunabadi barely acknowledged him, failing to stand up, and Ashraf humbled himself, honouring him, and sat in a lower place.[53]

Another important biographical dictionary is the *Riyaz al-janna* of Mirza Mohammad Hasan Hoseini Zunuzi (d. 1218/1803).[54] Zunuzi began his life in Khoy in 1172/1758 and ended it there. Along the way he studied in Karbala with major figures such as Behbahani and Mirza Mahdi Shahrestani and philosophy with Mirza Mohammad Mahdi Mashhadi in Mashhad; he also spent some time studying in Isfahan. The *Riyaz* is a massive biographical dictionary divided into eight *rawzas* by classes of people; the fourth is on 'ulama, philosophers, and Sufis and the only part published. It was completed in 1216/1802, just a couple of years before his death. In some cases, he draws upon earlier Safavid and post-Safavid sources like Afandi's *Riyad al-'ulama* and also influences later sources such as Khwansari's *Rawdat al-jannat*. As a poet himself, he often takes note of the poetry of the thinkers. Notices on Safavid philosophers and Sufis include Ibrahim the son of Mulla Sadra (whom he describes as the 'greatest of mystics'), Mir Fendereski, Sharif-e Lahiji also known as Qutb al-Din Eshkevari (d. *c.*1095/1684), 'Abd al-Razzaq Lahiji, Fayz Kashani, Jamal Khwansari, Hosein Tonakabuni, Rajab Ali Tabrizi, Mirza Rafi'a Naini (d. 1082/1671), Mir Damad, Qazi Sa'id Qummi, Sadeq Ardestani, and Fazel-e Hindi.[55] Given Ardestani's pivotal role in the tradition in the 18th century, he is described as the 'lord of the recent philosophers and the support of the divinising gnostics'. Other important entries include his teachers Mohammad Bidabadi, Ali Nuri (with whom he studied parts of the *Asfar* of Mulla Sadra and *Shawariq* of Lahiji), and Mahdi Naraqi, as well as Abol-Qasem Modarres Isfahani, Esma'il Khwajui, and 'Abd al-Rahim Damavandi.[56] He also includes notices on people he regarded as important but who seem to have been forgotten by posterity such as Mirza Naser al-Din Isfahani (d. 1191/1777), a philosopher who apparently was affiliated to the Mulla Sadra tradition and was personal physician to Karim Khan Zand in Shiraz.[57] Given his long notice on Bidabadi, study with Nuri, associated with Mirza-ye Qummi (Abol-Qasem Gilani, d. 1231/1816), it is quite likely he spent some time in the Bidabadi circle in Isfahan.[58]

Finally, there is the Sufi biographical dictionary *Tarayeq al-haqayeq* by Ma'sum-Ali Shah Naeb al-Sadr Shirazi (d. 1344/1926), a prominent Ni'matullahi Sufi of the Qajar period.[59] Because of his own affiliations, he tends to find Sufis among all manner of 'ulama and has been criticized for being an unreliable source. However, he is a valuable source for Qajar approaches to the question of mysticism and its contestations. He mentions those who died and witnessed the sack of Isfahan such as Fazel-e Hindi and Esma'il Khwajui; he also describes the latter as a Sufi master whose Sufi disciples included Mohammad Bidabadi, Mulla Mihrab Gilani (d. 1217/1802), and Mahdi Naraqi.[60] He is keen to present the confluence of jurists and Sufis—of *'urafa-yi mujtahidin* as he calls them—comprising in their ranks Bidabadi and Naraqi.[61] Other claims, which are more difficult to verify, include the suggestion that the jurist Seyyed Mahdi Bahr al-'ulum was called so because of his mastery of the esoteric and occult sciences (*'ulum-i ghariba*), and that Mulla Sadra, like the other philosophers of the high Safavid period, was a Nurbakhshi Sufi.[62]

Histories in the Persianate tradition often have very useful details about intellectual life. For the period of the Zand ascendency, there is *Gulshan-i murad* by Abol-Hasan Ghaffari-ye Kashani with an appendix by Mirza Baqer, with the original text completed in 1206/1791, some two years before the death of the author, and the appendix completed in 1210/1796.[63] The end of the first *maqala*

includes a short *tazkira* of scholars and poets. In this, six are mentioned in particular: Mohammad Baqer Behbahani, Aqa Mohammad Bidabadi, described as
a divine mystic (*'arif-i rabbani*), his teacher Esma'il Khwajui as a true spiritual
wayfarer (*salik-i masalik-i haqq*), Mirza Naser al-Din tabib Isfahani as a perfect
sage (*hakim-i kamil*), Mulla Mahdi Naraqi as the foremost scholar of his age, and
Mir Abol-Qasem Hoseini-ye Kashani.[64] For Khwajui and Bidabadi their role in
Isfahan is stressed. Isfahani is described as a 'Sinai' of philosophy and mysticism
who perpetuated the Platonic way. Naraqi has one of the longest mentions, partly
due to being a recipient of Zand patronage. The final figure was probably also a
Zand client, as posterity did not really think him worthy of a serious mention.

Similarly, local histories can be very instructive. The *Jami'-ye Ja'fari*, a local
account of Yazd in the 18th and 19th century by Mohammad Ja'far 'Tarab' Naini,
gives useful accounts of patronage and scholars.[65] The author had himself studied philosophy in Isfahan with Mulla Esma'il Isfahani (d. 1277/1860), who had
'inherited from his teacher Mulla Ali Nuri' and 'entered into the registers of the
philosophers of the Platonic persuasion'.[66] One important chapter mentions the
books, especially translations, that were available to buy in Yazd, including the
renditions of Mulla Sadra by Seyyed Ahmad Ardakani.[67]

Another local history is *Mirat-i Qasan* or *Tarikh-i Kashan*, completed in 1288/
1871 by 'Abd al-Rahim Zarabi 'Suhayl'-e Kashani, partly, it seems, for the court
of Naser al-Din Shah Qajar. Chapter four is on the notables, including a section
of notices on 'ulama and philosophers (*hukama*) such as Mohsen Fayz Kashani,
Mahdi Naraqi, and his son Ahmad Naraqi, as well as the Sufis and sayyids of the
city.[68] In particular the notice on Mahdi Naraqi is important for our purposes—
having studied in Isfahan, he spent most of his career teaching in Kashan, both
the rational and the scriptural disciplines. The author then gives a full account of
his family and the scholars among his descendants.

A similar work is the late Qajar *Farsnama-yi Nasiri* by the scion of the prominent Dashtaki family Mirza Hasan Fasayi (d. 1316/1898).[69] The work is part
of his attempt to recover his family endowments that dated back to the 15th
century. The text was already lithographed two years before his death. Much
more than just a family history or even a local history of Shiraz, it locates the city
within the wider history of the Qajars. It is an invaluable source on the 'ulama,
poets, shrines, and religious schools and endowments of Shiraz among other
things.

Finally, one of the key witnesses to 1722 and beyond was the famous Iranian
thinker and migrant to India, Mohammad Ali 'Hazin Lahiji (d. 1180/1766).[70]
Lahiji was born in 1103/1691 in Isfahan; his father Abu Talib, a scholar in his
own right and bibliophile, had migrated to Isfahan and died in 1127/1715.
Because of his descent from the Sufi Shaykh Zahed-e Gilani (d. 700/1301), the
preceptor of Shaykh Safi al-Din of Ardebil (d. 735/1334), his family enjoyed the

patronage of the Safavid Shahs, including Sultan Hosein and his son Tahmasp II.[71] He began his studies with his father-in-law, in exegesis, theology, and philosophy. Later, Hazin's teachers included a number of important philosophers and Sufis including Shaykh 'Inayat Allah Gilani and Akhund Masiha-ye Fasayi (with whom he studied works of the Avicennian tradition such as *al-Shifa'*, *al-Isharat wa-l-tanbihat*, and the controversies between Davani and Dashtaki in the 15th century),[72] Seyyed Hasan Taleqani (with whom he studied the texts of the school of Ibn 'Arabi), Mulla Mohammad Baqer 'Sufi' (with whom he studied *ishraqi* texts), and most famously Mulla Sadeq Ardestani (with whom he studied works of *hikmat* generally and who was said to have been killed in the Afghan attack in 1134/1722).[73] According to his own listing, he wrote a number of Arabic glosses on the Avicennian and *ishraqi* tradition already when he was in Isfahan.[74] His works suggest that the dominant mode of philosophical inquiry in Isfahan was a form of Avicennism, sometimes with *ishraqi* tendencies, sometimes with an inclination towards the mystical speculation of the school of Ibn 'Arabi, and other times a more established tradition influenced by Naser al-Din Tusi. An amalgam of the three is often associated with Mulla Sadra and his school—however, there is little evidence of his influence on Hazin. He lived through the siege of Isfahan in 1134/1722, during which two of his brothers died as well as his maternal grandmother and his library and possessions were ransacked.[75] In his *Tazkira*, Hazin recounts among the scholars who died during or just before the siege of Isfahan: Mirza 'Abd Allah Afandi, student of Majlesi II, collaborator on the *Bihar al-anwar* and author of the famous biographical dictionary *Riyad al-'ulama' wa-hiyad al-fudala'*, Mulla Baha al-Din Mohammad Isfahani [Fazel-e Hindi], Mirza Kamal al-Din Masiha-ye Fasayi, one of his teachers, and Mulla Hamza Gilani, student and anamneusis of Mulla Sadeq Ardestani, who himself is not mentioned, suggesting that he did indeed die some time before the siege of Isfahan.[76] However, he is the only source for some of this, and other sources give different dates for Hindi in particular. As Hazin wandered, he spent some time in Mashhad, which even at this point was not devoid of philosophers: in particular, he mentions his company with Mulla Mohammad Rafi'a Gilani and Mulla Mohammad Shafi'a Gilani.[77] The later returned to Isfahan as Shaykh al-Islam after Nader Shah retook the city from the Afghans in 1729. Kinship and hometown networks remained important and proliferated—the association of Gilanis with philosophy in this period is of critical importance. Hazin seems to have become embroiled, due to his earlier association with the Safavid court, in intrigues against Nader Shah in Shiraz and Lar due to the heavy taxation imposed to fight the revolts of Madani and Mohammad Khan Baluch. The assassination and the defeat of the revolt may have precipitated his flight from Iran.[78] Hazin left Iran in 1146/1734 having spent over a decade wandering around southern Iran in search of students and patronage for India, stopping first

at the court at Thatta and then arriving in Delhi in 1149/1737.[79] There he witnessed Nader Shah's sack of Delhi in 1739;[80] he had fled Iran because of Nader
Shah, whose court considered him an opponent because of his close relationship
to the Safavids. He alienated Mohammad Shah and the poets of Delhi and so
moved on to Patna in search of a patron. He ended up in Benaras, where he died
in 1180/1766. In his own listing of his works (most of which are not extant), he
numbers many glosses on philosophical texts such as *al-Fusus fi-l-hikma*, which
was popular in the Safavid period and attributed to al-Farabi, *al-Mutarahat*
and *al-Talwihat* of Sohrawardi, *al-Najat* and the metaphysics of *al-Shifa'*, *Sharh
Hayakil al-nur* of Davani, the ontology section of *al-Tajrid* of Naser al-Din Tusi;
some were treatises on subjects popular in the later Safavid period such as the
problem of human agency and responsibility (*khalq al-a'mal*) and the origina-
tion of the cosmos (*huduth al-'alam*).

So much for the contexts, and now we move onto the figures and the texts,
beginning in Isfahan in the earlier part of the 18th century.

Fazel-e Hindi

Seyyed Baha al-Din Tabatabai Isfahani, known as Fazel-e Hindi (d. 1137/1725),
was an important Safavid thinker in both the rational and scriptural disciplines.[81]
He came from a family of traders and scholars who had spent a generation or so
in western India, but he was born and grew up in Isfahan and became a major
court scholar—his most important work, *'Awn ikhwan al-safa fi talkhis ilahiyyat
al-Shifa'*, a paraphrastic epitome and commentary on Avicenna's work, was
dedicated in 1081/1670 to the Safavid Shah Soleiman.[82] His father, Seyyed Taj
al-Din (d. 1098/1687), was himself a scholar and one of his teachers.[83] Although
we do not know much about his other teachers, especially in philosophy, we
do know that he narrated hadith from Majlesi (who himself also narrated from
Seyyed Taj al-Din) and was married into the Majlesi-Khatunabadi family.[84] He
was prominent enough to have his own mosque and seminary called the Jami'-ye
Fazel.[85] Certainly after the death of Majlesi, he was the most prominent jurist
of the early 18th century and respected for his scholarship even more than the
mulla-bashi Mohammad Baqer Khatunabadi; Fazel-e Hindi may not have held
high office because of his views on Friday prayer.[86] The dominance of Akhbaris
in Isfahan at the end of the Safavid period may also account for his political
marginalization. We know much more about his students because his various
licences to them have survived.[87] For example, his prominent students included
Mirza 'Abdullah Afandi (close member of the Majlesi circle and someone who
had studied philosophy with the Khwansaris and with Fazel-e Hindi), Mulla
Na'ima Taleqani, Mohammad Esma'il Khwajui, and the poet Hazin Lahiji.

In seminary circles, he is best known for his major contribution to Shi'i juris-prudence, *Kashf al-litham 'an qawa'id al-ahkam*, completed in 1110/1689.[88] Apart from the commentary on Avicenna, he also wrote a commentary on the Avicennian summa *Hidayat al-hikma* of Athir al-Din Abhari, a short logical epitome entitled *Khulasat al-mantiq* completed 1073/1662, a contribution to the genre demonstrating the existence of God, *Ithbat al-wajib*, completed 1080/1669, a theological treatise dedicated to Shah Sultan Hosein in 1126/1714 enti-tled *Chahar ayina*, and a systematic but succinct philosophical summa dedicated to the Mughal emperor Aurangzeb, *Hikmat-i khaqaniyya*.[89] Most of his philo-sophical works stem from the period in which philosophy was barely contested in Safavid Iran. As such they represent an important Avicennian bridge across the Afghan occupation of Isfahan into the generation of students who continued to teach philosophy in the city and those who scattered to other parts of the country.

The epitome on logic is extremely dense and represents mere headings to be discussed in class. As such it probably reflects what he would have covered and does not constitute any contribution to logic—in fact, after the 16th century at least until the 19th century there is little logical writing in Iran, apart from some treatises on the Liar's Paradox. The coverage is also rather idiosyncratic drawing upon elements of Avicennian logic on definitions and essences, proof theory and types of propositions, and aspects of the definition and classifica-tion of the sciences. As such it is perhaps a more methodological propaedeutic to his classes. However, his engagement with the Avicennian tradition is better understood in his commentary on the *Shifa'*. In the logic section of the *'Awn*, he defends Avicenna especially against a 'recent scholar' (*fadil al-muta'akhkhirin*) on the syllogistic, especially the modal syllogistic—this is probably a response to Fakhr al-Din al-Razi.[90] His commentary on the metaphysics shows him not to stray much from the text or to engage contemporary thinkers. He asserts that the subject matter of metaphysics can only be the higher causes and being as such and not God in particular.[91] He defends Avicennian hylomorphism and substance-based metaphysics critiqued by the *ishraqi* school and by Mulla Sadra (without mentioning them).[92] Consistent with Avicenna, while acknowledging the superiority of the incorporeal and intelligible over the sensible, he rejects the existence of Platonic forms and the Platonic theory of numbers, contrary to the *ishraqi* tradition.[93] Finally, he rehearses the Avicennian proof for the existence of God and glosses his argument about divine simplicity; following Avicenna's radical contingency that is predicated on the fact that contingency arises from the duality of existence and essence in possible beings, he uses it to construct a cosmological argument for the existence of God as the sole simple being.[94]

In his work for Aurangzeb, one sees a greater engagement with the doctrines circulating in his time, although it remains a rather brief summa. It is consistent with the forms of Avicennism that came to dominate the curriculum in India, such as the commentary on al-Hidaya by Mulla Sadra. On the initial question of whether existence is a self-evident notion not requiring demonstration, he holds that it is true for our existence but not for existence per se or for God.[95] On the related question that comes from the Mulla Sadra tradition, while he holds that the notion of existence is shared between the Necessary and the contingent, it is essential to the former but not the latter. From this he argues against the modulated singularity of existence (tashkik al-wujud), which he surprisingly describes as the view of the 'commonality'; this view was in fact only held by Mulla Sadra and his followers.[96] Avicennians in the centuries before Fazel-e Hindi held that the chain of causality from God is one of essences, which are created (maj'ula), and not a chain of existence; he affirms it, again contrary to the reversal of this position by Mulla Sadra.[97] On the question of whether there is a mode of existence particular to the mind, he seems to remain neutral, stating that philosophers affirm it while theologians deny it.[98] We do know that this was an issue of contention among philosophers, with some critics of Mulla Sadra denying the utility of a concept of mental existence. His reticence is also surprising since the Avicennian tradition affirmed the existence of a mental mode of existence. While he retains the Avicennian proof for the existence of God, he affirms a more theological understanding of the incipience of the cosmos that for him must be temporal, based on the original creation of matter in time.[99] At times he can show his independence of the Avicennian school, for example, when he criticizes Naser al-Din Tusi's treatise on the nature of the intellect.[100] The text culminates with his proof for the existence of God, which follows early modern discussions but with a particular focus—especially since Khafri (d. 1535)—on the question of divine simplicity.[101] Fazel-e Hindi may not have been the most important Avicennian of the period—the Khwansaris probably had more claim to that, and their commentaries were more widely cited. However, as the leading jurist, he was influential and his very espousal of Avicennism and rejection of doctrines associated either with ishraqi thought or the new positions of Mulla Sadra played a role in the contestation of the latter and the slow uptake of his thought in the long period of the 18th century. He also represented an important strand in Avicennism—a more theologically attuned and committed one that again differentiated him from the Khwansaris and perhaps appealed to those who had some reservations about philosophical inquiry.

Na'ima Taleqani

Mulla Mohammad b. Mohammad Taqi known as Na'ima Taleqani (d. 1160/ 1747) came from a family of scholars based in Qom and Isfahan.[102] He himself was born in Isfahan and studied there, primarily with Sadeq Ardestani (but also with Fazel-e Hindi). Manuscript evidence places him in Isfahan in 1115/1703—the date of his copy of Jalal al-Din Davani and Mir Sharif Ali Jurjani's glosses on the *Sharh al-matali'*.[103] He is credited with his own gloss on this text and on other Avicennian texts such as *al-Isharat* and the theological treatise *Tajrid al-i'tiqad*. He seems at some stage to have been the keeper of the books at the royal library (*kitabkhana-ye Soltani*). During the siege of Isfahan in 1722, he escaped to Qom (a number of other figures fled there including Lutf Ali Azar and his family). There on the request of friends, he wrote his major work *Asl al-usul*, which he completed on 15 Jumada II 1135/March 1723. Soon after he left for his hometown of Taleqan, where he continued to write and teach until his death. He completed a treatise on the incipience of the cosmos (*huduth al-'alam*) in 1136/1724, *Fasl al-khitab fi tahqiq al-khitab* on the problem of the divine omnipotence and human agency, a gloss on the hadith collection *Tahdhib al-ahkam* in 1147/1734, and his major work on the afterlife, *Manhaj al-rashad fi ithbat ma'rifat al-ma'ad*, in 1151/1738 shortly before he died.[104]

In the introduction to the *Asl al-usul*, which he says he wrote on the doctrine of existence and its emanation, drawing upon the insights from mystical intuition, he mentions the Afghan attack on Isfahan:

> I was asked to write this when the age had taken up the sword of enmity against the people during the occupation of the city of Isfahan by the Afghan forces, and their killing of many of the inhabitants and of my fellow countrymen, and their pillaging of the city and the countryside around it and the putting to death of many believers, not least among whom were my friends, my companions and my family. I fled to the city of Qom—the city of sanctuary—may God preserve her from misfortunes and from the ravages of the Afghans. I found refuge there far from my family and home. But there the request was renewed—and I was obliged to comply—and I did so willingly and determinedly, setting forth the text with the assistance of God and arranging it with an introduction, there chapters and a conclusion, and I called it *Asl al-usul*.[105]

He refers to Mulla Sadra as the 'best of scholars' and cites his notions of the fundamental reality of being and priority in causality relating to being, and his notion that being is the principle of individuation (*tashakhkhus*).[106] His independent positions included a rejection of motion in the category of substance (*haraka jawhariyya*), and a rejection of Mulla Sadra's position on resurrection. On Mulla Sadra's espousal of the identity thesis (that knowledge entails a unitive act between the intellecting subject and object and especially the union of the human intellect and the active intellect), he attempts to reconcile his position with an 'explanation' of Avicenna's.[107] He defends Mulla Sadra's assertion that in the chain of causality from God, it is existence that emanates and not essence.[108] His cites Mulla Sadra's explanation of modulated monism but prefers Ibn 'Arabi's more radical position and cites approvingly the views of Sufis.[109] He describes the descent of being in terms of the manifestation of God through the archetypes (*a'yan thabita*) and insists that the singular reality of God is all that exists.[110]

His conception of philosophy remains consistent with Mulla Sadra, albeit with a more accentuated mysticism: true knowledge is predicated not only upon an esoteric and experiential gnosis of God but also upon the need to practise spiritual exercises and retreats (*riyadat wa-khalwat wa-mujahadat*). Through these acts, the mystic on the path can traverse the good path of ascent to the highest levels of this lowly earth and acquire the intimacy of the spiritual beings beyond, and through the process of negating the self attain the presence of the One.[111] He clearly associates himself through this with Sufis as he states that true knowledge is not perception but unveiling according to this group (*kashf 'ind ha'ula'i l-ta'ifa*). The aim is to become a divine mystic (*'arif rabbani*).

Alongside these features that demonstrate how the Ardestani legacy was the main conduit for the dissemination of the ideas of Mulla Sadra and his attachment to the Sufi tradition of Ibn 'Arabi, Taleqani weaves commentary on scripture into his philosophical exposition, considering philosophical inquiry to be parallel to exegesis. Much as is the method of Mulla Sadra, at the end of his discussion of how the divine attributes must be identical to the divine essence he cites various hadith.[112] He explains the emanation of existence from God in terms of the famous hadith of the 'hidden treasure'.[113] The conclusion mainly comprises his commentary on *surat al-ikhlas* and *ayat al-nur*.[114] Thus, in his oeuvre we can discern someone taking on the mantle of Mulla Sadra, albeit in a more pronounced mystical manner and critical of some of the key metaphysical doctrines he held. It is unclear whether it impacted on the fuller revival of the Sadrian tradition a few decades later—since none of his students' names are mentioned in the sources, this is perhaps no accident.

Damavandi

'Abd al-Rahim b. Mohammad Yunus Damavandi (d. 1160/1747) was also a student of Sadeq Ardestani and a Nurbakhshi Sufi.[115] He migrated from Isfahan to Karbala where he became the prayer leader at the shrine of Hosein. He seems to have studied with Shah Mohammad Darabi in Isfahan. Various mystical works of his are mentioned in the biographical sources, and some of them have survived in manuscript. Zunuzi describes him as an accomplished mystic, philosopher, ascetic, and sage. He seems to have written on the Shi'i tradition of Ibn 'Arabi with works on monism (*Risalat al-tawhid: Tahqiq ma'na wahdat al-wujud*), and on the concept of the perfect man (*Risalat hall al-rumuz al-radawiyya*, and *Risalat al-fuyudat al-husayniyya*), a *marginalia* on the exegesis *al-Safi* of Fayz Kashani, a couple of philosophical theological treatises on the incipience of the cosmos (*huduth al-'alam*) and on the nature of the divine decree and human responsibility of acts (*Risalat al-qada' wa-l-qadar*), as well as some esoteric commentaries on hadith (such as the famous hadith of Kumayl on the nature of reality that was much beloved of esoteric-minded monists).[116] His interest in this latter hadith as well as the sermon of enunciation (*khutbat al-bayan*) attributed to Ali demonstrates his affiliation to what is sometimes called Shi'i esotericism (*'irfan-i shi'i*).

His main work, *Meftah-e asrar al-Husayni*, is divided into 37 keys to the secrets; in it he describes Sadeq Ardestani as his teacher.[117] He argues that the esotericist's path has not been made clear by the philosophers and mystics who came before him, so he sees it as his duty to do so—based on his own mystical insights. He indicates that he wrote the work inspired by and probably in the presence of the shrine of Imam Hosein and that its title indicates the date of completion.[118] He repeatedly refers in the text to the Imam as his spiritual guide (*murshid*). Using *abjad* calculations, the title renders the value of 1159/1746, which would be when the text was completed. He probably died in Karbala.

He begins the text by distinguishing an exoteric from an esoteric path. The exoteric path might arrive at *knowledge* of God, but it is only through the esoteric that one arrives at God. That is the spiritual path—the path of Sufis, although he is careful not to use the word—citing the famous saying of the Prophet that includes the phrase 'the path (*tariqa*) is my actions'.[119] Keys VI and VII are dedicated to the distinction between knowledge and gnosis and depend on sayings of Imam Ali, whom he refers to as the *Qiblat al-'arifin*—a title commonly used later by the Bidabadi circle including Nuri. He cites a major text for the Sufis—the famous commentary of Kashani on the so-called hadith of Kumayl on the nature of reality.[120] He discusses repeatedly the ideas of the school of Ibn 'Arabi, citing the major figures and cites approvingly the views of the Sufis as the best path.[121] He consistently refers to Ibn 'Arabi as the leader of those who practise mystical intuition or kashf (*ra'is al-mukashifin*), and we see how he privileges the method of *kashf* over reason.[122] The influence of Mulla Sadra on a number of positions is also clear, and he cites him as Sadr al-muhaqqiqin (leader of the verifiers).[123] Later in the text, he even cites the famous four journeys as described in the work of Mulla Sadra.[124]

Damavandi makes a number of claims for Sufis that seem to go beyond one's expectations within a Shi'i context. First, he argues that the true mystics are part of the family of Mohammad.[125] Second, Key XIX is an interesting discourse on understanding the spiritual guide: alongside the notion that one has to have a *murshid*, and he who does not have one is a follower of Satan—a commonplace in Sufi discourse—he also defends the contemplation of the image of the spiritual master as a symbol of the contemplation of the true master who is the Imam.[126] This key is full of citations from the classical Sufi poets like Shabastari and Rumi. Third, in Key XXVIII he discusses the concept of the Mahdi and associates it on the one hand with the notion of the perfect man and the seal of saints in the school of Ibn 'Arabi, in which he makes a distinction between the absolute Mahdi who is awaited by the Shi'a and the many Mahdis who act as spiritual masters and reflect an expression of the absolute Mahdi through the process of *buruz* associated with the Nurbakhshi order.[127] The theory of projection (*buruz*) thus allows the Sufi master to be associated with the Mahdi as a projection of the Mohammadan reality; it was originally articulated by Seyyed Mohammad Nurbakhsh (d. 869/1464), the eponymous founder of the order to which Damavandi adhered.[128] He argues that the perfect spiritual guide is a *boruz-e kamel*—and is careful to distinguish this doctrine from the vulgar notion of metempsychosis. He complains that many of the exoteric scholars fail to understand these subtleties that even the Mahdi is a *buruz* of Imam Ali, the true pivot of the universe and the focus of the hearts of believers. In this vein, he recounts his vision that he received once when reciting the Qur'an that took him to the mosque of Kufa and before the prayer niche he encountered Gabriel who covered the horizon.[129] Gabriel addresses him and tells him that Ali is his *qibla* and the *qibla* of all believers and prophets. This confirms the superiority of *walaya* over *nubuwwa* and affirms the reason why Damavandi and those like him consistently refer to Ali as the *qiblat al-'arifin*. He does, however, repeat how he considers Imam Hosein to be his *murshid*—in a vision in 1154/1741 and again in Karbala at the head of the shrine in 1155/1742.[130] The Imam refers him back to the Mahdi. Fourth, he stresses in Key XXXI the importance for Sufis of spiritual practices as a means to arrive at God.[131]

What we see in Damavandi is the influence of Mulla Sadra on the more openly esoteric-minded thinkers of the period. His work exemplifies the esoteric Shi'i intellectual tradition, although in his other works that demonstrate the philosophical concerns of the period with the question of the incipience of the cosmos and squaring the causal efficacy of human agency with divine omnipotence, the influence of the Avicennian tradition can be seen.

Qutb al-Din Nayrizi

About Nayrizi (d. 1173/1760) we know quite a bit due to his role in the Zahabi Sufi order—and through him, we can trace lines of transmission and dissemination of philosophy and mysticism in the shrine cities of Iraq in the 18th century.[132] Seyyed Qutb al-Din Mohammad Shirazi Nayrizi began his initiation into

Sufism and hadith with Shah Mohammad Darabi (d. 1130/1718), author of a Sufi treatise entitled *Mi'raj al-kamal* on the need for a spiritual master, in Shiraz, and then studied philosophy for seven years in Isfahan with Sadeq Ardestani.[133] Darabi was not, however, his preceptor into the Zahabi order; that was his father-in-law Ali-Naqi Istahbanati (d. *c*.1129/1717).[134] He remained in Shiraz for some time and then moved to Najaf ten years before he died there. His works, mainly in poetry, include *Anwar al-walaya wa-mishkat al-hidaya*, a mystical commentary on a hadith popular at the time, *Misbah al-walaya, Fasl al-khitab*, also known as *Hikmat al-'arifin*, a long poem of around 6,000 verses on the nature of philosophy, *Kanz al-hikma, Mufarrij al-qulub, Risala-yi 'ishqiyya* on the nature of the erotic motion and issuance of the cosmos from God, and *Risala-yi ruhiyya* on the states of the Sufi adept's soul mixed with Avicennian psychology, as well as some commentaries on hadith popular in esoteric Shi'i circles, such as the recognition of the Imams through their luminous nature (*bi-l-nuraniyya*).[135] One of the most interesting sources on Nayrizi is the account of his daughter Umm Salama, whose *Jami' al-kulliyyat* is based on *Fasl al-khitab*.[136]

Nayrizi characterized his mode of philosophy as 'prophetic' and 'Alid' as well as the philosophy of mystics (*hikmat al-'arifin*); as such, it is distinct from Greek philosophy that is based on the 'fantasies of the philosophers'.[137] He strictly demarcates his own exercise—rooted in the Qur'anic notion of wisdom as a 'great good' (referring to Q. 2.269) that is divinely bestowed from the vanity of humanly constructed thought.[138] Given Nayrizi's metaphysical espousal of *wahdat al-wujud*, the key notion of monism that became the focus of controversy and philosophical discussion from the 18th century in particular (although it was much contested in Shi'i contexts before), he was known as the 'second Ibn 'Arabi'. Like many Sufi masters, he expressed his ideas in verse and penned most of these in Najaf at the shrine of Ali—most of his works are epic poems upon which his disciples and later followers wrote commentaries. Much of his work is exegetical. His association to the monism of Ibn 'Arabi is stronger than any affiliation to Avicenna or Mulla Sadra. While he accepts the latter's doctrine of the ontological primacy of existence (*asalat al-wujud*), he rejects the notion that existence is analogically and meaningfully shared (*ishtirak ma'nawi*) between God and the cosmos; existence is a singular reality with God as its primary referent and is not modulated.[139] On the related issue of what emanates primarily and simply from God, he sides with Mulla Sadra on it being existence, linking it to the Neoplatonic axiom of 'only one thing can issue from one'.[140] The influence of Ibn 'Arabi is striking throughout the whole text on the issue of monism and God as the true referent of the term existence.[141]

Nayrizi's corpus is arguably not strictly philosophical, even if he demonstrates a good understanding of the doctrines and arguments of Avicenna, the *ishraqi* school, and of Mulla Sadra. It is more in line with esoteric Shi'i *'irfan*, mixing the school of Ibn 'Arabi with meditations upon scripture. This coupled with the poetical style and his strong Sufi affiliation meant that his legacy remained primarily with the Zahabi initiates. However, mediated through some of his students, his work did resonate with the more scholastic generation of mystically inclined philosophers, unaffiliated to Sufi orders, in the seminary in the Qajar period.

Bidabadi

Nayrizi himself was a direct teacher of Bidabadi. Bidabadi's father Mohammad Rafi' Gilani was a well-known scholar, and he moved to from Mazandaran to Isfahan, settling in the suburb of Bidabad.[142] Bidabadi had been the recipient of the patronage of the previous Zand ruler, Ali-Murad Khan (d. 1785). Zunuzi says that he played a major role in the revival of the study of metaphysics in Iran and its effects were widely felt, even though some like Zunuzi himself were not direct students. He also indicates his role in establishing the study of the occult sciences alongside philosophy and mysticism. Bidabadi himself was a philosopher inclining to *theosis* (*hakim-i mutaallih*), which meant that he believed philosophy was a practice and way of life by which one acquires a resemblance to the divine (*al-tashabbuh bi-l-bari'*), as a mystic (*ahl-i sayr u suluk*), and as someone known for his piety and even miracles (*sahib al-maqamat wa-l-karamat*).[143] Another contemporary witness, the Ni'matullahi Sufi Mohammad Ja'far Kabudarahangi, known as Majdhub Ali Shah (d. 1238/1823), claims that the Bidabadi circle was renowned for their mystical and spiritual practices (*riyazat u mujahada-yi nafsani*) alongside their *'irfan* (mystical) orientation in their study of metaphysics.[144] More recent studies have traced the modern tendency of *'irfan* in the Shi'i shrine cities of Iraq back to the Bidabadi circle.[145]

Bidabadi had studied with Mirza Mohammad Taqi Almasi (d. 1159/1746),[146] who was the prayer-leader in Isfahan under Nader Shah, and the philosopher Esma'il Khwajui (d. 1174/1760), as well as Qutb al-Din Nayrizi—they had all been students of Mulla Sadeq Ardestani (d. 1134/1722), the leading philosopher (inclining towards mysticism) in Isfahan. In that sense, we might talk about one strand of 18th-century philosophy following the 'school' of Ardestani. We know very little about Ardestani apart from the claims of his saintly nature, the influence of Mulla Sadra upon him, and his interest in mysticism not just in theory but also in practice such that he was described in biographical sources as a 'divine mystic' (*'arif-i rabbani*).[147] Similarly, we know little about Khwajui beyond his role as a teacher in Isfahan whose students included, alongside Bidabadi, Mulla Mahdi Naraqi (d. 1209/1794), and Mulla Mihrab Gilani (d. 1217/1802)— apart from one treatise critiquing the unreality of time (defending Mir Damad's position on perpetual creation) and another on the mystical concept of the monism (*wahdat al-wujud*), most of his works that have been published are on the scriptural disciplines[148] Bidabadi's students included Mirza Abol-Qesem Modarres Khatunabadi (d. 1212/1797), Ali Nuri, Seyyed Sadr al-Din Dezfuli (d. 1258/1842), a renowned mystic associated with the Zahabi order who also did much to spread '*irfan* in the shrine cities of Iraq,[149] Mulla Mihrab Gilani (d. 1217/1802), described as a 'Sufi' and a member of the Zahabi order,[150] Mulla Nazar Ali Gilani (d. after 1206/1792), another member of the circle and author of an Arabic treatise *al-Tuhfa*,[151] Seyyed Ahmad Ardakani (d. 1245/1830) who translated *al-Mabda' wa-l-ma'ad* and *Sharh al-Hidaya* of Mulla Sadra into Persian,[152] and the prominent jurist Shaykh Mohammad Ibrahim Karbasi (d. 1261/1845).[153]

Bidabadi was famed for his asceticism and known as a spiritual master as well as teacher of *hikmat* texts—some Zahabi sources even describe him as a master in their order, although the reliability of the claim is doubtful.[154] Nevertheless, his association through his teacher and students with Zahabis is quite clear. Working as a grocer, he was a philanthropist and a skilled alchemist—this latter brings into focus the interest that his circle had in the occult. Some of his works read like ecstatic Sufi initiations. The short *Risala himmatiyya* is addressed directly to the adept and blends together exegetical comments on scripture with references to the school of Ibn 'Arabi to demonstrate not only that the spiritual path entails both the exoteric and the esoteric, faith and works and mystical experience, all oriented towards an understanding that only God exists.[155] Most of his other works are on Sufi topics and glosses on Qur'anic exegeses of Mohsen Fayz Kashani and Nizam al-Din Nishapuri (d. 730/1330).[156]

His main work, *al-Mabda' wa-l-ma'ad*, is a study, in three parts, of the nature of existence, of God, the creation of the cosmos and its expression in the human and the eschatological folding up of existence that follows, broadly, the themes and concerns of Mulla Sadra.[157] The first part begins with a rehearsal of Avicenna's famous proof for the existence of God, and then on the question of divine simplicity and the identity of the attributes and the divine essence, he moves into exegetical mode and draws upon the Shi'i theological tradition.[158] The rest of the part is then taken up with a mystical contemplation of the descent of being from God through the prisms of the language of emanation, of overflowing love, and the neoplatonic language of procession and reversion with an important Shi'i twist that the reversion is mediated through the perfect human (ultimately the Imam).[159] Given such a position, he defends the logical and not the temporal incipience of the cosmos. The second part on creation constitutes his physics, a mixture of Avicennian doctrines alongside a concern with the nature of the descent of the human soul and its faculties that allow it to return to its source. The third part on the afterlife seems to set aside the body; the destinations of different souls and their experiences after death and before the judgement as well as their final destination are discussed. But in all, one finds a recapitulation of the esoteric Shi'i notion that human souls are immortal—they always have been and always will be by virtue of their incorporeality and direct relationship with the divine command.[160] He does not refer to Mulla Sadra's theory of resurrection—in fact, no authorities are mentioned at all. One wonders whether the brief nature of the text, focused on the life cycle of the human soul—it is the origins, procession, and reversion of the human soul in relationship to God that is his concern—indicates its origins as notes emerging from his classes that seem to have focused on the ethical and spiritual practices of the self.

His glosses on *al-Asfar al-arba'a* of Mulla Sadra were published in the margins of the Tehran lithograph of 1282/1865, and another set of glosses on *al-Masha'ir* are in manuscript.[161] But they add little to what we know from the published texts. What is significant is that in the person of Bidabadi, we can discern the confluence of philosophy and mysticism not just in terms of the theoretical study but also the practice. His works attest to this interpretation, as do his networks of formation and knowledge dissemination. Bidabadi's circle, which later included Nuri, his most prominent student, embraced a number of scholars from his native region of Gilan and included his friend the prominent jurist Abol-Qasem Gilani, better known as Mirza-ye Qummi (d. 1231/1815) whose own interest in Sufism and philosophy was well known despite his critique of 'decadent' Sufis.[162]

Mahdi Naraqi

Mohammad Mahdi Naraqi (d. 1209/1795) was arguably the most important philosopher of the period and a prolific thinker who engaged critically with the work of Mulla Sadra, as well as continuing the Avicennian tradition through his commentaries, especially on *al-Shifa'*.[163] After his initial studies in Kashan (where he later returned to teach), he trained with Esma'il Khwajui and Mohammad Zaman Kashani (d. 1172/1759) in Isfahan.[164] As a polymath who wrote on a variety of issues and genres, he was described as one who 'unifies in himself the rational and the scriptural' (*jami' al-ma'qul va-l-manqul*).[165] Like others of his time, he did not have a direct affiliation to a Sufi order, but his work demonstrates the influence of some Nurbakhshi ideas. He also spent some time in Karbala studying *fiqh* with Vahid Behbahani and Yusuf Bahrani. He works in jurisprudence as well. In philosophy and theology his major works include a commentary on the *Metaphysics* of *al-Shifa'* of Avicenna in which he often adjudicates between the Khwansaris and Mulla Sadra preferring the former, *Jami' al-afkar wa-naqid al-anzar* completed in 1193/1779 on the proofs for the existence of God and Avicennian metaphysics as found in *al-Isharat*, *Qurrat al-'uyun*, a treatise of existence and essence that attracted the critical attention of Ali Nuri and Shaykh Ahmad al-Ahsai, which was also completed in 1182/1768, *al-Lum'a al-ilahiyya fi-l-hikma al-muta'aliya*, on the Sadrian tradition, *Anis al-muvahhidin*, a short treatise on the theological categories in Persian, *Mushkilat al-'ulum*, a miscellany that includes plenty of philosophical and logical arguments, and perhaps his most influential work on moral psychology, *Jami' al-sa'adat*, which draws upon the Persian *akhlaq* tradition and Aristotelian virtue ethics as well as the Shi'i ethics of Fayz Kashani.[166] After returning to Kashan, he was the Friday prayer leader and enjoyed the patronage of the Zand governor 'Abd al-Razzaq Khan; it was on the insistence of the latter that he led an embassy to Agha Mohammad Khan Qajar, who was besieging the city 1198/1784, to sue for peace.[167]

On the whole, Naraqi follows the school of Mulla Sadra, especially on the fundamental reality of being (*asalat al-wujud*) and the idea that what emanates from God is existence and not essence.[168] He seems to hold that the conceptual distinction of essence and existence in the phenomenal world does not map onto reality; like Mulla Sadra, he does not think that essences exist in extramental reality.[169] Yet, he recognizes that Mulla Sadra is not within the Avicennian school and consistently refers to him as the Shirazi mystic.[170] He also upholds the Sadrian infallibilist position on epistemology, which is based on the identity thesis and the process known as 'knowledge by presence' (*'ilm huduri*).[171] Consistent with Mulla Sadra and other thinkers of a broadly Platonist persuasion in the Safavid period, but contrary to Avicenna, he affirms the existence of an ontological realm known as the 'world of similitudes' (*'alam al-mithal*).[172] He is critical of a number of Sadrian positions. First, while he adopts the notion of modulation in existence (*tashkik al-wujud*), he considers it to be merely a logical concept and not something that pertains to actuality, and in fact in doing so he might be reflecting a more 'orthodox' Avicennism stemming from Naser al-Din Tusi.[173] Second, while accepting a mystical intuition for the unity of being (*wahdat al-wujud*), he does not think it can be rationally demonstrated or known.[174] He seems to be critical of Mulla Sadra's version of monism as well as of Ibn 'Arabi's—that is the main thrust of *Qurrat al-'uyun*. He argues concomitantly that the issue of the simple reality being all things (*basitu l-haqiqa kullu l-ashya'*) is not established.[175] It seems that his own sympathies lie with a metaphysical exposition that is a more Avicennian version of Mulla Sadra. With Avicenna, he affirms the actual plurality of contingent existents.[176] Third, on the incipience of the soul, he rejects the Sadrian doctrine that the soul is corporeal in its incipience and argues for its spiritual incipience (*ruhaniyyat al-huduth*) consistent with the Avicennian tradition.[177] Furthermore, on the question of the incipience of the cosmos, he sets aside Mulla

Sadra's theory of motion in substance as a means for reconciling an eternal cosmos with God's creative agency, and opts instead, following his teacher Khwajui, for Mir Damad's notion of perpetual creation (*huduth dahri*).[178]

None of his students were prominent philosophers—some were jurists and others Sufis. There was no one to take on his legacy, despite the fact that his philosophical ideas and influences were the most interesting in the period (and demonstrated a deep knowledge of the thought of philosophers who came before). He achieved fame at a time when Kashan was flourishing but Isfahan had recovered and the centre of culture and power was gravitating further north. Naraqi represents the culmination of an Avicennian tradition. While his commentary on *al-Shifa'* was read, it seems a Sadrian reading of Avicenna prevailed. The success of his contemporary Ali Nuri's establishment of Mulla Sadra at the heart of the curriculum meant that at least for two generations Avicennism was eclipsed from the intellectual landscape of Iran. Naraqi's ethical treatise, however, did have a lasting impact—it indicated an element of the rise in ethical thought that was soon married with mysticism in the Qajar period and inherited by the modern seminary.

Conclusions

What can we conclude about the developments in philosophy in the period from the sack of Isfahan to the consolidation of Qajar rule? The most obvious point is that philosophy continued to be taught and disseminated continuously in the various centres—not just Isfahan but also in Mashhad, Qom, Shiraz, Hamadan, and Kashan, as well as Najaf—across the country, in seminaries and beyond, in Arabic and in Persian and through new networks of scholars and not just a small elite in Isfahan. Shiraz and Mashhad had already seen the teaching of philosophy in the Safavid period but the other cities grew as centres focused on specific individuals.[179] Creativity was often pursued through the vehicle of commentaries and marginalia—as was often the case in the postclassical period—and these were often on the works of Avicenna. The 'school of Isfahan', which never had been a unified set of doctrines or methods, fractured in the period in which there were not strong school affiliations. What did, however, emerge was that the two major Safavid thinkers Mir Damad and Mulla Sadra entered the canon of the philosophical tradition to be read alongside Avicenna, Sohrawardi, and Ibn 'Arabi in the cultural milieu of the Persianate world. The Avicennian tradition remained the prime signifier of a philosophical training through the study of the *Shifa'* and *al-Isharat*—alongside the influential *Shawariq al-ilham* of 'Abd al-Razzaq Lahiji in philosophical theology—albeit supplemented in the margins by the texts of Mir Damad on the question of time, Mulla Sadra on existence, and the revival of Neoplatonic concerns with the so-called *Theologia Aristotelis* and various works attributed to al-Farabi.

Second, the period provides us with further evidence for the need to consider a more 'expansive' sense of philosophy. The thinkers of this period had strong theological positions and often also associated with Sufism or at least in the metaphysical tendency of mysticism which emerged in this period as *'irfan*. Nurbakhshis, Ni'matullahis, and Zahabis studied with philosophers, wrote philosophical treatises, and disseminated ideas among their own networks of peers and disciples, particularly in centres of Sufi learning such as Shiraz, Kashan, Kerman, and Tabriz. The mixing of what were distinct genres of writing in earlier periods continued the late Safavid trend towards more holistic works that considered the function of philosophy to be a complete way of thinking about reality, about the homologies between the books of revelation and of the cosmos, and an ethically committed way of life. Scriptural texts, Sufi aphorisms, mystical visions, the doxa of the ancients as well as poetic motifs all worked alongside apodictic arguments to establish philosophical positions. The demarcations between argument and dogma, exegesis and demonstration, became blurred.

Third, given the political instability of Iran and the ease with which scholars could retreat to the relative security—and obscurity—of the shrine cities in Iraq, these places became major centres for the teaching of philosophy and of Sufi practice as we saw in the cases of Damavandi and Nayrizi. For too long the intellectual history of Shi'i Islam since the Safavid period has focused on the fortunes of the hierocracy and jurists in the shrine cities. But lest we forget, the lure of these places also lay in the occult circles of initiation, the tekkes, the networks of philosophers and the teachers of Ibn 'Arabi, the logicians, and other theological entrepreneurs.

Finally, one could argue that none of the figures studied in this paper or who one might find in the 18th century constituted an original thinker—they were minor figures defending Avicenna or criticizing positions of Mulla Sadra and Mir Damad, or upholding the monism of Ibn 'Arabi. But they did play a critical role in opening up the canon that allows us to make sense of the significance of philosophy in the period. It is precisely through such an expansion of the canon that we can better understand the philosophical tradition, to set aside the assumption of perennial questions and central themes devoid of any diachronic analysis, that we can engage with these figures so that we can develop, in the words of Richard Rorty, a 'thick description of the institutional arrangements and disciplinary matrices' of that tradition:[180]

> I should want to include under 'intellectual history' books about all those enormously influential people who do not get into the canon of great dead philosophers, but who are often called 'philosophers' either

because they held a chair so described, or for lack of any better idea—people like Erigena, Bruno, Ramus, Mersenne, Wolff, Diderot, Cousin, Schopenhauer, Hamilton, McCosh, Bergson and Austin. Discussion of these 'minor figures' often coalesces with thick description of institutional arrangements and disciplinary matrices, since part of the historical problem they pose is to explain why these non-great philosophers or quasi-philosophers should have been taken so much more seriously than the certifiably great philosophers of their day. Then there are the books about the thought and influence of people who are not usually called 'philosophers' but are at least borderline cases of the species. These are people who in fact did the jobs which philosophers are popularly supposed to do—impelling social reform, supplying new vocabularies for moral deliberation, deflecting the course of scientific and literary disciplines into new channels.

The aim is not to create a new canon or to engage in a doxographical exercise but to focus on the nature of the practice of philosophy that, as specialists on Islamic thought have indicated, rests upon commentary traditions. It is thus often through the commentators and such minor figures that we can truly make sense of what, for example, was the Avicennian tradition of the 18th century, how texts were studied, which parts were studied and glossed, and how they were used to make sense of the intellectual preoccupations of their practitioners. Reconstruction for its own sake—or what might be termed antiquarianism—is not the purpose, even if earlier efforts to trace the intellectual history of the period from, say, 1500 and 1900 did little else but give a list of names, texts, and some ideas on their particularities that seem quite incommensurable to our notions of philosophy.

Notes

1. It was built in 1070/1660 for Mohsen Fayz Kashani (d. 1090/1679) by Shah 'Abbas II as part of his attempt to entice him to take the post of *Shaykh al-islam* of Isfahan. See Mohammad Taher Qazvini, *'Abbasnama*, ed. Ibrahim Dehqan (Arak: Intisharat-e Davudi, 1950), 256.
2. Reza-Qoli Khan Hedayat, *Rawzat al-safa-yi Nasiri* (Tehran: Intisharat-e Khayyam, 1339 Sh/1960), VIII: 493.
3. Sajjad Rizvi, 'The *takfir* of the philosophers (and Sufis) in Safavid Iran', in Camilla Adang et al. (eds), *Accusations of Unbelief in Islam: A Diachronic Perspective on Takfir* (Leiden: Brill, 2016), 244–269.
4. This work of Qummi's is available in a critical edition—Ata Anzali and S. M. Hadi Gerami (eds.), *Opposition to Philosophy in Safavid Iran: Mulla Mohammad Taher Qummi's Hikmat al-'arifin* (Leiden: Brill, 2017).
5. On the pivotal role of Nuri in continuing the teaching of philosophy and establishing Mulla Sadra (d. 1636) as the hegemonic reference for philosophy in Iran, see my 'Mulla Ali Nuri', in *Philosophy in Qajar Iran*, ed. Reza Pourjavady (Leiden: Brill, 2018).

6. Seyyed Hossein Nasr, *Islamic Philosophy from its Origins to the Present: Philosophy in the Land of Prophecy* (Albany: SUNY Press, 2006), 235–236. Interestingly, Nasr is remarkably silent about the 18th century and about even a major figure like Sabzavari (d. 1289/1873) in the 19th century.

7. Most clearly discernable in 'Muqaddima', to Sadr al-Din Shirazi, *al-Shawahid al-rububiyya fi-l-manahij al-sulukiyya*, ed. Seyyed Jalal al-Din Ashtiyani (Mashhad: Ferdowsi University Press, 1967), lxxiii–cxxi.

8. Nasr, *Islamic Philosophy from Its Origin to the Present*, 236.

9. Karim Khan (d. 1779) himself was no patron of the 'ulama—see John Perry, *Karim Khan Zand* (Oxford: Oneworld, 2006), 122.

10. Henry Corbin, *Histoire de la philosophie islamique* (Paris: Gallimard, 1986), 476–478.

11. Ata Anzali, *Safavid Shi'ism, the Eclipse of Sufism, and the Rise of 'Irfan*, unpublished PhD dissertation, Rice University, 2012, 116–118.

12. Ashtiyani, 'Muqaddima', to Mulla Na'ima Taleqani, *Asl al-usul*, ed. Seyyed Jalal al-Din Ashtiyani (Tehran: Imperial Iranian Academy of Philosophy, 1357 Sh/1978), iv.

13. 'Abd al-Nabi Qazwini, *Tatmim Amal al-amil*, ed. Seyyed Ahmad al-Hoseini (Qom: Kitabkhana-ye Ayatullah Mar'ashi, 1407/1986), 66, 78. See also Ata Anzali, *Safavid Shi'ism*, 112–113, 122.

14. Anzali, *Safavid Sufism*, 120; Rasul Ja'fariyan, *Siyasat u farhang-i ruzgar-i Safavi* (Tehran: Nashr-i 'ilm, 1388 Sh/2009), II: 1069. On this madrasa, see Seyyed Muslih al-Din Mahdavi, *Isfahan dar al-'ilm-i sharq, madaris-i dini-yi Isfahan*, ed. Mohammad-Riza Nil-furushan (Isfahan: Markaz-i Isfahan–shenasi, 1386 Sh/2007), I: 238–241.

15. Ja'fariyan, *Siyasat u farhang-i ruzgar*, II: 1069.

16. Mirza Mohammad sadiq Musavi Nami-ye Isfahani, *Tarikh-i Giti-gusha dar tarikh-i khandan-i Zand*, ed. Sa'id Nafisi (Tehran: Chapkhana-yi Iqbal, 1318 Sh/1939), 210, 278.

17. Tonakabuni, *Qisas al-'ulama'*, 172.

18. Cf. Mohammad Hashim Asaf, 'Rustam al-hukama', *Rustam al-tavarikh*, ed. M. Mushiri (Tehran, 1969), 447–450; Birgitt Hoffmann, *Persische Geschichte 1694-1835 erlebt, erinnert und erfunden: Das Rustam al-tawariḥ in deutscher Bearbeitung* (Bamberg: AKU Verlag, 1986), II, 734–739; Tonakabuni, *Qisas al-'ulama'*, 171–172; John Perry, 'The Zand dynasty', in Peter Avery, Gavin Hambly and Charles Melville (eds), *The Cambridge History of Iran Volume 7 From Nadir Shah to the Islamic Republic* (Cambridge: Cambridge University Press, 1991), 93–94; John Perry, *Karim Khan Zand* (Chicago: University of Chicago Press, 1979), 298–299; Mehdi Roschanzamir, *Die Zand-Dynastie* (Hamburg: Hartmut Lüdke Verlag, 1970), 97–103; Abol-Hasan Ghaffari-ye Kashani, *Gulshan-i murad [Tarikh-i Zandiya]*, ed. Ghulam-Riza Tabatabai-Majd (Tehran: Intisharat-e zarrin, 1369 Sh/1990), 687ff; Reza-Qoli Khan 'Hedayay, *Fihris al-tavarikh*, ed. 'Abd al-Husayn Navai and Mir Hashim Muhaddis (Tehran: Pazhuhishgah-i 'ulum-e insani va muṭala'at-e farhangi, 1373 Sh/1994), 300, 417, 421.

19. Nasrabadi, *Tazkira-yi Nasrabadi*, ed. Ahmad mudaqqiq-i Yazdi (Yazd: Intisharat-e danishgah-e Yazd, 1378 Sh/1999), pp. 217–302; see C.A. Storey, *Persian Literature: A Bio-bibliographical Survey* (London: Luzac & Co., 1972), I, pt. 2, pp. 818–821. For studies of the text, see Iraj Afshar, 'Le Tazkare-ye Nasrabadi: Ses données socio-économiques et culturelles', in Jean Calmard (ed.), *Études safavides*, Paris/Tehran: Institut Français de recherché en Iran, 1993, pp. 1–12. A work that does the same job for North India (but includes Safavid poets) in the late Safavid period is *Kalimat al-shu'ara'* of Mohammad Afzal Sarkhwush (d. 1127/1714), ed. 'Ali-Riza Qazva (Tehran: Kitabkhana, muza, va markaz-e asnad-e Majlis-e Shura-ye Islami, 1389 Sh/2010); he includes entries of Baha al-Din al-'Amili (43), Mir Damad (43), Sayyid Ali Khan Dashtaki Shirazi (100), Sarmad (101), 'Abd al-Razzaq 'Fayyaz' Lahiji (149); it was written in 1093/1682—see Storey, *Persian Literature*, I, pt. 2, pp. 821–823. Another important contemporary Indian work, completed in 1147/1735, is the *Safina-yi Khushgu* of Bindraban Das 'Khushgu', ed. Seyyed Shah 'Ata Kakvi (Patna: Label Litho Press, 1959)—entries include Hazin and Walih (pp. 291–294); see Story, *Persian Literature*, I, pt. 2, pp. 826–828.

20. Nasrabadi, *Tazkira-yi Nasrabadi*, 237.

21. Ali-qoli Valih Daghestani, *Riyaz al-shu'ara'*, ed. Seyyed Mohammad Naji Nasrabadi, 5 vols. (Tehran: Intisharat-e Asatir, 1383 Sh/2004); see Storey, *Persian Literature*, I, pt. 2, pp. 830–833.

22. Valih Daghestani, *Riyaz al-shu'ara'*, I: 181, 184, 212, 217–218, 628–629, II: 874, III: 1166–1168.

23. Lutf Ali Beg Azar, *Atashkada*, ed. Hasan Sadat Nasiri, 2 vols. (Tehran: Chapkhana-ye Haydari, 1337 Sh/1958). For a study, see Mana Kia, 'Imagining Iran before nationalism: Geocultural meanings of land in Azar's *Atashkadeh*', in *Rethinking Iranian Nationalism and Modernity: Histories, Historiographies*, eds. Kamran Aghaie and Afshin Marashi (Austin: University of Texas Press, 2014), 89–112.

24. Azar, *Atashkada*, ed. Mir Jalal al-Din Muhaddith (Tehran: Amir Kabir, 1378 Sh/1999), II: 46–47.

25. 'Abd al-Razzaq Beg 'Maftun' Donbuli, *Tajribat al-ahrar wa-tasliyat al-abrar*, ed. Hasan Qazi Tabatabai, 2 vols. (Tehran: Muassasa-ye tarikh o farhang-e Iran, 1349 Sh/1070).

26. Donbuli, *Tajribat al-ahrar*, I: 150

27. Donbuli, *Tajribat al-ahrar*, I: 151–160.

28. Donbuli, *Tajribat al-ahrar*, I: 160–161.

29. Donbuli, *Tajribat al-ahrar*, I: 177.

30. Donbuli, *Tajribat al-ahrar*, I: 177–178.

31. al-Hurr al-'Amili, *Amal al-amil*, ed. Seyyed Ahmad al-Hoseini, 2 vols. (Najaf: al-Matba'a al-Haydariyya, 1966).

32. 'Abdullah Afandi Isfahani, *Ta'liqat Amal al-amil*, ed. Seyyed Ahmad al-Hoseini (Qom: Kitabkhana-ye Ayatullah Mar'ashi, 1410/1990); idem, *Riyad al-'ulama' wahiyad al-fudala'*, ed. Seyyed Ahmad al-Hoseini, 6 vols., (Qom: Kitabkhana-ye Ayatullah Mar'ashi, 1981).

33. Seyyed Ahmad al-Hoseini, *Talamidhat al-Majlesi* (Qom: Kitabkhana-ye Ayatullah Mar'ashi, 1410 Sh/1990), 37–38.

34. Afandi, *Ta'liqat*, 112, 140–141.

35. Afandi, *Ta'liqat*, 86–87.

36. Afandi, *Ta'liqat*, 142.

37. Afandi, *Ta'liqat*, 309.

38. Afandi, *Ta'liqat*, 275.

39. 'Abd al-Nabi Qazvini, *Tatmim Amal al-amil*, ed. Seyyed Ahmad al-Hoseini (Qom: Kitabkhana-ye Ayatullah Mar'ashi, 1407/1986); Ghulam-Husayn Khudri, *Ta'ammuli bar sayr-e tatavvuri-ye hukama u hikmat-i muta'aliya* (Tehran: Pazhuhishgah-e 'ulum-e insani u mutala'at-e farhangi, 1391 Sh/2012), 312–314; Sayyid Muhsin al-Amin, *A'yan al-shi'a* (Beirut: Dar al-ta'aruf, 1986), VIII: 128; Modarres-e Tabrizi, *Rayhanat al-adab* (Tabriz: Maktaba-ye Khayyam, 1959), IV: 453.

40. Qazwini, *Tatmim*, 52–57.

41. Qazwini, *Tatmim*, 74–75.

42. Qazwini, *Tatmim*, 67–69.

43. Qazwini, *Tatmim*, 69.

44. Qazwini, *Tatmim*, 77–78.

45. Qazwini, *Tatmim*, 82–83.

46. Qazwini, *Tatmim*, 84–86.

47. Qazwini, *Tatmim*, 88–89.

48. Qazwini, *Tatmim*, 109–111.

49. Qazwini, *Tatmim*, 105–106.

50. Qazwini, *Tatmim*, 117.

51. Khudri, *Hukama' o hikmat-e muta'aliya*, 312–313.

52. Qazwini, *Tatmim*, 48–49.

53. Qazwini, *Tatmim*, 66.

54. Mirza Hasan Zunuzi, *Riyaz al-janna: al-rawza al-rabi'a*, ed. 'Ali Rafi'i, 5 vols. (Qom: Kitabkhana-ye Ayatullah Mar'ashi, 1370 Sh/1991).

55. Zunuzi, *Riyaz al-janna*, I: 82–86, 515–521, II: 154–155, III: 435–440, IV: 260–272, II: 311–319, II: 422–423, III: 60–62, III: 71–74, III: 11–22, III: 124–131, III: 315–316, II: 199–208.

56. Zunuzi, *Riyaz al-janna*, IV: 422–438, IV: 23–24, IV: 567–574, I: 524–525, II: 72–73, III: 433–434.

57. Zunuzi, *Riyaz al-janna*, V: 160–167; Mirza Muhammad Kalantar, *Ruznama*, ed. 'Abbas Iqbal (Tehran: Kitabkhana-ye Sanai, 1362 Sh/1983), 112; Mohammad Taqi Mir, *Buzurgan-e nami-ye Fars* (Shiraz: Danishgah-e Shiraz, 1368 Sh/1999), II: 836–838.

58. Zunuzi, *Riyaz al-janna*, I: 522–523.

59. Ma'sum Ali-Shah Shirazi, *Tarayeq al-haqayeq*, ed. Muhammad Ja'far Mahjub, 3 vols. (Tehran: Kitabfurushi-ye barani, 1966).

60. Shirazi, *Tarayiq al-haqayiq*, I: 285.

61. Shirazi, *Tarayiq al-haqayiq*, I: 198.

62. Shirazi, *Tarayiq al-haqayiq*, I: 222, 183.

63. Abol-Hasan Ghaffari-ye Kashani, *Gulshan-e murad [Tarikh-e zandiya]*, ed. Ghulam-Riza Tabatabai Majd (Tehran: Intisharat-e zarrin, 1369 Sh/1990). By contrast, the main chronicle, *Tarikh-e Giti-gusha* of Nami-ye Isfahani, shows no interest in 'ulama.

64. Ghaffari-ye Kashani, *Gulshan-e murad*, 388–396.

65. Mohammad Ja'far 'Tarab' Naini, *Jami'-ye Ja'fari*, ed. Iraj Afshar (Tehran: Anjuman-e asar-e milli, 1353 Sh/1974).

66. Naini, *Jami'-ye Ja'fari*, 134.

67. Naini, *Jami'-ye Ja'fari*, 599–605.

68. 'Abd al-Rahim Zarabi Suhayl-e Kashani, *Tarikh-i Kashan*, ed. Iraj Afshar (Tehran: Chapkhana-ye rangin, 1335 Sh/1956), 199–278; see Storey, *Persian Literature*, I, pt. 1, 350.

69. Mirza Hasan Husayni Fasai, *Farsnama-ye Nasiri*, ed. M. Rastigar, 2 vols. (Tehran: Intisharat-e Amir Kabir, 1367 Sh/1988); partial translation by Heribert Busse as *History of Persia under Qajar Rule* (New York: Columbia University Press, 1972). See also Elke Niewöhner, *Die Daštakis: Die Familiengeschichte des Autor Hasan Fasa'i im Farsnama-yi Nasiri* (Berlin: Klaus Schwarz, 2009).

70. Shirazi, *Tarayiq al-haqayiq*, III: 530; Aqa Buzurg, *Tabaqat a'lam al-Shi'a*, IX: 510–520; Sarfaraz Khan Khatak, *Shaikh Muhammad Ali Hazin: His Life, Times & Works* (Lahore: Sh. Mohammad Ashraf, 1944), who based himself on the earlier translation by Belfour.

71. Husayn Zahidi, *Silsilat al-nasab-i safaviya* (Berlin: Chapkhana-ye Iranshahr, 1342/1924), 103–115.

72. On Masiha who had been Shaykh al-Islam of Fars, see Nasrabadi, *Tazkira-yi Nasrabadi*, pp. 252–253. See Hazin Lahiji, *Tazkirat al-mu'asirin* (Lucknow: Newal Kishore, 1876), 942–949; Mir, *Buzurgan-i nami-yi Fars*, II: 832–834.

73. Hazin, *Tazkirat al-ahval* (Lucknow, 1831), 12–47; Khatak, *Hazin*, 17–23.

74. Khatak, *Hazin*, 156–234, based on Hazin's *Risala dar fihrist-i asatidha u tasnifat-i khud*, MS, Royal Asiatic Society of Bengal, 1778.

75. Hazin, *Tazkirat al-ahval*, 7–8; Khatak, *Hazin*, 7.

76. F. C. Belfour (trans.), *The Life of Sheikh Mohammed Ali Hazin* (Bombay: The Educational Publishing Co., 1911), 1–4.

77. Belfour (trans.), *Hazin*, 21–22, 40.

78. Hazin, *Tarikh u safarnama*, ed. Ali Davani (Tehran: Markaz-e asnad-e inqilab-e islami, 1375 Sh/1996), 245–251. Cf. Michael Axworthy, *The Sword of Persia: Nader Shah from Tribal Warrior to Conquering Tyrant* (London: Tauris, 2006), 137–143; Mana Kia, 'Accounting for difference: A comparative look at the autobiographical travel narratives of Hazin Lahiji and 'Abd al-Karim Kashmiri', *Journal of Persianate Studies* 2 (2009), 210.

79. Belfour (trans.), *Hazin*, 68, 92–95; Khatak, *Hazin*, 68.

80. Belfour (trans.), *Hazin*, 95–99.

81. Henry Corbin, *La philosophie iranienne islamique aux XVIIe et XVIIIe siècles* (Paris: Buchet/Chastel, 1981), 334–340; Rasul Ja'fariyan, *Ahval u asar-i Baha al-Din Isfahani mashhur bih Fazel-e Hindi* (Qom: Intisharat-e Ansariyan, 1416/1996); Seyyed Mohammad Baqer Musawi Khwansari, *Rawdat al-jannat fi ahwal al-'ulama' wa-l-sadat* (Beirut: al-Dar al-islamiyya, 1991), VII: 106–112; Muhammad Ali Modarres-e Tabrizi, *Rayhanat al-adab* (Tabriz: Maktabat Khayyam, 1959), IV: 284; Aqa Buzurg Tihrani, *Tabaqat a'lam al-shi'a* (Beirut: Dar ihya' al-turath al-'arabi, 2009), IX: 575–577; Mirza Hasan Zunuzi, *Riyaz al-janna*, ed. Ali Rafi'i (Qom: Kitabkhana-ye Ayatullah Mar'ashi, 1378 Sh/1999), II: 199–208.

82. Sections of the metaphysics of the text were published in Seyyed Jalal al-Din Ashtiyani (ed.), *Muntakhabati az asar-i hukama-yi ilahi-yi Iran*, rpt. (Qom: Daftar-e tablighat-e islami, 1378 Sh/1999), II: 661–698; other parts of his glosses on the first chapter of the *Metaphysics* of the *Shifa'* were published in Hamid Naji's edition of Avicenna's work (Tehran: Anjuman-i aṣar va mafakhir-i farhangi, 1381 Sh/2002); and now a full critical edition is being prepared—volume 1 on the logic has appeared recently edited by 'Ali Awjabi (Tehran: Muassasa-ye pazhuhishi-ye hikmat va falsafa-ye Iran, 1394 Sh/2015).

83. Ja'fariyan, *Ahval u asar-i Baha al-Din Isfahani*, 14–19.

84. Muslih al-Din Mahdavi, *Zindagi-nama-ye 'Allama-ye Majlesi* (Tehran: Hamayish-e buzurg-dasht-e 'Allama-ye Majlesi, 1378 Sh/1999), I: 375; Seyyed Shihab al-Din Mar'ashi, *al-Ijaza al-kabira* (Qom: Kitabkhana-ye Ayatullah Mar'ashi, 1414/1994), 326; Sayyid Ahmad al-Husayni, *Talamidhat al-'Allama al-Majlesi* (Qom: Kitabkhana-ye Ayatullah Mar'ashi, 1410 Sh/1990), 62–63.

85. Mahdavi, *Isfahan dar al-'ilm-i sharq*, I: 209–210.

86. Ja'fariyan, *Siyasat u farhang-i ruzgar*, I: 702.

87. Ja'fariyan, *Ahval u asar-i Baha al-Din Isfahani*, 22–29.

88. Baha al-Din Isfahani, *Kashf al-litham 'an qawa'id al-ahkam*, 7 vols. (Qom: Mu'assasat al-nashr al-islami, 1416 Sh/1995).

89. Baha al-Din Isfahani, 'Khulasat al-mantiq', ed. Majid Hadizada in *Nusus wa-rasa'il min turath Isfahan al-'ilmi al-khalid*, ed. Majid Hadizada (Tehran: Hasti-numa, 1386 Sh/2007), 195–202; idem, *Hikmat-e khaqaniyya*, ed. Ali Awjabi (Tehran: Miras-e maktub, 1377 Sh/1998).

90. Isfahani, *'Awn ikhwan al-Safa'*, ed. Awjabi, I: 204, 220, 221, 254.

91. Isfahani, *'Awn ikhwan al-Safa'*, ed. Ashtiyani, 669–673.

92. Isfahani, *'Awn ikhwan al-Safa'*, ed. Ashtiyani, 674–685.

93. Isfahani, *'Awn ikhwan al-Safa'*, ed. Ashtiyani, 685–693.

94. Isfahani, *'Awn ikhwan al-Safa'*, ed. Ashtiyani, 696–698.

95. Isfahani, *Hikmat-e khaqaniyya*, 124.

96. Isfahani, *Hikmat-e khaqaniyya*, 125.

97. Isfahani, *Hikmat-e khaqaniyya*, 130–132.

98. Isfahani, *Hikmat-e khaqaniyya*, 126.

99. Isfahani, *Hikmat-e khaqaniyya*, 142–145.

100. Isfahani, *Hikmat-e khaqaniyya*, 149–150.

101. Isfahani, *Hikmat-e khaqaniyya*, 157–158.

102. Al-Amin, *A'yan al-shi'a*, X, 81; I'timad al-saltana, *al-Ma'asir wa-l-asar*, ed. Iraj Afshar (Tehran: Intisharat-e Asatir, 1363 Sh/1984), 163, 182; Aqa Buzurg, *Tabaqat a'lam al-shi'a*, IX: 790; Seyyed Ahmad Hoseini, *Talamidhat al-'Allama al-Majlesi* (Qom: Kitabkhana-ye Ayatullah Mar'ashi, 1410/1989), 89; Khudri, *Hukama o hikmat-e muta'aliya*, 293–299; Corbin, *La philosophie iranienne islamique aux XVIIe et XVIIIe siècles*, 300–334; Zunuzi, *Riyaz al-janna*, V: 195–196.

103. Aqa Buzurg, *al-Dhari'a ila tasanif al-shi'a* (Beirut: Dar al-adwa', 1983), VI: 724.

104. Aqa Buzurg, *al-Dhari'a*, VI: 27, XI: 84, XV: 184, 2025, XVII: 9, 330, XXVI: 229. Taleqani, *Manhaj al-rashad fi ma'rifat al-ma'ad*, ed. Riza Ustadi (Mashhad: Bunyad-e pazhuhishi-ye Islami, Astan-e quds-e raẓavi, 1419/1998). The text on the incipience of the cosmos, alongside *Asl al-usul*, is cited in a list of philosophical and mystical texts in the Shi'i tradition in Mohammad Ja'far 'Majdhub Ali Shah' Kabudarahangi, *Mir'at al-haqq*, ed. Hamid Naji Isfahani (Tehran: Intisharat-i Haqiqat, 1383 Sh/2004), 68.

105. Taleqani, *Asl al-usul*, 2.

106. Taleqani, *Asl al-usul*, 16.

107. Taleqani, *Manhaj al-rashad*, II, 182–184.

108. Taleqani, *Asl al-usul*, 41–42.

109. Taleqani, *Asl al-usul*, 35–39, 94.

110. Taleqani, *Asl al-usul*, 61–68.

111. Taleqani, *Asl al-usul*, 175–176.

112. Taleqani, *Asl al-usul*, 40–41.

113. Taleqani, *Asl al-usul*, 69–71.

114. Taleqan, *Asl al-usul*, 145–164.
115. Qazvini, *Tatmim Amal al-amil*, 107; Seyyed 'Abdullah Shushtari, *al-Ijaza al-kabira*, ed. M. al-Hairi (Qom: Kitabkhana-ye Ayatullah Mar'ashi, 1989), 23; Aqa Buzurg, *Tabaqat a'lam al-Shi'a*, IX: 425–426; Zunuzi, *Riyaz al-janna*, IV: 433–434; Corbin, *La philosophie irani-enne islamique*, 340–393; Khudri, *Hukama o hikmat-e muta'aliya*, 366–367; Kabudarahangi, *Mir'at al-haqq*, 68; Anzali, *Safavid Shi'ism*, 248–258. Both Corbin and Ashtiyani claim he was Zahabi but Anzali provides good reasons for his association with the Nurbakhshis—as Ma'sum Ali-Shah also claims in his *Tarayeq al-haqayeq*, III: 163.
116. Copies survive in the Mar'ashi Library in Qom: MS 1952 contains *Fuyudat Husayniyya* (copy dated 1171/1757) and *Risalat al-tawhid* as well as some commentaries on hadith of Ali. See Aqa Buzurg, *al-Dhari'a*, IV: 281, VI: 218, XIII: 686, XVI: 1964, XXI: 5256, XXVI: 1365, 1560.
117. 'Abd al-Rahim Damavandi, *Sharh-i asrar-i asma-yi husna ya Meftah-e asrar-i husayni*, in Ashtiyani (ed.), *Muntakhabati az asar*, III, 705–933, 718. See Shirazi, *Tarayeq al-haqayeq*, I: 430.
118. Damavandi, *Meftah-e asrar-i husayni*, 705–706.
119. Damavandi, *Meftah-e asrar-i husayni*, 709, 712.
120. Damavandi, *Meftah-e asrar-i husayni*, 739ff.
121. E.g. Damavandi, *Meftah-e asrar-i husayni*, 751.
122. E.g. Damavandi, *Meftah-e asrar-i husayni*, 811, 829.
123. E.g. Damavandi, *Meftah-e asrar-i husayni*, 872.
124. Damavandi, *Meftah-e asrar-i husayni*, 906.
125. Damavandi, *Meftah-e asrar-i husayni*, 799.
126. Damavandi, *Meftah-e asrar-i husayni*, 803–810.
127. Damavandi, *Meftah-e asrar-i husayni*, 862–876. Cf. Anzali, *Safavid Shi'ism*, 253–255; Shahzad Bashir, *Messianic Hopes and Mystical Visions: The Nurbakhshiya between Medieval and Modern Islam* (Columbia: University of South Carolina Press, 2003), 53–54, 98–102.
128. Shahzad Bashir, 'The *Risalat al-huda* of Muhammad Nurbakš', *Rivista degli Studi Orientali* LXXV, 1–4 (2001): 87–137, especially 96–97.
129. Damavandi, *Meftah-e asrar-i husayni*, 875–876.
130. Damavandi, *Meftah-e asrar-i husayni*, 881–883.
131. Damavandi, *Meftah-e asrar-i husayni*, 886–897.
132. Shirazi, *Tara'iq al-haqa'iq*, II: 216–219, III: 97; Aqa Buzurg, *Tabaqat a'lam al-shi'a*, IX: 598–602; Khawari, *Dhahabiyya*, pp. 297–337; Ihsan Allah Istakhri, *Usul-i tasawwuf* (Tehran: Kanun-e ma'rifat, n.d.), 414–461; Mir, *Buzurgan-i nami-yi Fars*, II: 842–846; Khudri, *Taammuli bar hukama va hikmat-i muta'aliya*, 270–274; Anzali, *Safavid Shi'ism*, 204–221. Zunuzi in his *Riyaz al-janna* does not even mention Nayrizi. Most accounts from Zahabi sources such as Khavari and Istakhri cited are hagiographical; a Zahabi source that is more measured is Mohammad Khvajavi's introduction to his edition of Nayrizi, *Risala-yi ruhiyya va manhaj al-tahrir* (Shiraz: Kitabkhana-ye Ahmadi, 1977), 15–33.
133. Abol-Qasem Amin al-sadr Khuyi, *Mizan al-savab dar sharh Fasl al-khitab*, ed. Muhammad Khwajavi, 3 vols. (Tehran: Intisharat-e mawla, 1383 Sh/2004), II: 1201–1202. On Darabi, who narrated hadith from the students of Majlesi and his work that included a treatise on the 'imaginal realm' ('*alam al-mithal*), see Aqa Buzurg, *Tabaqat a'lam al-shi'a*, IX: 330–331; idem, *al-Dhari'a*, XXI: 4776; Mir, *Buzurgan-i nami-yi Fars*, II: 735–737; Anzali, *Safavid Shi'ism*, 222–246; Hazin, *Tazkirat al-mu'asirin*, 111–112 mentions his class with Darabi in *Usul al-kafi* and in Avicennian texts.
134. Khuyi, *Mizan al-savab*, I: 94, III: 1214; see Mir, *Buzurgan-i nami-yi Fars*, II: 841.
135. Aqa Buzurg, *al-Dhari'a*, I: 482, 2414, XIV: 2286, XVII: 119, XVIII: 152, XIX: 623, 1349, XX: 3085, XXIV: 2065. Nayrizi, *Anwar al-walaya*, ed. Muhammad Khwajavi (Qom: Darya-ye nur, 1383 Sh/2004); idem, *Misbah al-walaya wa-bahr al-manaqib*, ed. Mohammad Khwajavi (Tehran: Intisharat-e mawla, 1424 Sh/2004); Abol-Qasem Amin al-sadr Khuyi, *Mizan al-savab dar sharh Fasl al-khitab*, ed. Mohammad Khwajavi, 3 vols. (Tehran: Intisharat-e mawla, 1383 Sh/2004); Nayrizi, *Risala-yi 'ishqiyya*, ed. Mohammad Riza Zakir 'Abbas 'Ali (Tehran: Anjuman-e asar va mafakhir-e farhangi, 1383 Sh/2004); idem, *Risala-yi ruhiyya va manhaj al-tahrir*, ed. Mohammad Khwajavi (Shiraz: Kitabkhana-ye Ahmadi, 1977).

136. Umm Salama Begum Nayrizi, *Jami' al-kulliyyat*, ed. Mahdi Iftikhar (Qom: Kitabsarayi-ye Ishraq, 1386 Sh/2007).
137. Khuyi, *Mizan al-savab*, I: 22, 28.
138. Khuyi, *Mizan al-savab*, I: 50–51, II: 1024.
139. Khuyi, *Mizan al-savab*, I: 136, 259–261, 275, 505, II: 555–556, 570–571.
140. Khuyi, *Mizan al-savab*, III: 1576–1577, 1592–1593.
141. Khuyi, *Mizan al-savab*, I: 119, 206, 322, 380.
142. Qazwini, *Tatmim Amal al-amil*, 162; Khwansari, *Rawdat al-jannat*, VII: 124; Aqa Buzurg, *Tabaqat a'lam al-shi'a*, IX: 283.
143. Muhammad Hashim Asaf 'Rustam al-hukama', *Rustam al-tawarikh*, ed. M. Mushiri, Tehran: Amir Kabir, 1348 Sh/1969, 405–408; Zunuzi, *Riyaz al-janna*, IV: 422–438; Aqa Buzurg, *Tabaqat a'lam al-shi'a*, IX: 695–696; Anzali, *Safavid Shi'ism*, 258–262; Modarres-e Tabrizi, *Rayhanat al-adab*, I: 187–188; Shirazi, *Tarayeq al-haqayeq*, III: 98, 214–215; Modarres Gilani, *Muntakhab*, 166; Khwansari, *Rawdat al-jannat*, VII: 116–118; 'Abbas Qummi, *Fawa'id al-radawiyya fi ahwal 'ulama' al-ja'fariyya* (Tehran: Kitabkhana-ye Markazi, 1359 Sh/1980), 618–619; Khudri, *Taammuli bar hukama u hikmat-i muta'aliya*, 300–303. A number of works have been published on Bidabadi and some of his mystical works as well: 'Ali Sadrai Khui, *Ashna-yi haqq: sharh-i ahwal u akfar-i Aqa Mohammad Bidabadi*, (Qom: Intisharat-e Nihavandi, 1379 Sh/2000); 'Ali Karbasizada, *Hakim-i muta'allih-i Bidabadi: ihyagar-i hikmat-i shi'i dar qarn-i dawazdahum-i hijri* (Tehran: Pazhuhishgah-e 'ulum-e insani o mutala'at-e far-hangi, 1381 Sh/2002); 'Abd al-Rahman Hatim, *Ra'id al-'irfan al-Aqa Mohammad Bidabadi* (Beirut: Dar al-Hadi, 2002), 7–24; Mir Seyyed Hasan Modarres Hashimi, *Sharh-i Risala-yi sayr u suluk mansub bi Aqa Mohammad Bidabadi* (Isfahan: Kanun-e pazhuhish, 1376 Sh/1997); 'Ali Sadrai Khui, *Tadhkirat al-salikin: nama-ha-yi 'irfani-i Aqa Mohammad-i Bidabadi* (Qom: Nur al-Sajjad, 1385 Sh/2006); Mohammad Bidabadi, *Husn-i dil*, eds. Ali Sadrai Khuyi and Mohammad Khwajavi (Qom: Intisharat-e Nihavandi, 1376 Sh/1997).
144. Kabudarahangi, *Mir'at al-haqq*, 69–70. He had studied with Mahdi Naraqi and Mulla Mihrab Gilani and was acquainted with 'Ali Nuri, although his main teacher in *hikmat* was Mirza Mohammad 'Ali Isfahani who was a student of Bidabadi. On Isfahani, see Zunuzi, *Riyaz al-janna*, IV: 502–503; Mu'allim-e Habibabadi, *Makarim al-asar*, I: 70–71; Shirazi, *Tarayiq al-haqayiq*, III: 254–258.
145. E.g. Hatim, *Ra'id al-'irfan*, pp. 17–18, citing Sayyid Kazim 'Assar.
146. Qazwini, *Tatmim*, 82; al-Amin, *A'yan al-shi'a*, IX: 197; Modarres-e Tabrizi, *Rayhanat al-adab*, I: 168; Khwansari, *Rawdat al-jannat*, II: 88; Khudri, *Taammuli*, 264–266. Jalal Humai suggests in his *Tarikh-i Isfahan* that Almasi might have been the first person to teach the works of Mulla Sadra, but this is not corroborated in any source of the period.
147. Mohammad 'Ali Hazin-e Lahiji, *Tarikh u safarnama-yi Hazin*, ed. 'Ali Davani (Tehran: Markaz-e Asnad-e Inqilab-e Islami, 1375 Sh/1996), 192; Qazwini, *Tatmim*, 135; Shirazi, *Tarayeq al-haqayeq*, III: 165; Modarres-e Tabrizi, *Rayhanat al-adab*, I 104–105; Amin, *A'yan al-shi'a*, VIII: 128; Ashtiyani, 'Muqaddima', 97; Aqa Buzurg, *Tabaqat a'lam al-shi'a*, IX: 359–360; Khudri, *Taammuli bar hukama va hikmat-i muta'aliya*, 250–256.
148. Qazwini, *Tatmim*, 67; Aqa Buzurg, *Tabaqat a'lam al-shi'a*, IX: 62–64; Modarres-e Tabrizi, *Rayhanat al-adab*, II: 105–107; al-Amin, *A'yan al-shi'a*, III: 402; Modarres Gilani, *Muntakhab*, 48; Muslih al-Din Mahdavi, *Lisan al-arz ya tarikh-i takht-i fulad* (Isfahan: Muassasa-ye farhangi-ye Isfahan, 1370 Sh/1991), 115–117; Khudri, *Ta'ammuli bar hukama va hikmat-i muta'aliya*, 274–281; Seyyed Mahdi Rejai, *Ahval u asar-i Mulla Esma'il-i Khwajui* (Isfahan: Shahrdari-e Isfahan, 1378 Sh/1999).
149. Shirazi, *Tasayeq-e haqayeq*, III: 219; Seyyed 'Abbas Qaim-maqami, 'Athar o afkar-e Sadr al-Din "Kashif" Dezfuli', *Kayhan-i Andisha* 38 (1370 Sh/1991): 77–93 (82–85); Hatim, *Ra'id al-'irfan*, 20–24. He wrote a number of works in mysticism such as *Qasim al-jabbarin*, *Hidayat al-salikin*, *Misbah al-tariqa*, and *Mir'at al-ghayb*. He seems to have been the leader of a branch of the Zahabiyya as well.
150. Modarres-e Tabrizi, *Rayhanat al-adab*, V: 385; Shirazi, *Tarayeq al-haqayeq*, III: 255; Modarres Gilani, *Muntakhab*, 192; Khudri, *Taammuli bar hukama va hikmat-i muta'aliya*, 207. Gilani was also a student of the philosopher Mulla Mahdi Naraqi. He used to teach *Fusus al-hikam*, the *Mathnavi*, and the *Asfar*. He did not write much: a short treatise on the unity of being

(*wahdat al-wujud*), and a gloss on *Gawhar-i murad*, the Safavid mystico-theological text of 'Abd al-Razzaq Lahiji.

151. A'zam Rijali, *Asar u afkar-i hukama u 'urafa-yi mashhur-i Isfahan az qarn-i davazdahum ta 'asr-i hadir* (Isfahan: Daneshgah-e azad-e islami, 1383 Sh/2004), I: 67–78; Gilani, *Risalat al-tuhfa*, in Ashtiyani (ed.), *Muntakhabati*, IV: 677–880, and also in Nuri, *Rasail-i falsafi*, 71–312; Khudri, *Taammuli bar hukama va hikmat-i muta'aliya*, 316–319.

152. Khudri, *Taammuli bar hukama va hikmat-i muta'aliya*, 309–311; Seyyed Ahmad Ardakani, *Mirat al-akvan: Tahrir-i sharh-i Hidaya-yi Mulla Sadra Shirazi*, ed. 'Abd Allah Nurani (Tehran: Miras-e maktub), 1375 Sh/1996; idem, *Mabda u ma'ad*, ed. 'Abd Allah Nurani (Tehran: Markaz-e nashr-e daneshgahi, 1362 Sh/1983).

153. Mirza Mohammad Mahdi Lakhnavi Kashmiri, *Nujum al-sama'* (Qom: Maktaba-ye basirati, 1397/1976), I: 67–68.

154. Khavari, *Zahabiyya*, 325.

155. Bidabadi, *Risala himmatiyya*, ed. Ali Karbasizada, in *Nusus wa-rasa'il*, ed. Hadizada, 205–211.

156. Karbasizada, *Hakim-i muta'allih*, 173–174.

157. Bidabadi, *al-Mabda' wa-l-ma'ad*, in Seyyed Jalal al-Din Ashtiyani (ed.), *Muntakhabati az asar-i hukama-yi ilahi-i Iran*, IV: 375–418.

158. Bidabadi, *al-Mabda'*, 377–80.

159. Bidabadi, *al-Mabda'*, 381–385.

160. Bidabadi, *al-Mabda'*, 405–406.

161. Ashtiyani, 'Muqaddima', 98–99. Mulla 'Abd Allah Zunuzi (d. 1257/1841), a leading student of Nuri, cites these glosses extensively in his *Lama'at-e ilahiyya va ma'arif-e rububiyya*, ed. Seyyed Jalal al-Din Ashtiyani (Tehran: Imperial Iranian Academy of Philosophy, 1976), 425 (citing Bidabadi's gloss on the meaning of the divine attribute of 'life' from his marginalia on *al-Asfar*). The text was completed on 6 Rabi' 1240/October 1824 and dedicated to Fath Ali Shah. See Muṣṭafa Dirayati, *Fihristwara-yi dastnivisht-ha-yi Iran (Dina)* (Tehran: Kitabkhana, muza o markaz-e asnad-e Majles-e Shura-ye Islami, 1389 Sh/2010), VIII: 1075–1076.

162. Cf. Husayn Modarresi Tabatabai, 'Falsafa u 'irfan az nazar-e Mirza-ye Qummi', in *Qummiyyat: majmu'a-yi maqalat darbara-yi Qumm* (New Jersey: Zagros Publishers, 1386 Sh/2007), 183–195. On Qummi, see Modarres-e Tabrizi, *Rayhanat al-adab*, V: 42–44; Zunuzi, *Riyaz al-janna*, I: 522–523.

163. Zunuzi, *Riyaz al-janna*, IV: 567–574; Modarres-e Tabrizi, *Rayhanat al-adab*, VI: 164; Kashmiri, *Nujum al-sama'*, 319; Aqa Bozorg, *Tabaqat a'lam al-shi'a*, XII: 543–544; Khudri, *Hukama u hikmat-i muta'aliya*, 319–333; Anzali, *Safavid Shi'ism*, 262–268. See Juan Cole, 'Ideology, ethics, and philosophical discourse in eighteenth century Iran', *Iranian Studies* 22 (1989): 7–34; Reza Pourjavady, 'Mulla Mahdi Naraqi', in Reza Pourjavady (ed.), *Qajar Philosophy* (Leiden: Brill, 2018).

164. Not much is known about Mohammad Zaman Kashani beyond his origins, his teaching in Isfahan, and his burial in Najaf. Another famous student of his was Kamal al-Din Masiha-ye Fasayi, who was one of the teachers in philosophy of Hazin Lahiji. He wrote a gloss on Khwansari's supergloss on Khafri's gloss on the *Sharh al-Tajrid* of Qushji. Other works of his included treatises in law and a short critique of Sunni traditionalist hermeneutics known as the 'balkafa' entitled *Hidayat al-mustarshidin wa-takhti'at al-mubalkafin*. See Khwansari, *Rawdat al-jannat*, VII: 124; Qummi, *al-Favaid al-razaviyya*, 619; al-Amin, *A'yan al-shi'a*, IX: 414; Khudri, *Hukama u hikmat-i mutaaliya*, 269–270; Ali Sadrai Khuyi, *Kitabshinasi-yi Tajrid al-i'tiqad* (Qom: Kitabkhana-ye Ayatollah Mar'ashi, 1424 Q/2003), 131. To my knowledge only one work of his has been published: *Mir'at al-zaman*, ed. Mahdi Dehbashi (Tehran: Anjuman-e asar u mafakhir-e farhangi, 1384 Sh/2005), in which he defends the position of the unreality of time, an issue of debate in his time starting with Jamal Khwansari in the generation before him and then by his contemporary Esma'il Khwajui, who criticized it in his *Ibṭal al-zaman al-mawhum*, in *Sab' rasa'il*, ed. Seyyed Ahmad Tuysirkani (Tehran: Miras-e maktub, 1381 Sh/2002), 239–283.

165. Kabudarahangi, *Mir'at al-haqq*, 70.

166. *Sharh al-ilahiyyat min kitab al-Shifa'*, ed. M. Muhaqqiq (Tehran: McGill Institute of Islamic Studies, 1365 Sh/1986)—there is a fuller edition by Hamid Naji Isfahani, 2 vols. (Qom: Kungirih-e bozorgdasht-e Mulla Mahdi Naraqi, 1380 Sh/2001); *Jami' al-afkar*

wa-naqid al-anzar, ed. Majid Hadizada, 2 vols. (Tehran: Intisharat-e hikmat, 1423/2002); *Qurrat al-'uyun*, ed. Seyyed Jalal al-Din Ashtiyani (Tehran: Imperial Iranian Academy of Philosophy, 1357 Sh/1978); *al-Lum'a al-'arshiyya* (Karaj: Intisharat-e 'ahd, 1381 Sh/2002); *al-Lum'a al-ilahiyya fi-l-hikma al-muta'aliya*, ed. Seyyed Jalal al-Din Ashtiyani (Tehran: Anjuman-e falsafa-ye Iran, 1357 Sh/1978); *Anis al-muvahhidin*, ed. Seyyed Qazi Tabatabai with introduction by Hasanzada Amoli (Tehran: Intisharat-e Zahra, 1363 Sh/1984); *Mushkilat al-'ulum*, ed. Hasan Naraqi (Tehran: Muassasa-ye mutala'at va tahqiqat-e farhangi, 1367 Sh/1988); *Jami' al-sa'adat*, 2 vols. (Baghdad: Dar al-Nu'man, 1968)—see Cole, 'Ideology, ethics, and philosophical discourse', 20–34 for a study of this latter work.

167. Hasan Naraqi, *Tarikh-e ijtima'i-ye Kashan* (Tehran: Muassasa-ye mutalaat va tahqiqat-e farhangi, 1345 Sh/1966), 159–160.

168. Naraqi, *Jami' al-afkar*, I: 439; idem, *al-Lum'a al-'arshiyya*, 19–22; idem, *al-Lum'a al-ilahiyya*, 57–60.

169. Naraqi, *al-Lum'a al-ilahiyya*, 54–58.

170. Naraqi, *Sharh al-ilahiyyat*, ed. Mohaghegh, 19, 94, 103; idem, *Qurrat al-'uyun*, 109, 121, 178, 190, 196, 197, 201.

171. Naraqi, *al-Lum'a al-ilahiyya*, 76–78.

172. Naraqi, *al-Lum'a al-ilahiyya*, 111–115.

173. Naraqi, *al-Lum'a al-'arshiyya*, 22–25; idem, *al-Lum'a al-ilahiyya*, 65–70; idem, *Qurrat al-'uyun*, 79; idem, *Sharh al-ilahiyyat*, ed. Naji, I: 426–429.

174. Naraqi, *Qurrat al-'uyun*, 218–221. Cf. idem, *Jami' al-afkar*, I: 138–141.

175. Naraqi, *Qurrat al-'uyun*, 205.

176. Naraqi, *Qurrat al-'uyun*, 115–120.

177. Naraqi, *al-Lum'a al-ilahiyya*, 96–101.

178. Naraqi, *Jami' al-afkar*, I: 178–243; idem, *al-Lum'a al-ilahiyya*, 92–95.

179. Anzali, *Safavid Shi'ism*, 193–194.

180. Richard Rorty, 'The historiography of philosophy: Four genres', in Richard Rorty et al. (eds), *Philosophy in History: Essays on the Historiography of Philosophy* (Cambridge: Cambridge University Press, 1984), 69.

7

Of Mullas, Manuscripts, and Migration: Aspects of Twelver Shi'i Community Life in the 18th Century

ANDREW NEWMAN

Western-language scholarship on Iran's 18th century has long portrayed the period as one of widespread disorder and chaos, sandwiched between the relative stability of the Safavid and Qajar periods. By contrast with the field of Safavid studies, the field of 18th-century Iran studies has not experienced any great expansion either in numbers of academics addressing the period or in the range of topics covered since the 1979 Iranian Revolution. The few studies of 18th-century Iran that have appeared in the years since the Revolution have not fundamentally challenged the above, prevailing narrative.

At the same time, few studies, whether produced before or after the Revolution, specifically explored religious life on the ground over the period.

The present chapter seeks to commence a questioning of received wisdoms regarding 18th-century Iranian history, and the period's religious life in particular. This will be done by offering information on both the geographical associations and movements of Twelver Shi'i 'ulama over the century and on manuscript copies of key Twelver texts composed by scholars from the 3rd/9th to the 10th/16th centuries that can be dated to this period.

The results of this examination point to a degree of continuity in certain aspects of religious life and activity between late Safavid Iran and the 18th century to date not suggested in the extant secondary literature, whether produced before or after 1979.

The Received Wisdom

Nader Shah (*reg.* 1736–1747) expelled the Afghans, retaking from them the Safavid capital of Esfahan that they had seized in 1722, in 1732 deposed Tahmasp II Safavi, the son of Shah Sultan Hosein (*reg.* 1694–1722, d. 1726), ruled briefly in the name of the latter's infant son 'Abbas III, recaptured lands taken by the Ottomans and the Russians during the years immediately following 1722, deposed 'Abbas III in 1736, proclaimed himself shah, and invaded India.

Just as his understanding of the Safavid period as following a rise/decline paradigm and as conventionally spanning the years 1501 to 1722 set the tone for, and still influences, Western-language scholarship on Safavid Iran, so Edward Browne's (d. 1926) understanding of Iran's 18th century set the tone for subsequent discussions of Iran's 18th century as well.

For Browne, a fellow of Pembroke College, Cambridge, the fall of the Safavid capital to the Afghans in 1722 was the inevitable result of a decline in the social, political, and spiritual/moral fabric that had gripped Iran since at least the death of 'Abbas I (*reg.* 1587–1629).[1]

Problematic as Browne viewed the state of post-'Abbas I Iran, however, following the 1722 Afghan capture of the Safavid capital of Esfahan, for Browne Iran's situation only worsened.

Browne described the son and successor of the 'last' Safavid Shah Sultan Hosein, Tahmasp II as a *roi fainéant* (an idle king) and, in his descriptions of Iran's Afghan years deployed such terms as 'devastations', 'chaos and misery', and 'disastrous'.[2]

Browne depicted the rule of Nader as increasingly brutal. Nader ordered a massacre of Delhi's inhabitants, to the number of some 110,000, in retaliation for the killing of 'some' of his soldiers in a riot. Nader blinded his son when he suspected the latter's involvement in a plot to subvert him. Nader, too, was 'daily more detested' by his 'Persian subjects' owing to his 'increasing cruelty, tyranny, avarice and extortion . . . but most of all, perhaps, his attempt to impose . . . the Sunni doctrine'. Revolts were suppressed 'after much bloodshed'. Himself about to kill 'all his Persian officers and soldiers' in his largely Turkic and Uzbeg army, some of these took it on themselves to move first and assassinated Nader. Thus, for Browne, although Nader 'first appeared as its [Iran's] deliverer from the Afghan yoke, [he] now bade fair to crush it beneath a yoke yet more intolerable.' In the aftermath of Nader's murder, 'universal violence and lawlessness . . . prevailed in Persia.'[3]

As to the Zand period that followed, Browne concurred with, and cited, the assessment of Sir John Malcolm (d. 1833), in the latter's *The History of Persia*, that Karim Khan Zand (d. 1779), 'as contrasted with those who preceded and followed him . . . was a beautiful and fertile valley in the midst of an arduous journey over barren and rugged wastes.'[4] Browne added that at the height of his powers Karim Khan 'practically ruled over the whole of Persia except Khorasan.'[5]

A paradigm for the understanding of the period was thus well set when Laurence Lockhart, based, as Browne, at Pembroke College, Cambridge, in 1983 published his *Nadir Shah*, a volume that might be thought of as the first serious, detailed 'academic' attempt to come to grips with Iran's 18th century. Lockhart, who dedicated the volume to Browne's memory, consulted a much broader range of sources than had Browne[6]—comprising a large number of European-language and Persian sources.

To be sure, Lockhart's final judgement on Nader is a balanced one. He notes that medical issues later in life caused Nader to waiver between melancholy and 'outbursts of rage'. But, more so than had Browne, he also carefully notes Nader's accomplishments across a range of activities, addressing his military, statesman-like, and rulership qualities, his appearance and character, health, contributions to the arts (including his endowments to the shrine at Mashhad), and his attitude towards religion (including his relationship with the Twelver faith and his attitude towards Christians).[7]

Lambton's 1977 reference to the "tribalization' of Iran over the 18th century, as a result of, and further contributing to, the absence of the strong centralized state, glossed Browne's model. Perry's 1979 volume on Karim Khan, a political history, only reprised the earlier narrative for both the relevant years of the century and Karim Khan himself.[8] Over the years following the 1979 revolution, the study of 18th-century Iran failed to witness either the exponential growth in scholarly attention experienced in Safavid studies, or any fundamental challenge to the above, overly political narrative and, especially, to the Browne-'ite' attention to, and focus on, the damage/destruction wrought by Nader.

Avery's 1991 article on Nader in *The Cambridge History of Islam* broke no new ground in terms of sources or analysis and mainly focussed on the political.[9] Perry's article on the Zands in the same volume is, also, largely a political narrative. A subsection therein on 'government and society' referred to Malcolm's above-cited characterization of Karim Khan and his reign.[10]

These years have witnessed some attention being paid to Iran's economy in the 18th century, following on the new attention to the Safavid economy and largely penned by the same few authors.

In his work on the 18th century Floor, who had written extensively on the Safavid economy, consulted an extensive range of sources, especially those of the Dutch East India Company, as well as materials consulted by Browne and, especially, Lockhart.[11]

Nevertheless, the data and the many anecdotes culled from these sources—the latter based mainly on their authors' personal experiences in a limited number of locales—support the familiar narrative about the period. Thus, in an early work, although he notes some positive aspects of Nader's reign for the economy, Floor writes that Nader's 'contribution to the economy of Iran was mainly a destructive one', with any initially positive moves being 'negated' by 'subsequent oppressive behaviour'.[12] By contrast, Karim Khan Zand 'pursued a more just and responsible fiscal policy'.[13]

In his discussion of the specie/monetary challenges facing Nader, Matthee, also well-known for his work on the Safavid economy, does offer useful, if decidedly monetarist/economic explanation for some of the more 'oppressive' policies and actions of Nader's tax collectors and the importance of the booty seized at the conquests of Qandahar in 1738 and Delhi in 1739. But, taken together, the fuller picture of the entire century that he presents, his discussion only reinforces the Browne-ite vision of the period.[14]

Religious Life in the 18th Century

Beyond mention of Nader's apparent predisposition to the disestablishment of Twelver Shi'ism, the scholarship on the century to date has not been overly concerned with aspects of religious life and/or with the fate of Twelver Shi'ism either inside Iran or elsewhere.

Browne's mention of Nader's Sunni sympathies has been cited. Lockhart mentioned Nader's effort to force 'his Shi'a subjects to abjure their faith' but also noted his attention to Christians, both Iranian and foreign.[15] Perry only briefly addressed religious life under Karim Khan Zand. Noting that many 'ulama fled to Iraq at Nader's death, that Shi'ism was re-established in Iran under Karim Khan and that the latter's 'own religion was perfunctory at best', Perry also suggested Karim Khan regarded many classes of the 'ulama as 'parasites'.[16]

Prior to 1979, only Algar delved more deeply into the period's religious dynamic, in the process querying aspects of the Browne-ite narrative. In an article in the same 1977 volume in which Lambton spoke of the 18th century's tribalization, Algar noted that the 'Afghan invasion, for all its destructiveness, was only an episode', that Esfahan continued as a major centre of learning, and that Shi'ism 'maintain[ed] its dominance in Iran [and] demonstrated a vitality which manifested itself both institutionally and intellectually.'[17] Algar also discussed the Usuli/Akhbari polemic over the period.[18]

Nearly a decade later, in the aftermath of the Revolution, Cole's 1985 contribution on the Akhbaris and Usulis in the 18th century stands as the first detailed study of religious life 'on the ground' over the period.

For the present chapter the salient points of Cole's discussion of the course of the polemic after the fall of Esfahan comprise his suggestion that the capital's fall to the Afghans 'displaced hundreds of scholarly families' and that expropriation of vaqf by both the Sunni Afghans and Nader severely affected the 'ulama. However, Cole argued, Esfahan did remain an important centre of Shi'i Usulism, while Akhbarism flourished in the Iraqi shrine cities of Najaf and Karbala, to which so many fled.[19]

Cole's article highlighted the fortunes of the family of Baqer Majlesi (d. 1699).[20] Cole noted that some of the family left for Iraq. Others, he notes, retained religious offices across the Iranian plateau, still others married into families of local merchants and/or artisans and some emigrated to and found posts in India. Cole also noted that the eventual victory of Usulism over Akhbarism in Iraq had its roots in the continued, especially financial, ties between key clerics based in Iraq with family in Iran over the Zand period.[21]

More recently, Tucker, in his examination of the processes by which Nader undertook to legitimize his rule, also addressed Nader's policies with respect to Twelver Shi'ism. If perhaps only implicitly Tucker questioned the extent of Nader's supposed hostility to the faith and his rush to disestablish it. For Tucker, Nader's religious 'agenda' was more positive: he sought Ottoman recognition of the faith as the 'fifth' legal school less for theological reasons than for practical reasons, as such recognition would 'establish a legal framework that would absolve most Iranians of the legal charge of *kofr* (infidelity)'. Tucker also highlighted Nader's embellishment of such Shi'i shrines as that at Mashhad and those in Iraq which he did not see as anti-Sunni or anti-Ottoman per se.[22]

Scattered Centres: Shi'ism in the Safavid Period

In our 2013 *Twelver Shi'ism*[23] *tabaqat*[24] literature and information on manuscript copying were used to gauge the nature of Twelver scholarly activity over the centuries from the fall of Buyid Baghdad to the Sunni Saljuks in 1055 through the Mongols' 1258 capture of Abbasid Baghdad, the Safavids' capture of Tabriz in 1501, at which the faith was declared the realm's official *madhhab*, to the capture of Esfahan in 1722, the conventional date given for the end of the Safavid period.

The data over the entire period suggests the continuous presence of pockets of believers scattered across the entire, expanding Islamic world, thus underlining the fact that, as in the present so in the past, not all Shi'a were/are Iranian. Information presented by al-Tehrani suggests that these sites were also perceived as active centres of intellectual activity across the period. The data does suggest a lessening of scholarly activity across the region's centres from at least the 13th century, precisely those years when the faith began to face its greatest existential challenges, but a marked upturn in scholarly activity especially but not exclusively in Iran, from the middle 17th century.

At the same time, independent information on the later copying of texts composed by well-known Twelver scholars whose careers spanned the 9th to the 16th centuries points to the relative loss of access to, and the availability of, manuscripts of these works from 1055. Only in the later years of the 17th century, again especially but not exclusively with reference to Iran, does the data suggest there was any marked 'recovery' of access and the availability of such texts.

In neither instance was it claimed that the information gleaned from these sources was 'absolute' but rather that the information was interesting and 'indicative'.[25]

The Iran-based upturn in the 'fortunes' of Twelver Shi'ism in the later 17th century, it was argued, contrasts with the very limited 'reach' that the faith had achieved across all sectors of Iranian society in the century after Esma'il I (*reg.* 1501–1524), the first Safavid shah, established it as his new realm's official religion following capture of Tabriz by Safavid forces in 1501. In these years the limited understanding, let alone the acceptance of, the faith's key doctrines and practices as articulated in 'the texts' was especially evident in the years following the death of Esma'il's son and successor Tahmasp in 1576. In these years Sunnism was clearly revealed to still be very popular in some key cities. Too various manifestations of the same sort of heterogeneous, distinctly 'unorthodox' Shi'i-Sufi messianism that brought the Safavids to power quickly (re)appeared in both rural and urban areas.

The same limited 'popular' impact of the top-down imposition of the faith is observable in those parts of the Deccan, in southern India, where elites likewise adopted it as their realms' official religion.

By the end of the 16th century in neither Safavid Iran or the Deccan was the longevity/survival of the faith's establishment anything of a foregone conclusion. Indeed, the outbreak of a second great civil war at Tahmasp's death—the first, prolonged civil war had broken out at his father's 1524 death—portended the collapse of the Safavid realm altogether. By contrast, other already well-established centres of the faith in the Lebanon, 'Arab' Iraq, the Hijaz, and the Gulf continued active over the century.[26]

The faith's genuine, widespread, and 'popular' establishment and, in the process, the '(re)discovery' of its pre-Safavid legacy in Iran from the later 17th century had its roots in responses to a combination of external political-military as well as internal political-military but also spiritual challenges dating to the later 16th and early 17th centuries.

The external challenges faced by 'Abbas I were rooted in the incursions of and territory lost to the Ottomans and Uzbegs in the aftermath of Tahmasp's death and the outbreak of the second civil war period among and between the realm's key domestic constituencies. Millenarian risings by rural and urban elements continued apace after 'Abbas I's accession, by definition questioning the spiritual legitimacy of his rule. Concomitant with these was both the rise of Sufi orders and the reappearance of messianic veneration of Abu Muslim (d. 755) among urban-based artisanal and craft elements. Discontent among such elements, only accentuating such associations, was exacerbated by a series of natural disasters and domestic economic challenges made worse by the effects of specie outflow.

The existential scale of the challenges faced by the realm in these years is attested by, and encouraged, the corresponding magnitude and range of responses thereto.

Of primary concern herein are the responses to the domestic spiritual challenges.

These entailed a marked effort by the court and its affiliated constituencies to enhance the realm's commitment to the faith via the marked expansion of the realm's distinctly Twelver religious infrastructure—such as schools and mosques—, its ties to and official patronage of supportive Twelver religious scholars—who undertook the propagation of sympathetic interpretations of Shi'i doctrine and practice, increasingly utilizing Persian in the process—and its identification with and sponsorship of 'popular' but distinctly Shi'i religious practices.

Among the clergy the rise of popular affection for Abu Muslim and, over the century, growing Sufi-style popular discourse generated its own reaction, especially in the form of a series of treatises denouncing both. At the same time, such other, already observable 'internal' 'debates' as the legitimacy of Friday congregational prayer in the continued absence of the Imam were rekindled in the 17th century. Over the century such polemics were notable for their increasing use both of Persian and their reference to the Imams' traditions and rulings from works by pre-Safavid Twelver scholars.

Unsurprisingly, these same years witnessed a concomitant growth in the Iran-based production of manuscript copies of precisely such works, including many whose widespread accessibility had been extremely limited over the intervening centuries.

The interest in the traditions was particularly marked from mid-century. Copies of the 'four books' of the Imams' traditions produced between the onset of the Twelfth Imam's disappearance in the 870s and the 1055 capture of Baghdad by the Sunni Saljuks rare in subsequent centuries became distinctly accessible in this period. The interest in the traditions was further attested by four new collections thereof produced in the same time frame—including two works of the same Baqer Majlesi. The better-known of these two was the multivolume *Beḥar al-Anvar*, portions of which were completed by 1670 but which was only finished only after his death by his students and contained some 'rediscovered' pre-Safavid works in whole or in part.[27]

This project in particular spoke to Majlesi's own agenda for privileging the Imams' traditions in the midst of, and a means of rising above, the realm's ongoing spiritual discord. His 1687 appointment as the capital's *Shaykh al-Islam* only attests to the centre's approval of his 'project'.

By this time, then, key elements of the realm's very Shi'i religious infrastructure were in place—with only more to come, viz. the Chahar Bagh complex after the turn of the century—, key early manuscripts were once again extant, and there is concrete evidence that both elites and non-elites were both understanding and supportive of key dimensions of the faith's doctrine and practices. As formulated by such of those scholars of the period best-known today, these extended the claims to authority of senior clerics over the interpretation of both and undertaking of many of the latter that had been reserved for the Imams during their presence within the community.

But, the marked activity in Iran in these years did not preclude that elsewhere in the Shi'i world.

Thus, centres in Lebanon, Iraq, the Hijaz, and the Persian Gulf, as well as India—to be sure the Deccan states were now 'rolled up' and Shi'ism therein disestablished by the Mughals, who nevertheless were patrons of Iranian Shi'i scholars—continued active, as suggested both by the numbers of scholars associated therewith as well as manuscript copying activity. The faith even spread further to the East in these years, to modern-day Thailand and Sumatra.

Moreover, travel between all these centres of the faith was common throughout the period, attesting to their perceived vitality by contemporary scholars.[28]

The Faith in the 18th Century

Appendix I below presents information both on the scholars' geographical affiliations across the Shi'i world to the end of the 12th Islamic century, corresponding to the years 1689 to 1785.

Over this century, based on *nisba* alone, Iran does seem to have continued as by far the chief centre of activity in this period. In fact, the situation of the faith in Iran was very much improved over the years of the previous century both in terms of indicative numbers and also the range of locales associated with large numbers of scholars.

But the Persian Gulf communities were also more active than in the previous Islamic century. Sites in Iraq more than held their own over these years, as did sites in Lebanon and, to an extent, India. Afghanistan makes an appearance in this period but activity in the Hijaz seems to have dropped. [29]

The information available on manuscript copying in Appendix II, while, again, not to be taken as absolute, does suggest some lessening of copying activity. The *ṭabaqat* literature for the period also contains markedly fewer references to post-1722 manuscript copying.[30]

While *nisba*, as has been suggested however, is less than a precise tool by which to adjudge centres of scholarly activity, evidence of actual activity and movement by named individuals noted by al-Tehrani offers more nuance.[31]

In Iran, libraries are reported for the later 1600s: three are mentioned in Esfahan for the years prior to 1722, and a large library of over 1,500 volumes is reported for a scholar—Ibrahim al-Qazvini—who died in 1736. Another library is reported for an Esfahani living in Najaf prior to 1722, and in the years after 1722, an Iran-associated scholar donated his library to students in Najaf.[32]

There were also those who moved to India prior 1722, among them members of the Majlesi family, as also noted by Cole, but others as well. One went on to Hyderabad, although by now that city had officially lost its Shiʻi character,[33] three went to Najaf, one to Karbala, and one to Mecca.[34]

While some Iran-based scholars are specifically said to have fled the Afghan attacks, many also stayed in Iran. Thus three went to India, but one went from Esfahan to Amol, another from Esfahan to nearby Khvansar, two others from Esfahan to Qazvin, one of whom then went on to Tabriz, and others went to Luristan, Shiraz, and to Karbala. Seven are reported killed or captured in the Afghan attacks.[35]

Well after 1722 as well, however, two are recorded as having gone to Karbala and two to Hyderabad, in 1739 and 1747, and four to elsewhere in India and three to Najaf later in the century. But one who travelled to India later returned to Iran. Another, al-Husayn al-Jazaʼiri, who died in 1745 and was a grandson of Niʻmatallah al-Jazairi (d. 1701), another student of the same Majlesi, went to India and then came back to Najaf, apparently via Esfahan.[36]

Plague is reported in Khorasan in 1725, just four years after the fall of Esfahan.[37]

Iran-based scholars undertook the hajj in the decade after 1722 and in 1761.[38]

As for Bahrain and eastern Arabia in these years, from Bahrain in the years before 1722 scholars travelled to Mashhad, to Esfahan, and to India and then Shiraz. After 1722, Bahrainis went to Huwaiza, two went to India, and one each went to Iran and Najaf.[39]

Outside Iran local dynamics seem also to have played a role in informing movement: in the wake of Omani Ibadi attacks in 1717–1718, on Bahrain, one scholar is reported as having fled to al-Qatif, in eastern Arabia. Following attacks from the same quarter in 1738, one went to al-Qatif and others travelled to Shiraz or elsewhere in Iran.[40]

A school is reported in Bahrain in 1720, and before 1722 a poor Qatifi scholar studied hard there and was able to relocate to Bahrain. Libraries are also recorded in the area after 1722 and later in the century as well. In the later years of the century, a Qatifi was living in Mecca.[41]

To the west, manuscript activity is reported in Mecca in the early 1700s. A Meccan-born scholar was in India in 1722. Another taught scholars who came there in the 1740s. An apparently Iranian scholar was forced out of Yemen in 1747 by Zaydi elements, while another who died in 1765 visited all the major Shiʻi centres across the region, from Iraq to Iran and India, before settling in Lebanon's Jabal ʻAmil. A Hijazi left for Yemen to spread the faith and died there in 1781.[42]

As to Sham, a Syrian was living in Istanbul in the 1680s and ʻAmilis moved to Najaf and the Kazemayn in the years before 1722.[43]

Prior to the Afghan attack, a Lebanese settled in Hyderabad, but travelled there via Mecca and Khorasan.[44]

As to Iraq and the shrine cities, a library is reported in Iraq in the 1680s and another in Baghdad in the 1750s. Plague is reported in Baghdad in 1690, in Najaf in 1689, 1718, and 1773, and in Karbala in 1772, as well as Iraq generally in 1830.[45]

Circa 1730, an Iraqi travelled to Murshidabad, in Bengal, and bought some books, including works by al-Tusi, which the former later gave to students in Najaf. An Iraqi travelled to Iran but was killed in Istanbul in 1754, and, later in the century, a resident of Iraq studied in Fars and Gilan and then returned to Karbala.[46]

As to India, in the later 1600s, one India-based scholar came to Iran and settled in Shiraz, but two others came to Karbala, one before 1756.[47]

Manuscript copying of pre-Safavid-period texts and, especially of pre-1258 works and even some early Safavid-period works, is widely reported across the region, especially up to 1722 in Iran. Thereafter, al-Tehrani's references to copying at named sites or by copyists with *nisbas* taper off markedly.

Many of those copies that can be placed were made in Iran, albeit prior to 1722, at such sites as Larijan, Mashhad, Tehran, Hamadan, Qain, Tabriz, Kashan, and Natanz, many in Esfahan, including a copy of *al-Faqih*, as well as Qom, Sabzewar, Yazd, Kirman, and Shiraz.[48]

After 1722, copying of such texts is reported in Mashhad, as well as by scholars associated with Rayy, Qain, Kashan, and in Esfahan. In the latter a scholar started a copy of a work but only competed it after he had fled the Afghan attacks. Just a few years after 1722 a scholar in suburban Esfahan was involved in considerable copying activity, including some of the 400 *usul*.[49]

Outside Iran, prior to 1722, copies of earlier texts were made in Karbala, many in Najaf, one in Mecca, several in Jabal 'Amil, one in Istanbul, and one in Bahrain. In India, copies have also been dated to before 1722.[50]

In the years after 1722 through to 1785, copies were made in Najaf, Karbala, Yaman, Bahrain, Mecca, and al-Qatif.[51]

Pre-1722 copies of texts undertaken by scholars without a *nisba* and without a place name total some 30,[52] and there are but 12 post-1722 such copies mentioned.[53]

Conclusion

Generally speaking, studies of 18th-century Iran completed both before and after the Iranian Revolution have tended to focus on and reinforce a largely political narrative first mooted in Western sources more a century ago. This narrative sees the period as one marked by widespread disorder, political fragmentation, and economic downturn in between two periods of relative order and political centralization.

For the few who did consider the period's religious life in any detail, Algar and, since the Iranian Revolution, Cole and Tucker all assumed that by the time of the Afghan invasions Twelver Shi'ism had, indeed, achieved some 'traction' on the ground and remained not merely a viable but the dominant discourse in Iran over the century.

The present chapter has presented information both on geographical associations of Twelver Shi'i scholars and on the copying of key texts across the century. The information is not meant to be taken as absolute but rather as indicative.

On balance, both the manuscript data and references to copying activity cited by al-Tehrani do suggest a post-1722 drop-off in copying across the Shi'i world, although to be sure, the copying activity of the latter years of the previous century does suggest a very great number of a wide range of pre-1501 texts was now accessible to the community.

Copying did continue, however, and it continued across the same Twelver Shi'i Iranian and, especially, non-Iranian centres noted for their activity in the previous century.

The biographical information presented by al-Tehrani, while also indicative if not absolute, does suggest that Iran did continue to be associated with the largest number of scholars across this century—as it had in the previous century. But, this information also confirms that the Iranian and non-Iranian sites that were active in the previous century continued as such across the next century as well.

Continued preoccupation with narratives that highlight the political and the economic and thereby privilege 'decline' and 'destruction' overlooks the 'cultural'. Insofar as the latter can comprise religious life, at least, the present chapter suggests some grounds for arguing for a degree of continuity between the 18th and the earlier and perhaps also later centuries.

Notes

1. On Browne's Safavid 'narrative' and its continued reproduction in Safavid Studies, despite the post-1979 expansion of the field, see our *Safavid Iran: Rebirth of a Persian Empire* (London, 2006), 2f.
2. E. G. Browne, *A Literary History of Persia*, 4 (Cambridge, 1959), 134, 121, 133. The field has long been disposed to 'organizing' the region in terms of dates. Browne himself (ibid., 126–127) equated the 1722 battle of Gulnabad both with the 635 battle of Qadisiyya, when the Muslim Arab armies defeated the Sassanians, and the 1258 Mongol capture of Baghdad. This volume of Browne's work was originally published in 1924 as *A History of Persian Literature, 1500–1924*.
3. Ibid., 4: 121, 133–134, 136–138. Compared with the Safavid shahs, only Esma'il II and Mohammad Khodabandeh ruled for shorter periods of time, approximately two and nine years respectively. Unlike Nader, however, no sitting Safavid shah died from unnatural, i.e. violent, causes.
4. Ibid., 4: 139. Malcolm completed his work some twenty years before his death, over a century before the 1924 publication of this volume of Browne's *A Literary History*. For further

references by Browne to Malcolm, see ibid., 4:137, 140–141. For Browne's reference to Malcolm in the former's discussion of the early Qajars, see 4:144. Browne's attention to Nader's barbarity in fact also echoes the attention thereto in the lengthy account of Malcolm (London, 1815, 2: 44–108, esp. 2: 98f). For further uses of Malcolm, see nn6, 10.

5. Ibid., 4: 139–140.

6. Browne utilized such primary works as those by the Jesuit Tadeusz Kruszinski (d. 1756), who left Iran in 1725, and Jonas Hanway (d. 1786), who borrowed much from an earlier French work, a Persian history of the Zands, as well as Malcolm and R. G. Watson's (d. 1892) history of Iran completed in 1866, covering events to 1856. On Hanway, see Lockhart, *Nadir Shah* (London, 1938), 308–310, and, also, n9.

7. Ibid., 266–281, 274, 276. Lockhart's bibliography runs to 14 pages. He discussed the most important of his sources in Appendix III (292–313). On Nader's early career, see also Lockhart's later *The Fall of the Safavi Dynasty and the Afghan Occupation of Persia* (Cambridge, 1958), 304f.

8. A. K. S. Lambton, 'The Tribal resurgence and the Decline of the bureaucracy in the eighteenth century', in T. Naff and R. Owen, eds., *Studies in Eighteenth Century Islamic History* (Carbondale, Ill., 1977), 108–129; J. Perry, *Karim Khan Zand: A History of Iran 1747–1779* (Chicago, 1979).

9. P. Avery, 'Nadir Shah and the Afsharid Legacy', *The Cambridge History of Iran, Vol. 7: From Nadir Shah to the Islamic Republic*, P. Avery et al., eds. (Cambridge, 1991), 3–63. To be sure, Avery did, for the first time, draw from Muhammad Kazim Marvi Yazdi's '*Alam-ara-ye Naderi*, completed between 1747 and 1796, but see, nevertheless, esp. 54, on Nader's 'increasing violence and cruelty'; 57, on his subjects' view of his effort to displace Shiʿism; 58, and the 'withdrawal of his Iranian subjects' trust' forcing him to reply more on non-Iranian levies; 59, on 'the sufferings of the Iranian people which were their principal legacy from "the last Asiatic conqueror"'. Perry's article on Nader in *EI2* echoes these discussions and their tones. M. Axworthy, in his *The Sword of Persia: Nader Shah, from Tribal Warrior to Conquering Tyrant* (London, 2006), does discuss Nader's 'military revolution' and argues that Nader might have developed a dynasty that could have resisted later Western imperial expansion. (See also his 'The Army of Nader Shah', *Iranian Studies*, 40/5 (2007), 635–646.) Nevertheless, in the books' final chapter, Axworthy highlights Nader's increasing debility due to illnesses and the cruel manner in which he sought additional finances as he moved east to put down rebellions. It also details his growing distrust of close associates and other family members. Axworthy notes some political and military successes but concludes that Nader's reign 'was a failure and a disaster for his country' both during his reign and also for 'the suffering that collapse [of his "regime"] brought about in later years (285–286)'.

On the date of '*Alam-ara-ye Naderi*, see E. S. Tucker's 'Explaining Nadir Shah: Kingship and royal legitimacy in Muhammad Kazim Marvi's 'Tarikh-i "Alam-ara-yi Nadiri"', *Iranian Studies*, 26/1–2, 95. In a private communication, M. Axworthy noted that Lockhart's reference (297) to a manuscript of vols 2 and 3 as dated 1171/1757 was 'likely to be reliable'.

10. J. Perry, 'The Zand Dynasty', *The Cambridge History of Iran, Vol. 7: From Nadir Shah to the Islamic Republic*, P. Avery et al., eds. (Cambridge, 1991), 64–103, esp. 95f. Perry notes, for example, Karim Khan's 'tolerance and magnanimity shown to all classes' (102) and cites Malcolm's sympathetic portrait. Perry's article on Karim Khan in *Encyclopedia Iranica* (*EIr*) in fact closes with Malcolm's above-cited evaluation, also cited by Browne. See n4 above. A. H. Zarrinkub's 'Karim Khan Zand', *EI2*, echoes the received wisdom.

11. See W. Floor, *A Fiscal History of Iran in the Safavid and Qajar Periods, 1500–1925* (New York, 1998); idem, *The Afghan Invasion of Safavid Persia, 1721–29* (Paris, 1998); idem, *The Persian Gulf: The Rise of the Gulf Arabs, The Politics of Trade on the Northern Persian Littoral, 1730–1792* (Washington, DC, 2007), a collection of his earlier articles; and idem, *The Rise and Fall of Nader Shah: Dutch East India Company Reports, 1730–1747* (Washington, DC, 2009).

12. Floor, *A Fiscal History*, 238.

13. Ibid., 249.

14. R. Matthee, *The Monetary History of Iran: from the Safavids to the Qajars* (London/New York, 2013), esp. 152, 155–158. Matthee notes the limited nature of the economic 'bump' from the treasure Nader seized at both cities and the extent to which barter and copper still dominated

local trade (168); the latter observation, however, in fact suggests some limits to the impact of fluctuations in specie over the period. The anecdotal evidence cited by Matthee is collected from Dutch commercial sources, other foreign, and some Persian accounts. The expertise and experience, and biases, of all of these are largely unexplored. The author of one source (cited on 170, 172, 174–175), the German Samuel Gottleib Gmelin (1745–1774), was in fact a physician, a naturalist, and a botanist. See the 1784 preface by Peter Simin Pallas to *Travels Through Northern Persia, 1770–1774*, W. Floor, transl. and ann. (Washington, DC, 2007), xvii–xxvii. Outside areas of his immediate expertise, Gmelin's information, second-hand at the very least, and his judgements can only be adjudged problematic. For examples of the former, see Floor's annotations on 288, nn31, 32, and Gmelin's discussions of a murder that occurred some years before his arrival on the scene (188–189) and of the personal drinking habits of a local ruler (11).

15. See Lockhart's short summary, 'Nadir's Attitude Toward Religion', in *Nadir Shah*, 278–281.
16. Perry, *Karim Khan*, 220–222. Perry's later (2011) *EIr* article reprised his earlier discussion. In both Perry noted that Karim Khan endorsed Twelver Shi'ism and approved of stipends for key religious figures but refused pensions to many classes of 'ulama, including students and sayyids, regarding them as 'parasites'. In both contributions Perry noted that *ta'ziyeh* commemorations of Imam Hosein death at Karbala further developed in this period. In the *EIr* article Perry concludes that 'Shi'ism as a component of Iranian identity, which came under threat during Nader Shah's attempts to make peace with the Ottoman Turks, reasserted itself fully under the Zands.' To be sure, in his *Karim Khan* (ibid.), Perry did challenge earlier suggestions that Karim Khan persecuted Sufis. See also Perry, 'The Zand Dynasty', 97. Zarrinkub's brief *EI2* article on Karim Khan does not address religion at all.
17. H. Algar, 'Shi'ism and Iran in the Eighteenth Century', in Naff and Owen, eds., 290, 301–302.
18. Algar, 'Shi'ism and Iran in the Eighteenth Century', 300. The Akhbari/Usuli discourse is otherwise unnoticed in the pre-1979 scholarship on Nader and Karim Khan cited above. See also nn19, 22.
19. J. Cole, 'Shi'i Clerics in Iraq and Iran, 1722–1780: The Akhbari-Usuli Conflict Reconsidered', *Iranian Studies* 18/i (1985), 5–6. The article, together with Cole's *Roots of North Indian Shi'ism in Iran and Iraq* (Berkeley, 1988), highlighted the importance of relations between Twelver centres in Iraq, Iran, and India.

    Published a year before Cole's article, S. A. Arjomand's *The Shadow of God and the Hidden Imam*, Chicago, 1984, contained but minimal reference to the faith during the Afshar and Zand periods, though the Akhbaris and Usulis were mentioned (215–217, 221–222). M. Momen offers a brief discussion of religion in 18th-century Iran in his *An Introduction to Shi'i Islam* (New Haven, 1985), 124–127. Momen also noted the flight of Shi'i scholars from Iran to Iraq after 1722 and argued for the consequent decline of Esfahan as a centre of scholarship. Reprising the Browne paradigm, Momen characterizes Nader's reign as having 'degenerated into savage executions and fruitless military campaigns' after Delhi and the Afshar period as a whole as 'troublesome and turbulent'. Momen did note that Nader failed in his efforts to displace the faith in Iran. H. Halm's brief discussion of the 18th century in his *Shi'ism* (Edinburgh, 2nd ed., 2004; originally published in 1991) (94–97) noted Nader's hostility to the faith and the 'ulama, the flight of 'many' to Iraq, and the eventual victory of the Usulis over the Akhbaris. In his 'Aspects of Akhbari Thought in the Seventeenth and Eighteenth Century', in N. Levtzion and J. Voll, eds., *Eighteenth-Century Renewal and Reform in Islam* (Syracuse, 1987), 133–160, E. Kohlberg focused more on the doctrinal differences between the two. In a broadly similar vein, see R. Gleave, *Scripturalist Islam: The History and Doctrines of the Akhbari Shii School* (Leiden, 2007) and his earlier *Inevitable Doubt: Two Theories of Shi'i Jurisprudence* (Leiden, 2000). For an historical discussion of the dispute, see Gleave, *Scripturalist Islam* and, more recently, our own *Twelver Shi'ism, Unity and Diversity in the Life of Islam, 632 to 1722* (Edinburgh, 2013), s.v.
20. Majlesi has long been adjudged a religious fanatic whose influence over the last two Safavid shahs played a determinant role in Safavid 'decline'. Most recently, R. Matthee referred to Majlesi's 'nefarious influence' at court in his *Persia in Crisis*, London, 2012, 253, and to Majlesi's 'unleashing a wave of persecution' against the Sufis that, Matthee admitted, however, 'is otherwise poorly documented [*sic*] (202)'. Nearly a decade before W. Floor had pointed

to the lack of evidence for al-Majlesi's role in any such persecution; see Floor, 'The *Khalifeh al-Kholafa* of the Safavid Sufi Order', *Zeitschrift der Deutschen Morgenländischen Gesellschaft*, 153/1 (2003), 79–80, and our *Safavid Iran*, 241n64.

On the longstanding hostility to Majlesi in Safavid Studies and, indeed, Iranian Studies as a whole, see our 'Baqer Majlesi and Islamicate Medicine: Safavid Medical Theory and Practice Re-examined', in A. Newman, ed., *Society and Culture in the Early Modern Middle East: Studies on Iran in the Safavid Period* (Leiden, 2003), 371–396, and idem, *Safavid Iran*, ix, 3.

21. Cole, passim, using a manuscript copy of 'Mir'at al-Ahwal-e Jahan-nama' by Aqa Ahmad Behbehani (d. 1819). The work has since been published in Tehran, 1370.

22. E. Tucker, *Nadir Shah's Quest for Legitimacy in Post-Safavid Iran* (Gainesville, 2006), 83. Tucker briefly refers to the Akhbari/Usuli polemic (40, 128n44). The volume was based on Tucker's 1992 PhD dissertation. Tucker also authored the careful entry on Nader in *EIr*. Tucker's reference to Nader and Mashhad recalls that of Lockhart, cited above.

23. Newman, *Twelver Shi'ism*.

24. The term refers to the Muslim biographical literature in Islam in which individuals or groups are organized by the century in which they lived. In this case the source used was the multivolume *tabaqat* work by the well-known Shi'i scholar Agha Bozorg al-Tehrani (d. 1970) for the fifth to the twelfth Islamic centuries, that is, from approximately 1009 to 1785, *Tabaqat A'lam al-Shi'a*, 6 vols, ed. A. N. Munzavi (Qom, n.d.).

25. On the caveats of using al-Tehrani, based as it is on *nisba*, see Newman, *Twelver Shi'ism*, 11. Note that both sources of the above data are based on the Islamic calendar; thus, the relevant volume of al-Tehrani (vol. 6) covers the 12th Islamic century, that is, from 1689 to 1785.

Note also that many, if not most, of those listed by al-Tehrani did not have a *nisba* of any sort. Where they did, however, the volumes' indices cross-referenced his subjects by their *nisba*. The temptation would be to consult only the entry for the *nisba* itself (e.g. Bahrani, Tabrizi, etc.) under which are listed all the individuals with that *nisba* by their proper name, and count them. The more advisable method is to examine each and every individual entry from page 1.

26. Newman, *Twelver Shiism*, 155–176.

27. These first four collections of the Imams' traditions comprise *al-Kafi*, compiled by Mohammad b. Ya'qub al-Kulayni (d. 941), *al-Faqih*, of Mohammad b. Ali, Ibn Babawayh (d. 991) and two compilations produced by Mohammad b. al-Hasan al-Tusi (d. 1067). In the Safavid period, another set of 'three Mohammads'—Mohammad b. al-Murteza, Fayz al-Kashani (d. 1680), Mohammad b. al-Hasan, al-Hurr al-'Amili (d. 1693), and Mohammad Baqer Majlesi—produced four collections. Al-Kashani completed his *al-Wafi*, still largely unexplored by scholars in the field, by 1658; al-Hurr completed his *Wasa'il al-Shi'a* by 1677. See our *Twelver Shiism*, 62, 131, 179. *Maladhdh al-Akhyar*, Majlesi's other multi-volume collection of the Imams' statements, arranged by *fiqh* chapters, has been published (Qom, 1408/1987), but has yet to be critically addressed by the field.

28. Newman, *Twelver Shiism*, 177–202.

29. This appendix corresponds to portions of Appendix I in our *Twelver Shiism*.

30. The active use of Persian across the period is mentioned frequently, for original works and translations. See al-Tehrani, 6: 277, 282, 371, 819, 81, 22, 562, 107, 706, 69, 146, 391, 805, 607, 615, 742. On the use of Persian, see our *Twelver Shi'ism*, 168–170, 180, 182–184, 186–187, 188, 193–196, 198n15, 200n47.

31. On *nisba*, see our *Twelver Shiism*, 11, 210–211.

32. Al-Tehrani, 6: 15f, 565, 86, 393, 272, 632, 13. See also 327 for a post-1722 library.

33. See Newman, *Twelver Shi'ism*, 53, 168, 178, 193, 194, 195, 201, 213.

34. Al-Tehrani, 6: 368–369, 363, 263, 640.

35. Al-Tehrani, 6: 542, 515, 57, 751, 360, 173, 242, 173, 471, 66, 390, 764, 59, 360, 594, 533, 686, 488. On one scholar, a student of Baqer Majlesi, who wrote a book in Esfahan during the Afghan siege, see 6: 141–142.

36. Al-Tehrani, 6: 173, 211, 314, 550, 618, 286, 552, 748, 582, 368, 670, 263, 96, 425, 632, 723, 272, 150, 427, 273, 226, 314, 630, 280, 697, 193.

Sufis are mentioned, some in Shiraz, in the decades after 1722. See 598, 559, 808.

37. Al-Tehrani, 6: 23.

38. Al-Tehrani, 6: 34, 476.

39. Al-Tehrani, 6: 3, 26, 38, 25, 26, 831, 185, 684. In the years before 1722 one local scholar was arrested by the Safavids and taken to Iran (6: 542).

40. Al-Tehrani, 6: 736, 09; 453, 816; 469; J. Cole, 'Rival Empires of Trade and Imami Shiism in Eastern Arabia, 1300–1800', *International Journal of Middle East Studies*, 19/2 (May, 1987), 194f.

41. Al-Tehrani, 6: 180, 418, 772, 770.

42. Al-Tehrani, 6: 302, 275, 410, 539, 833.

43. Al-Tehrani, 6: 11, 42, 373, 540.

44. Al-Tehrani, 6: 145–146.

45. Al-Tehrani, 6: 216, 684, 47, 181, 103, 44.

46. Al-Tehrani, 6: 775, 403, 715.

47. Al-Tehrani, 6: 521, 42, 216.

48. Al-Tehrani, 6: 57, 101, 116; 280, 482, 290, 350, 838, 190, 287, 482, 559, 113, 200, 313, 366 of *al-Faqih*, 612, 630, 632, 697, 715, 736, 814, 411, 493, 616, 654, 575, 423, 340, 467, 213, 262, 309, 340, 376, 442, 461, 470, 509, 580, 594–596, 738, 759, 808, 809, 123, 124, 181.

49. Al-Tehrani 6: 66, 144, 738, 390, 448–449, 376, 363, 544, 611. On the texts comprising the 400 *usul*, the very earliest collections, many contemporary, of the Imams' statements, on which see E. Kohlberg, 'al-Usul al-Arba'umia', *Jerusalem Studies in Arabic and Islam*, 10 (1987), 128–66.

50. Al-Tehrani, 6: 11, 96, 121–122, 202, 307, 592, 652, 660, 670, 681, 789, 821, 301, 229, 253, 211, 253, 504, 581, 181, 297–298.

51. Al-Tehrani, 6: 795, 181, 689, 769, 771, 821, 504, 624–625, 242–243, 821.

52. Al-Tehrani, 6: 56, 82, 83, 94, 138, 146, 159, 159–160, 201, 258, 290, 294, 367, 389, 441, 473, 572, 588–589, 626, 705–706, 711, 737, 751–752, 760, 779, 784, 803, 819, 823–834, 835–836.

53. Al-Tehrani, 6: 82, 83, 89, 201, 626, 642–643, 649, 649, 667, 685, 705, 764.

54. Portions of both these appendices were first published as such in our *Twelver Shiism*, published by Edinburgh University Press, 2013.

Appendix I: The Manuscript Evidence, Manuscript Copying Across the Centuries[54]

	12th c.	13th c.	14th c.	15th c.	1494–1543	1544–1591	1592–1640	1641–1688	1689–1722	1723–1785
Al-Kāfī of al-Kulaynī (338/245 datable)										
	0	1	2	1	0	28	24	158	17	10
Al-Faqīh of al-Ṣadūq (d. 991) (98/83)										
	1	0	0	0	0	4	9	52	9	2
Tahdhīb of al-Ṭūsī (d. 1067) (462/366)										
	0	0	2	2	6	28	42	221	34	17
Al-Istibṣār of al-Ṭūsī (203/174)										
	0	4	0	0	1	5	34	111	8	4

	12th c.	13th c.	14th c.	15th c.	1494–1543	1544–1591	1592–1640	1641–1688	1689–1722	1722–1785
Works by al-Ṭūsī (d. 460/1067)										
al-Nihāyā (22/10)										
	6	2	0	0	1	1	0	3	0	1
Al-Mabsūt (38/30)										
	5	5	0	0	0	1	5	6	0	3
Al-Khilāf (23/16)										
	3	1	1	0	0	1	2	2	0	1

Work	14th c.	15th c.	1494–1543	1544–1591	1592–1640	1641–1688	1689–1722	1722–1785		
Kitāb al-Ghayba (1/0)	0	0	0	0	0	0	0	0	0	0
Al-Tibyān (*tafsīr*) (27/21)	14	4	1	1	0	0	1	0	0	0
Works by al-ʿAllāma al-Ḥillī (d. 1325)										
Qawāʿid al-Aḥkām (241/1650)	0	13	13	18	17	24	18	49	9	8
Taḥrīr al-Aḥkām (79/60)	0	15	15	8	7	26	5	8	0	0
Mukhtalaf al-Shīʿa (82/66)	0	7	2	1	1	13	6	20	4	4
Tadhkirat al-Fuqahā (51/43)	0	2	2	1	1	9	3	5	4	1
Nihāyat al-Wuṣūl (35/27)	0	5	5	1	0	0	1	3	1	2
Khulāṣat al-Aqwāl (54/20)	0	0	0	1	1	9	5	1	0	1
Kashf al-Murād (27/18)	1	2	2	4	0	3	0	4	1	0

Appendix II: Scholars by Region, Fifth-Twelfth Islamic Centuries/Eleventh-Eighteenth Centuries AD

5th Islamic Century 1009–1105	6th Century 1106–1202	7th Century 1203–1299	8th Century 1300–1396	9th Century 1397–1493	10th Century 1494–1591	11th Century 1592–1688	12th Century 1689–1785
Iran 107 including	Iran 241 including	Iraq 65 including	Iran 71 including	Iran 59 including	Iran 190 including	Iran 530 including	Iran 975 including
Tus/Nishapur 27	Rayy 43	Hilla 22	Qum 8	Astarabad 11	Mazanderan 38	Isfahan 81	Isfahan 177
Rayy 13	Qum 32	Baghdad 19	Shiraz 7	Gurgan 5	Khurasan 30	Mashhad 67	Shushtar 91
Qazvin 11	Tus/Nishapur 29	Wasit 7	Tabaristan 7	Yazd 5	Shiraz 23	Astarabad 50	Mashhad 81
Gurgan 9	Qazvin 21	Kufa 4	Kashan 6	Kashan 4	Kashan 17	Shiraz 50	Qazvin 48
Isfahan 9	Kashan 19	Najaf 2	Astarabadi 5	Isfahan 4	Isfahan 15	Kashan 19	Shiraz 47
Qum 9	Hamadan 17		Amol 4	Amol 4	Qazvin 9	Qazvin 15	Kashan 44
	Varamin 10		Rayy 3	Sabzewar 3	Tabas 9	Tabriz 11	Tabriz 37
	Isfahan 8		Yazd 3	Gilan 2	Tabriz 9	Qum 9	Qum 29
			Khurasan 3	Khurasan 2	Qum 8		Gilan 25
			Isfahan 2	Qum 2	Yazd 7		Astarbad 24
			Tus/Nishapur 2	Shiraz 2			Sabzewar 21

Iraq 59
Baghdad 28
Basra 14
Kufa 10

Syria 15
Aleppo 11
Damascus 3

Lebanon 11

Iraq 61
Baghdad 15
Hilla 13
Najaf 13
Kufa 11

Syria 25
Aleppo 20

Gulf 4

Iran 50
Qum 7
Yazd 4
Isfahan 4
Hamadan 4
Daylam 2
Rayy 2
Nishapur 2

Gulf 13
Bahrain 11
Ahsa 2

Syria 12

Iraq 66
Hilla 33
Karbala 5
Kufa 5
Wasit 5
Najaf 3
Baghdad 2

Syria 20
Aleppo 16
Damascus 4

Lebanon 18

Jabal Amil 52

Iraq 43
Hilla 15
Najaf 8
Baghdad 3

Gulf 21

Jabal Amil 80
'Amili' 65
Juba 7
Mays 6

Iraq 54
Najaf 17
Jazair 15
Hilla 9

Gulf 27

Iraq 166
Najaf 79
Jazair 38
Hilla 12

Lebanon 121
Jabal Amil 118

Gulf 95

Gulf 203
Bahrain 102
Maqab 16
Qatif 15
Awal 14
Khatt 12
Diraz 9
Ahsa 8
Mahuz 5

Iraq 191
Najaf 80
Jazair 47
Kazemain 25
Karbala 14
Hilla 9

Lebanon 119

5th Islamic Century 1009–1105	6th Century 1106–1202	7th Century 1203–1299	8th Century 1300–1396	9th Century 1397–1493	10th Century 1494–1591	11th Century 1592–1688	12th Century 1689–1785
Tripoli 10	Bahrain 4	Aleppo 11	Jabal Amil 13	Bahrain 13	Bahrain 18	Bahrain 53	Jabal Amil 96
						Ahsa 10	
Jabal Amil 1		Hims 1	Karak 2	Ahsa 4	Ahsa 5	Qatif 2	India 42
				Qatif 4	Qatif 3		Kashmir 11
							Hyderabad 2
Egypt 7	Egypt 3	Lebanon 4	Gulf 6	Syria 4	Herat 7	India 34	Afghanistan 10
		Jabal Amil 4	Bahrain 6	Herat 4			Herat 8
			Hijaz 4	Hijaz 4	India 6	Hijaz 27	Hijaz 9
			Yemen 2	India 1	Yemen 5		Yemen 4
							Syria 3

8

The Persian Economy in the Eighteenth Century: A Dismal Record

WILLEM FLOOR

Safavid period

Introduction

We don't have quantitative data on the economy of Safavid Persia. The only quantitative data that we have are from the English (EIC) and Dutch East Indies Companies (VOC), but these only concern their own trade. As we have incomplete information on their market share for many individual commodities, which share, moreover, fluctuated over time, we cannot extrapolate these data for the sector as a whole. Nevertheless, the EIC and VOC records provide most of our understanding of the functioning of international trade, the monetary system, and other aspects of the Persian economy. Other, often impressionistic, data on the economy are found in travelogues and local histories. Unfortunately, most of the available information only concerns certain parts of the country, so that we are mostly in the dark as to the situation in regions not covered by these sources. All this allows us to give only a rough picture of the contours of the economy of Safavid Persia and of its most general trends and developments.

The information situation is worse with regard to eighteenth-century Persia. The EIC and VOC still operated in Persia and produced quantitative data, but these are incomplete in case of the EIC. Both Companies probably also had a lower and even a declining market share. For the second half of the eighteenth century there are also quantitative data for the trade with Russia, but here also we have no idea about its market share. Furthermore, there is a significant drop in the number of travelogues written during this period, and their number can be counted on two hands. In short, given the scarcity of data, and their weighing factors, the economic situation in eighteenth-century Persia can only be sketched with a broad brush. I will do so by describing how the situation was in Persia around 1700, first by assessing its human resources, the structure of the economy, and international trade, followed by a discussion of the individual economic sectors. Thereafter, I indicate to what extent the economic conditions in Persia changed after 1722, when it was conquered and occupied by the Afghans, the Russians, and the Ottomans, and thereafter, when the country was in almost perpetual state of war.

Population

Not much is known about the size of Safavid Persia's ethnically, linguistically, and religiously diverse population, which probably did not total more than 7 million by 1700. We have no data on its annual growth and related data (e.g., birth, mortality), but it must have been below one percent per year, in harmony with what is known for other non-industrial countries prior to 1900. About 15 percent of the population lived in urban areas, the home of the country's elite (military, bureaucratic, commercial, and religious). These were mostly small towns, because only Isfahan and Tabriz were major cities, i.e., had over 100,000 inhabitants. The elite employed a large part of the urban population, both as domestic servants and in their various professional fields. The remainder of the urban population were self-employed in trades, crafts, and market gardening. It is estimated that some 60 percent of the population lived in villages, making a living mainly as subsistence farmers, while some 25 percent of the population were engaged in pastoralism. There was some internal migration, either a movement to areas with high agricultural peak demand or to work in urban areas. However, it is not known how important such movements were. Most of the population (95 percent) was illiterate. We have no definite information about the standard of living,[1] which most likely fluctuated with the ups and downs of agricultural output, negatively influenced by droughts, locusts, and epidemics. Inflation, which at times was high, bedeviled the economy and mostly hit the urban poor, as evidenced by occasional bread riots. The basic features characterizing this state of affairs did not change fundamentally change in the century after 1700.[2]

Economic Structure

We have no information on capital formation and consumption or on economic growth in Persia's economy. In normal times the bulk of investments took place in housing, followed by the production of the various tools and implements necessary for economic activities. The construction of public works (palaces, markets, mosques) and infrastructure (irrigation canals, caravansaries, bridges) were the other main investments that took place. Given the nature of the economy, it is not too far-fetched to assume that the abovementioned economic indicators fluctuated in harmony with agricultural output. The structure of the economy most likely reflected the occupational distribution of its population. This meant the agricultural sector contributed some 80–90 percent to GNP, while the artisanal and services sector added the remaining 10–20 percent. However, Safavid Persia was not a single economic unit. Due to the lack of proper roads, which were rather camel and mule tracks, each major region had to be self-sufficient in all or most of its basic needs. This meant that the production pattern in each province of necessity mirrored that in the others, and there was little specialization.[3]

To a large extent the villages were autarkic where most of their needs were concerned. They were mainly inhabited by subsistence farmers, i.e., they produced their own food with some surplus, made their own clothes and footwear, and were engaged in some off-farm activities. The same held for the pastoral groups. Nevertheless, these villages and pastoral communities needed to market their surplus to the nearest market towns to be able to obtain those goods that they could not make themselves. Therefore, there was trade with outsiders, but this was limited, and exchange was mainly based on barter, except in areas producing cash crops like raw silk or goat down (*kork*). These market towns, in their turn, had to exchange the commodities they had collected from their rural hinterland and those that were produced within their own borders with other parts of the country, or to export them. Moreover, some of these towns supplied goods that were unique (Kerman *kork*) or were of a very high quality (brocade, velvet). Or climate conditions made it possible to cultivate products that could not be grown elsewhere, like citrus fruit (*morakkabat*), or in larger quantities than elsewhere (e.g., silk, rice). This had as a consequence that there was some trade and internal exchange between the different parts of the country, despite the fact that the country both politically and economically was still in a fragmented state. The agricultural sector had little to offer for export. Persia's only major cash crop was raw silk, which was mainly produced in the provinces of Gilan and Shirvan. Other agricultural products were also exported, including goat down, wheat, and dried fruit, but their monetary value was insignificant.[4] Some horses were exported to India, but most of this trade originated in Central Asia rather than Iran.

The national currency was the silver *'abbasi* (for trade, taxes) and the copper *qazbegi* (for retail, wages), whose value fluctuated with prices in the markets for these two metals. However, the effect of the resulting inflation and monetary depreciation does not seem to have impacted the standard of living of the lower classes, because most people lived in rural areas that were at best marginal to the monetized economy.[5] Also, the incomes of those urban trades and crafts that were agriculture related fluctuated in consonance with farm incomes (and certainly with the level of agricultural production) rather than with urban incomes.[6]

Role of the State

The role of the state was limited and restricted to three areas: (i) revenue collection, (ii) defense, and (iii) limited public services. The state's involvement in the economy was very limited. It maintained some royal manufactories to produce high-quality textiles and some arms, but otherwise it did not have a pronounced presence, either in capital formation or in consumption expenditure. Most of its expenditures were pensions, stipends, wages, and other forms of payments to members of the royal family, the bureaucracy, and the army.[7]

To pay for all these expenditures, the state collected taxes from land, animals, manufacturing, trade, customs, and rents from state monopolies (*qoruq*), in addition to fines, confiscation, and gifts. Taxes were mostly paid in kind, probably around 80 percent of the total. Although no reliable data are available, the total amount collected was given as some 700,000 *tumans* around 1700.[8]

The government was not directly involved in tax collection, but sold the right to do so to the highest bidder. These bidders included governors, customs farmers, and the Mint master. All of them had to make a profit on their investment and, therefore, collected more than of the official assessment through extortion, illegal taxes, and the sale of lower-ranking offices within their jurisdictions. An important characteristic of the functioning of the fiscal system was the state's, and by extension the landlord's, ability to raise the level of the extraction of the surplus above what was customary. The working of the fiscal system displayed the same characteristics as that of the political patrimonial system, that is, it was both centralized and decentralized. It was centralized in the sense that the political center set the number of taxes, the rates, and the rules for collection, but decentralized because it was conducted by tax farmers or state-appointed tax collectors. Tax collection therefore was not implemented using universal and objective principles, but rather on particular and subjective ones. This personalized and arbitrary system led to a situation where confiscation became a fixture of the tax system. The bulk of the tax burden fell on the shoulders of the rural and urban population. Most important, the tax system was not aimed to stimulate economic and social development. In fact, it was a kind of formalized spoils system, permitting the elite to remain or become rich at the expense of the vast population that lived and sweated in poverty (features held in common with many if not most preindustrial societies). Because of the arbitrary nature of tax collection, the system discouraged accumulation of capital, and thus improvement of the economic system. The operation of the fiscal system, therefore, was but a logical consequence of the operation of the political economy in general just like in any pre-industrial state.[9]

Only once did the state try to get directly involved in the economy and exploit one of its natural resources, viz., the establishment of the raw silk export monopoly by Shah Abbas I from 1619–1629. This was mirrored by an attempt to control part of its international trade by concluding a commodity package-based annual contract with the VOC.[10] Apart from an attempt by Reza Qoli Mirza in 1739–1740 to control the silk trade,[11] these short-lived attempts were not repeated thereafter, as they did not deliver the expected results. Moreover, they were difficult to manage effectively.

International Trade

Although Persia was mostly self-sufficient, it needed to import certain products which it could not produce (pepper, spices), or could not produce enough of (metals, sugar), or that were wanted by the wealthy (luxury fabrics). We have no information about the size of international trade in relation to the economy, but it was most likely about 5–7 percent of GNP. The apparent lack of importance of international trade is indicated by the nature of its imports, i.e., mostly goods consumed by the moneyed class. However, on the other hand, international trade was the only source of specie/bullion for Persia and as such had a more significant role in the economy than its size would indicate. The vast majority of these imports were consumer goods; very little was for productive use. Persia had to pay for those imports and, therefore, it exported unprocessed agricultural goods (raw silk, cotton, wool, dried fruit, wheat, and animals), which likewise were all consumption goods. There was very little export of manufactured products; the export of carpets and textiles, which became significant trade items in the following century, had not yet begun.[12] Because Persia lacked important export products and had neither gold nor silver, it was a dirt-poor country. The agricultural sector contributed most to its GDP, but it had only one really important cash crop, viz., raw silk. As the proceeds of its exports were insufficient to pay for its imports, Persia had a structural balance of payment deficit. Therefore, it was forced to pay for part of its imports in specie or bullion. Since it had neither gold nor silver mines, how did Persia obtain these funds? Fortunately for Persia, the trade deficit was mainly with India, for Persia had a positive trade balance with the Ottoman Empire and Russia as well as due to revenues from invisible trade. If the trade deficit with India was higher than the positive trade with the Ottomans and Russia, Persia usually temporarily imported less and/or depreciated its currency. Persia's major trading partners were above all India (main imports were textiles, spices, sugar, rice, indigo, and metals), followed in importance by the Ottoman Empire and Russia.[13]

Monetary Issues

In the absence of a banking system, there were few alternatives to holding large amounts of money both for trade and for liquid savings (partly as a precaution against bad times); that is, the velocity of money was low, and there was a widespread tendency to hoard. Tampering with the weight or quality of the currency increased the value of the state's considerable holdings of older high-quality coins and made available more currency, which therefore allowed collection of more revenue and prevented the flight of most current money. The price, however, was inflation and the upheaval of exchange relations. Inflation, which at times was high, combined with a structural balance of payments deficit with India (partly offset by a surplus elsewhere), bedeviled the economy, and mostly hit the urban poor, as most people in the rural areas were not part of a monetized economy.[14] The main obstacle to a sovereign monetary policy was the perennial threat that through the working of Gresham's Law all remaining good coin would be driven out by money thus manipulated. Throughout the later seventeenth century, an undervaluation of silver at the mint accounted for much of the export of silver, without, however, automatically leading to an influx of gold. Hardly less important for the nature and volume of monetary circulation were the periodic devaluations of the currency. These had the double objective of raising revenue for the treasury and of stemming the outflow of specie. The consequences of these measures, however, tended to be negative: they reduced an already low level of confidence in ready money and reinforced tendencies to hoard or to export the remaining good coins.[15]

Agriculture

Agriculture and its ancillary activities remained the occupation of 80–90 percent of the population. Its main crops was wheat, barley, rice, raw silk, and tobacco, in addition to minor crops such as millet, lentils, peas, beans, and all kinds of fruit. Most of the output of these crops were for domestic consumption, while some of it was exported (silk, tobacco, dried fruit, cotton) abroad or to neighboring regions. In particular, the export of raw silk was important because it yielded a relatively large amount of ready cash.

There were four kinds of landed property: (i) *khasseh* or crown land used to pay for the upkeep of the royal court and bureaucracy, (ii) *mamalek* or state lands mainly used for the maintenance of the military readiness of tribal levies and provincial bureaucracies. These two types of property were exempt of taxation. The two other types of property were (iii) *vaqf* or endowments, mainly used for the financing of ecclesiastical expenditures or for the use of private endowment entitlement holders, and (iv) *molki* or private property, which represented the smallest part of landholdings, mostly held by absentee landlords. *Owqaf*s were partly exempt from taxation, but private property was not. Peasants received part of the production depending on their input. As a general rule, if they contributed labor and animals they would receive 40 percent, while the providers of the other three inputs (land, seed, and water) would each also receive 20 percent. The peasants' share fluctuated depending on the imposition of corvées, additional fees, debt, and the like. Through off-farming activities (charcoal, weaving, hunting, etc.) they tried to improve their income and standard of living.[16]

Like in other preindustrial societies, cultivation methods and tools were primitive and less productive than they could have been, given the right incentives. Simple ploughs, harrows, spades, winnowing forks, and the like were used, often locally made by migrant artisans. Where irrigation occurred, methods were wasteful, although water was the main limiting factor of production. Apart from human labor the other main energy input was provided by animals, both on-farm (plowing, harrowing) and off-farm (transport of the surplus). A similar unproductive attitude existed toward Persia's forestry and fisheries resources, because there was no major effort to exploit and develop them.[17]

Industry

There was manufacturing in the towns, in small workshops employing fewer than 10 persons, which were organized in guilds. Their output was mostly for local and regional use. The most important handicraft branch was that of textiles, weaving a variety of fabrics and floor coverings, both expensive and cheap versions thereof. As noted above, neither carpets nor fabrics were important for export. Other branches of artisanal activity included activities such as construction, metal working, leather working, and food processing crafts. A special kind of artisanal employment was that of those who worked in so-called royal manufactories, which produced mainly products needed by the royal court (costly textiles) and the army (military supplies), while such products were also purchased on the market. Some towns supplied goods that were unique (Kashan tiles) or were of a very high quality (Kerman shawls, Kashan velvets). Labor conditions were poor, and child labor was normal. There were six long (8- to 10-hour) working days, Friday being the day off. There also were holidays (*Moharram, Eyd al-Fitr*, etc.). Wages depended on market conditions and skilled workers earned more than less or unskilled workers.[18]

Mining

Despite a wealth of minerals in its subsoil, mining was barely undertaken. Due to primitive mining techniques, and lack of water, transport, and energy sources near potential sites, mining was almost impossible. Although copper in particular was mined near most urban centers, output was insufficient to meet local demand, and large quantities of copper were imported. Also, Persia had neither gold nor silver deposits that could be cost-effectively mined. The cost of extracting precious metal ore simply made it impossible to make a profit on it, as is suggested by a saying quoted by Tavernier: *noqreh-ye Kervan dah kharjeh nuh hasel*—the silver of Kervan: ten in expense for nine in yield.[19] As a result, the country had to import much of its metal needs. The only successful mining operation, in terms of profitability, was that of turquoise in Khorasan.[20]

The Eighteenth Century: Afshar Period

Introduction

There was no change in the structure of the economy of Persia after the fall of the Safavids in 1722. Nevertheless, there were developments that significantly impacted the size of the economy and the way in which it functioned. So as not to repeat what I have said about Safavid Persia, in the following I only focus on those aspects of the economy that underwent change after 1722, for Persia anno 1730 or 1770 was not the same as Persia anno 1700. What was different? The invasion of Persia by the Ghilzay Afghans, followed by an eight-year occupation, crippled the economy. Many people died, trade was greatly disturbed, and the country was robbed blind by the invaders. When they were finally defeated and evicted, Persia was a bankrupt country. Its treasury was empty, and although the Afghans had been expelled, large parts of the country were still occupied by foreign powers. Although the Afghans conquerors had occupied most of central Persia, they did not control the entire Safavid realm. The Ottomans invaded the country in 1722, seizing Persia's Western Caucasus provinces (Armenia, W. Georgia, Shirvan, and Daghestan), most of Azerbaijan, including Tabriz, as well as Kurdistan and Hamadan, all of which they held until 1735. The Russians held all the provinces around the Caspian eastern seaboard from Darband to Rasht until 1732. In the northeast and east, Malek Mahmud Sistani took hold of Khorasan and Sistan until 1726.[21] Of course, the new rulers of Persia wanted to end this occupation, which led to war, consequently draining the country of its remaining meager resources.

Population

Due to the Afghan invasion, occupation, and subsequent wars a large number of people were killed, and Persia needed people to create wealth and pay taxes. Above I wrote that although we don't know the size of Safavid Persia's population by 1700, it was probably about seven million. However, we do know that thereafter the population dropped in size. How do we know this? There were serious military conflicts from 1715 until the end of the eighteenth century. Cities like Mashhad, Kerman, Shamakhi, Tabriz, Shiraz, Yazd, Kermanshah, and Isfahan, to mention but the most important ones, had lost much of their population by 1730 due to famine and the plague as well as to sieges, and their subsequent sacks and killings by Abdali and Ghilzay Afghan, Lezgi, Ottoman, and Nader Shah's troops.[22]

An overview of the occurrence of epidemics in eighteenth-century Persia suggests that in addition to war and famine this must have led to a reduction in population size. During the Afghan occupation a plague broke out in Gilan that allegedly lasted 10 years, and many died, according to Hazin. The Dutch only reported an outbreak in the summer of 1727, which lasted till October and claimed many lives.[23] In 1731, the area from Hamadan to Barbarud, near Borujerd, was ravaged by the plague, and 200,000 people were said to have perished. The plague was also said to have scoured Kashan, Baghdad, and Kermanshah. The survivors had fled into the mountains and many even fled to Isfahan, Shiraz, Qazvin, and Soltanabad.[24] In Sirjan, the plague had struck toward the end of May 1735 and was slowly making its way toward Kerman. Already 30 people had died in Kerman. On May 25, the town officials made public that all sincere and believing Moslems should go to the mosques to pray and give alms to make the plague go away. By July the plague was over. In the period prior to that day, some 50 to 60 people had died every day, but this was mainly ascribed to the heat, so there may not have been a plague at all, it was suggested.[25] In 1735, plague had broken out at Ganjeh during the siege of that city.[26] In October 1737, the plague broke out in Qom where 6,000 people died. As a result the town was empty, because the population had fled, while the plague also broke out at Golpeygan.[27] In early 1737, the new city of Aq-su that had been built south of Shamakhi suffered the plague, and 9,000 people died.[28] In early 1738, the plague broke out in besieged Qandahar.[29] In 1739, the Russian consul reported the plague at Kashan, but Iranians said that no other "sickness prevailed than usual in the fruit season."[30] In 1741, there was an outbreak of a pestilential disease in Kong, either the plague or cholera; 40–50 people per day died, and there were not enough able-bodied people to bury the dead.[31] In 1757, Karim Khan Zand had to cease his campaign in Khuzestan against the Banu Ka'b due to an outbreak of the plague, which also had broken out in Soleymaniyeh (Kurdistan) in 1757–1758.[32] In 1760 there was an outbreak of pestilence in Kurdistan, and from 1760–1767 a severe epidemic in Mazandaran.[33] Tiflis and Georgia had recurrent epidemics of the plague in the second half of the eighteenth century. In 1770, some 8,000 people died of the plague in Tiflis, "without counting the dead in the villages."[34] In 1773 there was plague in Soleymaniyeh (Kurdistan) and in Basra in Iraq, as well as on both sides of the Persian Gulf.[35] In 1774 there was a severe epidemic of plague in Kermanshah.[36] In 1784 Agha Mohammad's troops at Tehran suffered from "the plague, which is peculiar to this area" (vaba' keh khasseh-ye an molk ast).[37] In 1797 and 1798 there was again an outbreak of plague in Soleymaniyeh.[38]

Data for Isfahan suggest that its population amounted to 550,000 in 1710, 240,000 in 1727, and 50,000 in 1736, or a reduction by 90 percent in 25 years![39] The substantial drop in the size of the population of Isfahan was due to the collapse of Safavid rule after the nine-month siege of Isfahan (1722), when many people died from hunger, fled, or were killed. The fall and sack of Isfahan was followed by the harsh rule of the Afghan invaders, which further reduced the number of inhabitants.[40]

The rule by their successor, the liberator of Persia, the later Nader Shah, was as destructive, and his rule led to more internal killings and migration.[41] The almost constant state of war during most of the eighteenth century, leading to recruitment of soldiers, fiscal oppression, famine, rebellions, and more killings, continued to have a downward pressure on population size, and the occasional outbreak of epidemics was not helpful either to stop this trend. Immigration of nomadic groups from Afghanistan and Central Asia that were recruited for Nader's army partially offset this downward trend, but many of them died in military conflicts, and they did not add to the country's productive capacity in a significant way. The result was a smaller population with less productive capacity. It was also a more rural population, because urban people tended to migrate to rural areas, and settled villagers probably joined nomadic groups.[42]

Agriculture

Given the fact that Persia was an agricultural economy and that labor was one of the main inputs for agriculture meant that given the significant drop in population, there must have been less output. One might, of course, argue that there existed an enormous scope for the increase of productivity in Persia. Peasants and land were underemployed, and given the right incentives, were able and willing to produce more. Such an increase in output, however, was only possible through the introduction of an increasingly diversified package of crops due to a better use of existing underutilized resources, i.e., labor and land, but that did not happen. A more likely scenario is that the loss of life in rural areas was partly offset by the influx of urban dwellers. However, these were mostly unskilled labor, and therefore, their contribution probably was marginal in the beginning. Also, many rural people were drafted for military operations. Because most of its agriculture was rain-fed, Persia with fewer people could not put more land under production, an obvious choice to boost output.[43] But it was not only that there were fewer people, the same was true for animals. Apart from death due to illness, lack of fodder, and the like, there also was the requisitioning of animals by the army for its operations. With fewer people and animals, both the major energy inputs in agriculture, output had to drop. Less production had as a consequence that the level of normal revenues also declined.

Role of Government

Although Persia had fewer people and, therefore, lower revenues, this need not have crippled the functioning of the state, because with a lower population size there also were lower expenditures. Therefore, could not the economy have functioned like the one in 1700, be it at a lower level? In short, the economy need not necessarily be in imbalance. The short answer is NO! Because the reality was that the government was bankrupt and needed resources wherever and in whatever manner it could get hold of them, as there was a structural need for money to finance the military operations throughout Persia. In 1700, estimated government revenue was 0.7 million *tumans*. In 1735 the Dutch estimated that Tahmasp Qoli Khan (the later Nader Shah) needed 25,000 *tumans* or Dfl. 10.6 million each month to pay his 125,000-man army, or about 36 percent of the revenues of 700,000 that the Safavids raised during normal years.[44] After the Afghan occupiers had been expelled, Persia still faced a much reduced revenue base. Its major earner of specie, raw silk was not available to the central government after 1722. The Caucasus provinces included major producing areas of raw silk and together with Gilan, the other major producers of raw silk, were Persia's major earners of foreign exchange. However, these provinces were in the hands of respectively the Ottomans and the Russians until 1735. Azerbaijan was not only a major province in size, but also important economically as a major producer of agricultural products (having generally higher rainfall and higher population than most other provinces). Qandahar, the seat of the Ghilzay Afghans, was a major trade emporium, a center for trade between India, Persia, and Central Asia. In short, if the government wanted to increase its revenues, it had no choice but to regain control over rebellious and occupied provinces. It was only after 1732, when the Russians—and after 1735, when the Ottomans—withdrew from the Caspian and Caucasus provinces that silk revenues were available again to the central government. However, regaining occupied territory and control over its wealth and resources would only resolve some of Persia's financial problems. Nader's control over the Caucasus provinces and Azerbaijan remained tenuous and very costly, and the same held for Kermanshah.[45] Thus, the cash revenues that these provinces provided were not always available and were in lower quantities due to labor supply problems, and sometimes they absorbed them due to the need to suppress local rebellions.

Thus, it seems that the fiscal problems of the government became worse rather than better after it had regained control over all its provinces. According to Hanway, in the 1740s the army's wage bill alone amounted to five million pounds (two million *tumans*) per year, while the annual revenues were supposed to yield a similar amount (5.7 million pounds or 2.3 million *tumans*), half of it from the conquered areas in India (see Table 8.1). However, except for the conquered parts of India and the provinces of Gilan and Mazandaran, the kingdom was so impoverished by rapine that, in Hanway's estimation, it might only pay one quarter of the normal revenues.

These amounted to 2,387,000 pounds or 41 percent of the total. Thus, if only one quarter of these would be paid, revenue would be about 590,000 pounds, with total revenue of some 3.9 million pounds. This constituted a significant shortfall of funds, contributing to local rebellions, abandonment of land, further plunder, and debasement of the currency.[46] We cannot be sure whether Hanway's figures are correct, but it is clear that this contemporary observer realized that Nader Shah's manner of operation was unsustainable. The funds just

Table 8.1 **Estimated revenues of the provinces in good times in 1743**

Province	Mildinars	Pounds
India, conquered provinces	12,500,000	3,125,000
Qandahar and Herat	1,000,000	250,000
Khorasan	2,000,000	500,000
Astarabad	50,000	12,500
Mazandaran	400,000	100,000
Gilan	500,000	125,000
Shirvan, Georgia, part of Daghestan	1,500,000	375,000
Erevan, Persian Armenia	2,000,000	500,000
Persian Iraq (Qazvin, Esfahan, Fars)	1,500,000	375,000
Azerbaijan (incl. Tabriz, Ardabil)	1,500,000	375,000
Total	22,950,000	5,737,500

Source: Hanway, *An Account*, vol. 2, pp. 26–27.

were not there, which, if Nader Shah did not find other means to raise funds, he had to demand more from the population, which had to led to more oppression, which led to rebellions, resulting in bloody suppression.

Nader's large army of more than 200,000 soldiers[47] also must have had some growth impact on the economy.[48] After all, the soldiers were also consumers. However, the general insecurity, the tyrannical behavior of the officials, the low government payments for the goods it bought, the high cost of living for the craftsmen, and the crushing weight of the high fiscal burden resulted not only in eliminating the potential growth impact of these expenditures but in actually reducing economic growth. In addition, the army's operations seem to have had a negative impact on the productive capacity far beyond the area of the immediate military theater. The soldiers often extracted more than the locally available surplus, sometimes at artificially lower than market prices and sometimes by just taking things without paying for it. Consequently, agricultural productive capacity suffered due to a significantly reduced population as well as due to the incessant demand for pack animals because of their high mortality rate during army operations.[49]

Given that the usual revenues sources were not able to yield the higher level of fiscal burden that was imposed upon them on a sustained basis, how did the central government deal with that problem? How was Nader going to finance the deficit, and where would he get the additional funds needed? Most of these taxes were spent on defense and pensions, the defense budget being as high as 40 percent by the 1740s. Hence, additional taxes were imposed on the population to cover the budgetary deficit. Therefore, Nader Shah again took to extracting cash money from the population, which was enforced by beatings and sometimes even killings. Nader publicly stated that he "could not care less if the whole country was ruined and whether there was trade or not, the only thing that interested him was to dress and maintain his troops."[50] In October 1736, tax collectors were seen going about with sticks, swords, and hatchets, tormenting and beating people to get the additional 12,000 *tumans* assigned to Isfahan and proportionally to other cities.[51] He further forced the merchant community, including the EIC and VOC, to pay large sums of cash and provide services, sometimes very expensive ones.[52] Particularly oppressive was the demand of the loan of ships to ferry troops to Oman, to stop fleeing rebels, or to help overcome the Arab crews of the royal navy, who had mutinied. One such loan was very expensive for the VOC, when one of its ships took a Persian ambassador to India, which shipwrecked near Karachi. There was no compensation for this loss or for the services rendered, and the same held for those Persian subjects who were forced to provide similar services.[53] To get more revenues, Tahmasp II confiscated part of *vaqf* land in 1732, followed by Nader Shah, who confiscated most of it in 1737.[54] To raise more revenue, Nader not only confiscated lands, but in 1738 he also ordered a new land assessment made to get a better knowledge of the tax base. This was the best assessment made up till then and served the state well into the nineteenth century, and, most important, enabled Nader Shah to collect more revenues.[55]

International Trade

The volume of trade in Persia fell precipitously after the Afghan occupation, and in particular international trade suffered considerably. The major commercial operators, Armenian, Banyan, and Persian Muslim merchants, as well as the Dutch and English Companies, were forced to reduce their activities considerably. VOC trade suffered a 50-percent loss in gross profits during the Afghan occupation, and even more during the Afshar period (see Table 8.2). The mercantile community, which had hardly any trade under Afghan rule, had hoped for a revival of trade in the 1730s, which did not materialize. The country was in shambles, money was scarce, and trade only occurred in small lots with long credit.[56] Fewer people, who were heavily taxed, meant less purchasing power, meant less demand for non-vital products, meant less international trade, meant lower customs revenues and other trade related revenues. By 1730, most of the Safavid coinage had already been exported. Matters grew worse when in July 1731, the *mo'ayyer-bashi*, of Isfahan, who also served as the city's governor, announced that, henceforth, Afghan money would cease to be legal tender. What followed was a total standstill of the little trade that remained, causing many people to flee the city.[57]

Like in the agricultural sector, there was the unreliability of the availability of pack animals and fodder. The supply of these animals and their feed was vital for trade, because without them nothing could be moved in the country. In normal years, the size of the herds was determined by levels of disease, famine, and drought, all three of which had a crippling effect on transportation capacity and its cost. However, now also had to be added the impact of war, with its

Table 8.2 **Gross profits of the VOC's Persian Directorate by decade (1700–1754)**

Years	Amount (in Dutch guilders)
1700–1709	402,859
1710–1719	363,728
1720–1729	185,856 (includes Basra)
1730–1739	72,587 (includes Basra)
1740–1749	73,912 (includes Basra)
1750–1754	137,131 (includes Basra)

Source: VOC 2762, chapter 15.

destruction of property and, in particular, of requisitioning of animals, leading to high freight rates. Growing insecurity further increased the cost of escorting caravans and commercial transaction costs in general.[58] Also, sometimes the government demanded so much cash, usually from merchants and minorities, that the money supply was inadequate to carry on normal trade. Most trade via the Persian Gulf went through Bandar Abbas, although after 1737 the role of Bushehr started to increase, to overtake the role of Bandar Abbas in the 1750s.[59]

This development was due to the particular characteristics of the Persian economy. As before, Persia suffered from a lack of exportable commodities besides silk and some minor products. As silk production had gone down, the traditional export surplus and the corresponding inflow of specie with the Ottomans may have diminished. To some extent, this was offset by a larger trade surplus with Russia, as goods that normally would have been carried to the Levant were now exported via Russia. This held in particular for raw silk.[60] However, the trade surplus with the lands lying to the northwest appears to have been smaller than the trade deficit with India (and Asia in general). We lack definitive data, but the export of silver (and to some extent gold) to Asia, unbalanced by an inflow from the north and west, may well explain the sudden rise of the role of copper in international trade and the greater use of copper for domestic trade. In 1735 the government in Persia decreed the gold–silver ratio to be 1:11. This was much higher than in Europe (1:15), and, more importantly, higher than in the Ottoman Empire. Therefore, merchants in Persia who accepted silver suffered a loss.[61]

As a consequence, trade was dead in Isfahan in 1737, also because its population had shrunk to 10 percent of its size 40 years earlier. Transport between cities was difficult and risky due increased banditry, arbitrary confiscation of pack animals by the authorities, high fodder prices, and so forth.[62] This was one of the reasons that the European East Indies Companies wanted to close down their office in Isfahan, which only the EIC succeeded to do in 1740.[63] The situation of depressed trade due to military operations, shortage of money, and government interference with the market, which had begun after 1722, became structural after Tahmasp II (1730). This led to more direct interference by the state into trade by forcing merchants and/or craftsmen to sell only to it at low prices, or by forcing them to buy goods from government warehouses, or by trying to control the silk and *kork* trade after 1739.[64] Forced orders to supply Nader's army caused much dismay among the tradespeople and craftsmen in Isfahan in 1740, according to Kalushkin, the Russian agent in Isfahan. Lerch, a German physician in Russian service, wrote that in 1745 in Resht there were 15 caravanserais for merchants, which were all almost empty. He only saw one caravan moving from Tabriz to Resht. In Darband, a caravanserai with 150 shops had just been built at the orders Nader. They were all empty, and no merchant was in sight. Lerch, who was in Persia in 1745–1747, noted that wherever he went merchants were exposed to oppression. Nader even heavily fined Russian merchants in Shamakhi, Tabriz, Ardabil, and Isfahan. The merchants in Resht did not have the money, and the visiting Russian embassy lent them the money. Golitsin, the ambassador, ordered all Russian merchants to depart Persia for Astrakhan. Only those who had to wind up business stayed. Armenian merchants also departed for Astrakhan. Russian diplomats noted that trade in Persia was dead because the merchants were bankrupt; many therefore left Persia.[65]

The decline in the level of VOC sales in Afshar Persia was also reflected in the decline of the gross profits of its Persian directorate as compared with the preceding and following period. Table 8.2 shows that the Afshar period was a commercial low point for the VOC. It was so bad that even during the Afghan occupation the VOC had been able to realize more profits. It is true that the profits during the Afghan period mostly came from trade at Basra, but the VOC also traded with Basra during the Afsharid period.[66]

These profit rates were inflated, however, because they were gross figures. If corrected for loss on the export of specie, the loss due to overly high book rates for Persian currency, the government debt to the VOC and loss of interest thereon, as well as the cost of the various loans of money, services, and ships to the Persian government, trade results were negative after 1730, if not earlier.[67] The possible positive effect of Nader's three-year remission of taxes in 1739 was short-lived, as in 1744, Nader demanded retroactive payment of the remitted taxes. Likewise, the moderate revival of trade in Mashhad after the return of the army from India was incidental and temporary. Hanway related that when he visited Mashhad in 1744, the town had become totally ruined and trade was depressed.[68]

The oppression and permanent state of war under Nader Shah, followed by the ruinous Afsharid succession war, resulted in depressed international trade, an indication of a domestic economy in crisis. In 1770, the German traveler and careful observer of the situation in northern Iran, Samel Gmelin concluded: "The Persians are less wealthy and impoverished because of oppression by Nader Shah and *even more so* [my italics] due to the revolts that followed his death as well as the internal wars."[69] The relative peaceful interlude of Karim Khan Zand's reign was too short to improve this situation. Moreover, succession wars started again after his death in 1779 and were finally ended only in 1796 when the Qajar contender was able to defeat the last Zand pretender and take Mashhad and Tiflis.

Monetary Situation

One other way to raise money quickly was to interfere with the monetary system, something that previous rulers also had done. At various times during this troubling period, the government in need of revenue used monetary manipulation of one kind or another for this purpose. The usual method was either by raising the accountancy value of the existing coins or by reducing the weight of coins, principally by clipping old coins. Such measures usually were accompanied by a ban of the export of good coins and the bullion it was made of. Another time-honored way of raising revenue through monetary manipulation was to tax the export of specie. In October 1732, Tahmasp Qoli Khan issued a decree stipulating that the export of (European) gold ducats was only allowed on payment of a duty of 5 percent, to be paid in so-called white, i.e., silver money.[70]

In 1732, Tahmasp II ordered that silver and copper money had to be accepted "as is," without the demand of any premium.[71] This decree represents a unique step in Persia's monetary history. It meant, after all, that henceforth copper was not token money anymore, and that Persia implicitly had adopted a tri-metallic system in the sense that gold, silver, and copper coins had officially fixed rates of exchange. It appears that the decree was indeed rescinded, for nothing is reported about its application; yet it was a signal of things to come. The new coins struck by Nader Shah in 1736 did not address the problems that had caused the tightness in the money market, however, and in particular the adverse gold–silver ratio compared to conditions in the Ottoman Empire. Also, as always, a lack of bullion caused government revenue receipts in ready money to fall short. Therefore, Nader Shah again took to extracting cash from the population.[72] In addition, in 1735 Nader Shah temporarily devalued the copper money by declaring that, henceforth, the double *paisa* copper coin was worth a single *paisa*, involving a devaluation of 50 percent. In early 1736 he rescinded that decree, and for a while the double *paisa* copper coin was counted at its normal value.[73] This shows once again that there was an official rate of exchange between copper and silver. For although payments took place in copper money, the tax obligation was calculated in silver, and henceforth people had to come up with twice as much copper as before to meet the tax obligation.

In March 1737, both copper and silver money was so scarce in Kerman that merchants did not care whether they were paid in silver (previously the preferred medium) or copper as long as they were paid.[74] To fill his empty coffers Nader Shah needed additional funds. Therefore, in January 1738, if not earlier, Nader decided to devalue his currency. The new regulations caused *abbasi*s to become scarce. The Dutch, who were allowed to export specie, found it difficult to obtain cash. Copperware at this point had become so prominent in the money markets that buyers even differentiated between the types of copper offered. There was Hamadani copper and Kermani copper, which was of almost the same quality as Qazvin copper. Hamadani copper was not always obtainable. Demand for copper was at times so brisk that it led to panic buying.[75]

In March 1739, Nader Shah defeated the Mogul emperor Mohammad Shah and conquered his capital Delhi. As a result, Nader acquired an enormous booty, which he carried to Persia. The total estimated value of the spoils brought from India ranges from 30 million to 87 million pounds, with various sources claiming that half was in specie or coin. Feeling militarily and financially secure after his Indian conquest, Nader Shah attempted to merge the monetary system of Persia with that of India to facilitate trade with Persia's main trading partner. To integrate the Indian and the Persian monetary system, the new Persian monetary system adopted the Mogul gold *mohur*, known in Persian as *mohr-e ashrafi*, weighing almost exactly 11 grams. This means that Nader abandoned his attempt to model the monetary system after the Spanish real of eight, widely used in long-distance trade at that time.[76]

Whatever the goal of the monetary reform of 1740, it mattered little to the Persian population or to those trading with Persia. Despite the enormous booty that Nader Shah had brought from India and the new coins that he had struck, commerce was still mostly carried on with copper. This reality suggests that the basic parameters of Persia's monetary situation had not changed at all. Given the new and large supply of bullion one would expect that Persia's problem of tight money supply was resolved, at least in the short, if not the medium term. However, that did not happen, for despite the major influx of booty into Persia after the conquest of India in 1739, much of that was hoarded by Nader Shah himself as well as his commanders. In fact, Nader Shah had instituted a policy whereby all gold and silver that he could lay his hands on was transferred to his treasury, or hoarded rather, in Kalat-e Naderi. Yet copper continued to hold its dominant place in the market.[77]

The Zand Period

What, if anything, changed under the Zands? In some respects the Zand rulers were worse off than their Afsharid predecessors. Persia's population had been reduced significantly in size and, moreover, was exhausted and impoverished after more than 30 years of war, high taxation, and oppression.[78] The Zands ruled over a much smaller Persia. By 1759 Karim Khan Zand (r. 1750–1779) had emerged as the victor in the struggle for control over Persia, be it that some parts such as Khorasan were left under Afsharid authority (as vassals to the Afghan Dorranis), while other parts (the Caucasus provinces, Gilan, Talesh, Mazandaran) remained semi-autonomous. Although these Khans (except Khorasan) formally recognized Karim Khan as their overlord after 1763, they paid token submission to him, both in terms of tribute and military support. Also, Zand rule was marred by rebellions, wars, and dynastic strife. Certainly it was less than under the Afsharids, but the necessary funds to finance military operations (in particular the one-year siege of Basra) were a drain on the economy.[79]

International Trade

Trade prospects remained depressed, because the population had been decimated and financially weakened by the succession of wars[80] and further decreased under the Zands. The VOC director in Bandar 'Abbas proposed closure of operations in Persia in 1747, which finally happened in 1766. The spending of the Kalat treasury hoard gave a short-lived boost to trade. However, this was but a temporary phenomenon that soon was deflated due to renewed fighting among Nader Shah's successors, for money remained scarce and trade in the Persian Gulf was still dominated by barter and (partial) payments in copper and a variety of silver and gold coins, in particular after 1754.[81] Trade in the Persian Gulf remained relatively large and important, but at a much reduced level. The East India Company almost completely stopped trading in the Gulf and, henceforth, trade was mainly carried on by local and British so-called country traders.[82] A similar development may be observed concerning the trade with Russia. After an initial upsurge in trade after 1751, there was a drop in 1756, after which it settled at a much lower level for the next decades, as shown in Table 8.3. The good news was that trade with Russia continued to be advantageous for Persia; the resulting large deficit on its trade balance Russia had to pay for in cash.

Trade with Persia's other important trading partner, the Ottoman Empire, also suffered a considerable decline, in particular after the Ottoman withdrawal from Persian territory in the Caucasus in 1735. A series of military conflicts occurred between the two states, which was not beneficial to the development of trade relations. Also, in the 1740s the raw silk-producing areas in the Caucasus were negatively effected by the revolt of the Lezgis and the subsequent pacification campaign.[83] During the ensuing Persian-Ottoman wars in the 1740s, raw silk played an important role as an economic weapon, for Nader Shah had given his merchants orders not to sell any silk to Turkey.[84] Declining raw silk exports (see Table 8.4) had a significant impact on the trade of Aleppo and Izmir, where imports of cloth (which Persian merchants bought with the proceeds of raw silk sales) had dropped off by more than 50 percent.[85]

Despite the relatively peaceful interlude of Karim Khan Zand's reign, succession wars started again after his death in 1779 and were finally ended only in 1796 when the Qajar contender was able to defeat the last Zand pretender and take Mashhad and Tiflis.[86] A British traveler observed in 1790 that "[m]anufactures and trade are at present greatly decayed in Persia, the people having had no interval of peace to recover themselves since the death of Kerim Khan to the present

Table 8.3 **Volume of Russian trade with Persia, 1750–1769**

Year	Export	without duties	Import	without duties	duties
1750	48.5	–	847.6	819.0	6.3
1751	22.4	–	437.9	366.9	6.8
1752	410.9	336.8	485.3	387.7	14.3
1753	588.6	497.5	813.1	689.1	16.4
1754	444.0	258.6	313.1	179.7	46.0
1755	355.3	188.9	339.6	275.8	37.6
1756	169.5	129.9	150.0	112.5	18.5
1757	249.5	222.4	239.8	189.7	17.7
1758	362.2	–	241.7	–	–
1759	212.5	17.2	129.7	105.2	5.4
1760	142.8	69.9	144.6	122.0	25.4
1761	138.0	82.8	115.7	97.0	17.7
1762	207.0	127.4	269.1	230.0	28.6
1763	115.3	109.8	392.1	330.0	26.8
1764	256.1	146.0	482.6	425.0	40.6
1765	283.0	163.9	254.5	214.6	38.2
1766	92.8	–	282.1	253.5	–
1767	251.6	216.3	240.4	219.6	13.5
1768	190.9	123.4	382.0	362.9	23.3
1769	317.5	269.0	408.8	367.1	21.9

Source: N. G. Kukanova, "K voprosu o torgovle Rossii v Iranom v 50–80e gody XVIII v.," in N. A. Kuznetsova, ed., *Iran*, Moscow, 1977, p. 75, table 2.

period, but if a regular and permanent government were once again to be established, there is little doubt but they would flourish."[87] This is what finally happened, though it took some more years to do so.

Monetary Situation

The twelve years following Nader Shah's death in 1747 were marked by political chaos, leaving the currency situation confused. There was no monetary uniformity in the country. Although the new authorities continued to strike coins using the Indian weight standard, they found it difficult to maintain a viable currency.

Table 8.4 **Raw silk exports to Turkey during selected years by quality category in *man***

Date	Harir-e kenar	Harir-e elvan	Harir-e Gilan
1132/1719	12,665	870	9,972
1141/1728	19,819	329	3,862
1156/1743	3,400	70	624
1182/1769	3,606	74	–
1195/1780	635	55	–

Source: Zarinehbaf-Shahr, *Tabriz*, p. 175, table 20.

Many local rulers struck their own coinage and arbitrarily fixed their accounting value. Both silver and gold were priced out of the market. The denominations of the silver coins remained the *'abbasi* and its fractions; those of the copper coins are not known. The situation in Khorasan was little better. Under Nader Shah's Dorrani successors in Khorasan and Afghanistan, the rupee continued to circulate, probably as the main trade coin. In the Persian Gulf region, exports in this period mainly consisted of cash. Payments for imported goods were in principle accepted in all kinds of currencies, but in practice were restricted to only a few. The main currencies were the Indian gold rupee, the Persian silver rupee, and the silver *naderi*s. The relative importance of copper was further bolstered by the fact that the alloy of the silver *mahmudis* was very bad. Faced with structurally tight money supply and widespread debasement of the coinage, in 1763, Karim Khan Zand first tried to alleviate this situation by having the British agree to a voluntary ban on the export of specie. It was evident that Persia's negative trade balance could only be rectified by developing the export trade or by reducing imports. As this was not possible in the short term, another way to deal with the problem was to "correct" the weight and/or alloy of the coinage to make it less attractive for export. To that effect the government collected the old silver and copper money and struck new currency of less weight and/or alloy in 1768. Nor did Persia's shaky economic conditions improve under Karim Khan's successors.[88]

Conclusion

To conclude, the fall of the Safavid dynasty in 1722 was the end of an era. The population of Persia had been plundered and had suffered war and famine. The downward trend in the size of the population and the revenue base led to a greater fiscal burden for the population, both in relative and absolute terms, and thus to less purchasing power. This led to banditry, and thus less internal security and hence to less trade and higher commercial transaction costs. Consequently, the productive base of the country needed time and the right socioeconomic and political parameters to recuperate. This did not happen, due to Nader Shah's belligerent policies. Nader Shah won most of his battles against his neighbors, but his victories were all short-lived and, unlike after previous founders of dynasties, all his territorial gains were lost by his immediate successors—while in the process he crippled the remaining productive capacity of the economy. Trade suffered because of the reduced purchasing power of the decreasing and over-taxed population, the higher overheads for trade due to payment of "protection money," other demands made on traders, and depreciation of the coinage.[89] As a result, trade results were the worst since the VOC, Persia's single most important foreign trading partner, had started to trade with Persia in 1623. Although I pointed out at the beginning of this chapter that the VOC data cannot be used as a pars pro toto for Persia's entire trade, all other sources (British, Armenian, Georgian, and even some Persian ones) give a similar impression of a downturn in trade.

Concerning monetary policy, the Afghan conquerors followed the Safavid model, and so did Tahmasp II, who was reinstated in 1729. Nader Shah reduced the weight of the coins, as did Karim Khan Zand (as of 1766), by increasing the value of the existing coins against the *tuman*, the unit of account. None of these measures was effective, owing to the difference in the gold–silver ratio between the Ottoman Empire and Persia, which made accepting silver more expensive than copper. As a result, there was a flight into copper, and after 1734 copper coins were not used as tokens anymore, but as full-bodied coins. Because of the small number of mints, which only struck coins intermittently, a shortage of copper coins developed as well, given the sudden huge demand. Consequently, copper in whatever form became also a major form of payment, while barter trade was widely practiced as well to resolve the monetary crunch.[90]

In short, eighteenth-century Persia was a rather isolated, barely developed state, which did not constitute a national economy, as it was made up of a number of regional economies that in great many respects were autarkic. Its ethnically, linguistically, and religiously diverse population was mostly rural and was probably not higher than six million by 1800. About 10 percent lived in urban areas, who were self-employed in trades, crafts, services, and market gardening. The rest of the population was engaged in subsistence farming and pastoralism. Taxes were farmed out, government revenues were spent on payments to the ruling family, the administration, the religious class, and, above all, on military expenditures. The structural balance of trade deficit, inflation, and lack of sufficient exports resulted in depreciation of the currency.

Notes

1. For a failed attempt to do so, see Roman Siebertz, *Preise, Löhne und Lebensstandard im safa-vidischen Iran: Eine untersuchung zu den Rechnungsbüchern Wollebrand Geleynssen de Jonghs (1641–1643)* (Vienna: Verlag der Österreichischen Akademie der Wissenschaften, 2013). For my review of this book, see *Der Islam* 91/1 (2014), pp. 236–239.

2. For details, see Willem Floor, *The Economy of Safavid Persia* (Wiesbaden: Reichert, 2000), chapter 1.

3. Willem Floor, *A Fiscal History of Safavid and Qajar Iran* (New York: Bibliotheca Persica, 2000), chapter 1.

4. For a detailed discussion, see Willem Floor, *Agriculture in Qajar Iran* (Washington, DC: MAGE, 2003); idem, *The Economy*, chapter 7.

5. Rudi Matthee, Willem Floor, and Patrick Clawson, *The Monetary History of Safavid, Afsharid and Qajar Iran* (London: IB Tauris, 2013), chapter 1.

6. An exception were those areas that produced cash crops such as raw silk (Gilan, Shirvan) and down or *kork* (part of Kerman), see Floor, *The Economy*, pp. 254–248.

7. Floor, *Fiscal History*, chapter 2; idem, *The Economy*, chapter 2.

8. Floor, *Fiscal History*, pp. 67–68.

9. For a detailed discussion, see Floor, *A Fiscal History*, chapter 1; also Gideon Sjoberg, *The Preindustrial City: Past and Present* (Glencoe: Free Press, 1960); Patricia Crone, *Pre-industrial Societies* (Oxford, 1989).

10. Rudolph P. Matthee, *The Politics of Trade in Safavid Iran* (Cambridge: Cambridge University Press, 1999); Willem Floor and Mohammad H. Faghfoory, *The First Dutch-Iranian Commercial Conflict* (Costa Mesa: Mazda, 2004), chapter 1.

11. On this attempt to control the silk trade, see Floor, *Nader Shah*, pp. 240–242 (John Wiley and Sons Ltd.).

12. For the marginal role of Persian carpets and textiles in Persia's exports, see Floor, *The Persian Textile Industry in historical perspective 1500–1925* (Paris: l'Harmattan, 1999), pp. 60–92, and idem, "The Import of Textiles Into Seventeenth Century Safavid Persia," *Eurasian Studies* 4 (2007), pp. 107–141; republished in Thompson et al., eds., *Carpets and Textiles in the Iranian World 1400–1700* (Oxford–Genoa: Ashmolean Museum—Bruschettini Foundation, 2010), pp. 31–48.

13. Floor, *The Economy*, chapters 5 and 6.

14. An exception were those areas that produced cash crops such as raw silk (Gilan, Shirvan) and down or *kork* (part of Kerman); see Floor, *Economy*, pp. 254–258.

15. Matthee, Floor, and Clawson, *The Monetary History*, chapters 1–4.

16. Floor, *The Economy*, chapter 7; idem, *Fiscal History*, pp. 38–60.

17. Floor, *The Economy*, pp. 282–289, 293–300.

18. Floor, *The Economy*, pp. 309–326; idem, *The Persian Textile Industry in Historical Perspective, 1500–1925* (Paris: Harmattan, 1999), pp. 16–28.

19. Jean-Baptiste Tavernier, *Les Six voyages de Turquie et de Perse*, 2 vols. (Paris: G. Clouzier, 1676), vol. 1, p. 373.

20. Floor, *The Economy*, pp. 303–308; idem, *The Traditional Crafts of Qajar Iran* (Costa Mesa: Mazda, 2003), pp. 186–210.

21. Laurence Lockhart, *Fall of the Safavid Dynasty* (Cambridge: Cambridge University Press, 1958), pp. 123, 212–273, 279–280, 308–312, 341–359.

22. Willem Floor, *The Rise and Fall Nader Shah* (Washington, DC: Mage, 2009), pp. 7–8, 29, 40, 211, 225; idem, *The Afghan Occupation of Persia, 1722–1730* (Paris: Cahiers Studia Iranica, 1998), pp. 29–30, 47, 50, 60–61; Lockhart, *Fall*, pp. 99, 127–128.

23. Mohammad Ali Hazin, *Tarikh-e Hazin: shamel avakher-e Safaviyeh, fitneh-ye Afghan, saltanat-e Nader Shah va ahval-e jam'i az bozorgan* (Tehran: Kitābfurūshī-i Tayād, 1332/1953), p. 44; Floor, *Afghan Occupation*, p. 258.

24. Floor, *The Rise and Fall of Nader Shah* (Washington, DC: Mage, 2009), p. 8, n. 26; *A Chronicle of the Carmelites in Persia and the Papal mission of the seventeenth and eighteenth centuries*, 2 vols. (London: Eyre and Spottiswoods, 1939), vol. 1, pp. 579, 621.

25. Floor, *Nader Shah*, p. 182.

26. Floor, *Nader Shah*, pp. 44, 47.
27. Floor, *Nader Shah*, p. 225.
28. Floor, *Nader Shah*, p. 70.
29. Floor, *Nader Shah*, p. 77.
30. Hanway, *An Account*, vol. 1, p. 322.
31. Cyril Elgood, *A Medical History of Persia and the Eastern Caliphate: The Development of Persian and Arabic Medical Sciences from the Earliest Times until the Year A.D. 1932* (Cambridge: Cambridge University Press, 1951), p. 413.
32. Austen Henry Layard, 1846, "A Description of the Province of Khuzistan," *JRGS* 16, p. 43; J. D. Tholozan, *Histoire de la peste bubonique, 1er Mémoire—en Perse* (Paris: G. Masson, 1874).
33. Tholozan, *Histoire*.
34. Marie-Félicité Brosset, *Histoire de la Géorgie*, 2 vols. in 3 (St. Petersburg, 1849–1857), vol. II/2, p. 241.
35. Carl Ritter, *Die Erdkunde in Verhaeltnis zum Natur und Geschichte der Menschen* (Berlin: G. Reimer, 1822–1859), p. 59.
36. Georg Sticker, *Abhandlungen aus der Seuchengeschichte* (Giessen: A. Töpelmann, 1908–1910), p. 269.
37. E'tezad al-Saltaneh, Ali Qoli Mirza, *Eksir al-Tavarikh* (Tehran: Visman, 1370/1991), p. 34.
38. Sticker, *Abhandlungen*, p. 275.
39. Floor, *The Economy*, p. 3.
40. Floor, *The Afghan Occupation*, pp. 150, 154, 161, 171, 174, 179, 183, 186.
41. On migration, see, e.g., John Perry, "Forced Migration in Iran during the Seventeenth and Eighteenth Centuries," *Iranian Studies* 8/4 (1975), pp. 199–215; Floor, *Nader Shah*, pp. 40, 217, 222.
42. Laurence Lockhart, *Nadir Shah* (London: Luzac, 1938); Willem Floor, *The Rise and Fall Nader Shah* (Washington, DC: Mage 2009), pp. 29, 35, 42, 60.
43. This situation, of course, also must have resulted in a drop in effective demand. However, this was offset by the influx of nomads from Central Asia, Baluchistan, and Afghanistan, who served in Nader's army and increased demand for food, fodder, animals, and related equipment. It was this additional demand that caused the nationwide oppression of the population.
44. VOC 2357, Gamron to Batavia (24/08/1735), f. 282–283. He usually paid his soldiers monthly in cash. VOC 2546, Relaes lopers, Sept. 1740, fol. 1700. The money had to be transported on mules. The official charged with such money transport took the animals by force and paid for them a price fixed by himself. In 1744, a payment of 50,000 crowns or 5,000 tumans required 130 mules. Jonas Hanway, *An historical account of the British trade over the Caspian Sea*, 4 vols. in 3 (London: n.p., 1753), vol. 1, pp. 234–235.
45. Axworthy, *The Sword*, pp. 230–252, 258; Lockhart, *Nadir Shah*, pp. 170–172, 197–211; Floor, *Nader Shah*, p. 95.
46. Hanway, *An Account*, vol. 2, pp. 26–27.
47. According to Mohammad Kazem Marvi, *'Alamara-ye Naderi*. ed. Mohammad Amin Riyahi (Tehran: 'Alam, 1369/1990), vol. 3, p. 1088, in 1746 when Nader held court in Mashhad, there were allegedly some 220,000 men in his army camp.
48. On the size of Nader's army, see Michael Axworthy, "The Army of Nader Shah," *Iranian Studies*, 40/5 (2007), pp. 635–646. On Nader's policies and activities in general, see Michael Axworthy, *The Sword of Persia: Nader Shah, from Tribal Warrior to Conquering Tyrant* (London: I. B. Tauris, 2009) (notably pp. 249–250 and 260).
49. Hanway, *An Account*, vol. 2, p. 26; M. R. Arunova & K. Z. Ashrafiyan, *Gosudarstvo Nadir Shaxa Afshara* (Moscow, 1958), chapter 6; John Cook, *Voyages and Travels through the Russian Empire, Tartary, and Part of Persia*, 2 vols. (Edinburgh, printed for the author, and sold by E. & C. Dilly, 1770), vol. 2, pp. 315–316, 323, 328–331, 400; Floor, *Nader Shah*, pp. 7, 36–40, 61–62, 85; idem, *Fiscal History*, p. 237.
50. N.A., VOC 2322, Isfahan to Gamron, 22 March, 1733, f. 376vs.
51. N.A., VOC 2416, Isfahan to Gamron, 26 Oct. 1736, fol. 2539–2540; VOC 2416, Isfahan to Gamron, 14 April 1737, fol. 1315.
52. Floor, *Nader Shah*, pp. 4, 18–19, 25, 50, 110, 113, 116–118, 120–130, 132–136, 139–161, 163–164, 201–202, 213–215.

53. Floor, *Nader Shah*, pp. 142, 164, n. 202, 165 ("[E]verybody and anything, be it human being, animal or vessel on both sides of the Persian Gulf were pressed to do royal service.").

54. Floor, *Fiscal History*, pp. 234, 241; the policy of expropriating *vaqf* was announced at the Moghan in the spring of 1736—see Axworthy, *The Sword of Persia*, p. 171, and James Fraser, *The History of Nader Shah* (London, printed by W. Strahan, for the author, 1742), pp. 121–122.

55. Floor, *Fiscal History*, pp. 242, 336.

56. Floor, *Nader Shah*, p. 220.

57. Floor, *Nader Shah*, p. 10.

58. Floor, *Nader Shah*, pp. 181, 186, 225.

59. Floor, *Nader Shah*, pp. 224–225, 231.

60. Floor, *The Economy*, pp. 237–240; N. G. Kukanova, *Ocherki po istorii russko-iranskikh torgovykh otnoshenii v XVII–pervoi polovine XIX veka* (Saransk: Mordovskoe knizhnoe izd-vo, 1977), ch. 3. The Russian merchants paid in goods, silver and copper. The presence of Russian troops in the Caspian provinces until 1732 also meant that additional specie was available, in particular copper. VOC 2252, f. 695 (11/09/1729).

61. Marvi, *'Alam-ara-ye Naderi*, vol. 1, p. 377 (one *methqal*, meaning 24 *nokhud* and therefore 4.61 g, of gold = 550 *dinar*; one *methqal* of silver = 50 *dinars*).

62. Floor, *Nader Shah*, pp. 223–224.

63. Floor, *Nader Shah*, pp. 19, 43, 88, 230.

64. Floor, *Nader Shah*, pp. 226–230; idem, *Textile Industry*.

65. Arunova and Ashrafiyan, *Gosudarstvo*, p. 247; Johan Jacob Lerch, "Nachricht von der zweiten Reise nach Persien . . . von 1745 bis 1747," *Magazin für die neue Historie und Geographie an gelegt von D. Anton Friedriech Büsching*, vol. 10 (Halle: Johann Jacob Curt, 1776), pp. 378, 402, 432.

66. Floor, *Nader Shah*, p. 219.

67. Floor, *Nader Shah*, pp. 249–251.

68. Axworthy, *The Sword*, p. 250; Hanway (1753), vol. 1, p. 256 (". . . plainly shews how rapid a progress Nadir Shah made in the ruin of Persia, even of his favourite city."). On the demand of payment of the remitted taxes, see Floor, *Fiscal History*, pp. 237–238.

69. Gmelin 2007, p. 318.

70. Matthee, Floor, Clawson, *Monetary History*, p. 148.

71. VOC 2255, Isfahan to Gamron, May 30, 1732, fols. 1991–1992.

72. N.A., VOC 2416, Isfahan to Gamron, Oct. 26, 1736, fol. 2539–2540; VOC 2416, Isfahan to Gamron, April 14, 1737, fol. 1315.

73. Matthee, Floor, and Clawson, *Monetary History*, pp. 149–153.

74. N.A., VOC 2417, Kerman to Gamron, March 19, 1737, fol. 4170; J. A. Saldanha, *The Persian Gulf Précis*, 8 vols. (Calcutta: Superintendant of Govt. Printing, 1906) (reprint Gerrards Cross: Archive Editions, 1986), 1:51, Feb. 25, 1737. (In Kerman, "silver money was at one hundred per cent. Exchange. . . . old copper at Carmania was twenty nine Shahees that maund . . . Abbases at five Shahees, or Black Money or old Copper.")

75. Matthee, Floor, and Clawson, *Monetary History*, p. 156.

76. Matthee, Floor, and Clawson, *Monetary History*, pp. 158–159.

77. Lockhart, *Nadir*, p. 254; Matthee, Floor, Clawson, *Monetary History*, pp. 161–162.

78. VOC 2710, f. 1480; Willem Floor, *The Rise of the Gulf Arabs: The Politics of Trade on the Northern Persian Littoral 1730–1792* (Washington, DC: MAGE, 2007), pp. 87–93.

79. John Perry, *Karim Khan Zand* (Chicago: Chicago University Press, 1979); Bakikhanov, *The Heavenly Rose-Garden: A History of Shirvan & Daghestan*, translated by Willem Floor and Hasan Javadi (Washington, DC: MAGE, 2010), pp. 138–149; Samuel Gottlieb Gmelin, *Travels through Northern Persia 1770–1774*, translated and annotated by Willem Floor (Washington, DC, MAGE, 2007), pp. 11–12, 97–100.

80. Perry, *Karim Khan Zand*, pp. 246–271.

81. Floor, *The Persian Gulf: The Rise of the Gulf Arabs. The Politics of trade on the northern Persian littoral 1730–1792* (Washington, DC: MAGE, 2007), pp. 90, 202; Matthee, Floor, Clawson, *Monetary History*, p. 173.

82. A. A. Amin, *British Interests in the Persian Gulf 1747–1780* (Leiden: Brill, 1976), chapter 7.

83. Lockhart, *Nadir Shah*, pp. 197–211.
84. Hanway, *An Account*, vol. 1, p. 40.
85. Fariba Zarinebaf-Shahr, *Tabriz under Ottoman Rule (1725–1730)*, unpublished dissertation University of Chicago 1991, pp. 177–181; Bruce Masters, *The Origins of Western Economic Dominance in the Middle East: Mercantilism and the Islamic Economy of in Aleppo, 1600–1750* (New York, 1988), p. 31; Reza Sha'bani, *Tarikh-e ejtema'i-ye Iran dar 'asr-e Afshariyyeh* (Tehran: Novin, 1359/1980), pp. 431–455.
86. Perry, *Karim Khan Zand*, pp. 297–302.
87. William Francklin, *Observations Made on a Tour from Bengal to Persia in the Years 1786–1787* (London, 1790), p. 147.
88. Matthee, Floor, and Clawson, *Monetary History*, p. 175.
89. Floor, *Nader*, chapter 5.
90. Matthee, Floor, and Clawson, *Monetary History*, chapter 5.

9

Tribal Resurgence in the Eighteenth Century: A Useful Label?

WILLEM FLOOR

The Problem

The term tribal resurgence is almost invariably used as if the term explained some process or development, but nobody cared to define what this precisely entailed.[1] The contributors apparently consider the term self-explanatory and assume that the readers know what they were referring to. I for one still don't know what the users of this term mean to convey by this term. Lambton, who first used this term in connection with eighteenth-century Iran, did not explain what she meant by it either.[2] Lambton just posited that there were two tendencies in the eighteenth century; one was tribal resurgence and the other a decline of the bureaucracy. In her view both were caused by the collapse of the central government. She noted that such a phenomenon was not new, because the tribes had already reasserted themselves after the death of Abbas I, and that by the end of seventeenth century there was an upsurge of tribal activity at Iran's borders.

According to the dictionary, resurgence means "a continuing after interruption; a renewal," and also "a restoration to use, acceptance, activity, or vigor; a revival." Reassertion means among other things "to make other people recognize again your right or authority to do something, after a period when this has been in doubt" or "to start to have an effect again." None of these meanings are entirely satisfactory in this context, but let's assume that Lambton and those who used the term in this conference meant to say that there was an increased presence felt of tribes through violent and/or unruly behavior.[3] In fact, later she qualified it as "the changed position of the tribes."[4] If that is acceptable, then we should ask ourselves why Lambton excluded the situation in the sixteenth century from her

analysis. For that century was the scene of much tribal resurgence and reassertion, as Lambton would call it, both at the border and in the interior of Iran. The
Safavid family itself was part of the Aq-Qoyunlu tribal group that governed much
of Iran (Esma'il I was just an Aq-Qoyunlu pretender in another guise). Therefore,
can we characterize the Safavid chief's victory over the other Aq-Qoyunlu pre-
tenders as tribal resurgence? Moreover, Esma'il I's reign was marred by regular,
sometimes long and drawn-out, warfare against tribal and other local interest
groups in Khuzestan, Gilan, Mazandaran, Khorasan, Kurdistan, and Shirvan. Was
this tribal resurgence or tribal suppression by a rival tribal group? Things were not
much better under Tahmasp I, who also had to deal with tribal revolts in various
parts of his realm. In addition, there were two Qezelbash civil wars (1524–1532
and 1577–1587), which also were a form of tribal resurgence. However, Lambton
does not include that period in her analysis, for unknown reasons. Maybe she
assumed that there was (a) no decline of the bureaucracy and (b) no breakdown
of central government in that century. However, if both in the sixteenth and eighteenth century there was much tribal resurgence, why is the one different from the
other or not? Also, as Lambton did not define the exact meaning of "decline" and
"breakdown," how are we going to measure such developments? Was the fact that
Khorasan was overrun by Uzbeks for many years a sign of breakdown of central
government? If not, when do we determine that such decline has taken place?

The Disagreement

Because of the above and other reasons that I discuss below, I don't think that the
label "tribal resurgence" is a very useful one. I deliberately use the term "label" to
convey the fact that scholars invariably use this term without taking the trouble to
explain it or look beyond its immediate connotation. To gauge the usefulness of
this term I think it is necessary to understand the context in which it is used, that
is, within the structure of Iran's political system, because it is only then that we may
also better understand terms such as "decline of the bureaucracy" and "breakdown
of central government," if indeed such developments took place. Therefore, I briefly
outline the main characteristics of that political system, after which I discuss
whether the terms "tribal resurgence" and "decline of the bureaucracy" enlighten
us as to the functioning of the political system of eighteenth-century Iran.

Iran's Political System

Safavid Iran was a preindustrial state. Communications were badly developed,
and the population was diverse in language, ethnicity, and religion. Outside the

cities, which may have housed 15 percent of the population, people were either sedentary, living in villages, or pastoralists, migrating annually in tribal groups. The pastoral population probably constituted 25–30 percent of the whole and increased during unsettled times.

The Safavid, Afsharid, and Zand political system was patrimonial—that is, the shah was the sole source of political power. His dominance was reinforced by his religious standing as spiritual guide of the Safavid order. His will was executed through the civil bureaucracy, and if need be, by the army. Both were loyal to the shah rather than to the political system. This did not change, even though the size, organization, and implementation tools of the bureaucracy and army changed over time. Hence, political rule, relations, and responsibilities were highly personalized. This meant that the members of the civil, religious, and military inner circle surrounding the shah derived their influence and power from their proximity to the shah. Thus, it was not so much their functions and responsibilities that gave them their power, but the knowledge that they held their functions for the shah or for one of his important magnates.

In keeping with this patrimonial structure, the shah took care to be aware of what his immediate advisors and executives were doing. Therefore, he allowed direct access to his person by a great many people outside his group of close advisors. Contemporary observers were surprised to see that the common people could approach the shah with their complaints on all kinds of occasions.[5]

The shah's personal household was a model for a patrimonial system that permeated society, a society that itself was composed of a large number of subordinate patrimonial households that vied with each other both vertically and horizontally to increase their influence and power. For those at the bottom of society this meant getting the ear of someone higher on the ladder, and so on, all the way to the ruler. At all levels there were rivalries, scheming, and conflicts between patrimonial households of the same rank. The shah, to further his own authority, encouraged and manipulated such rivalries. The conflicts both managed tensions and reinforced the primacy of the shah and the stability of the political system. The system thus did not usually eradicate those who fell out of line but rather doled out castigation and punishment and then brought dissenters back into the fold again or replaced them with family members.[6] Thus, accommodation rather than confrontation was the guiding principle of the patrimonial system.

This patrimonial system clearly was not "Oriental despotism,"[7] if we conceive that as a rigid tip-down system of authority. Rather the patrimonial system was centered around the figure of the shah, who acted as a force binding it together. The system also had checks and balances in that the shah had to respect "right, reason, custom, and Islam,"[8] as well as the self-interest of those who supported the system he headed. Failure to do so could lead to rebellion, to weakening of the central authority, and even to the fall of the dynasty.

Because of the underdevelopment of the communications system and the high cost of absolutist central control, the shah exercised selective control only. That, is provincial, local, and other leaders were given responsibility but not real authority. This served to minimize initiative, to foster obedience, and, above all, to maximize uncertainty. To reduce the risk of the rise of local power bases, governors were usually rotated annually, sometimes even more often. The shah also aimed to increase his hold on the local rulers through the judicious use of military force and other coercive measures. Various local rulers were therefore permitted to continue to exercise their traditional role in a precisely circumscribed way, which served to formalize their submission to the center.[9]

From the above it is clear that Iran was a rather weak state with a weak central government. The various administrative jurisdictions enjoyed self-government to a large extent, as did many corporate groups, such as tribes, guilds, and village communities. As long as the corporate groups paid their taxes and did not try to tilt the balance of power, they were allowed to administer their own internal affairs without too much governmental interference. This policy did not stem from some democratic notion, but rather from the fact that the power elite did not have the manpower to extend its sphere of influence to all layers of society. Furthermore, the difficulty of communications greatly hampered the effectiveness of the central government. In the outlying provinces all this forced the central government to rely on the local elites. This cooperation between the central government and the local influential families enhanced the position of both. The central government was thus assured of powerful local support, which gave a boost to its not infrequently unstable rule.

Therefore, the central government concentrated on one task, viz., the collection of taxes, neglecting other functions such as the provision of public services and the maintenance of order, leaving these functions to the local elites.[10] Many government offices were sold to the highest bidder, and the collection of taxes was farmed out. But not only the wealthy and powerful shared in the spoils. A whole army of clients, relatives, and other supporters also profited from their patrons' positions. They often acted as the agents of their patrons and/or the subtenants of offices and of tax farms. Thus, local government constituted the backbone of Iran's administrative system or bureaucracy. Its main function was to levy of taxes and maintain law and order. Local "dynasties" of kalantars, sheikhs, kadkhodas, zabets, and so forth guaranteed stability, the steady flow of funds, and taxes. But this decentralization of power did not mean that the center relinquished its sovereignty; rather it served to underscore that sovereignty, because the center could intervene whenever it wished to do so.[11]

Tribal Resurgence: System-Neutral

What the above implies is that when there was a challenge to the central government's authority and sovereignty, which even might lead to its overthrow,
this did not mean that the administrative system was done away with. In fact,
what we see is that each new set of rulers (Aq-Qoyunlu, Safavid, Ghilzay, Afshar,
Zand, Qajar) had recourse to and relied on local structures that remained in
place irrespective of who ruled. Certainly, the upper echelon of bureaucracy may
have been wiped out and/or replaced, but it could be and was easily replaced,
and the new rulers and their magnates linked with the local administrators to
facilitate tax payments and maintenance of law and order.

Similarly, whether the ruler was Ghilzay, Afshar, or Zand, none of them
changed the structure of society or the essentials of the political system. All of
them had been part of that system, their own previously subordinate patrimonial household had now become the central patrimonial household. The only
change in the political system was the rationalization of the legitimacy of the
new shahs, because none of them were Safavids, although the new rulers all married Safavid women. Whereas the Ghilzays relied on the force of power, the later
Nader Shah Afshar made an effort to acquire legitimacy and first ruled as Safavid
viceroy then as regent, after which he had himself crowned by acclamation,
while the Zands for the same reasons of legitimacy likewise ruled as viceroys
for the Safavids.[12] Also, in a great many cases during the Afshar and Zand period
many of the hereditary governors, or at least members of their family, remained
in power.[13] This held even more so for subordinate local officials such as *kalantars*, *kadkhodas*, *zabets*, and sheikhs. Thus, there was no structural change in the
political system, and therefore, the increase or decrease of tribal forces or tribal
resurgence made no difference in how the system functioned, although some of
its administrative methods may have been adapted. Therefore, the term "tribal
resurgence" suggests more than it actually means; it was incidental and did not
upset the structure and nature of the political system.

Decline of the Influence of the Bureaucracy?
Not Really

Let's now have a look the alleged decline of the bureaucracy, the other major
development that Lambton observed during the eighteenth century. This question seems to be a no-brainer. Let's have a look at the facts. Mahmud and Ashraf
Ghilzay killed hundreds if not thousands of top-level bureaucrats and destroyed
most Safavid records. Moreover, some of Nader's generals destroyed much

of the remaining records a decade later.[14] If this did not led to a decline of the bureaucracy, what did then?

The same Mahmud, as ruler of much of Iran, started to realize that he might have acted somewhat too hastily when destroying much of Iran's bureaucracy and its records. He may have been a leader of the Ghilzay Afghans and allied tribes, but tribal does not necessarily mean that its leadership is antibureaucratic or anti-central control. On the contrary, control is what tribal leadership of a large confederacy is all about. Also, Ghilzay leaders had long held a position in the Safavid bureaucracy as the *kalantar*s of Qandahar. They were no novices to bureaucratic practice and, therefore, they sought advice and recreated the central bureaucracy. Mahmud Ghilzay had Mirza Sami'a write the *Tazkerat al-Moluk*, a state manual that detailed how the country was managed and who should pay how much in taxes and which officials received how much in payment for what kind of function.[15] Mahmud also had a full-fledged "cabinet" and staff to manage the country's affairs, including a *qurchi-bashi* (commander of the Qezelbash levies) and a *qollar-aghasi* (commander of the royal slaves)![16] His successor Ashraf did likewise; he had Mirza Rafi'a write the *Dastur al-Moluk*,[17] another state manual, and also had his own "cabinet" and related staff, exactly like that of his predecessor in composition. Both rulers struck coins after the Safavid model and had a bureaucracy to write their *farman*s, letters, and other documents. Although the Afghan reign was too short to assess how well their central bureaucracy had developed, there is no doubt that its reach was obeyed throughout their realm. For there was a strong central government. Both Mahmud and Ashraf were obeyed in the outlying parts of Iran they controlled. Their governors carried out their orders and instructions, for which they received robes of honor and made use of the local administrative structure to raise funds and get things done.[18] Tahmasp II Safavi from the very beginning kept a court-in-exile that in composition reflected that of his father. He also had a "cabinet," had an administrative organization to write documents and keep records, and struck coins. After he regained the throne at the end of 1729, nevertheless, even he felt the need for more information, for in 1731, his *vaqaye'-nevis*, Mirza Naqi Nasiri wrote the third Safavid state manual.[19]

In short, there is no doubt that there was a decline in the size of the central bureaucracy, but did that mean that there was also a decline in its capability? The authors of the three state manuals all were scions of bureaucratic families, who were already part of the bureaucratic system prior to the Safavid dynasty and also served its successors. Therefore, they were easily able to write these manuals as they knew the system and how it functioned very well and were able to rely on their family's records to recreate any datum that was needed. In particular, Mirza Naqi Nasiri's book is telling in this respect as he was able, for example, to provide precise information on the titles and honorifics of each official in the bureaucratic system and the number of troops the various governors had to maintain.

Does the lack of records at the central level and the strong countercurrent from the central government to recreate a central administrative capability not show how right Lambton was? In the following I discuss that in my view that was not the case, while I also discuss how the central government dealt with and overcame the lack of a central database in a practical manner. Lambton argued that "[t]he decline of the bureaucracy was also probably a contributory factor militating against the growth of a slave army. It was no longer capable of administering such an army." While recognizing that without a tax assessment it was difficult to provide and pay troops, Lambton further asserts that "already before the fall of the Safavids the complicated administrative machinery for allocating the funds to its military and civil officials had ceased to function effectively."[20] This last statement does not seem to be borne out by the facts. First, it would seem that there was a system in place to keep good records. The so-called third Safavid state manual describes the task of the *daftardar* or archivist as follows:

> His function is to prevent the royal books that are in the secretariat from being eaten by mice and from dirt and dust as required. Each one of them is kept at a fixed place and he does not allow an outsider [to the administration] to see [them]. After the year has come to an end the book of that year is taken to the storage space, where they are kept. In the morning, before the department heads are present in the secretariat he arranges the books in their places and when the clerks are finished with the books and go outside of the secretariat he closed the books and kept them so that nothing would happen to them.[21]

It was unlikely that this system still existed in 1731, at least in Isfahan,[22] when the above quoted text was written, but the detailed description suggests that it certainly did prior to 1722.

Second, this is confirmed by a careful observer like Engelbert Kaempfer, who in the mid-1680s noted that the Safavid fiscal administration was well organized and that it kept good records. He wrote: "The chamber of the *lashkar-nevis* deals with the salaries of officials, courtiers, soldiers, artisans and servants, listing with exactness the name of each one, his place of birth, where he lives, his function, his salary, and what day after day has been paid or paid in advance (*with great exactness down to the cent*) and making the calculation of how much has to be paid to each."[23] This contemporary appreciation of the effectiveness of the administration is also borne out by other data, such as referred to in the next paragraph.

Third, from the surviving Safavid chancellery documents it is clear that whenever a claimant asked for confirmation of his salary, stipend, or some other form of payment, the Safavid bureaucracy was able to trace the original document(s) awarding the payment, the documents making changes therein or awarding the payment to an heir, and any other relevant factor.[24] The following gives an example of such a document (in a very abridged form) from 1706, or in a period, when according to Lambton the Safavid bureaucracy no longer functioned effectively. The document concerns a request from the heirs of Mirza Beg Fendereski to have the *soyurghal-e abadi* of their father of 30 *tumans* transferred to them. The assets office (*sarkar-e avarajeh*) of Azerbaijan confirmed that indeed such an amount had been granted to the deceased by a decree dated Safar 1078/July–August 1677, which was based on an edict by Abbas II from Rajab 1076/January 1666, and that the allotment was charged to the following listed sources. Moreover, another amount, which is named, was allotted by an edict dated Shavval 1034/July 1625, while the document ends with a detailed reasoning of how the inheritance was going to be transferred. In short, this document shows a bureaucracy that had records and could find individual documents in 1713 going back to the original grant in 1625; not so bad for an allegedly failing bureaucracy.[25]

It is, of course, true that this task became almost impossible in the absence of most of these records at the central government level after their destruction in 1722 and 1732. This may explain why under Tahmasp II and his successors the system of awarding revenue assignments to government officials was replaced by direct payments. This system obviated a connection between the tax assessment and the provision of troops. Nevertheless, there was a need to get a better understanding of the country's fiscal resources, as financial needs were high and urgent, which is exactly what Nader ordered in 1737–1738. The result was what has been called the best fiscal assessment made up till then, an assessment that was still used by the Qajars, when conditions had returned to normal.[26] Now, if this is true, then this high-quality output cannot have been produced by a bureaucracy in decline nor could it have been because "the old administrative tradition lingered on."[27] Therefore, we have to assume that the administrative apparatus was still quite capable and effective at doing their jobs. The fact that the relevant documents and know-how about the situation in the provinces and their districts were kept by families of bureaucrats, both at the national and the local level, facilitated such a task, of course.

The above means that there was no financial or administrative impediment to form a slave army. There was just a conscious and explicit choice not to raise such an army as there was neither need nor comparative advantage to having it. The Qajars later on under more normal circumstances did not create a slave army either. However, more importantly, how true is my argument that the local structures were the backbone of the bureaucracy? Lambton herself already pointed out that local leaders emerged when central government broke down.[28] These local leaders, however, did not emerge *sui generis* or function in a political vacuum as she seems to imply, but continued to be the executive arm of the central government, even though some local leaders may have acted independently for a period of time. In fact, Lambton herself writes that these officials were absorbed by the Safavid administration and likewise by the administration of succeeding regimes. The *kalantar* of Fars, Mirza Mohammad, had to ask permission to retire in 1760, which indicates he was very much an official in service of the central government that had appointed him in the first place. The breakdown of central government during the successions wars (1748–1759) did not change that; it only emphasized the fact that the local administration was the backbone of the system. Moreover, it was not a ramshackle system, but rather one that functioned quite effectively as a bureaucracy, as is clear from the surviving documents of that period.[29]

Take, for example, the patrimonial household of Ebrahim Khan of Qarabagh. He had started out as a lowly *beg* of the subordinate Javanshir tribe in the Qarabagh area, served for a time in Nader's army, fled in 1738 and went into hiding, became a bandit in 1747, and then with his band was able to take control in Qarabagh and sometimes over a larger area. Like the Afshar and Zand rulers at the national level, "his officials were his brothers and their sons, his children, and were all noted *beg*s. Each of them, in property and wealth, retainers, and splendor, was equal to the khans of other *velayats*."[30] In the service of his court and provincial bureaucracy he employed *minbashis, yuzbashis, monshis, eshiq-aghasis, keshikchis, yasavols, nazers,* and so forth.[31] He also had good fiscal records. "All the tribesmen of Qarabagh, who were listed in the rolls and registers, formed the cavalry," in exchange for tax-exempt status. When mercenaries had to be hired, even the tax-exempt tribes paid contributions in cash (*towjih*) and kind, but when serving in the army, feed for their horses and cost of gear was at the Khan's expense.[32] This does not sound like a bureaucracy in decline, and if Ebrahim Khan's case is an example of tribal resurgence, then I must say tribes remarkably behaved like effective components within the national political and administrative structure.

Discussion

Above I have shown that increased activity by tribes had no impact whatsoever on the nature and structure of the political system of Iran. After their conquest of Iran, the Ghilzays, Afshars, Zands, and Qajars did not establish a new political order or start a reorganization of the existing societal structures. Rather they imposed themselves upon the existing situation, putting their own people in positions that had been occupied by members of the previous power elite. On the local level they left the system as it was, as they did with the holders of the offices there. Local influential families and tribal chiefs were left in their places and merely "converted" into supporters of the new regime. They also made sure that their central government was strong, and they bloodily suppressed any sign of disobedience.

There is no doubt that the central Safavid bureaucracy was debilitated by the killing of hundreds, if not more, of its members and the destruction of most records in Isfahan in 1723. However, the new central governments quickly acquired information about the way in which the system was supposed to work (confirming the above observation that nothing changed), adapted themselves quickly by changing the method of the payment system (direct payments instead of revenue assignments),[33] established a new database through their reliance on the backbone of the system, viz., the local bureaucrats and chiefs, and continued with a new set of tax records as if nothing had changed. In short, tribal resurgence does not explain what happened in Iran at the end of the seventeenth and throughout the eighteenth century. The tribal elite were part of the political system that had its ups and downs, its ebbs and floods. Likewise, the bureaucracy was not in decline; the moment a new central government had securely installed itself, it established a financial administration at the national level, linking with the provincial and local level to ensure that its lifeblood, taxes, were collected and paid.

Notes

1. Michael Axworthy was the only other participant who queried the usefulness of the term "tribal resurgence" at the conference; his comments on this matter appear on pages 2 and 53 in this volume.
2. A. K. S. Lambton, "The tribal resurgence and the decline of the bureaucracy in the eighteenth century," in Thomas Naff and Roger Owen, eds., *Studies in Eighteenth Century Islamic History* (Carbondale: Southern Illinois University Press, 1977), pp. 108–129, 377–382 (notes).
3. Lambton, "The Tribal Resurgence," p. 108.
4. Lambton, "The Tribal Resurgence," p. 120.
5. Willem Floor, "The Secular Judicial System in Safavid Persia," *Studia Iranica* 29 (2000), pp. 13–19.
6. For example, in 1505 Esma'il I intervened militarily in Gilan-e biyeh-pas to call Amireh Hosam al-Din to order, who remained in power despite continued defiant behavior. Budaq 94; Qomi I, 87; Monshi 1, 31; Hoseyni 221–222; Qomi 1, 141; Shirazi 44. A similar operation took place in Mazandaran in 1518, where the rebellious local ruler was allowed to continue in office. Shirazi, *Takmelat*, pp. 56–58; Bidlisi, *Cheref-Nameh*, vol. 2, p. 534; Qazvini, *Tarikh*, p. 278. Despite the enmity that existed between the Shirvanshahs and the Safavids, Shah Esma'il I allowed the son of his slain foe to govern Shirvan. Khatunabadi 441; Dorn 590; Qomi 1, 139; Shirazi 58–59, 135. Likewise, Tahmasp I forgave his brothers, Sam Mirza

and Alqas Mirza after they had rebelled. Tahmasp also pardoned Malek Soltan Mahmud for his support of Sam Mirza's rebellion. Monshi 57. Abbas I twice intervened in Arabistan to call Sayyed Mobarak to order, but each time reinstated him. Minorsky, "Musha'sha'," *Encyclopedia of Islam*.[1]

7. For a discussion of the various forms of despotisms, see Richard Koebner, "Despot and Despotism: Vicissitudes of a Political Term," in *Journal of the Warburg and Courtauld Institutes* 14, 3/4 (1951), pp. 275–302; Sven Stelling-Michaud, "Le mythe du despotisme oriental," in *Schweizer Beiträge zur allgemeinen Geschichte*, 18–19, 1960–1961, pp. 328–346; Melvin Richter, "The Concept of Despotism and l'Abus des Mots," in *Contributions to the History of Concepts*, 3, 2007, pp. 5–22.

8. For the importance of these concepts, see, for example, Nezam al-Molk's *Siyar al-moluk*, al-Ghazali's *Nasihat al-moluk*, and Keykavus's *Qabusnameh*.

9. The position of the *valis*, such as the rulers of Georgia and Kurdistan come to mind.

10. See on the tasks of government G. Sjoberg, *The Pre-Industrial City: Past and Present* (Glencoe: University of Illinois Press, 1960), pp. 244–252; see also Willem Floor, "The office of *kalantar* in Qajar Persia," *Journal of the Economic and Social History of the Orient* (JESHO), vol. 14 (1971), pp. 253–268.

11. For a detailed discussion, see Willem Floor, *The Fiscal History of Safavid and Qajar Iran* (New York: Bibliotheca Persica, 2000), chapter 1.

12. Willem Floor, *The Rise and Fall Nader Shah* (Washington, DC: Mage, 2009); idem, *The Afghan Occupation of Persia, 1722–1730* (Paris: Cahiers Studia Iranica, 1998); Laurence Lockhart, *Nadir Shah* (London: Luzac, 1938); John Perry, *Karim Khan Zand* (Chicago: Chicago University Press, 1979); Lambton, "The Tribal Resurgence," pp. 116–120, 127.

13. Mirza Naqi Nasiri, *Titles and Emoluments in Safavid Iran: A Third Safavid State Manual*. Translation and commentary by Willem Floor (Washington, DC: MAGE, 2008).

14. Lambton, "The Tribal Resurgence," p. 112.

15. Mirza Sami'a, *The Tadhkirat al-Muluk*, ed. and translated by Vladimir Minorsky (London, printed for the Trustees of the "E. J. W. Gibb memorial," published by Luzac, 1943).

16. Floor, *The Afghan Occupation of Persia, 1722–1730*, pp. 175–176.

17. Mirza Rafi'a, *Dastur al-Moluk: A Safavid State Manual*. Translated and annotated by Willem Floor and Mohammad Faghfoory (Costa Mesa, CA: Mazda, 2007).

18. Willem Floor, *The Afghan Occupation of Persia, 1722–1730* (Paris: Cahiers Studia Iranica, 1998), pp. 175–176, 236, 322; Rudi Matthee, Willem Floor, and Patrick Clawson, *The Monetary History of Safavid, Afsharid and Qajar Iran* (London: IB Tauris, 2013).

19. Nasiri, *Titles and Emoluments*; Matthee, Floor, and Clawson *The Monetary History*.

20. Lambton, "The Tribal Resurgence," pp. 111–112.

21. Nasiri, *Titles and Emoluments*, p. 73. The same text offers descriptions of the tasks of other fiscal officials.

22. For example, it may still have existed in provincial centers as evidenced by the library of the shrine of Imam Reza, which has an extensive collection of fiscal documents from the Safavid period, see Abu Fazl Hasanabadi and Elaheh Mahbub, "Introducing the Safavid Documents of the Directorate of Documents and Publications of the Central Library of the Holy Shrine at Mashhad (Iran)," *Iranian Studies* 42/2 (2009), pp. 314–326.

23. Engelbert Kaempfer, *Amoenitatum Exoticarum politico-physico-medicarum fasciculi V, variae relationes, observationes & descriptiones Rerum Persicarum* (Lemgoviae [Lemgo, Germany]: Typis & impensis H.W. Meyeri, 1712), p. 89 (my italics).

24. See the text of many documents in Renate Schimkorheit, *Regesten publizierter safawidischer Herrscherurkunden* (Berlin: Klaus Schwarz, 1982), pp. 296–453.

25. Schimkorheit, *Regesten*, pp. 380–383.

26. Floor, *Fiscal History*, pp. 242, 336.

27. Lambton, "The Tribal Resurgence," p. 112.

28. Lambton, "The Tribal Resurgence," pp. 120–121.

29. See, for example, the many detailed and varied administrative documents in K. P. Kostiyan, ed., *Persian Documents of the Matenadaran—Decrees* (1652–1731), vol. 3 (Yerevan: National Academy of Sciences, 2005); idem, *Persian Documents of the Matenadaran*, (1734–1797), vol. 4 (Yerevan: Nairi, 2008); Magali A. Todua and Ismail K. Shams, eds., *The Collection*

of *Persian Firmans of Tbilisi*, 2 vols. (Tiflis: Central Historical Archives of Georgia, 1989); Mamad Taqi Musavi, *Orta asr Azarbaijan tarikhina dair fars-dili sanadlar XVI–XVIII asrlar* (Baku: Elm, 1977).

30. George A. Bournoutian, *A History of Qarabagh: An annotated translation of Mirza Jamal Javanshir Qarabaghi's Tarikh-e Qarabagh* (Costa Mesa: Mazda, 1994), p. 136.

31. Bournoutian, *A History*, pp. 133, 136.

32. Bournoutian, *A History*, p. 133. For the similar case of Lotf Ali Khan of Darband, Qubeh, and Saliyan as well as of Hedayat Khan of Gilan, see Samuel Gottlieb Gmelin, *Travels through Northern Persia 1770–1774*, translated and annotated by Willem Floor (Washington, DC: MAGE, 2007), pp. 25, 43, 99, 101–102, 148.

33. Although this was a significant change, it was not a structural one, because already under the Zands this system was not universally applied and it was not adopted by the Qajars.

10

Iranian-Russian Relations in the Eighteenth Century

GOODARZ RASHTIANI

Introduction

With the expansion of relations between Iran and Russia in the Safavid period, especially after the reign of Shah Abbas I, and with the travel of representatives and ambassadors between Isfahan and Moscow, conditions were provided for the further growth of commercial transactions. Generally, the Safavid government had a privileged position in such relations. However, the last years of the reign of the Safavids coincided with the weakening of the central government in Iran, and relations between the two countries hit rock bottom, because at the time the central government in Russia, ruled by Peter the Great (1682–1725), was strengthening, characterized by territorial expansion to the south. This triggered the beginning of a new era in relations between the two countries, whose consequences and outcomes have been some of the most important issues of Iran's foreign relations in the centuries that followed.

The period from the fall of Isfahan (1722) to the rise of the Qajar dynasty (1795) is of great importance in historical studies in terms of relations with Tsarist Russia, because Iran's political sovereignty was confronted with a rising power on the northern border. Therefore, identification of various aspects of this historical period is considered a prerequisite to understanding political relations between the two countries later.

This period begins with the campaign of Peter I to the Iranian coasts of the Caspian Sea from Daghestan to Astarābād. This event meant the first attempt to change the relations between the two countries and develop territory toward areas which were historically part of the territory under Iran's sovereignty. The rise of Nader Shah thwarted the Russians from consolidating its position in those areas and made them return to their former borders.[1] During the rule of the Zand dynasty (1750–1794), the northern territories, particularly the Caucasus, were greatly neglected and, after the death of Karim Khan Zand (1751–1779), Georgia became Russia's protectorate in 1783. This provided the pretext for the interference of the Russian government in Iran's relations with the Caucasus khanates. The campaign of Agha Mohammad Khan Qajar (1789–1797) to this region and two periods of war with Russia during the reign of Fath Ali Shah (1797–1834) culminated in the Gulistan (1813) and Turkmenchay (1828) treaties. Additionally, the Tsarist government managed to achieve a superior economic position over Iran through diplomacy, such that Russia took the monopoly of trade in the Caspian Sea.

Hence, the eighteenth century began with an imbalance in relations between the two governments and Russia's dominance over parts of Iran and ended with an extensive campaign by Russia for further territorial development in Iran. In the middle of this century, there was a relatively long period with different characteristics than before, the most important of which included territorial development to the south, occupation of parts of Iran and establishment of military bases in those parts, conclusion of a number of treaties, exit from the occupied territories of Iran, efforts for a making an alliance against the Ottomans, Russia's attempts to spread its influence on Armenians and Georgians, and Russia's monopoly on trade and shipping in the Caspian Sea.

Interestingly, unlike the usual tradition of the time (and in contrast to Iran's relations with other countries), although significant developments had occurred in relations between the two countries and extensive military campaigns were mounted to the northern parts of Iran, none of them led to confrontation and war with Iran, which was an unusual phenomenon in international relations. On the other hand, although there was no military conflict between the two countries in this period, the Russians made extensive efforts to attract Armenians and Georgians (coreligionists of the Russians), to establish relations with the Caucasus khanates, to seize business opportunities in the Caspian Sea, and to establish commercial and military bases on the Iranian coasts of the Caspian Sea—which developments altogether can be referred to as "quiet encroachment," which made it easier for Russia to achieve victory in wars in the beginning of nineteenth century.

Diplomacy on the Eve of Crises: Relations with Russia during the Late Safavid Period

In the era of Shah Soltan Hossein (1694–1722), relations between Iran and Russia became quite different from the past and underwent fundamental changes. The rise of Peter I, who made changes in the industry, commerce, and culture of Russia in the early eighteenth century, led to the emergence of Russia as a global power, and these developments had a profound effect on Iran.

Many historical studies mention the mission of Israel Ori (1658–1711) as the first envoy of the Peter the Great to the Safavid court. However, it seems that he was not more than an adventurer and was not accepted even as the representative of Iran's Armenians, although he was in contact with some of Karabakh landlords. With letters of introduction from Leopold I[2] and Johann Wilhelm II,[3] he went to Russia through Poland[4] and, in his correspondence with Peter the Great, called for the liberation of Armenians from the domination of Iran and Ottoman, citing letters from a number of Iranian Armenians.[5]

Ori, with a delegation of 33 people, went to Iran in 1708. The French ambassador and some Catholic priests, due to a religious distrust of Armenians and Orthodox, banded together to thwart Ori's intentions.[6] The existing documents indicate that liberation of Armenians was just a pretext for Ori for gaining economic benefits and tax exemptions for export and import of goods between Iran and Russia.[7]

The Embassy of Artemy Volynsky and Its Achievements

At the same as he was fighting in northern Europe and with the Ottomans, Peter the Great also showed interest to Iran and Central Asia. The first relations were established with the Khanate of Khiva in 1700 and with Turkmen merchants, and the claim that gold had been found in the estuary of Oxus River (Amu Darya) had drawn the attention of Peter to the east more than ever. Sending ambassadors to Central Asia and Iran was another plan of Peter at the time. Accordingly, Bekovich-Cherkassky was sent to Transoxiana in May 1714, and Ivan Buchholz went to Khiva in November 1714.

In this context, Artemy Petrovich Volynsky, one of the young officers close to Peter, was appointed as the Russia's ambassador to Iran. In addition to signing a trade agreement with Iran, Volynsky was assigned the responsibility to conduct comprehensive studies on the geographical situation, communication ways, military forces, and ways of access to India.[8]

In addition to providing the necessary information, the achievements of this embassy were very important for Volynski and Russia from the perspective of trade relations, because an important trade agreement was signed between the two countries (in July 1717), based on which Russian merchants were allowed to trade throughout Iran and purchase silk as they wished. Moreover, Russia was given permission to establish a consulate in Isfahan (and later in Gilan),[9] and the

Iranian government pledged to protect Russian citizens from attacks of thieves and bandits.[10]

This contract is important in several aspects of the history of relations between Iran and Russia. First of all, it was the first formal bilateral agreement between the two countries. Secondly, it caused a great influx of Russians to commercial markets in Iran. The third point is that residence of the Russian consul in Iran was a special right awarded to that government, and subsequent events all indicated the important role of this Russian official in the regulation of bilateral relations between the two countries, particularly defending the interests of Russian merchants. As we will see, the Russian consul had a deputy or deputies in other towns such as Shamakhi, located in the eastern Caucasus, who were responsible for facilitating the realization of Russia's goals. Fourth, this contract was referenced as a basis for all future agreements between the two countries by the end of the Zand dynasty, and two paragraphs from it (concerning the residence of the Russian consul in Iran and free trade of Russians) were included in all subsequent contracts.

In letters to Shah Soltan Hossein in December 1721, Peter the Great appointed Semeon Avramov as the Russian consul in Rasht and Alexis Baskakov as his deputy in Shamakhi. Peter also asked Iranian rulers for their freedom of activity and residence and to provide necessary facilities for Russian merchants.[11] Trade development was so important for the Russian government that following the looting of Russian merchants' property in Bukhara, Peter the Great personally ordered Avramov to address the case according to the 1717 contract (June 1721).[12] Based on a report from another Russian merchant indicating the non-payment of his claim by local rulers in Iran,[13] Peter ordered the Russian consul in Rasht and his deputy in Shamakhi to secure redress for the lost rights of this merchant.[14]

Military Campaign of Peter the Great to the Caucasus and the Caspian Sea

The three main plans of Peter the Great in dealing with Iran were as follows:

1. The establishment of a safe trade route between Russia and India through the Caspian Sea and then through Khiva and Bukhara or Iran.
2. Full surveillance of Iran's silk trade.
3. Having the upper hand in the Caspian Sea (this was contingent on the achievement of two other objectives).
4. Preventing Ottoman expansion to the Eastern Caucasus and Caspian Sea

After the siege and fall of Isfahan by the Afghans in 1722, the looting of Russian merchants' property by Davoud Khan Lezgi provided the necessary pretext for Peter's attack. After arriving in Astrakhan on July 15, 1722, he addressed the King and people of Iran in a statement and assured that security would be provided for all.[15] Before leaving Astrakhan, Peter sent a person named Boris Turkestanov to King Vakhtang VI, the governor of Georgia, to inform him of his impending arrival in Iran and warn him to avoid war with Turkey.[16]

His campaign started from Astrakhan in July 1722 with 242 warships, 22,000 infantrymen,[17] 2,000 Kazakhs (the Kazakhs residing in Terek Valley), 22,000 Ghalmoughs, 30,000 Tatars, and 5,000 sailors. This 9,000-strong fleet, headed by General Terani, was sent overland.[18] After arriving in Derbent, Peter did not head to the south. Lockhart believes that Peter initially decided to continue ahead along the Caspian coast, but later he found that he could not do so without enough provisions—and he could not receive provisions from Astrakhan due to adverse seasonal conditions. Hence, he reluctantly avoided heading to the Caucasus. The arrival of an Ottoman ambassador also affected this decision of Peter the Great. Damat Ibrahim Paşa, the Prime Minister, had sent this ambassador to dissuade Peter from heading to Shirvan and thereby risking war between the two countries.[19]

Russian forces seized almost the whole western (Baku, Salyan, and Lankaran) and southern (Anzali and Rasht) coasts of the Caspian Sea a couple of weeks later. But the goal of Russia in relation to the liberation of Armenians and Georgians was not accomplished and other regions of the Caucasus were occupied by the Ottomans. A treaty was agreed in 1724 in Istanbul whereby Russia and the Ottomans recognized each other's possessions in the Caucasus and the Caspian Sea.

The Results of the Persian Campaign of Peter I

In his description of the results of Peter's attacks on Iran, Lockhart argues that Peter's expectations were not met in this campaign. In particular, he could not extend effective help to King Vakhtang or other Christian leaders in Transcaucasia. Furthermore, the cooling of Russia's relations with Turkey was an imminent possibility, and many people, about one-third of Peter's forces (33,000 people), lost their lives in this military campaign.[20] Altogether, 130,000 of them died in Iran at the time.[21] Considering that Russia had a garrison of 30,000 soldiers in those areas, about one-third of them died of disease,[22] exceeding the number of those who lost their lives as a result of fighting with the clans and tribes of those areas. These people died not because of war, but because of climatic conditions in northern Iran. This region for half a year has warm and humid weather, which was unbearable for the Russians. Lack of sanitary facilities and epidemics also accelerated the rate of mortalities.

Peter the Great's failure to push into Georgia brought catastrophic consequences for Vakhtang and led to his removal from the Georgian government by Tahmasp II. Finally, Vakhtang took refuge in Russia.[23] Another of Peter's unaccomplished goals was the revival of trade between Britain and Iran through Russia. A few months before his death, Peter the Great asked a merchant named Richard Mainwaring, who was bound for England, to discuss this with his comrades in London. In this regard, Jonas Hanway writes, "Although Peter was aware of many problems with this plan, he did not anticipate all of its difficulties. His death put an end to this issue and British merchants who feared the risks of trade via Russia prevented the implementation of this plan until an unexpected event occurred in 1738 and opened new windows for commercial activities."[24]

The following year, the Russians made efforts to legalize their possessions in Iran through signing a contract with Ismail Beg, the ambassador of Tahmasp II. However, this contract was not approved by the king,[25] and from this time onwards, the Russians efforts were focused more on the basis of the agreement made with the Ottomans in 1724.

Nader Shah: A Return to the Former State and Formation of a Boundary between the Two Countries

With the rising power Tahmasp Gholi Khan (later called Nader Shah), Iran adopted a stricter policy toward the presence of the Russians. Astarabadi states that the first relations of Nader Shah with Russia date back to late 1728, when he sent a message through Tahmasp to the Russian court and required them to evacuate Gilan. In a report sent to London in October 1728, Ostanian pointed out that when Iran became united under a prince, his first decision would be to reclaim the Russian possessions and expel them from that part of Asia, which is referred to as the Muslim heritage.[26]

Nader's policy toward Russia was initially focused on the evacuation of occupied territories. Accordingly, in 1728, he warned Avramov that if his military campaign against Abdali Afghans were to be successful, the Russians residing in Iran should get on board the ship and return to their own country.[27] Avramov adds, "When he was going to return to Russia in January 1729, he asked Tahmasp's Etemad Al-Doleh [Tahmasp's vizier] why that prince does not request help from the Russians against his enemies? He replied that if Tahmasp does so, Nader Shah will not serve him anymore and his position will be precarious."[28]

Once the position of Nader Shah was fully consolidated, he sent a letter to Anna Ioannovna, the Empress of Russia (1730–1740), and called for the immediate evacuation of the occupied areas of Iran. The Russian government also referred this issue to its commanders based in Gilan.[29] According to Astarabadi, it can be concluded that the Russians had developed their possessions at that time and also dominated Soltanieh.[30]

Ultimately, a treaty was signed between Peter Shafirov and Mirza Mohammad Ibrahim Mostofi in Rasht in January 1732 under which it was decided that the Russians evacuate Gilan, Mazandaran, and Astarābād. The Russians pledged that in the case of evacuation of the Caucasian lands by the Ottomans, they would also transfer the lands to the north of the Kura River (Baku and Derbent) to Iran. Another provision of this treaty was the free trade of Russian merchants in Iran and permission for the residence of the Russian consul in Iran.[31]

Empress Anna, in April 1732, announced the approval of the Treaty of Rasht and called it binding for her government. In a separate letter, she appointed Avramov as the Russian ambassador to Iran and reiterated that Shafirov and Vasili Levashov also continue their services in Iran. In an order issued to General Levashov on August 31, 1733, Empress Anna asked him to cooperate with Nader and peoples of the Caucasus in the fight against the Ottoman Empire.[32]

From then on, Nader had congenial relations with Russia, as he frequently sent greetings on the occasion of the accession of Russian monarchs, including Elizabeth Petrovna (1741–1762), expressing his hope for the continuation of friendship between the two countries. In another letter, Nader stated that despite all conflicts between the two countries, he hoped that intimacy and congeniality between Iran and Russia would be strengthened. He reiterates the same hope in a letter to a Russian minister.[33]

Treaty of Ganja (1735)

In 1733, Sergei Golitsyn, Russia's ambassador went to Isfahan to visit Nader, at the request of Empress Anna, and asked to accompany the Persian army on campaign.[34] After returning from Daghestan in August 1734, Nader started war with the Ottomans and the siege of Ganja. Nader's first campaign in Daghestan increased the sensitivity of the Russians to his presence close to the borders of Russia. Hence, in letters to him in October 1734, the Russian Foreign Ministry urged him to clarify the objective of his presence in Daghestan.[35]

It seems that Golitsyn's good relationship with Nader enabled him to reassure the Russian government that Nader's actions were merely aimed at dealing with Daghestan insurgents and were not to the detriment of Russia's interests. At the same time Prince Golitsyn provided Nader with the necessary equipment for siege warfare: heavy artillery and engineers. Given the weakness of the Iranian army at this time in siege artillery, this assistance of Russia was greatly useful and shows the Russians' firm decision to support Iran to defeat the Ottomans.[36]

At this time, Nader negotiated with Golitsyn on the Russian evacuation of the remaining provinces of Iran. During these negotiations (at Ganja), Golitsyn reported to Empress Anna that the Iranians were calling for the destruction of the Chapel of the Holy Cross (constructed by Peter the Great to the north of Darband for the use of Russian troops). But Golitsyn did not refuse to abandon this place to the Iranians.[37]

The Russians, facing an imminent war against the Western powers because of the Poland Crisis in Europe, and risking the emergence of an alliance between Iran and Turkey in the East, decided to withdraw their military forces from these areas in the hope that an alliance with Iran would serve Russian interests as well, or better.

Therefore, during the siege of Ganja in 1735, Baku and Derbent were evacuated; it was agreed that the captives of both sides be released, and the Soulak River in northern Daghestan would be the border between the two countries.[38] The important point of this treaty was the determination of the boundary between Iran and Russia because there were no clear boundaries between the two states before that time.[39]

This treaty also strengthened the alliance of Iran and Russia against the Ottomans.[40] The Soulak river remained as the boundary of the countries until the Treaty of Gulistan in 1813. After the return of Golitsyn, Nader appointed Mirza Kafi Naseri Kholafa as Iran's ambassador to Russia and sent him to that country with many gifts.[41] In a letter, he also congratulated Empress Anna on her victories against the Ottomans.[42]

While Nader was in Daghestan, some Russian agents expressed concern about Nader's movements on the borders of Russia and speculated that these could lead to an invasion of Russia under the pretext of chasing Daghestani insurgents.[43] In addition, Nader received news indicating that the Russians were involved in stimulating these insurgents and harboring them.[44] Russians support for the Daghestani rebels is an interesting topic, but it is mentioned only in this source.

At the same time that Iranian forces were fighting in Daghestan, based on a report of Kaloshkin suggesting that Tahmasp (now deposed) might try to flee to Russia disguised as a German, the Russian government in May 1738 ordered Jünger, chief of the military police in Astrakhan, to carefully control all ports, harbors, and police stations to prevent Tahmasp from entering Russia, in order to avoid problems for Iran-Russia relations.[45]

The need to fight the common enemy of both countries (i.e., the Ottoman Empire) underlay long negotiations on an alliance between Iran and Russia.[46] Interestingly, although the governments of Iran and Russia had placed great emphasis on unity and joint action against the Ottoman Empire, this plan was never put into action,[47] because neither of them wanted to give up their short-term and long-term interests in favor of each other's interests. Hence, they failed to forge an effective alliance against the Ottomans. On the other hand, Ottoman diplomacy had the necessary experience and cleverness not to act against Iran and Russia at the same time.

Another aspect of relations between Iran and Russia was related to Nader Shah's plan for the establishment and development of shipping in the Caspian Sea—something which was overtly and covertly opposed by Russia, and they spared no effort to thwart measures of John Elton, who was serving Nader Shah in the execution of this plan.[48]

Nader Shah's Proposal to the Russian Empress

One of the interesting points, mentioned in the *History of 'Alam-ara-ye Naderi* and later in other resources, is Nader Shah's proposal of marriage to the Russian empress, Anna. According to a report of Mohammad Kazem Marvi, when Kaloshkin was returning to Russia, Nader Shah wrote a letter and sent many gifts to the Russian empress and proposed to marry her in order to strengthen the unity of the two royal families. Based on the same report, Empress Anna's reply was equivocal; she suggested that Nader Shah should travel to St. Petersburg so that they could get better acquainted with each other.[49] After the conquest of Khiva (in 1740), Nader Shah released 12,000 Russian prisoners who had been captured by Uzbeks during the attack of Begović Cherkaski in 1714–1715.[50] It seems he renewed his proposal again at the same time, but it was rejected.[51]

Nader Shah Policy on the Caspian Sea

As already noted, the Russians had increased their activities in the Caspian Sea since the era of Peter the Great, and they had monopolized shipping in this sea. Due to the insecurity and slow road transport for the passage of commercial caravans through Daghestan, and also due to the absence of diplomatic relations that could have regulated commercial arrangements between Russia and the Central Asian khanates, the continuation of Russian dominance over the Caspian Sea was of great importance. On the other hand, in the third decade of the eighteenth century, British merchants were more active in Russia with the aim of the booming transit of goods in the Caspian Sea.

This coincided with Nader Shah's initiative for the establishment of the navy in the Caspian Sea, in which Nader Shah and British merchants had many interests in common. Although many historians argue that Nader Shah's failures in Daghestan and the need to send supplies by sea to Daghestan were the main motivation of Nader Shah for the establishment of the Navy in the Caspian, it should be taken into account that this plan may already have been on his mind in the early days after his accession in 1736. In response to a request from Empress Anna Ioannovna suggesting the alliance of Iran and Russia against the Ottomans, Nader Shah responded with a letter on December 18, 1736, making the entry of Iran into this alliance conditional upon Russia providing him with a ship to suppress Turkmen rebels and sending 100 sailors and 100 carpenters to the Persian Gulf to build a ship for him.[52] The Russians did not agree to this request.[53]

With the arrival of John Elton, a British merchant, at the Caspian Sea, Nader Shah's dream was closer to coming true. In December 1734, Empress Anna had given a concession to British merchants according to which transit of goods to Iran via Russia was subject to a three-percent tax. Based on this, John Elton started his business in Kazan for the transit of goods via Russia to Iran and assigned Captain Woodruff the responsibility of building a ship in Kazan for this purpose.[54] Upon completion of construction of the ship, named the Empress of Russia, Elton and Woodruff loaded it up with goods for Iran, sailed down the Volga River to the south, and arrived in Anzali in June 1741 after crossing the Caspian Sea. On arrival, they managed to meet Reza Qoli Mirza. The Vicegerent of Iran seized the opportunity and declared the freedom of British merchants to trade with Iranians, by issuing an order to all provinces and the Beylerbey.[55]

During the presence of Nader Shah in Daghestan (in 1741–1743), Elton drew greater attention by sending a shipment of Rasht rice to Derbent.[56] But the Russians were unhappy with these activities and created many problems for Elton and his colleagues, including notably an incident in which Woodruff was arrested and beaten by a Russian officer. Elton lodged a complaint with Iranian officials and personally went to Nader Shah's camp to the northwest of Derbent, a meeting which apparently made a strong impression on Nader.[57]

In subsequent meetings between Nader Shah and Elton, the issue of shipping and shipbuilding was further discussed. At the end of these negotiations, in 1743, Nader Shah appointed John Elton, titled Jamal Beig, to be the head of Iranian shipbuilding and ordered him to build some European-style ships.[58]

Elton established the shipping centers and headquarters in Langarud and Lahijan. His services to Nader Shah did not remain hidden to the Russians, including the Russian consul in Gilan. Lockhart believed that the Russians feared that if Nader Shah could have established a stronghold on the southeastern corner of the Caspian, enabling him to deploy a fleet there, then it would have been easy for him to attack Russia. Since the Russian government had regarded the Caspian Sea for a long time as a Russian sea, any attempt by others to take control over it was considered a threat.[59]

When Sherbatov, the Russian ambassador to Nader Shah's court, received reports on the appointment of Elton as the head of the Iranian shipbuilding project, he immediately issued letters of protest. As a result of his protests, British merchants appointed Jonas Hanway, a partner of one of the affiliated businesses, to go to Iran and investigate the charges against Elton. Hanway realized that Elton was at the service of Nader Shah engaging in shipbuilding in Langarud.[60] The British promised to pay Elton an annual salary of 400 pounds sterling and appoint him to a qualified position in the British Navy.[61]

In February 17, 1745, in response to Lord Triole, Elton wrote that, despite what might have been assumed, not only he was not at the service of the Iranian government, but also all his attempts were directed at improving the economic situation of Britain in Iran and, for this purpose, he had tried to meet Nader Shah in any way.[62]

A report of Bakunin, the successor of Aparov, indicating the construction of two frigate ships and four smaller ships, as well as four big boats by Elton, further angered Russian officials. The Russian Company tried to force Elton to give up serving Nader Shah. As Elton refused all these promises and requests, Nader Shah called him the noblest Christian. As Elton's activities expanded over time, Russian acts of sabotage increased. First, the Russian government banned the transit of goods through Russia for delivery to Elton or anyone associated with him. Then the Russians insisted on the purchase of two British ships in the Caspian Sea and their passage under the flag of Russia.

Finally, in November 1746, Elizabeth issued an order whereby all concessions related to the transit of goods through the territory of Russia, transferred to the British government based on the 1734 treaty, were canceled. According to this order, the relevant merchants were required to avoid sending goods to Iran and transferring their property abroad.[63]

Despite all the hindrances of Russia, Elton remained at the service of Nader Shah and made earnest efforts to reintegrate and organize the Iranian Navy on the Caspian. In a report addressed to the Governor of Astrakhan, dated July 30, 1746, it was mentioned that Iranian ships in the Caspian Sea demanded that Russian ships give them a military salute. He ordered that, until they received any special instruction from Petersburg, Russian merchant ships quickly hide their guns as soon as encountering Iranian ships, so that the Iranians could not expect them to give a military salute.[64]

Nader Shah was killed in June 1747, leaving the whole country in chaos, and as a result, Elton's shipbuilding endeavor was closed down. In October 1750, Haj Jamal Foomani asked Elton for help in dealing with Mohammad Hassan Qajar, who was trying to capture Rasht. Elton not only refused his request but also declared his readiness to join Mohammad Hassan Qajar in December of that year. This led to the killing of John Elton by Haj Jamal Foomani and pro-Russian peasants in Gilan in 1751.[65]

There is little information about what happened to the Caspian Sea fleet. According to a report of Professor Puliktov from Tbilisi, one of the ships built by Elton was burned near Rasht in 1752 (AH 1165) at the instigation of the Russian government. In addition, the remains of the second ship were visible near Langarud up to less than a century ago.[66] After the death of Nader Shah, the Russian government put an end to business activities of the British in Russia and the Caspian Sea.

Quiet Encroachment: Expansion of Russian's Sphere of Influence during the period of the Zand Dynasty

With the death of Nader Shah, a new era in relations between Iran and Russia began, which we have referred to as the "quiet encroachment of Russia in Iran" in this chapter. Quiet encroachment means applying a kind of policy with the help of other economic, diplomatic, and social tools based on which, in the absence of a strong central government in Iran, Russia managed to start penetrating into the northern parts of Iran from the second half of the eighteenth century at the lowest possible cost. Political fragmentation on the shores of the Caspian Sea and the Caucasus, the historical background of monopolized control over the Caspian Sea, negligence of the Zand rulers toward the northern parts of Iran, and some grounds for a shift toward the northern neighbor were the most important factors that encouraged the Russians "to execute this policy.

As in the era of Peter the Great, there were also some programs for conducting expert studies on Iran in this period. These studies, aiming at providing information for the realization of Russia's policies, involved a wide range of studies related to geographical conditions; to roads, trade routes, ports, and harbors; and to demographic and social characteristics of different regions of Iran. After the death of Nader Shah, a new wave of studies and mapping in different parts of Iran began. The visits of Igumnov in 1764, Baghlan Aslanov in 1764–1765, and Mirzabeygi Volganov[67] in 1776 to Iran and, most importantly, studies by Samuel Gottlieb Gmelin[68] are some examples of Russian researchers' efforts to describe the natural conditions of the region, gathering information about military and naval forces in the north of Iran and the Caucasus, and climatic conditions there.

As previously mentioned, the reign of the Zand dynasty coincided with the empowerment of Catherine II (1762–1796 AD), who is argued by historians to have been the most powerful Russian ruler after Peter the Great. The policy of "quiet encroachment" was continued during Catherine's rule, though it shifted to actual invasion in the final year of her reign.

Although there was no threat from Iran against Russia, Catherine was thinking about intervention in the eastern Caucasus and northern Iran from the first days of her reign. Initially, she constructed a fortress in Mozdok located on the bank of Terek River in 1763. Later, this fortress became the main base and played a crucial role in Russia's influence in the region.[69] In addition, she ordered the construction of a series of fortifications like Mozdok, Georgievsk and Kizlyar, and the rebuilding Chapel of the Holy Cross in the North Caucasus in 1776. These became a solid base for her military campaigns and those of her successors.[70] In the same year, by sending a delegation to the Governor of Derbent, Fath Ali Khan, Catherine asked the Iranian government to allow the Russians to use Derbent to attack the Ottomans by land. Without promising anything to the Russians, Fath Ali Khan discussed the proposal with Karim Khan Zand. It seems that the Russians had already moved to Derbent before securing the cooperation of Iran. Although Golestaneh reports that the Russian troops were defeated by Fath Ali Khan,[71] it seems actually there wasn't a battle between them and Fath Ali Khan didn't agree to the passage of Russian soldiers from Darband.

Karim Khan Zand's relations with Russia were at a low level; his rule was mainly focused on the southern parts of Iran. Hence, this caused further orientation of Gilan, Derbent, Georgia, and Karabakh toward Russia.[72]

At the end of Karim Khan reign, when Iran was involved in a war with the Ottomans in Basra, the Russians sent an ambassador to Shiraz and called for a joint action against the Ottoman Empire. Unlike in 1766–1767, this proposal was agreed to by Karim Khan, but his death left this plan undeveloped.[73]

With the final conquest of Crimea in 1782, Russia's policy on its southern borders focused on the Caucasus. The Russian empress gave Prince Grigory Aleksandrovich Potemkin-Tavricheski responsibility for the settlement and final conquest of the Caucasus. He appointed his cousin, General Pavel S. Potemkin, as the commander of Russian forces in the Caucasus. General Potemkin actively established extensive communication with Armenians, Georgians, and other Caucasian khanates.[74]

Therefore, on the eve of the rise of Agha Mohammad Khan Qajar, in addition to complete mastery over the Caspian Sea and trade there over the past four decades, the Russians had constructed some major fortifications in the northern Caucasus and also caused Georgia to be its protectorate under an agreement in 1783. Moreover, close relations were established with Armenians and the Gilan, Derbent, and Karabakh khanates.

In fact, the Qajar government was heir to a severe crisis in relations with Russia and was confronted with a dilemma between confrontation with Russia in the Caucasus (the policy Agha Mohammad Khan followed) or acceptance of the loss of the eastern Caucasus. Fath Ali Shah chose the first option, to his cost.

Conclusion

From the late Safavid period, the nature of relations between Iran and Russia fundamentally changed, as the Russian army under the command of Peter I occupied areas of northern Iran for the first time and comprehensively planned for expansion of its influence. Poor geographical conditions for Russian soldiers, local resistance in Daghestan, and wider strategic requirements (e.g., the balance of power and fear of war with the Ottomans) caused the Russians to limit their plan after the establishment of military bases in 1722. Until a decade later, Russia's policy was mainly focused on maintaining the status quo and legitimizing their occupation through bilateral agreements (with Ismail Beg and the Afghan Ashraf) and the Ottomans (the 1724 treaty).

The rise of Nader Shah led to the withdrawal of Russia from occupied territories without any war between the parties, a unique event in the history of Iran. Another important achievement during Nader Shah's reign was the exact determination of the border area and selection of Soulak River as the frontier. Despite congenial relations between the two countries and frequent exchange of ambassadors and representatives, there were ambiguities and conflicts on two issues. The first issue was Russia's monopoly on shipping in Caspian Sea (leading to the effort to block development of Iran's shipbuilding industry), and the second was the Russians' support for the rebels in Daghestan, which led to the cooling of relations between the two countries.

With the death of Nader Shah and the renewal of domestic crises, the Russian government, in addition to pursuing its former priority on the development of trade with Iran, began its policy of "quiet encroachment" in northern Iran and the Caucasus (learning from the negative consequences of the military campaigns of Peter the Great). Not only would this covert policy not much disturb the sensitivity of the Zand government, it was also far less costly than military presence and also avoided conflict with the Ottomans. The permanent presence of the Russian consul in Gilan until the end of the eighteenth century, while political relations between the two countries had reached rock bottom, is clear evidence of the Russian government's intention to increase its sphere of influence in Iran. Hence, a tendency to side with Russia could be observed among some of the northern Iranian the Caucasus khanates in the second half of the eighteenth century. After observing the inability of the central government in Iran, Russia signed bilateral agreements with these local rulers, a good example of which is the protectorate treaty with Georgia in 1783. What came out of this action for Russia was the advancement of its policy at the lowest material and spiritual cost. Documents from the eighth decade of this century attest well to the extensive preparations of the Russian government to develop the policy of quiet encroachment further and expand its possessions across the Caucasus and northern Iran.

The rise of Agha Mohammad Khan (who, like Nader Shah, was the output of internal energy in Iranian society in the rapid regeneration of missed opportunities) showed that he would spare no effort to suppress the inclination of local rulers toward Russia. However, the natural outcome of the conflict of interests between the two countries could not be delayed indefinitely, as was shown by Catherine's large military operation to seize the Caspian Sea and the Caucasus. As a result of the attack in 1796, which was commanded by General V.Zubov, Russian troops overran most of the territory of the Caspian Sea and the Caucasus without any resistance. By this time, an invasion of inland areas of Iran looked possible. Catherine's death and the peaceful policies of her successor, Pavel I, only delayed the final collapse of relations between the two countries and the first decade-long Russo-Persian war (1804–1813).

Notes

1. For more details about life and the rule of Nader Shah see Michael Axworthy, *The Sword of Persia* (London, 2006).
2. Holy Roman Emperor, King of Germany, Hungary, and Bohemia (1640–1705).
3. Elector Palatine (1690–1716).
4. George A. Bournoutian, *Armenian and Russia (1626–1796): A Documentary Record* (Mazda Publisher, California, 2001), doc. no. 49.
5. Ibid., doc. no. 46.
6. Laurence Lockhart, *Soqut-e Safaviyeh va ayyam-e istila-ye Afaghaneh dar Iran*]The fall of the Safavi dynasty and the Afghan occupation of Persia[translated by Ismail Doulatshahi (Tehran, 1383/2004), p. 54.
7. George A. Bournoutian, *Armenian and Russia (1626–1796): A Documentary Record*, docs. no. 82–83.
8. Ibid., doc. no. 77.
9. On December 21, 1721, Peter asked Soltan Hossein to agree that Baskakov to be the vice consul of Shamakhi. See *Asnadi az ravabet-e Iran ba Rusiyeh az payan-e Safaviyeh ta avval-e Qajar* [Documents of Iran–Russia relations from the Safavid to the Qajar], documents translated from Russian to Persian by Rahim and Behruz Mosalmanian Qobadiani, edited by Hoseyn Ahmadi (Tehran, 1378/2008), doc. no. 3.
10. O. A. Nikonov, *Iran v veneshnepoliticheskoi strategy Rossiskoi imperi v 18 veke* (Vladimir, 2014) [О. А. Никонов, *Иран во внешнеполитической стратегии Российской империи в XVIII веке.* Владимир, 2014], p. 71.
11. *Asnadi az ravabet-e Iran ba Rusiyeh*, doc. No. 7.
12. AVPRI (*Archive of Foreign Policy of Russian Empire–Moscow*), F. 77, Russian–Persian Relations, Op. 1, year 1721, D. 2, pp. 1–8 [АВПРИ: Архив внешней политики Российской империи ф. 77. Сношения Россиии с Персией, Оп. 1, г. 1721, д. 1, лл. 1–8].
13. AVPRI (*Archive of foreign policy of Russian Empire–Moscow*,) F. 77, Russian–Persian Relations, Op. 1, year 1721, D. 2, p. 12.
14. *Asnadi az ravabet-e Iran ba Rusiyeh*, doc. no. 9.
15. Mohammad 'Ali Jamalzadeh, *Tarikh-e Ravabet-e Rus va Iran* [History of relations between Russia and Iran] (Tehran, 1372/1993), pp. 175–177; Abdol Hosein Navai, *Ravabet-e siyasi va eqtesadi Iran dar dowreh-ye Safaviyeh* [Political and economic relations of Iran during the Safavid] (Tehran, 1377/1998), pp. 238–240.
16. P. G. Butkov, *Materialiy delya novoi istoriai Kavkaza c 1722 po 1830 god* [П. Г. Бутков, *Материалы для новой истории Кавказа с 1722 по 1803 год*, СПб. 1869.] (St. Petersburg, 1869), vol. 1, p. 15.

17. Almost all of them had participated in the war with Sweden.

18. Alexander Gordon, *The History of Peter the Great, Emperor of Russia: A Short Account of the Author's Life* (Aberdeen, 1755), vol. 11, p. 284.

19. The most complete description of Peter's attack has been done by Lockhart, *Soqut-e Safaviyeh*, pp. 160–165.

20. Peter Henry Bruce, *Memoirs of Peter Henry Bruce, esq., a military officer, in the services of Prussia, Russia, and Great Britain. Containing an account of his travels in Germany, Russia, Tartary, Turkey, the West Indies, &c., as also several very interesting private anecdotes of the Czar, Peter I, of Russia* (London, 1782), p. 356.

21. The resources used by Butkov suggested that the numbers of deaths were between 45,000 and 200,000. But it seems that the maximum was 130,000 people. Butkov, *Materialy delya novoi istorii Kavkaza*, vol. 1, p. 141.

22. Currently, the place where the Russians were buried is known as "Russians' Graveyard," located around Gaskar.

23. After hearing that Peter planned to attack Iran, Vakhtang went to Ganja and waited for him. He also contacted the representatives of Yerevan, Azerbaijan and Armenia with a view to an attack on the Lezges. Without receiving any response from Peter the Great, Vakhtang stayed in Tbilisi for a while. As his supplies were running out, he sent a messenger to Peter and asked how long he must wait for him in Ganja. When it became clear that Peter would not go beyond the limits of Derbent or enter the Caucasus for fear of a confrontation with the Ottomans, Vakhtang returned to Tbilisi in disappointment. Not long after this, he was deposed at the order of the Shah and after a while took refuge in Russia. See: Lockhart, *Soqut-e Safaviyeh*, pp.213–214 and Alexander A. Tsagareli, *Perepiska Gruzinskikh tsareih i vladetelnihk knazeih c gasudaryami Russiskimi v XVIII stoletii* (St. Petersburg, 1890), pp. 142–143.

24. J. Hanway, *An Historical Account of the British Trade Over the Caspian Sea: With the Author's Journal of Travels from England Through Russia Into Persia, and Back Through Russia, Germany and Holland. To which are Added, the Revolutions of Persia During the Present Century, with the Particular History of the Great Usurper Nadir Kouli* (London, 1754), vol. I, p. 13. Here Hanway refers to efforts made by the famous John Elton for the revival of this trade. In a trade treaty between Russia and England (1734), it was stipulated that British merchants could send their goods through Russia to Iran and vice versa by paying a tax of 3%.

25. Butkov, *Materialy delya novi istoria Kavkaza*, vol. 1, p. 55.

26. Lockhart, *Soqut-e Safaviyeh*, p. 304.

27. TSADA (*Archive of old Documents–Moscow*), С. Абрамов, *Дневная Записка в: Центральный архив древних актов* (ЦАДА), Персидские дела 1726 г., № 6, p. 101.

28. Ibid., p. 103.

29. Mirza Mehdi Khan Astarabadi, *Tarikh-e Jahangosha-ye Naderi* (Tehran, 1368/1989), pp. 178–184.

30. Ibid., p. 109.

31. *Asnadi az ravabet-e Iran ba Rusiyeh*, doc. no. 31; Vladimir Minorsky, *Tarikhche-ye Nader Shah*, translated by Rashid Yasemi (Tehran, 1313/1944), p. 14; Lockhart, *Soqut-e Safaviyeh* F. 77: Russian–Persian Relations, year 1732, D. 5, pp. 51–52.

32. O. P. Markova, Rossiia *Zakavkaz'e i mezhdunarodnie otnosheniia v 18 veke* (Moscow, 1966), [О. П. Маркова, *Россия, Закавказье и международные отношения в XVIII в.* Москва, 1966.], p. 120, Asnadi az ravabet-e Iran ba Rushiye, doc. no. 35.

33. Abdol Hosein Navai, *Ravabet-e siyasi va eqtesadi Iran dar dowreh-ye Safaviyeh*, pp. 244–248.

34. *Asnadi az ravabet-e Iran ba Rusiyeh*, doc. no. 42; Mirza Mehdi Khan Astarabadi, *Tarikh-e Jahangosha-ye Naderi*, p. 227.

35. AVPRI (*Archive of foreign policy of Russian Empire–Moscow*), F. 77, Russian–Persian Relations, Op. 1, year 1734, D. 1, pp. 20–21.

36. Reza Sha'bani, *Tarikh-e ejtema'i-ye Iran dar doureh-ye Afshariyeh* [The Social history of Iran in the era of the Afsharid] (Tehran, 1369/1990), vol. 2, p. 919.

37. Michael Axworthy, "The Army of Nader Shah," in *Iranian Studies*, vol. 40, no. 5, December 2007, p. 640; Markova, *Zakavkaze i mezhdunarodnie otnosheniia v 18 veke*, p. 122.

38. T. D. Iozefovich, *Dogovory Rossia c Vostokom* (St. Petersburg, 1869), Т. Д. Юзефович, *Договоры Россия с Востоком*, СПб. 1869]., pp. 203–207.

39. Before this contract, Astarabadi believed that Niazabad was the border of Iran and Russia. Mirza Mahdi Khan Astarabadi, *Tarikh-e Jahangosha-ye Naderi*, p. 261; *Asnadi az ravabet-e Iran ba Rusiyeh*, doc. no. 39; Mohammad Hoseyn Qodsi, *Nader Nameh* (Mashhad, 1339/1960), pp. 375–376; Gholamali Vahid Mazandarani, *Majmu'eh-ye 'ahdnamehha-ye tarikh-i Iran* [Iran's historical conventions] (Tehran, 1350/1971), p. 87.

40. Butkov, *Materialy delya novi istoriia Kavkaza*, vol. 1, p. 135.

41. Ibid., 255.

42. AVPRI (*Archive of foreign policy of Russian Empire–Moscow*), F. 77: Russian–Persian Relations, Op. 2, D. 96, pp. 4–6.

43. S. R. Kishmishev, *Moharebat-e Naderi* [original Russian title: Походы Надир-шаха в Герат, Кандагар, Индию и события в Персии после его смерти, Тифлис, 1889], translated by 'Oun-al-Saltaneh, manuscript no. 21444 in Majlies Library (Tehran), p. 257 A.

44. Ibid., pp. 257 A and 257 B.

45. *Asnadi az ravabet-e Iran ba Rusiyeh* [Documents of Iran–Russia relations from the Safavid to the Qajar], doc. no. 53.

46. Michael Axworthy, "The Army of Nader Shah," p. 643.

47. *Asnadi az ravabet-e Iran ba Rusiyeh*, doc. no. 52.

48. Ibid., doc. no. 68.

49. Mohammad Kazem Marvi, *'Alam-Ara-ye Naderi*, edited by Mohammad Amin Riyahi (Tehran, 1369/1990), p. 318.

50. Mirza Mahdi Khan Astarabadi, *Tarikh-e Jahangosha-ye Naderi* (Tehran, 1368/1989), p. 359.

51. Mohammad Kazem Marvi, *Alam Ara-ye Naderi*, p. 339. Mohammad Kazem Marvi *'Alam Ara-ye Naderi*, edited by Mohammad Amin Riyahi (Tehran, 1364/1985), vol. 3, pp. 1074–1075.

52. *Asnadi az ravabet-e Iran ba Rusiyeh*, doc. no. 51.

53. Reza Sha'bani, *Tarikh-e ejtemai-e-e Iran dar dowreh-ye Afshariyeh* [The Social history of Iran in the era of the Afsharid], p. 876; Sir Dadvar Abutorab, *Tarikh-e nezami va siyasi Iran dar dowreh-ye Nader Shah Afshar* [Political and military history of Iran during the reign of Nader Shah Afshar] (Mashad, 1380/2001), p. 737.

54. Laurence Lockhart, *Niruy-e darya'i-ye Nader Shah* [The Navy of Nadir Shah], translated by Gholam Hossein Mirza Saleh, in *Majalleh-ye Bastanshenasi va Tarikh*, no. 9 (Tehran, 1369/1990), vol. II, p. 421.

55. Sha'bani, *Tarikh-e ejtema'i-e Iran*, pp. 877–881.

56. Sir Dadvar Abutorab, *Tarikh-e nezami va siyasi-ye Iran dar dowreh-ye Nader Shah Afshar*, pp. 742–743.

57. Laurence Lockhart, *Niru-ye darya'i-ye Nader Shah*, pp. 63–64.

58. Ibid., p. 350.

59. Ibid., p. 64.

60. Ibid., p. 66.

61. Sir Percy Sykes, *Tarikh-e Iran* [History of Iran], translated by M. T. Fakhr Gilani (Tehran, 1363/1984), vol. II, p. 391; Hanway J. *The Revolutions of Persia: Containing the reign of Shah Sultan Hosein, with the invasion of the Afghans, and the reigns of Sultan Mir Maghmud and his successor Sultan Ashreff. To which is prefixed, a chronological abridgement of the Persian monarchy from its first foundation* (London, 1753), vol. 1, p. 302. See website: http://reader.digitale-sammlungen.de/en/fs1/object/display/bsb10366648_00001.html, vol. 1, p. 302.

62. Gholamhoseyn Zargarinejad, *Ruzshomar-e tahavollat-e tarikhi-ye Iran dar 'asr-e Qajariyeh* [Chronology of developments of Iran in Qajar era] (Tehran, 1386/2007), p. 315.

63. H. L. Rabino, *Velayate Dar-al-Marz-e Iran*, translated by Jafar Khomamizadeh (Tehran, 1350/1971), p. 540.

64. Abolghasem Taheri, *Tarikh-e ravabet-e siyasi ba bazargani-ye Iran va Englis* [History of commercial and political relations between Englan and Iran] (Tehran, 1354/1975), vol. I, p. 228.

65. H. L. Rabino, *Velayate Dar-al-Marz-e Iran*, p. 543; Sir Dadvar Abutorab, *Tarikh-e nezami va siyasi-ye Iran dar doureh-ye Nader Shah Afshar*, p. 743.

66. V. G. Gajiev, *Razgrom Nader Shakha v Daghestan* (Makhachkala, 1966) [В. Г. Гаджиев *Разгром Надир-шаха в Дагестане*. Махачкала, 1966]., p. 205.

67. AVPRI (*Archive of foreign policy of Russian Empire–Moscow*), F. 77: Russian–Persian Relations, Op. 5, D. 2, p. 59.
68. He was born into a family of scientists from Tübingen in 1744. His father was a pharmacist and surgeon, and his uncle was an eminent scientist. At the age of 18, he got his medical degree from Leiden University in the Netherlands and then became interested in seaweeds. He was appointed to the chair of botany at University of St. Petersburg when he was only 22 years old. He was the first European specialist in the natural sciences to visit Iran. During his mission, He collected many samples from Gilan and Mazandaran. Samuel Gottlieb Gmelin, *Travels Through Northern Persia, 1770–1774*, translated by Willem Floor (Washington DC, 2007).
69. Fitzroy Maclean, *Sheikh Shamel Daghestani* [Original title: To Caucasus, the end of all the earth: an illustrated companion to the caucasus and Transcaucasia], translated by Kaveh Bayat) Tehran, 1370/1991), p. 28.
70. *Asnadi az ravabet-e Iran ba Kavkaz* [Some documents of the relations between Iran and Caucasus] (Tehran, 1372/1993), p. 9; Mahmoud Afshar Yazdi. *Siyasat-e Urupa dar Iran* [Europe's policy in Iran] (1358/1979), p. 47.
71. Golestaneh, *Mojmal al-Tavarikh*, pp. 340–341.
72. O. A. Nikonov, *Iran v veneshnepoliticheskoi strategy Rossiskoi imperi v 18 veke*, p. 331.
73. AVPRI (*Archive of foreign policy of Russian Empire–Moscow*), F. 77, Russian–Persian Relations, Op. 6, years 1774–1800, D. 15, p. 126.
74. For more information, see the correspondence of Russian officials with local authorities of the Caucasus gathered in books: George A. Bournoutian, *Armenian and Russia (1626–1796): A Documentary Record*.

Bibliography

Abdol Hosein Navai, *Ravabet-e siyasi va eqtesadiye Iran dar doureh-ye Safaviyeh* [Political and economic relations of Iran during the Safavid] (Tehran, 1377/1998).

Abolqasem Taheri, *Tarikh-e ravabet-e siyasi ba bazargani Iran va Englis* [History of commercial and political relations between Englan and Iran] (Tehran, 1354/1975).

Abdalhassan Golestaneh, *Mojmal al-Tavarikh*, Edited by Modarres Razavi (Tehran, 1344/1965).

Alexander Gordon, *The History of Peter the Great, Emperor of Russia: A Short Account of the Author's Life* (Aberdeen, 1755).

Asnadi az ravabet-e Iran ba Rusiyeh az payane Safaviyeh ta avval-e Qajar [Documents of Iran–Russia relations from the Safavid to the Qajar], documents translated from Russian to Persian by Rahim and Behruz Mosalmanian Qobadiani, edited by Hossein Ahmadi (Tehran, 1378/2008).

Asnadi az Ravabet-e Iran ba Kavkaz [Some documents of the relations between Iran and Caucasus] (Tehran, 1372/1993).

Fitzroy Maclean, *Sheykh Shamel Daghestani* [original title: To Caucasus, the end of all the earth: An illustrated companion to the caucasus and Transcaucasia], translated by Kaveh Bayat (Tehran, 1370/1991).

George A. Bournoutian, *Armenian and Russia (1626–1796): A Documentary Record* (Mazda Publisher, California, 2001).

Gholamali Vahid Mazandarani, *Majmu'eh-ye 'ahdnamehha-ye tarikhi-ye Iran* [Iran's historical conventions] (Tehran, 1350/1971).

Gholamhoseyn Zargarinejad, *Ruzshomar-e tahavvolat-e tarikhi-ye Iran dar 'asr-e Qajariyeh* [Chronology of developments of Iran in Qajar era] (Tehran, 1386/2007).

Samuel Gottlieb Gmelin, *Travels Through Northern Persia, 1770–1774*, translated by Willem Floor (Mage Publishers, 2007).

H. L. Rabino, *Velayat-e Dar-al-Marz-e Iran*, translated by Ja'far Khomamizadeh (Tehran, 1350/1971).

J. Hanway, *An Historical Account of the British Trade Over the Caspian Sea: With the Author's Journal of Travels from England Through Russia Into Persia, and Back Through Russia, Germany and Holland. To which are Added, the Revolutions of Persia During the Present Century, with the Particular History of the Great Usurper Nadir Kouli* (London, 1754).

J. Hanway, *The Revolutions of Persia: Containing the reign of Shah Sultan Hosein, with the invasion of the Afghans, and the reigns of Sultan Mir Maghmud and his successor Sultan Ashreff. To which is prefixed, a chronological abridgement of the Persian monarchy from its first foundation* (London, 1753). See website: http://reader.digitale-sammlungen.de/en/fs1/object/display/bsb10366648_00001.html

Laurence Lockhart, *Niru-ye darya'i-ye Nader Shah* [The Navy of Nadir Shah], translated by Gholam Hossein Mirza Saleh, in *Bastanshenasi va Tarikh*, no. 9 (Tehran, 1369/1990).

Laurence Lockhart, *Soqut-e Safaviyeh va ayyam-e istila-ye Afaghaneh dar Iran* [The fall of the Ṣafavī dynasty and the Afghan occupation of Persia], translated by Ismail Doulatshahi (Tehran, 1383/2004).

Mahmoud Afshar Yazdi, *Siyasat-e Urupa dar Iran* [Europe's policy in Iran] (1358/1979).

Michael Axworthy, "The Army of Nader Shah," *Iranian Studies*, vol. 40, no. 5, December 2007, 640.

Michael Axworthy, *The Sword of Persia, Nader Shah, from Tribal Warrior to Conquering Tyrant* (London, 2006).

Mirza Mehdi khan Astarabadi, *Tarikh-e Jahangosha-ye Naderi* (Tehran, 1368/1989).

Mohammad 'Ali Jamalzadeh, *Tarikh-e ravabet-e Rus va Iran* [History of relations between Russia and Iran] (Tehran, 1372/1993).

Mohammad Hossein Qodsi, *Nader Nameh* (Mashhad, 1339/1960).

Mohammad Kazem Marvi, *'Alam Ara-ye Naderi*, edited by Mohammad Amin Riyahi (Tehran, 1369/1990).

Peter Henry Bruce, *Memoirs of Peter Henry Bruce, esq., a military officer, in the services of Prussia, Russia, and Great Britain. Containing an account of his travels in Germany, Russia, Tartary, Turkey, the West Indies, &c., as also several very interesting private anecdotes of the Czar, Peter I, of Russia* (London, 1782).

Re'za Sha'bani, *Tarikh-e ejtema'i-e-e Iran dar dowreh-ye Afshariyeh* [The Social history of Iran in the era of the Afsharid] (Tehran, 1369/1990).

Rudi Matthee, "Rudeness and Revilement: Russian–Iranian Relations in the Mid-Seventeenth Century," *Iranian Studies*, vol. 46, no. 3, 2013, 333–357.

S. R. Kishmishev, *Moharebat-e Naderi* [original Russian title: Походы Надир-шаха в Герат, Кандагар, Индию и события в Персии после его смерти, Тифлис, 1889], translated by 'Oun-al-Saltaneh, manuscript no. 21444 in Majlies Library (Tehran).

Sir Dadvar Abutorab, *Tarikh-e nezami va Siyasi-ye Iran dar dowreh-ye Nader Shah Afshar* [Political and military history of Iran during the reign of Nader Shah Afshar] (Mashad, 1380/2001).

Sir Percy Sykes, *Tarikh-e Iran* [History of Iran], translated by M. T. Fakhr Gilani (Tehran, 1363/1984).

Vladimir Minorsky, *Tarikhche-ye Nader Shah*, translated by Rashid Yasemi (Tehran, 1313/1944).

IN RUSSIAN:

AVPRI (*Archive of foreign policy of Russian Empire–Moscow*) F. 77, Russian-Persian Relations [АВПРИ: Архив внешней политики Российской империи ф. 77. Сношения Россиии с Персией.].

TSADA (*Archive of Old Documents–Moscow*), С. Абрамов, *Дневная Записка в: Центральный архив древних актов* (ЦАДА), Персидские дела 1726 г., № 6.

P. G. Butkov, *Materialiy delya novoi istoriia Kavkaza c 1722 po 1830 god* (St. Petersburg, 1869) [П. Г. Бутков, *Материалы для новой истории Кавказа с 1722 по 1803 год*, СПб. 1869.].

V. G. Gajiev, *Razgrom Nader Shakha v Daghestane* (Makhachkala, 1966) [В. Г. Гаджиев, *Разгром Надир-шаха в Дагестане*. Махачкала, 1966].

O. P. Markova, *Zakavkaze i Mezhdunarodnie otnosheniia v 18 veke* (Moscow, 1966) [О. П. Маркова, *Россия, Закавказье и международные отношения в XVIII в.* Москва, 1966.].

O. A. Nikonov, *Iran v vneshnepoliticheskoi strategii Rossiskoi imperii v 18 veke* (Vladimir, 2014) [О. А. Никонов, Иран во внешнеполитической стратегии Российской империи в XVIII веке. Владимир, 2014].

T. D. Iozefovich, *Dogovari Rossii c Vostokom* (St. Petersburg, 1869) [Т. Д. Юзефович Договоры России с Востоком, СПб. 1869].

Alexander A. Tsagareli, *Perepiska Gruzinskikh tsareih i vladetelnihk knazeih c gosudaryami Russiskimi v XVIII stoletii* (St. Petersburg, 1890) [Александр А. Цагарели, Переписка грузинских царей и владетельных князей с государями российскими в XVIII столетии, С.-Петербург, 1890].

11

Persia 1700–1800: Some Views from Central Europe

GIORGIO ROTA

As is well known, narrative sources from the last few decades of Safavid rule, either Persian or Europen, are not particularly abundant in number. As far as the latter are concerned, the fall of the dynasty in 1722, caused and followed by foreign invasions, and the outbursts of anarchy and civil war subsequent to the death of Nader Shah Afshar (1747) and Karim Khan Zand (1779) had, among other effects, that of making the relations with Europe, the presence of Europeans in Persia and, therefore, the production of European narrations and documents much more difficult than they had finally become, after a slow start, during the second century of Safavid rule.

After the Safavid period, interest in Persia in the courts and chancelleries of Europe most probably decreased, also thanks to the decline of the Ottoman empire as a military threat and, thus, diminished need for an Eastern ally against the Ottomans: nonetheless, interest certainly did not fade away altogether. For instance, the Venetian Senate wrote a letter to Nader Shah as late as 3 March 1742, although only with the limited and traditional aim of recommending a Catholic missionary, the Capuchin Niccolò da Girgenti, to the goodwill of the ruler:[1] in other words, Persia, despite the various 'revolutions' it experienced during the first decades of the 18th century, had not disappeared entirely even from the political horizon of the Republic of Venice, which by that time had become a second- or even third-tier European power and had ceased to play any political or military role of note on the international scene.[2] Larger powers pursued more substantial aims: the Swede Johan Otter travelled to Persia in 1736 to establish diplomatic relations between France and Nader Shah, and Simon de Vierville was sent there in 1751 to gather information on the political and economic state of the country.[3]

Therefore, and precisely on account of this perhaps decreased but still lingering interest, it is not really surprising that the *Haus-, Hof- und Staatsarchiv* in Vienna, which might appear an unlikely place, should hold a relatively large amount of interesting documents in European languages concerning Persia in the 18th century. They are 'Central European' insofar as they are preserved in a Central European capital and at a certain point were deemed significant by a Central European power. While their authors came from at least five different countries, this was a time in which modern nationalism was still unknown and, thus, it is more than likely that ethnic or geographical origin mattered to these men less than their political allegiance. The following is a concise description of these documents, their authors, and, in a necessarily sketchy and incomplete manner, their contents.

From the point of view of the date of its redaction (and not of its author's permanence in Persia), the earliest is the *Relazione dell'Ambasciata fatta al Re di Persia, dal Padre Felice Maria da Sellano, Missionario Cappuccino della Provincia dell'Umbria, dall'Anno 1699 sino all'Anno 1702*[4] (in Italian), which seems to have been written down in the summer of 1702. Its author, Father Felice Maria da Sellano, had spent several years in Persia as a missionary and had returned to Rome to report on the state of the Capuchin mission, when news arrived of fresh Apostolic Armenian 'persecutions' against the missions in Tbilisi and Ganjeh. He was thus sent back to the Safavid court as a Papal ambassador to enlist the support of Shah Soltan Hoseyn (1694–1722) against the new threat. He left Rome on 3 February 1699 and travelled via Florence, Venice, Innsbruck, Vienna,[5] and Belgrade to Constantinople. He then sailed to Trebizond, whence he travelled on via Erzurum, Erevan (the first city in Safavid territory), Tabriz, Qom, and Kashan, finally reaching Isfahan on 17 November 1700.[6] After some not always easy dealings with the Persian officials, he left the Safavid capital on 21 April 1701 and reached Rome on 28 June 1702. As is the case in many accounts written by missionaries who lived in or travelled to Safavid Persia, da Sellano's virtually only interest lies in his embassy, the state of the Catholic missions in the country, the dangers they face, and the fruits they might bear. As a consequence, he does not really describe Persia, its inhabitants, or its government but simply provides occasional remarks, such as those on the poor climate and bad quality of the water in Qom. However, he carefully records details about the protocol of Royal audiences and meetings with various Persian officials and governors: his memoirs, compared to other available sources, would therefore make excellent material for a case study of a European embassy on the eve of the Safavid collapse, along the lines set by Rudi Matthee in two important articles.[7]

Mémoires des Voyages Faits dans l'Empire Turc, et le Royaume de Perse[8] is the title of an excerpt, in French, from a longer travel account: the whereabouts of the full text of the *Mémoires*, if it still exists, are presently unknown. Its author, Ferdinand Amadeus von Harrsch (1661 or 1664–1722),[9] travelled to Persia for leisure: the end of the Nine Years' War (1688–1697), where he fought in the Imperial army and reached the rank of *Generalquartiermeister* (quartermaster general), gave him the time for what he calls *des Voyages un peu extraordinaires*. From another excerpt in the same manuscript[10] we gather that his original plan had been a journey around the world along the route Germany—Holland—Cadiz—Veracruz—Mexico City—Acapulco—the Philippines—China—*Indiam Orientalem*—Persia—Turkey—Europe.[11] However, in a third section of the manuscript[12] he states that after leaving Isfahan he travelled to Erzerum, 'from where I came'.[13] Indeed, in Spain he had been dissuaded by 'reputable men' (*von achtbaren Männern*) from going ahead with his project.[14] Von Harrsch must have left Germany some time in 1698 (or in 1699 at the latest), and on 29 January 1701 he was back in Vienna:[15] a few months later the War of the Spanish Succession (1701–1714) broke out, allowing him to resume his old profession. Whereas he was in Persia before Father da Sellano, it is reasonable to surmise that the reopening of the war against France delayed the writing of the *Mémoires*: the fact that the title of *Selecta quaedam* mentions him as a count allows us to determine that at least our copy of this excerpt (and perhaps the text itself) was compiled after 12 July 1714, when the title of *Reichsgraf* (Imperial Count) was bestowed on von Harrsch.[16] Despite their relative brevity, the *Mémoires* touch upon a number of subjects: Isfahan and its main monuments, the Persian landscape, the organization of the government, the ruler, the Persians' way of dressing and their nature and habits, the kind of things one could sell in the country, the ethno-religious minorities living in the Safavid capital (including the Catholic missionaries), the differences between Persians and Turks, and so on. We also find odd information, such as the estimates current in Persia at the time of the age of the Mughal ruler Owrangzib (1658–1707), who was variously reported to be 118 or 128 years old.[17]

Von Harrsch does not seem to have been biased, in one way or another, regarding Persia and the Persians. For instance, he remarks on the aridness of the countryside and the lack of trees and wood, but is ready to praise the Persians' ability to build irrigation systems. The Persians hold the Christians for impure but:

> sont incomparablemet plus traittables que les Turcs [. . .] si la Perse n'etoit pas si excessivement loing de chez nous, elle meriteroit qu'on y fit des voyages; mais comme cela ie [*sic*] ne le conseille point à qui que ce soit, car il y a trop de risque par la Turquie, avant que d'y pouvoir etre.

The 'sweetness' and the good manners of the Persians have, however, a negative side. Whatever *tant d'auteurs, qui ont pris plaisir, d'agrandir les choses de loing* may have written, the Persians are less brave than the Turks: *on hait la guerre, la craint*. Despite the shortness of his stay, von Harrsch grasped the weakness of the Safavid political leadership and the danger that a conflict would pose to the dynasty's survival: among other things, he writes that the Shah *n'est pas trop aimé* by his subjects, since his good nature allows abuses on the part of the State officials.[18] The above-mentioned lack of bias also appears in those parts of the *Mémoires* devoted to religion in Persia. Born in the Duchy of Württemberg as the son of a Protestant pastor, von Harrsch served in the armies of at least two Catholic powers (Venice and the Empire) before converting to Catholicism some time after he returned from Persia, probably in connection with his marriage.[19] He states that in Persia *tout le monde a la liberté, de vivre et croire à sa mode*, with the exception that Muslims are not allowed to become Christians. In this regard, he does not conceal the fact that the Catholic missionaries had failed in their aim to spread Christianity among the Muslim population and states that they may have converted 'at most' one hundred people during the one hundred years of their presence in the country: one thing Persians and Turks have in common is *le mépris de nostre Religion*. Moreover, he mentions the failure of the Papal embassy led by Palma Pignatelli (in Persia in 1698–1700) to achieve any substantial result, the apostasy of two Augustinian priors in Isfahan,[20] and the conversion to Islam of the two Sherimanian brothers, which had been caused by the fear of losing a legal litigation against another Armenian, the infamous Philippe Zagly, who had also become a Muslim before them. In any case, eighty years after a conversation on this topic between Shah 'Abbas I (1587–1629) and Pietro della Valle,[21] the Persians were still of the opinion that Ali and St. George were one and the same person, which caused a certain amount of interest in buying golden medals with the image of the saint *comme on les fait à Nuremberg et Augsbourg*. Von Harrsch also devotes a few lines to the Zoroastrians, noting their poverty and low social status as well as the fact that *ils croient la transmigration des âmes comme les Banianes*. As for the latter, who, according to von Harrsch, live in great numbers in Isfahan together with *autres Indiens*, they have idols which have a purely symbolic value, and *ils se moquent de ceux qui les traittent d'Idolatres*, as if they would not know that there is only one Supreme Being.

The *Mémoires sur les affaires de Perse et de Turquie*,[22] also in French, is the work of lieutenant colonel P. G. F. de Bohn, an Imperial officer who dedicated it to 'His Royal Highness, *monseigneur* the Duke of Lorraine and Bar, Grand Duke of Tuscany, etc.', that is, the future Holy Roman Emperor Franz I Stephan (b. 1708, r. 1745–1765), Duke of Lorraine and Bar as Franz III (1729–1737), and Grand Duke of Tuscany as Francesco II (1737–1765). As de Bohn himself explains in the introduction to his memorandum, from 1724 he lived ten years in the Ottoman empire (presumably in Constantinople) as a free man and four more years as a prisoner after his role as an informant to the Habsburg court was discovered. His account is, however, brief and slightly misleading for a reader who is not already familiar with the events. In fact, de Bohn was a Dane and a double agent. Sent by the court of Vienna, he entered the service of the Hungarian prince and former rebel leader, Ferenc II Rákóczi (1676–1735), in exile in Turkey since 1717, and became the latter's secretary and cartographer: de Bohn, who was a lieutenant colonel in the Imperial army, held the same rank at the small court of the Prince. In 1734 he travelled to Paris, on his own initiative according to the introduction of the *Mémoires*, or sent by either Rákóczi or another redoubtable enemy of the Habsburgs, Claude Alexandre (Ahmed Paşa) de Bonneval (1675–1747), according to other sources. There he was unmasked as a spy, arrested and imprisoned in the Bastille, and finally freed at the end of 1738, after the end of the War of the Polish Succession between France on one side and Austria and Russia on the other (1733–1738).[23] Back to Austria, de Bohn failed to secure a commission as an officer in the Imperial army, which was then fighting against the Turks in the War of 1735–1739, triggered in part by the conflict over the Polish throne. Therefore, having more free time on his hands than he would have liked, he decided 'to sweeten the bitterness' caused by forced idleness through study: since he wished to be helpful to the House of Habsburg, he produced an instrument to frustrate the hostile plans of the Ottomans. The *Mémoires* have the formal appearance of a scholarly work, complete with footnotes and, occasionally, quotations from other sources. Much of the essay does concern the Ottoman empire, but more than half of the *Mémoires*'s 42 folios are devoted to Persia. The work is remarkable in so far as, despite its late date, it still presents Persia not only as a useful ally against the Ottomans but, indeed, as the only useful ally. Despite the Ottomans' internal problems and recent costly campaigns in Persia,[24] as de Bohn writes, they remain a formidable foe as the war of 1735–1739 shows: they are not only the arch-enemy of the House of Habsburg but are incessantly supported and incited by the French. The other Christian powers bordering on the Ottoman empire (Russia, Poland, and the Republic of Venice) are not, for different reasons, in a condition to support the Emperor effectively with 'powerful and reliable diversions' in the case of war:[25] Unlike them, Persia is, being sufficiently strong to withstand an Ottoman offensive, remote enough to prevent communication between the enemy troops engaged on its soil and those fighting in Hungary, and finally *solide et durable* in its hostility to the Ottomans. Another important aspect of the *Mémoires* is de Bohn's claim that he had the possibility, in the period of the vizierates of Ibrahim Paşa and Topal Osman Paşa, to see 'most' of the plans produced at the Ottoman court for the war against Persia together with reports written by Ottoman officers stationed at the Persian border. This had prompted 'old Ragoczi' to charge him with the task of drawing maps to instruct the Sultan and his ministers. In other words, de Bohn seems to have gathered his information on Persia exclusively in Constantinople, and mostly from Ottoman sources,[26] although he may have drawn on de Bonneval's strategic considerations as well as, perhaps, Krusinski's expertise. His description of Persia starts in a most flattering way: *la Perse est en ellemême un roiaume très puissant qui ne le cédes* [sic] *guére à l'Empire Ottoman ni en étendue, ni en fertilité, ni en richesses, ni en nombre d'habitans.* De Bohn repeats traditional commonplaces, such as that of the 'natural mildness' of the Persians: *le Gouvernement Persan, quoi que despotique, étant naturellement doux et moderé par le génie de la Nation qui n'incline point à la tyrannie,* indeed a striking statement when one thinks that it was made under the reign of Nader Shah. Interestingly, he claims that the Imperial court planned to send an agent to Persia 'to safeguard its interests' there, but the project had been interrupted by the 'defeat and total ruin' of the Afghans (1729). He also writes that France kept a 'minister' in Persia until 1732 (when he had to leave the country on account of an illness) whose task was preventing the Persians from waging war on the Ottomans at a time when the King of France might 'need' the latter against the Emperor. A new envoy was chosen in 1734, with the mission of negotiating peace between the Persians and Ottomans, but de Bohn did not know if he was ever sent.[27] De Bohn does not mention Nader Shah's conquest of Delhi but writes that he 'punished' the Mughals for fomenting unrest among the Afghans and forced them to cede Kabul. This may mean that the *Mémoires* were written between the conquest of Kabul (end of June 1738) and the battle of Karnal (24 February 1739), or not long after the latter event, when news of it had not yet reached Europe.[28] It is however also possible that de Bohn simply found the sack of Delhi too embarrassing for the reputation of his hero. Indeed, elsewhere he writes that the Safavid house 'just became extinct (*vient de s'éteindre*) with the death of Shah Tahmasp [II] and of his only son', but not that they had been deposed by Nader Shah. It is not clear whether this version of the events is due to lack of information or, as is perhaps more likely, an attempt to gloss over the real circumstances of Nader Shah's seizure of power and, ultimately, betrayal of his Royal masters: the latter possibility would be consistent with de Bohn's constant praise of Nader Shah. Shah Tahmasp II and his two sons (not only one) were murdered in May or June 1739 by Nader Shah's son.[29] The Dutch in Isfahan were informed of the execution of the former rulers on 3 July:[30] if de Bohn was genuinely unaware of the fact that the princes had been held prisoners since 1736,[31] he must have completed the *Mémoires* before the news of their death reached Europe.

The next document chronologically, likewise in French, is the *Etat present des affaires de la Perse, sur le rapport, qu'en a fait le S.r Gustave Ferdinand Gyllenram, Officier Suedois, étant de retour de Perse à Constantinople le 17/28 Janvier 1753.*[32] The text is a translation, seemingly of an interview or a conversation (*rapport*) with Gyllenram rather than of a written account: the translator may have been a Swede as well, as the double Julian and Gregorian dating seems to suggest.[33] Gustav Ferdinand Gyllenram (1727–1753) and his brother Daniel Fredrik (1718–1752) arrived in Persia in 1748, where they served as military officers.[34] Sadly, Gyllenram never completed his journey back to Sweden and passed away in Constantinople in the same year 1753; his brother had died in Persia the year before. At least one other letter written by the two brothers is known: in it they promised to send 'a short description of what had gone astray in Persia' after the dethronement of Shah Soltan Hoseyn, but it is not known whether the latter document was ever penned.[35] At the beginning of the *Etat present des affaires de la Perse*, Gyllenram makes it clear that the plot to murder Nader Shah was not led by his nephew and successor, the future 'Adel Shah Afshar (1747–1748), but by Mohammad Khan Qajar. Then he goes on to describe the first years of the rule of Shahrokh Shah Afshar (1749–1796) in Khorasan: while the Swedish officer's prediction that *les choses ne pourront pas long tems* [sic] *en rester là*, that is, with the region under a blind ruler and not taking any part in the struggle for Persia, was very reasonable, surprisingly it was proved wrong by later events. Continuing, Gyllenram briefly deals with Shah Esma'il III Safavi (1750–1773) and his *vakil-e dowleh*, Karim Khan Zand (1751–1779), pointing to the mutually beneficial relationship between the eighteen-year-old Shah[36] and his 'minister': the former owed his throne less to his rather shaky dynastic rights than to his capable strongman, whereas the Khan benefited from acting in the name of a member of the Safavid house and not his own. As for Erek'le II, King of 'Georgia',[37] he did not side either with Shahrokh Shah or Shah Esma'il III, and the conquests he had made were in self-defence against the Afghans and the Lezghians rather than part of a truly expansionist strategy. Gyllenram remarks that these conquests had drawn much attention from abroad due to the geographical position of Georgia and the presence there of merchants and travellers who could report about them, but they are not necessarily more significant than the events taking place on the Iranian plateau: and indeed, during the second half of the 18th century the destiny of Georgia was, once more, mostly shaped outside the borders of the country. As for the Afghans of Kandahar, they invaded Khorasan under their new ruler Ahmad Shah Dorrani (1747–1773) in 1750 but were beaten back by the Kurds retaining control of Herat: according to rumours they had among them a brother of Ebrahim Shah's, named Rahim Mirza, as a puppet Afsharid pretender. Gyllenram states that Ja'far Khan exerted *autorité souveraine* in Khorasan just as Karim Khan did in eastern and central Persia.[38] Finally, he concludes with a series of predictions (this time accurate) and assessments: political stability in Persia may lie very far in the future, since at the moment Kandahar is 'very difficult' to recover; the Afghans in Azerbaijan (*Agouans occidentaux*, as he calls them) are unruly and will have to be forced into submission; Erek'le II will not submit until a new ruler occupies the Persian throne in a stable way; and Shah Esma'il III will find it difficult to subdue Khorasan since the local Kurds want to preserve their own independence.[39]

It is more difficult to establish the authorship and the date of composition of the *Notices abrégées sur l'Etat actuel du Gouvernement du Royaume de Perse, tirées des notes d'un temoin oculaire*, which consists of four *notes* and the *Extrait*

d'une lettre de Monsieur Malivoire à l'Internonce Imperial et Royal[40] *en dâte* [sic]
Bagdad le 8e May 1798[41] (all in French). This eyewitness (*temoin oculaire*) and
the writer of the *Notices abrégées* are not the same person. The first *note* deals
with the career of Agha Mohammad Khan Qajar and the internecine strife that
followed the death of Karim Khan: from it we learn that the anonymous eyewitness visited the court of Karim Khan in Shiraz in 1768 and 1770, where he
became personally acquainted with Agha Mohammad Khan, and that this section was compiled between the early summer of 1795 and 11 September of the
same year, when the Qajar chief defeated Erek'le II and sacked Tbilisi. The second *note* deals with the current affairs of Khorasan, Herat, Sistan, and Kandahar
and provides a sketchy history of the Dorrani dynasty: Shahrokh Shah is mentioned as being still alive, and Zaman Shah Dorrani (1793–1800) is described
as being at the height of his power.[42] The third is a sequel to the previous narra-
tion of the events of the reign of Agha Mohammad Khan (with significant mistakes as far as the story of the conquest and sack of Tbilisi is concerned), and
the fourth deals with the murder of the founder of the Qajar dynasty and the
accession of Baba Khan,[43] who is described as a brave and skilled leader who
is loved by his soldiers and the people. His main challenger at the time when
the text was written was a Zand pretender, a 'nephew' of Karim Khan's named
Mohammad (or Mohammad Zaki) Khan, who was living in Bushehr when Agha
Mohammad Khan was murdered.[44] Despite factual inaccuracies in his telling of
past events, the anonymous author is remarkably accurate in his assessments
of current affairs and predictions of future developments: the Russians 'have
deserted' Erek'le II in his fight against Agha Mohammad Khan; *il faudra plusieurs
années* before Zaman Shah can re-establish order everywhere in his kingdom
(with hindsight, one may say that the author was overly optimistic here); the
sons of Shahrokh Shah won't be able to succeed him because the province will
be invaded either by the Persians or the Afghans; Persia will enjoy a long period
of peace under Baba Khan 'unless the Russians' attack it.[45] Then the *Extrait
d'une lettre* follows. Its author, Malivoire, calls Baba Khan *l'usurpateur actuel* and
provides more details on both the rebellion of Mohammad Khan Zand and an
attempt on the life of the ruler, thus implying that Baba Khan's position on the
throne was far from assured. Finally, the *Extrait d'une lettre* closes with some
information on the Wahhabis. Malivoire mentions an earlier letter of his dated
31 March, which suggests that von Herbert-Rathkeal's interest in the events in
Persia and Mesopotamia was not episodic but could rely on a steady flow of
information from Baghdad (and maybe from elsewhere).[46] *Monsieur* Malivoire
was the *cancelliere* ('secretary') of the French consulate in Baghdad.[47] As for the
anonymous eyewitness who provided the information for the *Notices abrégées*,
we have seen above that he was twice in Shiraz, in 1768 and 1770: so was Jean-
François-Xavier Rousseau (1738–1808),[48] who thus seems a likely candidate

for being the author. Between 1781 and 1808 he was the consul of France in Baghdad and Basrah[49] and therefore, at least for some time, Malivoire's superior. Of course, it would be interesting to know why two diplomats of the French Republic were informing the Imperial government about the situation in Persia on the eve of Napoleon's expedition to Egypt.

All of the above-mentioned works, which I have described in only a rather concise manner, deserve to be published because of what they contribute in terms of factual information on the history of Persia as well as what they convey about the history of the knowledge of Persia in Europe and its image in the eyes of the European readers of the time. Given the fact that the convenor of the conference whose proceedings are collected in this volume is one of the few living authorities on Nader Shah, I thought, perhaps paradoxically, that it might be of some interest to present here the text of a document that *does not* mention Nader Shah. The title of the essay is *Varij ragionamenti sopra lo stato presente, e la Crisi, in cui la Persia si trova*, that is, 'Various considerations concerning the present state of Persia and the crisis in which it finds itself.'[50] Neither the name of the author nor that of the addressee is stated. As far as the latter is concerned, given the present location of the document it would be logical for this to have been the Holy Roman Emperor or some prominent member of his government: however, the text contains no specific reference to Austria (or to any other European country[51]), its government or its ruling family. As for the author, he provides virtually no information about himself other than stating that he was not in Persia when he wrote his account of the country, but '800 leagues away'. He also writes that those who have not been in the Caucasus can hardly realize the importance of the fortress of Darband to Russia, which seems to imply that he had actually been there and could therefore fully grasp the implications of this aspect.[52] The mention, in the opening lines of *Varij ragionamenti*, of the Ottoman invasion of Venetian Peloponnese in 1715 might point to some special connection between this theatre of war and the anonymous author or the addressee.[53] On the other hand, this was at the time the most recent conflict between Christian powers and the Ottomans, and one in which Austria had played a most prominent role: referring to it thus would have been quite natural in a memorandum addressed to a European (not necessarily Austrian) official or politician. Likewise, the use of the then-standard Italian place name *Morea* (instead of *Peloponneso*, current today) would have been normal for any Italian-speaker of that period and therefore does not point to a specific geographical origin of the author. The account is written in very correct Italian: this, together with the fact that the expression *padshah-e alampanah* is transcribed without /h/ (a sound that is lacking in Italian and therefore possibly difficult for a mother-tongue speaker to recognize in other languages), seems to point to the author of the text being of Italian origin.[54] Likewise, the form *Esciref* (for Ashraf, the name of the second Afghan ruler of Persia) is not a mistake but indicates the effort to render the sound /sh/ according to the rules of Italian orthography (in Italian /sh/ does not occur before another consonant, hence the need to add an /i/ which is supposed to remain unpronounced). Occasional and not always accurate mention of earlier episodes of European and Middle Eastern history, as well as the likewise not always accurate use of terms from Classic or Humanist sources (such as, for instance, *Bactria, Hircania*, Scythians), may point to a formal education that was either superficial or distant in time when *Varij ragionamenti* was written.

While some of the personal and place names mentioned in the text (e.g., *Ardevil, Casbin, Ispahan*) follow spellings current in earlier or contemporaneous Italian sources, others (for instance, *Mahmud, Harat, Candahar*) are remarkably correct. The anonymous author's translations of *padshah-e alampanah* and *dowlat-e aliyeh* ('monarch and master of the world' and 'universal State' respectively) are formally only slightly incorrect but not incorrect in substance, and the chosen spelling (as in the case of *Esciref* for Ashraf) shows the influence of Turkish pronunciation, which is not surprising. All this seems to indicate a good knowledge of the Persian language as well. Also remarkable is the precision with which the author reports the title of a prominent Georgian feudal lord, the *eristavi* of Ksani: *chisnis eristavi* instead of the correct form *Ksnis eristavi*, whereby in Italian /ch/ is pronounced /k/.

The death of Peter the Great, explicitly mentioned in the text, and the beginning of Ashraf's rule over Persia represent the most easily detectable *termini post quos* for the completion of *Varij ragionamenti*: the Czar passed away on 8 February 1725 and Ashraf was crowned as Shah on 26 April of the same year.[55] The text, however, appears to have been composed a bit later, perhaps in 1726 or not very late in 1727. Several pieces of evidence lead to this dating. The anonymous author mentions the failed Ottoman advance on Isfahan which took place 'last year' (that is, in 1725) as well as the massive desertions of Turkish and Kurdish soldiers which occurred during the same campaign, but not Ashraf's victory over the Ottomans or the subsequent peace treaty between the two sides (20 November 1726 and 13 October 1727, respectively).[56] Malek Mahmud Sistani is mentioned as the master of Khorasan: this powerful local ruler was defeated by Tahmaspqoli Khan/Nader Shah in December 1726 and put to death in March 1727.[57] Finally, Iese/Mustafa Paşa (1724–1727), the brother of the deposed King Vakht'ang VI of Kartli (1711–1714 and 1719–1723), is said to be still in Tbilisi, no longer on the throne but scheming to oust the Ottoman governor and be reinstated in his place. Clearly, either the fact that Iese/Mustafa Paşa was largely powerless as a ruler misled the anonymous author into thinking that he had been deposed, or he had heard of the presence of an Ottoman *beylerbeyi* in Tbilisi and therefore concluded that the King must have been deposed: in fact, Iese died in 1727 in his double capacity of king and Ottoman governor of Kartli.[58] Thus, the latest possible *terminus ad quem* seems to be 20 November 1726 (Ashraf's victory over the Ottomans) or the first months of 1727.

It would be tempting to ascribe the authorship of *Varij ragionamenti* to the Ragusan traveller and diplomat Florio Beneveni.[59] Beneveni crossed Persia on his way to Bukhara and sent at least three letters to the Russian court from Shamakhi (not far from Darband) between 1 October 1719 and 1 July 1720.[60] He left Bukhara on 8 April 1725 and reached Astrakhan (via Khiva) on 17 September,[61] that is, at a time when Malek Mahmud Sistani was still alive and in power.[62] Once back in Russia, Beneveni expressed the desire to visit his homeland again after an absence of many years, and he was granted a passport on 18 December 1727: after that, all traces vanish, and we do not know if he ever saw Ragusa again.[63] These dates are compatible with our suppositions about the dating of *Varij ragionamenti* presented above: in the worst case, this presumption would only force us to move the date of the composition of the work forward by a few months, that is, before the time when the news of the Ottoman-Afghan peace became public knowledge in the European capitals.[64] Beneveni 'knew Persian, Turkish, and Tatar very well'[65] as well as, of course, his own mother tongue, Italian. The anonymous author's familiarity with a relatively unusual place name such as 'Black Russia' (*Russia Negra*), which may hint at a good knowledge of Russian history and geography, as well as what seems to be a certain pro-Russian stance (or, at least, an uncritical acceptance of information originating from Russian sources)[66] might also contribute to confirming this attribution.

Beneveni had at least one other Italian with him, his *Kammerdiener* Nicolò Minier, who was back in Moscow in April 1724.[67] Minier seems a somewhat less likely candidate for the authorship of *Varij ragionamenti*: nonetheless, it is interesting to note that, when referring to Malek Mahmud Sistani in one of his letters, he mentions him as the ruler of 'the province of Shegistan' (*provincij Shegistanskoj*),[68] while the anonymous author uses the form *Segestan*.

On the other hand, the report's main focus on the situation in western Persia (which may be explained by the interest the Austrian court, if the latter really was the original addressee of *Varij ragionamenti*, presumably had in a region in which the Ottomans were heavily involved) and, above all, the circumstance that Asadollah Khan of Herat is described as still alive (he had actually died in 1719–1720[69]) seem to militate against an attribution to men (like Beneveni and Minier) who spent years in Central Asia and must have been well acquainted with the situation in Afghanistan. On another occasion, the anonymous author speaks of 'Adel Girey (1719–1725) as if the latter were still the reigning *Shamkhal* of the Qumuq, whereas 'Adel Girey was defeated and deposed by the Russians in 1725.[70] Most probably, however, this is simply a case of the author of *Varij ragionamenti* (be he Beneveni or not) not being able to keep track of the fate of a lesser local ruler on

the fringes of an expanding Russian empire, and as such not particularly significant from the point of view of the authorship and dating of the work: yet one may
remark that, in general, the anonymous author's knowledge of the 'Tatars' living
in the Caucasian region does not appear to be very thorough. In the only Italian
text written by Beneveni that was accessible to us,[71] he employed the forms *Irat,
Candehar, Astrahan*, and *Astrabat*[72] (unlike the author of *Varij ragionamenti*, who
wrote *Harat* and *Ira, Candahar, Astracan, Esterabad*): nonetheless, he may have
used these forms due to his addressing a Russian readership and the need to con-
form to Russian spelling and pronounciation. On the other hand, he writes *sciah*
(for 'shah'), *Sciruan, Augani* (for 'Afghans'), and *Ispahan*[73] just as the anonymous
author does. A more detailed comparison of the two texts, as well as the search
for possible evidence of regional linguistic variations, should however be left to a
specialist in Italian philology.

The anonymous author wrote at a time when the political situation in Persia
was still very fluid. He saw the Ottomans as the strongest force in the country and
those who were best placed to achieve their strategic aims. His speculations on the
fate of Persia and the next moves of the actors operating on the local political scene,
as well as his assessment of the power relations between them, were of course cut
short by the quick and spectacular rise of Tahmaspqoli Khan/Nader Shah, who
decisively defeated the Afghans in 1729 and wrested Tabriz from the Ottomans
in 1730: this does not necessarily mean that such speculations and assessments
were unfounded or wrong at the time when they were made, but it may remind
us of how difficult it is to write about current geopolitical matters (today just as
three centuries ago) and shake our confidence a little bit further regarding the
statements and predictions of present-day 'experts' (on the Middle East or other
hotspots). This portrayal of a very brief phase in Persia's history is, in addition to
the factual information, the most interesting aspect of *Varij ragionamenti*.

Although the Italian text of the document can be found in the Appendix, an
English summary will probably be not unhelpful.[74] Our text opens in a rather
classic way with an indictment of the Turks: they are the most barbarous and
cruel people living on the face of the Earth, they have devoted themselves to
the destruction of the Christians and of all the 'nations' that refuse to submit
politically to them, and in them a false religious doctrine is coupled with a brutal nature (fol. 87a). According to our author, the Ottoman claim to universal
monarchy rests on several pillars: the possession of 'the three metropolises of
the three parts of the world', that is, Constantinople, Cairo, and Baghdad; and
sovereignty over the birthplaces of the three great lawgivers, Moses, Jesus, and
Muhammad, over the places where they announced their revelations and over
their resting places[75] (fol. 87b).

Then the author assesses the situation of Ashraf and his Afghans. Given the
imperial claims of the Ottomans, the anonymous author does not see how they

could possibly accept a compromise with Ashraf. The latter, however, is obliged to sue for peace since Isfahan, which possibly has a population of 120,000,[76] 'has been isolated for six years from the nearby regions': its soil not being fertile, the food supply of the capital depends on Lorestan and the territory between Isfahan itself and Hamadan. These two regions, however, have been occupied by the Ottomans (the former 'two years ago' and the latter 'last year' on occasion of the Ottoman advance against the Persian capital) and a famine is probably raging there since 'everybody knows that the Turks lay waste wherever territory they set foot on', which in turn means that Isfahan, too, is presumably experiencing a food shortage.[77] Finally, Ashraf cannot receive reinforcements from Kandahar, now probably in the hands of Mir Mahmud's younger brother,[78] who might even invade Persia one day in order to assert his rights over the throne[79] (fol. 88a). Ashraf can count on an army of 40,000, of whom perhaps as few as 5,000 are Afghan veterans, the rest being motley troops of limited value (*truppe racoltitie*).[80] The Turks and the Kurds who had joined him 'during last year's campaign' must have returned to their country after discovering his weakness, and in so doing they must have convinced their countrymen that Ashraf was not God's envoy, sent to reform and purify Islam from the 'abuses' introduced to it,[81] and to restore Ottoman greatness by fighting against the 'German Christians'—as the Turks themselves had superstitiously believed. Finally, there was yet another, more important factor of which the anonymous writer was absolutely convinced. Shah Tahmasp II had established himself two years earlier in Mazandaran and presently controls the provinces of Tabarestan and Astarabad as well, which can provide up to 20,000 fighters: because of the struggle between the Ottomans and Afghans, the anonymous author believes (although he is '800 leagues away from the theatre of war' when writing) that the Shah cannot have failed to raise a 'powerful army', leave his strongholds, conquer Qazvin, and threaten Isfahan, thereby forcing Ashraf to seek peace with the Porte (fol. 88b). Given that Ashraf cannot leave Isfahan for fear of an Ottoman attack, the Shah must have become master of the countryside, which in turn would induce the populace to join him, thinking that the Ottomans are actually supporting the Safavid house.[82]

Be that as it may, if the Ottomans hold out, writes the anonymous author, they will conclude peace on favourable terms and force Ashraf to recognize the Sultan as 'the supreme ruler of Mohammedanism', thereby reducing the Afghans to the same vassal status as the Crimean Tatars and the Regencies of the Barbary Coast. If the Turks would act rationally and were not blinded by 'ridiculous superstition', they would conquer Isfahan and thereby acquire a 'general right' (*dritto generale*) over Persia; if they operate otherwise, they cannot rest assured of Ashraf's loyalty, as he would certainly exploit any favourable chance that might arise after the Ottomans withdrew their forces. The Ottomans might want to find an agreement with the Afghans in order to incite them against the Russians

without engaging in open conflict with the latter: however, Ashraf is unable to
invade Gilan because the Afghans are not used to warfare in mountainous and
wooded regions and are not able to force their way through narrow defiles.[83] And
the Afghans can only enter Gilan through the *Serdab* [Sardab] Pass, which forty
grenadiers can defend against 'any powerful army' (fol. 89a). Whatever agreement the Ottomans may reach with Ashraf, they would certainly not include
the Russians in it, who would therefore 'be left to their own devices' (fols. 89a–
89b). A very good decision (*ottimo partito*) for the Russians would have been to
strengthen Shah Tahmasp II's 'good cavalry' with infantry and march on Isfahan
together with him via Qazvin at the same time as the Ottomans marched from
Baghdad to the Persian capital: this would have obliged Ashraf to abandon
Isfahan, and the Russians would have acted in conformity with their treaty of
1724 with the Ottomans, whereby they pledged to reinstate Shah Tahmasp II
on the Persian throne.[84] Instead, they preferred to watch idly. As a consequence,
once the Ottomans have disposed of the Afghans, it may be the Russians' turn,
since 'there is nothing more certain' than the fact that, after they have reached
a *modus vivendi* of any sort with Ashraf, the Ottomans will ask Russia to cede
Gilan: if they do not do this immediately it is only in order to recover from the
latest Persian campaign and to be able to put the claim forward more forcefully
later.[85] The Ottomans hope that Muscovy will cede Gilan through diplomacy
and without fighting—and the anonymous author is of the opinion that the
Russians will comply.

The Ottomans rightly 'court' Gilan because it is the 'most populated and richest province of the Persian monarchy' and the only one that has escaped the
ravages of the civil war.[86] In Gilan there are 25 cities, between 'good' and 'medio-
cre', and a very large number of villages (fol. 89b). It produces 3,000 bales of
silk every year at 100 pounds (*libbra*) each,[87] large quantities of golden brocade
and silk cloth, 'very good' saffron, fruits, vegetables (*legumi*), and 'an incredible
quantity of very good rice', of which some is exported to the rest of Persia but
most to Russia:[88] all of this is paid for in cash. Not only is Gilan self-sufficient
but it provides many other regions with what they need, and 'the Orientals hold
it for the equivalent of the Kingdom of Egypt.' The Shah used to draw 60,000
tomans revenue from Gilan, corresponding to about 2,000,000 German florins.[89]
According to the terms of the Treaty of Constantinople, Ottomans and Russians
were not supposed to share a border and the territory ruled by Shah Tahmasp
II was to be the buffer between them. While the Russians respected these terms
carefully, the Turks broke them by conquering Ardabil,[90] which lies 'at the
mouth' (*sopra le fauci*) of Gilan and had been granted to Shah Tahmasp II precisely because it is so easy to enter Gilan from that city. Gilan is but an eight-hour
march from Ardabil and can be entered through a pass called *Beias evler*, whose
inhabitants are Sunnis and wait for the Ottomans 'with great eagerness.'[91] This is

the only point through which one can move artillery, ammunition, 'and the rest' (fol. 90a). The Ottomans could therefore invade Gilan without being hindered by the Russians and force them to evacuate the province (fols. 90a–90b). The Russians are indeed too weak in Gilan to be able to stop the Turks: they have no cavalry, they can receive reinforcements from the motherland only with great delay, and sometimes sea storms wreck the fleets carrying troops, as happened in 1722 and 1724.[92] In contrast, the Ottomans are fully in control of Armenia and 'Media' through which they can transfer troops, ammunition, and food supplies from Asia Minor. And since the fame of the great wealth of Gilan whets the 'ravenous mind' (*animo ingordo*) of the Turks, they will not fail to conquer it. Should the Russians want to put Shah Tahmasp II on the throne of the whole of Persia, they are bound to fail since they cannot supply him with the necessary number of troops to conquer Isfahan and, at the same time, garrison Gilan properly. Furthermore, the Ottomans would certainly make peace with Ashraf and support him against both Shah Tahmasp II and the Russians, which would in turn lead to an open breach (*rottura*) between the Porte and Russia that, in Persia, can only be harmful to the latter.

The Ottomans have always been mistrustful of the ruler of Georgia, *Vactan Kan* (King Vakht'ang VI), and now that he is in exile in Russia they are afraid that the Russians may induce him to rouse trouble in his kingdom, which is presently occupied by the Turks themselves. *Vactan Kan* will certainly promise Russia 'mountains of gold' to convince her to move against the Ottomans, but he is not 'loved' by the Georgian grandees and therefore he does not enjoy much support in the country (fol. 90b). The only possibility for him to come back is Russia giving those grandees guarantees that he has abandoned any feeling of hate and rancour towards them and would therefore act in full harmony with them; in their turn, the grandees would rise against the 'tyrannical Turkish yoke' and restore their country to its previous freedom (fols. 90b–91a). The only Georgian feudal lord loyal to *Vactan Kan* is *chisnis Eris tavi*,[93] who can raise 5,000 warriors. *If all the Georgian grandees were united, they could cause a significant distraction for the Ottoman forces in case of a breach between the Porte and Russia.*[94] The anonymous author is of the opinion that Ottoman hostility towards *Vactan* is nothing but a direct consequence of the hostility that the *beylerbeyi* of Georgia, *Isac Pascia* (İshak Paşa),[95] nurtures for *Vactan*'s brother, Mustafa Paşa. The latter has converted to Islam and is currently in Tbilisi, from where he offers the Sultan large amounts of money in order to be appointed *beylerbeyi*. *Isac Pascia* is aware of these attempts and stokes the Ottoman court's fear of *Vactan* in order to prevent his own demotion from governor in favour of Mustafa Paşa, who won much credit at the Porte for the role he played in subduing Georgia.

Outside of Gilan, the Russians are the masters of Shirvan, with the 'impregnable fortress' of Baku and its 'large territory', and of the 'ancient fortress' of

Darband, which is dominated by a castle (also said to be 'impregnable') built on a very high rock. Darband is located 'between Shirvan and Asian Albania': known during antiquity as 'the Caspian Gates', according to the 'histories of the Persians' it was built by Alexander the Great at the most favourable place to stop Scythian raids into Persia, and its southern walls touch the Caspian Sea[96] (fol. 91a). The fortress is defended by seventy pieces of ordnance on its eastern side, whereas its western side is surrounded by very high mountains with narrow passes, where 'a few carbines can deny passage to larger armies'. Peter the Great and his army reached Darband in 1722 during his campaign to subdue the 'Scythians, or local Tatars', who were once Persian subjects but 'prepared novelties' thanks to the disruption and chaos caused in Persia by Mir Mahmud's siege of Isfahan.[97] Peter gave audience to the governor of the fortress, who had come to welcome him, and told him that he had arrived from far away to help his friend the Shah against his rebels, according to the request of the Shah himself. Then he asked the governor to allow him to enter Darband 'in order to see that renowned fortress'. The governor obliged in perfect good faith, whereupon Peter 'acted in the same way as Louis XIV in Strasbourg':[98] he placed a garrison of 4,000 soldiers[99] in the fortress and ordered the governor to leave immediately together with his family. People who have not visited those lands cannot realize the importance the fortress of Darband holds for Russia, which would be 'at great risk' without its possession given the chaotic state in which Persia finds itself (fol. 91b). Indeed, the fortress 'cuts the communications between the Scythians, or *Chingi* Tatars'.[100] These are the same Tatars, or 'Sarmatian Scythians', who conquered Persia and then, 'at the beginning of the 13th century', invaded and ferociously devastated Hungary and Poland at a time when the throne of the Holy Roman Empire was vacant between the death of Friedrich II of Hohenstaufen and the election of Rudolf I of Austria.[101] Having finally been repulsed, some of them settled down in the Crimea and others further east, in 'eastern Albania', where they created several 'princedoms'; 'those who live in the Kingdoms of Astrakhan and Kazan are the subjects of the Czar of Muscovy.' In 'Albania', on the coast of the Caspian Sea, there are three 'princes': the most powerful of them is called *Sciamkal bei* and is a vassal of Persia and of Russia at the same time. The other two rulers are *Andre Bei* and *Murtasà Bei*,[102] both Persian vassals: together with *Sciamkal bei* they can field 80,000 men. Their territories lie between the fortresses of Darband and *Terchi*,[103] both of which are held by the Russians. West of Darband is where the Lezghis live. They are also Persian subjects: however, they rose in rebellion a few years earlier, have conquered Shirvan and 'now' they have submitted to the Ottomans, since the latter got close to their territory thanks to the conquest of Ganjeh.[104] North of Darband live those Tatars who are more correctly called *Chingi*; they can count on 100,000 warriors. 'All these Tatars' planned to conquer Darband, open their way through Albania, join forces first with 'those three princes'[105] and then with the Tatars of Astrakhan and Kazan, and finally invade 'Muscovy' together (fol. 92a), thereby 'freeing their Muslim brothers from the Christian yoke'. And they would have succeeded in their design if Peter the Great, with his swift march on Darband, 'had not surrounded some and cut the communications among the others'.[106] The anonymous author reports that, in the opinion of the Persians, the appropriate title for the 'Czars of Muscovy' should simply be Grand Duke (*gran Duca*) on account of their possession of Muscovy and 'Black Russia' (*Russia Negra*):[107] because of their possession of the 'vast Tatar country' (*vasto paese tartaro*), they deserve the name 'Emperor of Tartary', since the region was an empire from the 13th century to the end of the 14th. 'All these Tatars' are Sunnis like the Ottomans, and the proximity of the latter makes them nurture great hopes: if there is an open war between Russia and the Porte, 'there are no doubts' that the Ottomans will find a great deal of support among the Tatars, although many of them are within reach of the above-mentioned fortresses of Darband and Terki. Darband has a harbour that could easily receive a fleet, but the *Chingi* filled it in the 13th century; Peter the Great wanted to have it dug and restored, but he was prevented from doing so by his untimely death. There are no other ports in the surroundings, and therefore naval squadrons are exposed to danger in the case of storms, as the events of previous years have shown.[108]

Besides Ashraf, who is the master of Isfahan and its surroundings, and the Lezghis who have conquered Shirvan (also known as Hyrcania),[109] there is Malek Mahmud, the Khan of Sistan (*Segestan*): 'committing a great treason' (*con grande fellonia*) against his legitimate prince he has become the lord of Bactria,[110] which is 'nowadays' called Khorasan (*Horassan*) and is reckoned to correspond to one-fifth of the Kingdom (*monarchia*) of Persia (fol. 92b). Furthermore, the usurper Asadollah (*Esadulah*) rules over the Kingdom of Herat, which was called *Ira* during Antiquity: he too rebelled against his 'natural ruler' and made himself independent.[111] All these 'new rulers' have bolstered up their position, and 'in a short time' they cannot fail to attack each other in the hope of increasing their dominions. As a consequence, peace is very far away for Persia, 'and perhaps it will need several decades before it comes' (fol. 93a).

Appendix: Varij ragionamenti sopra lo stato presente, e la Crisi, in cui la Persia si trova

Non vi è individuo nel genere umano, che sentendo il nome Turco, non venga in cognitione di un popolo il più barbaro, e crudele, che il vasto ambito della terra in se contenga; di una natione, ch'è inimica giurata del nome Christiano, all'estermino dello istesso tutti i suoi pensieri, e consigli dirigendo; di gente, che non tende, che alla ruvina di tutti, ed alla universal desolatione di quei, sopra i

quali per la loro spietata sorte prevale; conforme senza addurne infiniti deplor-
abili esempij de' passati secoli; ne nostri giorni la Morea nel 1715; e molto più
gl'anni scorsi la Persia con indicibil tragedia, ed esterminio inreparabile ne speri-
mentarono. La erronea credenza Mahometana conformandosi al genio brutale
de suoi credenti, ordinagli nell'alcorano non solo l'esterminio, sia per fas, ò nefas
di tutte le nationi, che ad ella soggettarsi repugnano; ma vuol anche, che frà
tutti i Mahometani non vi possa esser, che un solo Sovrano; e formandosi più
Sovranità, i sovrani debbano frà di se à tal segno perseguitarsi, che vinti, sca-
ciati, ed uccisi tutti gli altri; quello, che in ultimo prevale, debba esser l'unico
Sovrano de' Mahometani. Sultan Ahmed gran Signor de' Turchi pretende esser
l'unico, e legittimo herede di tal Sovranità, si per aver i suoi antenati con la occu-
patione di due Imperij, 40: Regni, è moltissime [**fol. 87a**] Provincie propagato
ampiamente l'alcorano; come anche obedendo alla predetta ordinatione della
sua credenza, perseguitando, e facendo aspre guerre à tutti i Sovrani della stessa
sua setta, gli avevano tutti uccisi, ed esterminati; il più potente frà quali essendo
stato Saladino ultimo sultano di Eggitto, fù questo vinto, ed ucciso da Sultan
Selim gran Signor de Turchi; il quale per conseguenza essendosi reso padrone di
Medina, e Mecca patria, e Mausuleo dell'impostor Mahometo, si fece proclamare
Monarcha universale non solo de' Mahometani, ma anche dell'Universo, per il
titolo, che possedendo le trè Metropoli dè trè parti del mondo Constantinopoli
dell'Europa, Babilonia dell'Asia, gran Cairo, ò pure Faraunia dell'Africa, pretend-
eva egli dover essere riconosciuto da tutta la terra per tale; aggiungeva à predetti
il titolo della possessione de' Santi luoghi, dove erano nati i tre Legislatori, Moise
in Eggitto, Giesù in Nazaret, e Mahometo in Medina; dove avevano publicato le
leggi, che sono il monte Sinai, la Palestina, e l'Arabia; dove anche erano sepolti,
cioè il Monte Oreb, Gerusalemme, e Mecca. Per tutte queste apparenti raggioni
li Sultani di Constantinopoli s'immaginano anche il di d'oggi aver un ius, e diritto
alla universal Monarchia di tutta la terra, il che superstitiosamente si lusingano,
che un di arivar debba, perciò essi s'intitolano <u>Padiscia alem pena</u>,[112] e la loro
potenza <u>devlet alie</u>, il primo volendo significare Monarcha patrone del mondo,
ed il secondo potenza universale. Essendo le predette tutte cosse impresse nel
orgolio [**fol. 87b**] Turchesco, sembra cossa assai ardua ad esser compresa dalla
parte de Turchi in qual maniera si possa comporre un accommodamento frà
il gran Signor ed Esciref, e far una pace stabile. Non vi è cossa più certa, che
Esciref domandi la pace per trovarsi in angustie, ed assai debole; si ritrova in
angustie primieramente, perche bisogna suppor, che attualmente in Ispahan
siano circa 120 m[ila]: anime frà combattenti, e gli habitanti di detta Città, il territorio della quale non è fertile, che con la grande industria de' coltivatori, i quali
mancando per le intestine guerre, non puol quello esser di alcun utilità à tanto
popolo, il mantenimento del quale dipendendo inremediabilmente dal Loristan,
e dal paese intraposto, frà hamadan [*sic*], e detta Ispahan, ed il primo essendo

da due anni in quà in poter de' turchi, ed il secondo l'anno antecedente invaso dall'essercito Turco, quando questo marchiò verso la metropoli mentovata; ed essendo à tutti ben noto, che per dove passa il turco tutto ruuina [*sic*], e desola, bisogna creder per cossa certa che vi regni una grandissima carestia non solo, ma anche terribil famina; Ispahan da sei anni in quà non ha communicatione con alcun paese vicino, onde necessariamente bisogna che sofri grandissima penuria di ogni cossa.

Esciref è oppresso anche dalle angustia [*sic*] per non poter aver soccorsi da sua gente da Candahar, dovendo supporsi, che in quel regno habbia prevaluto il partito del cadetto di Mir Mahmud, che vi si trova personalmente sostenendo i suoi dritti, [*sic*] e chi sà che non venghi un giorno con armata mano à disputar al Esciref la Capitale di Persia à se dovuta per esser stata conquistata dal suo fratel maggiore [**fol. 88a**]. Non potendo dunque Esciref avver rinforzi di truppe da Candahar non puol avver che pocho residuo de suoi veterani avghani, e forse non più di cinque milla, il resto della sua armata di circa 40.000: uomini non essendo composta che di truppe racoltitie; forze incomparabilmente inferiori al numeroso essercito Ottomano; e quelli Turchi, ò Curdi, che nella campagna dell'anno passato si gettarono al suo partito, avvendo visto la debolezza di lui, e la somma carestia nel paese, bisogna pur creder, che non averano mancato abbandonandolo, ritornarsene alla loro patria, imprimendo ne turchi un concetto tutto differente, di quello, che superstitiosamente avevano concepito, che Esciref fosse un messo di Dio mandato per riformare gli abusi introdotti nel mahometanismo, e perciò riaquistare [*sic*] l'anticha gloria ottomana guerregiando vittoriosamente contro i Cristiani germani, che avevano ofuscato ne passate guerre lo splendore del glorioso nome musulmano con reiterate, e generali battaglie guadagnate sopra d'essi Turchi. Ciascheduna delle predette raggioni è sufficiente ad obligar Esciref à mendicar la pace. Ma vi è un'altra più potente, e veridica, che io benche mi ritrovi a 800: leghe discosto da quel teatro di guerre, la tengo per indubitabile, ed è, che Sciah Tamas già da due anni rinserrato nella provincia di Masanderan, avvendo anche in sua devotione le provincie di Taberistan, ed Esterabad, abbondante di militia, potendo fornire fino 20.000: uomini, prevalendosi della favorabil occasione delle discordie de Turchi, ed avgani non averà mancato di formar potente armata, sortir da detta Provincia, ricuperar Casbin, e minaciar Ispahan. Ed Esciref [**fol. 88b**] non potendo scostarsi da Ispahan per tema dell'avvicinamento de Turchi, Tamas si sarà reso padrone del paese apperto, ed i Persiani credendo, che i Turchi agiscono per Tamas per restituirlo nel trono paterno, non mancarano di ripiglar coraggio, ed unirsi al loro natural Prencipe. Sia come si voglia se i Ottomani tengono fermo non solo farano una pace avantaggiosa, ma anche obligarano Esciref à riconnoscer il gran Signor per Supremo Sovrano del Mahometanismo, anzi soggettarsi à lui conforme allo stesso sono subordinati li Tartari della Crimea, e gli barbari dell'Africa.

Anzi se i Turchi aggissero da senno, non lasciandosi acciecar dalla ridicola super-
stitione, s'impadronirebbero d'Ispahan, scaciandone di li Esciref, ed essendo
padroni della capitale, aquistarebbero [sic] un dritto [sic] generale sopra tutto il
restante della Monarchia; facendo altrimenti non saprei, come possono assicu-
rarsi della lealtà di Esciref, perche al slontanarsi dell'Essercito Turco, non man-
carebbe di prevalersi d'ogni favorabile occasione. Se non vogliamo dire, che i
Turchi s'accommoderano con gli avgani per fomentar questi contro li Russi, non
volendo essi comparire nella scena in tal caso Esciref non sarà in stato di invader
Ghilan, per che le sue truppe non son accostumate à battersi ne paesi montag-
nosi, e boscosi, ne sforzar distretti angusti, non avvendo essi che un solo passo
detto <u>Serdab,</u> per penetrar in Ghilan, che da 40: soli granatieri puol essere guar-
dato contro qualsisia potente armata. Finalmente facendosi un accomodamento
di qualsisia maniera frà ottomani, e Esciref, si ha da supporre, che li primi [**fol.
89a**] non farano alcuna mentione in qualunque trattatto de' Russi, quali essendo
esclusi, si vedrano abbandonati alle proprie loro misure. Sarebbe stato per essi
ottimo partito, che marchiando i Turchi da babilonia [sic] verso Ispahan, essi
anche fornendo Sciah Tamas di fanteria, essendo lo stesso provisto di buona
cavalleria, con esso si fossero portati dalla parte di Casbin verso Ispahan, per
divertire Esciref, il quale vedendosi attacato con due potenti armate non
avverebbe mancato abbandonar Ispahan, e cercarne scapo [sic]. In tal caso i
Russi operato averebbero conforme il trattatto concluso con Turchi in
Constantinopoli l'anno 1724: nel qual trattatto si obliga la Russia di rimetter
Tamas sul trono paterno. Ma di già che hano voluto sempre stare per cossi dire,
con le mani alla cintola, potrebbe ben arivare che la festa degli avgani, fosse la
vigilia de' russi, attesoche non vi è cossa più certa, che composti gli ottomani con
gli augani, comincierano li primi à metter in campo le loro pretensioni sopra la
provincia di Ghilan, e domandar la cessione di essa da' Russi, e se ciò non faces-
sero immediatemente accomodatisi con gli augani, sarebbe per pigliar lena dalla
longa, e fatigosa guerra di persia [sic] per pocho tempo, e poi con maggior vigore
disputar con Russi. Sperano i Turchi, ed io son della stessa opinione, che la
Moscovia cederà Ghilan in virtù de' trattatti, senza, che sia d'uopo venir alle
mani, e con giusta raggione l'amoreggiano, perche è la più popolata e opulente
provincia della persiana Monarchia, e la sola, che di tante è restata illesa. Ghilan
contiene nel suo recinto vinticinque Città frà buone, e mediocri, senza contarne
il grandissimo numero de' villaggi, perche pare una intiera [**fol. 89b**] popula-
tione, produce 3.000: balle di seta l'anno, pesante 100: libre la balla, vi sono rich-
issime manifatture di stoffe di seta, e d'oro; produce ottimo safrano, ed varij
legumi, ed incredibil quantità di ottimo riso, che si asporta [sic] nel rimanente
della Persia, ma molto più in russia [sic]; abbonda de' frutti delitiosi d'ogni
genere, à segno che non avendo bisogno di alcun paese vicino, fornisce à molti il
bisognevole, ed il tutto à denaro contante; e vien stimata dagli orientali

equivalente al regno d'Eggitto. Le entratte, che il rè di persia [*sic*] ritirava da questa provincia, erano 60.000: tomani, che fano circa 2.000.000 de' fiorini di Alemagna. Nel trattatto fatto in Constantinopoli della spartitione di Persia frà Tahmas, Russi, e Turchi, questi due ultimi non dovevano esser confinanti, ma Tahmas doveva intramezar frà essi, il che fù trattatto con grandissima cautela da' russi per evitar di aver confinanti in quelle parti i Turchi, i quali infrangendo il detto trattatto, s'impadronirono della Città di Ardevil posta sopra le fauci di Ghilan, la qual Città conforme il trattatto, doveva restar à Tahmas, non per altro fine, che per aver un passaggio commodo in quella provincia; Da ardevil [*sic*] alle frontiere di Ghilan non vi sono, che otto ore di camino, il territorio però della predetta Città confina con li limiti della Provincia di Ghilan, nella quale si scende per un passaggio detto <u>beias evler</u>, habitato da mahometani della setta de' Turchi detta <u>Sunni</u>, da' quali sono anhelati con grand'ansietà. Questo è l'unico passaggio, per il quale si puol transitar artiglieria, munitioni, e resto. Dunque i Turchi per questo passo facendo irrutione in detta provincia senza poterne esser impediti da' Russi, presto obligarebbero [**fol. 90a**] questi abbandonarla. I Russi sono assai deboli in Ghilan per poter opporsi alla irrutione delle numerose truppe ottomane; mancano di cavalleria, e non possono ricever rinforzi dal loro paese, se non molto tardi, e qualche volta, come arivò gia per due volte cioè l'anno 1722: e l'anno 1724: quel mar cattivo fà nafragar [*sic*] flotte intiere; al contrario i Turchi padroni di tutta la Media, Armenia, ed à tali conquiste confinando l'Asia minore, che facilmente puol fornire, e numerose truppe, e provisioni si di guerra, che di bocca, e la fama delle grandi richezze di quella provincia alettando l'animo ingordo d'essi, non mancarano di soggettarla al loro Imperio, e d'agregarla alle passate conquiste. Supposto anche, che i Russi voglino metter alla testa della Monarchia Sciah Tamas, nianche in ciò riuscir potrano, perche non possono dargli truppe sufficienti per la conquista di Ispahan, e guardar ben presidiata la provincia di Ghilan, fuor che avrano ben à temer i Turchi, i quali agiustatisi con Esciref, indubitabilmente lo soccorreranno contro Tahmas, e Russi, onde si verrà ad una aperta rottura frà gli ottomani, e Russi, la quale non puol esser, che perniciosa alli ultimi in Persia.

I Turchi hano sempre avuto gelosia del Prencipe di Georgia Vactan Kan, il quale anche al di d'oggi gli da gran ombraggio, per essersi questo ricovrato in Russia, ne dubitano, che fomentato da quella, possi causar qualche turbolenza, ed inquietargli nel possesso del regno di Georgia. detto [*sic*] Prencipe non mancarà di prometter montagne d'oro alla Russia per impegnarla con Turchi, non essendo però amato da' grandi del paese, non ha in quello grand'appogio ; una sol cossa puol essergli proficua, che la Russia assicurasse detti grandi, che Vactan deposto [**fol. 90b**] deposto [*sic*] ogni odio, e rancore passarebbe con loro perfetta, e leale intelligenza, ed essi per scuoter il tirannico giogo Turchesco, pensar voglino, à riaquistar [*sic*] la pristina libertà alla loro patria. Il detto Prencipe non ha che un solo grande, che tien le sue parti, e che puol armar cinque milla combattenti, ed é chiamato chisnis Eris tavi. *Intendendosi* [*sic*], *che se tutti i grandi della Georgia si unissero veramente d'animo, e di forze, e si venisse à qualche rottura frà Russi, e Turchi non mancarebbero far à questi grandissima diversione.*[113] Credo io dunque, che questa grande gelosia, che i Turchi hano del Prencipe Vactan non deriva da altro, che dalla grande Gelosia, che Isac Pascia Beglerbei di Georgia concepisce del fratello del predetto Vactan, chiamato Mustafâ pascia, che si è fatto Turco, e si ritrova in Tiflis, ofrendo somme al Gran Signor per il governo di Georgia, ed il beilerbei consapevole di questi maneggi, fà concepire alla Porta grande ombra di Vactan, affinche alla sua esclusione il divano non si induca à rimetter il governo della Georgia al fratello di questo, il quale per servitij resi al gran Signor nel sottometergli tutta la Georgia si è aquistato [*sic*] gran merito apresso la porta ottomana.

I Russi fuor della Provincia di Ghilan sono padroni nella Provincia di Scirvan, che è l'anticha Hircania della inespugnabil fortezza di Bacù con ampio territorio; possiedono anche l'anticha fortezza di Derbent posta fra i confini del Scirvan, e della albania [*sic*] Asiatica, questa fortezza dai antichi detta Porte Caspie fù eretta da Alessandro Macedone conforme le istorie Persiano [*sic*] in sito avantagiosissimo per frenar le incursioni dei Sciti nella Persia, le sue mura verso il midi sono bagnate dal mar Caspio, verso l'aquilone è dominata da una fortezza inespugnabile posta sopra un altissimo [**fol. 91a**] rocco, munita di 70: pezzi di batteria, all'oriente, si come dalla parte del occidente, è cinta d'altissime montagne con angusti passaggi, dove poche carabine possono disputar il passo à esserciti numerosi. L'anno 1722: Pietro primo Czar di Moscovia, venuto verso il mar Caspio per rafrenare la baldanza de Sciti, o tartari di quelle parti, che altre volte soggetti alla Persia, per trovarsi al'ora [*sic*] questa in grandissime confusioni, essendo la sua capitale cinta di assedio da Mir: Mahmud avgano infestissimo ribelle di quella corona, meditavano novità, s'avicinò avanti questa fortezza con la sua armata; Il Sultan Governatore di essa per il rè di Persia, non tardò di venir incontro con magnifico seguito à Sua Maestà Russiana; la quale accoltolo benignamente, disse al Governatore, che era venuto da tanto lontano per soccorrer il rè di Persia suo amico contro i suoi rubelli, conforme, che dallo stesso rè era stato richiesto, e perciò domandava entrar in Derbend per veder quella fortezza tanto rinomata; Il Sultano gli ofri [*sic*] l'entrata sotto buona fede, dove entrato senza più prolongare, agi [*sic*] della stessa maniera, che Luigi 14: in Strasburgh, mettendovi guarniggione di 4.000: Russi in quella fortezza, ordinando al Governatore, che si ritirasse da essa incontinente con la sua famiglia. In tal maniera passò quella nobilissima fortezza sotto il dominio Russo. Chi non è stato in quelli paesi difficilmente potra [*sic*] concepire di che importanza sia quella fortezza alla Russia, senza la quale suposto le confusioni di Persia si sarebbe messa in grandissimo rischio. Perche la fortezza di Derbend taglia la communicatione di tutti i [**fol. 91b**] Sciti, ò pur Tartari Chingi. Questi sono quei Tartari, o pur Sciti

Sarmatici, che nel principio del secolo 13: vacando l'Imperio di Occidente per la morte di Federico secondo di Svevia, e prima dell'elevatione al Imperial trono di Rodolfo primo austriaco, avvendo conquistato la Persia, fecero crudeli invasioni nella Ungheria, e Polonia, devastando con incredibil desolationi quelli floridi Regni, ma finalmente respinti, parte restò nella Crimea, e parte avvendo ricolato più in dietro si ritirò nell'Albania Orientale, dividendola in varij principati, quelli che habitano ne' Regni di Astracan, e Casan sono soggetti al Czar di Moscovia; in Albania sopra le spiagie del caspio [*sic*] vi sono tre prencipi, il più potente detto Sciamkal bei [*sic*], era feudatario si de' Persiani, come anche della Russia, gli altri due ricevevano il loro feudo solo dai Rè di Persia, l'uno de quali si chiama Andre Bei, e l'altro Murtasà Bei, e benche il Sciamcal [*sic*] bei sia il più potente, tutti 3: però insieme possono armar 80.000: uomini, e le pianure del loro paese poste sono frà Derbent, e Terchi, ed ambe queste fortezze appartengono alla Russia. Verso l'occidente di Derbent sono i Lesghi, essi anche alla Persia soggetti, contro la quale però ribellatisi, gli anni scorsi rapirono alla stessa la provincia di Scirvan, ed ora si son fatti feudatarij de' Turchi, essendo questi con l'ocupatione di Gangia avicinati à loro confini, al Nord di Derbend gli tartari detti propriamente Chingi, potenti di 100.000: combattenti, il dissegno di tutti questi tartari era di occupar Derbend, aprirsi il camino nell'Albania, congiungersi con quei trè Prencipi, e poi tutti unirsi con li tartari di Astracan, e Casan sudditi [*sic*] della Russia, e tutti giunti insieme invader la mos- [**fol. 92a**] covia [*sic*] liberando i loro fratelli mahometani dal giogo de' Christiani, il che gli sarebbe riuscitto, se il Czar Pietro non avesse acelerato la sua marchia con l'essercito verso derbend [*sic*] non avesse rinserrato gli uni, e tagliato la communicatione con gli altri. Non pare fuor di proposito di mentovare quello, che i Persiani dicono de Czari di Moscovia, che per titolo di possessione della Moscovia, e russia [*sic*] Negra non gli convien, che il titolo di gran Duca, ma per il vasto paese tartaro che occupa, essendo stato anticamente Imperio dal secolo 13: fino all'ultimo del 14: gli conviene il nome di Imperator di Tartaria. Tutti questi Tartari sono di credenza Mahometana della setta di Sunni, che è quella da ottomani professata, dall'avicinamento de' quali non mancano concepir alte speranze, e senza dubio, se si vien ad una guerra apperta frà la Russia, e Turchi, troverano questi aiuti considerabili da essi tartari, benche una gran parte siano servati dalle prenominate due fortezze. La fortezza di Derbent tiene un porto assai commodo per recettione di una flotta, ma nel secolo 13: li Chingi lo riempirono, il Czar Pietro primo aveva meditato farlo nettare, e svotare, ma prevenuto da immatura morte, non pote [*sic*] esseguir si buon dissegno; in quelle vicinanze altri porti non vi sono, percio le flotte al sofiar di vento contrario, sono esposte al periglio, come gli essempij degl'anni passati fecero chiaro.

Fuor del rubelle Esciref padrone di Ispahan, e contorni; e gli Lesghi conquistatori di Scirvan, o Hircania; vi è anche Malik mahmud [*sic*] Kan di Segestan che con grande fellonia contro il suo legittimo Sovrano si è reso patrone della Bactriana, oggi detta horassan [sic], dove essercita Sovranità; la Bactriana è stimata la quinta parte della Monarchia [**fol. 92b**]. Nel Regno di Harat, da antichi detto Ira regna l'usurpator Esadulah [sic], questo ancora solevatosi contra il suo natural Prencipe sotrasse quel regno alla di lui ubbidienza rendendosi indipendente. Tutti questi nuovi Sovrani inmancabilmente essendosi stabiliti, frà qualche tempo non possono mancar di offendersi gli uni con gli altri per l'ambitione di stender il loro dominio, per conseguenza la tranquillità della Persia è assai lontana, e forse ne tirerà à molti Lustri[114] [**fol. 93a**].

Notes

1. Vienna, Haus-, Hof- und Staatsarchiv (hereafter: HHStA), *Handschriften Rot 134*, fols. 69a–71a: interestingly, the ruler is addressed as *Tahmas Kulikan* [...] *Imperatori Persarum*.
2. More than that cannot be said with certainty about the attitude of the *Serenissima* towards Persia in political matters after 1722, since the final reports to the Senate of the Venetian ambassadors at the Ottoman Porte seem to have disappeared and the dispatches of the same ambassadors still await an in-depth study.
3. Jean Otter, *Journal de voyages en Turquie et en Perse, 1734–1744*, ed. Alain Riottot (Paris: L'Harmattan, 2010), pp. 31–33; M. Gharavi, 'Un médecin des Lumières: Simon de Vierville et et son voyage en Perse', *Moyen Orient et Océan Indien* (1994): pp. 35–155 (pp. 43–45 on the genesis of the mission); Florence Hellot-Bellier, *France–Iran: Quatre cents ans de dialogue* (Paris: Association pour l'avancement des études iraniennes, 2007), pp. 77–80. As far as Austria is concerned, cf. *infra*, footnote 46.
4. HHStA, *Handschriften Rot 134*, fols. 1a–58a. Another copy is in HHStA, *Staatenabteilungen ausserdeutsche Staaten, Persien*, Kart. 1 (Konv. 1691–1753), fols. 31a–42a.
5. Along the way he obtained letters supporting the missionaries from the Grand Duke of Tuscany, the Senate of Venice and the Emperor.
6. *A Chronicle of the Carmelites in Persia*, ed. H. Chick, 2 vols. (London: I. B. Tauris, 2012) (1st ed., London 1939), vol. I, p. 499.
7. Rudi Matthee, 'Negotiating across cultures: The Dutch Van Leene Mission to the Iranian court of Shah Soleiman, 1689–1692', *Eurasian Studies*, 3 (2004): pp. 35–63; idem, 'A sugar banquet for the Shah: Anglo-Dutch competition at the Iranian court of Šah Sultan Hosein (r. 1694–1722)', *Eurasian Studies*, 5 (2006) (*Liber Amicorum: Études sur l'Iran médiéval et moderne offertes à Jean Calmard*, ed. Michele Bernardini, Masashi Haneda, Maria Szuppe), pp. 195–217.
8. HHStA, *Handschriften Weiß 706/30*, fols. 25a–43a.
9. And not von Harrach, as in *Quellen zur Geschichte Afrikas, Asiens und Ozeaniens in Österreichischen Staatsarchiv bis 1918* (Munich: K. G. Saur Verlag, 1986), pp. 22, 261, which is the source of the false attributions appearing in Giorgio Rota, 'Some Remarks on Wine Consumption as a Political Factor Under the Safavids', in *Wine Culture in Iran and Beyond*, ed. Bert G. Fragner, Ralph Kauz, and Florian Schwarz (Vienna: Verlag der Österreichischen Akademie der Wissenschaften, 2014), p. 235, and Rudi Matthee, *Persia in Crisis* (London: I. B. Tauris, 2012), p. 330. On his life, cf. Eduard Freiherr von Feuchtersleben, 'Die Grafen von Harrsch', in *Oesterreichische Zeitschrift für Geschichts- und Staatskunde*, 54 (1837), pp. 213–216 and 55 (1837), pp. 217–219; *Die Belagerung von Freiburg im Breisgau 1713: Tagebuch des österreichischen Kommandanten Feldmarschall-Lieutenants Freiherrn von Harrsch*, ed. Freiherr von der Wengen (Freiburg i. Br.: Eugen Stoll, 1898), n. 44, pp. XL–XLI and pp. 400–401. I would like to thank Prof. Leopold Auer, former director of the Haus-, Hof- und Staatsarchiv, for pointing to the existence of *Quellen* which, despite the occasional misprints, remains a

most precious tool in dealing with the collections of the HHStA. Finally, I am indebted to the author or authors of http://de.wikipedia.org/wiki/Ferdinand_Amadeus_Freiherr_von_Harrsch, which suddenly and unexpectedly clarified the 'mystery' of the name of the author of the *Mémoires*.

10. HHStA, *Handschriften Weiß 706/30, Selecta quaedam ex compendio vitae Ferdinandi Amadei Comitis ab Harrsch partim Latine partim Gallice, post reditum ex Peloponneso, vulgo Morea, scripto*, fols. 21a–25a.

11. Ibid., fols. 24a–24b. Von Harrsch writes here that, to the best of his knowledge, no German had yet made such a journey. However, a fellow Austrian officer had already travelled around the world (although partly unwillingly) a few years earlier: cf. Karl Rudolf Wernhart, *Christoph Carl Fernberger, der erste österreichische Weltreisende (1621–1628)* (Vienna: Europäischer Verlag Wien, 1972), pp. 5, 29–30, 33–34.

12. HHStA, *Handschriften Weiß 706/30, Anno 1700. Arrivée à Constantinople*, fols. 43b–53a.

13. Ibid., fol. 43b. In the *Mémoires* he mentions the portion of Persia that he saw *depuis Erivan iusqu'à Ispahan*.

14. Von Feuchtersleben, 'Die Grafen von Harrsch', p. 213.

15. HHStA, *Handschriften Weiß 706/30, Suite de ces Memoires [sic] après le retour de la Perse et Turquie*, fol. 53b. This section covers fols. 53b–105a.

16. Von Feuchtersleben, 'Die Grafen von Harrsch', p. 219. *Die Belagerung von Freiburg*, p. 400, seems to suggest a slightly earlier date.

17. Owrangzib was about 80 years old when von Harrsch was in Persia. Interestingly, the Carmelite Fr. Fulgenzio di S. Giuseppe wrote a few years later, clearly on the basis of rumours that he had heard either in Persia or India, that Owrangzib died in 1702 at the age of 104: cf. Alberto Dallolio, 'Un viaggio in Oriente alla fine del secolo XVII', *L'Archiginnasio. Bullettino della Biblioteca Comunale di Bologna*, 2 (1907): p. 90.

18. Being a professional officer may have helped von Harrsch to realize or sense the decline in military matters described in Matthee, *Persia in Crisis*, pp. 216–222.

19. Ines Peper, *Konversionen im Umkreis des Wiener Hofes um 1700* (Vienna and Munich: Böhlau Verlag and Oldenbourg, 2010), p. 86 states that 'während Protestanten im kaiserlichen Heer durchaus bis in den Generalsrang gelangen konnten, erleichterte doch die Zugehörigkeit zur katholischen Kirche den Aufstieg. Die Übertritte junger protestantischer Offiziere können auch nicht selten mit Heiratsplänen in Verbindung gebracht werden.'

20. John M. Flannery, *The Mission of the Portuguese Augustinians to Persia and Beyond (1602–1747)* (Leiden–Boston: Brill, 2013), pp. 94–102. Cf., however, also Giorgio Rota, 'Conversion to Islam (and sometimes a return to Christianity) in Safavid Persia in the sixteenth and seventeenth centuries', in *Conversion and Islam in the Early Modern Mediterranean: The Lure of the Other*, ed. Claire Norton (Abingdon: Routledge, 2017), p. 59.

21. During which the Shah explained to della Valle that the two were also the same as the Spanish Santiago and the Armenian St. Sergius: cf. *Viaggi di Pietro della Valle*, 2 vols. (Brighton: G. Gancia, 1843), vol. I, pp. 658–660.

22. HHStA, *Lothringisches Hausarchiv K137* (fols. not numbered).

23. *Lettres de Turquie (1730–39) et Notices de César de Saussure gentilhomme de la cour de S.A.S. le Prince François Rákóczi II* [. . .], ed. and Hungarian trans. Coloman de Thaly [Kálmán Thaly] (Budapest: Académie hongroise des sciences, 1909), pp. 170–173, 299–302; Heinrich Benedikt, *Der Pascha-Graf Alexander von Bonneval, 1675–1747* (Graz–Cologne: Hermann Böhlaus Nachfolger, 1959), pp. 107–109 (but cf. also pp. 94, 101–103, and 105). Both de Saussure and Benedikt confirm that de Bohn was personally acquainted with Bonneval. Actually, after Rákóczi had become a 'mere instrument' of the latter, Bonneval himself became the main object of de Bohn's spying: cf. ibid, p. 107. Together with the French ambassador at the Porte, de Villeneuve, Bonneval and Rákóczi formed a dangerous 'anti-Habsburg triumvirate': cf. Hermann E. Stockinger, 'Die Apostasie des Pascha-Grafen Alexander von Bonneval (1675–1747) und europäische Stimmen zum "Fall" Bonneval', in *Wahrnehmung des Islam zwischen Reformation und Aufklärung*, ed. Dietrich Klein and Birte Platow (Munich: Wilhelm Fink, 2008), p. 119. De Bohn played a vital role in keeping the contacts among the three men, and, according to *Lettres de Turquie*, pp. 173, 302, it was the shock and the chagrin caused by

the news of de Bohn's treason that caused the fatal illness which within a few months killed the Prince. De Bohn presumably met Father Judasz Tadeusz Krusinski as well, the author of *The History of the Late Revolutions of Persia*, who was Rákóczi's confessor and, according to Joseph von Hammer, *Geschichte des Osmanischen Reiches*, 10 vols. (Pest: C. H. Hartleben, 1827–1835), vol. VII, p. 367, 'divided his loyalty' between the Hungarian prince, the Grand Vizier Ibrahim Paşa, and the Imperial ambassador. Likewise, he must have been acquainted with the Hungarian renegade and printer Ibrahim Müteferrika, who was 'liaison officer' to Prince Rákóczi from 1717 to 1738: cf. Orlin Sabev, 'Political and Mental Borders: Austrian-Ottoman Relations in the First Half of the Eighteenth Century and the First Ottoman-Turkish Printing Press', in *Kommunikation und Information im 18. Jahrhundert*, ed. Johannes Frimmel and Michael Wögerbauer (Wiesbaden: Harrassowitz Verlag, 2009), p. 98. After 1739, P. G. F. de Bohn, that is, Poul Bohn (1697–1759), remained in Austrian service, eventually reaching the rank of *Feldzeugmeister* (General of Artillery). He is buried in Vienna, in the Cathedral of St. Stephen. His cousin was General Herman Jensen Bohn (1672–1743), who had a distinguished career in Russian service and was appointed commanding officer of a Russian expeditionary force to Persia in 1726: cf. G. L. Grove, 'Bohn, Herman Jensen', in *Dansk biografisk Lexicon*, ed. C. F. Bricka, 19 vols. (Copenhagen: Gyldendalske Boghandels Forlag, 1887–1905), vol. II, pp. 468–469, and idem, 'Bohn, Poul', ibid., pp. 469–470, according to which Poul travelled to Persia when he still was Rákóczi's secretary (it is not clear whether he did it as a private person or as an Ottoman officer). For a less than flattering anecdote on Herman Jensen, cf. *Memoirs of Peter Henry Bruce, Esq.* (London: T. Payne and Son, 1782), pp. 166–167.

24. De Bohn quotes rumours, according to which the Ottomans lost more then 200,000 soldiers in Persia. Father [Judasz Tadeusz] Krusinski, *The History of the Late Revolutions of Persia*, ed. du Cerceau, 2 vols. (London: J. Osborne, 1740; reprint New York, Arno Press, 1973), vol. II, p. 193, and later (1757) Father Leandro di S. Cecilia (quoted in *Chronicle of the Carmelites*, vol. I, p. 580) wrote of 150,000 casualties.

25. De Bohn assessed correctly and with great foresight the threat that a powerful Russian state would have posed to both Austria and Poland after its final victory over the Turks. However, here he may simply have followed Bonneval, who 'in Rußland erblickt [...] die Gefahr für die Zukunft der zivilisierten Welt': cf. Benedikt, *Der Pascha-Graf*, p. 101.

26. Ibrahim Paşa was Grand Vizier in 1718–1730 and Topal Osman Paşa in 1731–1732; 'old Ragoczi' is of course Prince Ferenc II Rákóczi.

27. The 'minister' who returned in 1732 is clearly a mistaken hint at Ange de Gardane, the French consul in Isfahan who left his post in 1730: cf. Hellot-Bellier, *France–Iran*, p. 74. The second envoy is certainly the above-mentioned Johan Otter.

28. On the battle of Karnal and the sack of Delhi (22 March 1739), cf. Laurence Lockhart, *Nadir Shah* (London: Luzac and Co., 1938), pp. 135–140 and 145–149; Michael Axworthy, *The Sword of Persia* (London: I. B. Tauris, 2006), pp. 198–205. News of the great victory arrived in Isfahan on 23 June, four months after the battle: cf. ibid., n. 21, p. 320. Kabul was formally ceded by the Mughal Emperor in mid-May 1739: cf. Lockhart, *Nadir Shah*, pp. 125, 152–153; Axworthy, *The Sword of Persia*, pp. 190, 212–213. The latest major contribution to the study of Nader Shah is Foad Sabéran, *Nader Chah ou la folie au pouvoir dans l'Iran du XVIIIe siècle* (Paris: L'Harmattan, 2013).

29. Axworthy, *The Sword of Persia*, pp. 219–220; cf. also Lockhart, *Nadir Shah*, pp. 176–177.

30. Axworthy, *The Sword of Persia*, n. 22, p. 321.

31. In comparison, the above-mentioned Otter knew both that the former rulers were held in captivity and that they were finally murdered, although information about their death clearly reached him only after he had left Isfahan on 12 April 1739: cf. Otter, *Journal de voyages*, pp. 84, 86, 98.

32. HHStA, *Staatenabteilungen, Persien*, Kart. 1. Its folios are inconsistently numbered.

33. Sweden adopted the Gregorian calendar in 1752.

34. For these and the following details on Gustav Ferdinand Gyllenram, his brother, and their journey to Persia, cf. Bahram Sohrabi, 'Early Swedish Travelers to Persia', *Iranian Studies*, 38 (2005): pp. 642–645. The article does not make clear which rulers or leaders the Swedish

brothers served during this rather troubled period of Persian history, apart from perhaps the short-lived Ebrahim Shah Afshar (1748–1749).

35. Ibid., p. 644.

36. Shah Esma'il III was 17 years old in 1750 according to John Perry, *Karim Khan Zand* (Chicago–London: The University of Chicago Press, 1979), p. 23.

37. Erek'le II ruled over K'akheti (eastern Georgia) between 1744 and 1762, and over united K'akheti and Kartli (central Georgia) between 1762 and 1798.

38. Gyllenram wrongly states that Ahmad Shah died during the same campaign, whereas he ruled until 1773. For brief outlines of the history of Khorasan under Shahrokh Shah, cf. ibid., pp. 8–10; Christine Noelle-Karimi, *The Pearl in Its Midst* (Vienna: Verlag der Österreichischen Akademie der Wissenschaften, 2014), pp. 121–127. On Ja'far Khan Kord-e Za'faranlu, cf. ibid., pp. 109, 121–125: he was blinded in October 1753. He is mentioned in passing in *The History of Afghanistan: Fayz Muhammad Katib Hazarah's Siraj al-tawarikh*, English trans. R. D. McChesney and M. M. Khorrami, 3 vols. (Leiden–Boston: Brill, 2013), vol. I, p. 20.

39. In fact, Kandahar was in Persian hands for the last time under Nader Shah, who conquered it in 1738 and held it until his death: cf. Lockhart, *Nadir Shah*, pp. 112–120. Karim Khan finally found himself forced to massacre the 'western Afghans' in 1759: cf. Perry, *Karim Khan*, pp. 79–81. Ordered to submit by Agha Mohammad Khan Qajar (1785–1797), Erek'le II refused, placing his hopes in the Treaty of Georgievsk (1783), which had turned his kingdom into a vassal state of Russia; betrayed and deserted by the Russians, he had to face the Persian invasion of Georgia and the sack of Tbilisi (1795). Finally, Shah Esma'il III or, more accurately, Karim Khan Zand, never tried to conquer Khorasan.

40. That is, Peter Freiherr von Herbert-Rathkeal, who was the Imperial ambassador (*internuntius*) at the Sublime Porte during the years 1779–1788 and 1792–1802: cf. https://db.donjuanarchiv.at/pub/DJA/BOT.pdf?AspxAutoDetectCookieSupport=1.

41. HHStA, *Staatenabteilungen, Persien*, Kart. 2 (Konv. Persica 1810–1819). Another copy of the same document is listed in *Verzeichnis der orientalischen Handschriften in Deutschland*, vol. XXXVII, *Islamische Handschriften*, part 5, *Thüringen*, ed. Florian Sobieroj (Stuttgart: Franz Steiner Verlag, 2001), n. 36, p. XXX (MS, G. B. f. 30, Jena).

42. Shahrokh Shah was to be captured and executed by Agha Mohammad Khan in 1796: cf. Perry, *Karim Khan*, p. 10. For a brief outline of Zaman Shah's reign, cf. Noelle-Karimi, *The Pearl in Its Midst*, pp. 129–130. Cf. also *The History of Afghanistan*, vol. I, pp. 71–100.

43. Baba Khan is never mentioned here as Fath-Ali Shah (1797–1834).

44. His name was Mohammad Khan b. Zaki Khan: cf. Mirza Fazlo'llah Shirazi Khavari, *Tarikh-e Zu'l-qarneyn*, ed. Naser Afshar Farr, 2 vols. (Tehran: Vezarat-e farhang va ershad-e eslami, 1380), vol. I, p. 77. Mohammad Khan's rebellion is not mentioned in Perry, *Karim Khan*, but he appears in the genealogical table of the Zand dynasty, ibid., p. 296 (he was a cousin of Karim Khan's). It seems unlikely that Mohammad Khan is one and the same person as the unnamed Zand prince who, according to a British document dated 21 August 1807, lived in Bushehr 'until very lately': cf. Kamran Ekbal, 'Ein britischer Plan zur Restauration der Zand-Herrschaft aus dem Jahre 1807', *Die Welt des Islams*, 22 (1982): p. 44 (and also pp. 46–47). This article is valuable for its mention of the contacts between British diplomats and Zand princes, but it is otherwise replete with factual, conceptual, and even logical mistakes.

45. Khorasan was definitively conquered by Baba Khan/Fath-Ali Shah in 1803 (cf. Noelle-Karimi, *The Pearl in Its Midst*, pp. 216–217), and the Russians indeed attacked Persia. As for Afghanistan and Zaman Shah, cf. *supra*, footnote 42.

46. Interestingly, David Marshall Lang, *The Last Years of the Georgian Monarchy, 1658–1832* (New York: Columbia University Press, 1957), pp. 207–208, mentions the Austrian 'influence' at the court of Ali Morad Khan Zand (1781–1785). Emperor Joseph II (1765–1790) was one of the European rulers to whom Erek'le II addressed himself in 1781–1782 with the request of funds to raise a body of troops trained in the European way in the hope, ultimately, to escape Russia's mortal embrace: cf. ibid., pp. 180–181; Luigi Magarotto, *L'annessione della Georgia alla Russia (1783–1801)* (Pasian di Prato: Campanotto Editore, 2004), pp. 30–32.

47. Von Hammer, *Geschichte des Osmanischen Reiches*, vol. VIII, n. e) p. 344: the word *cancelliere* appears in Italian in the original text. Cf. also http://gams.uni-graz.at/hp/pdf/35_Brieflisten.pdf.

48. Hellot-Bellier, *France–Iran*, p. 81.

49. Ibid., pp. 82–83. Rousseau lived between the two cities until 1802, when he settled down in Aleppo. On him, see also Irène Natchkebia, 'Joseph Rousseau on Georgia and the Planned Indian Expedition (1807)', *Journal of Persianate Studies*, 1 (2008): pp. 230–233 and n. 14, p. 238; Jean Calmard, 'The French Presence in Safavid Persia: A Preliminary Study', in *Iran and the World in the Safavid Age*, ed. Willem Floor and Edmund Herzig (London: I. B. Tauris, 2012), pp. 318–323.

50. HHStA, *Staatenabteilungen, Persien*, Kart. 1 (Konv. 1691–1753), fols. 87a–93a.

51. Russia is mentioned, since at the time Russian forces occupied parts of Persian territory.

52. Cf. *infra*, footnote 60.

53. Cf. *infra*, footnote 59.

54. Unless *Varij ragionamenti* is a translation, in which case we should of course speak of an Italian translator. I tend however to exclude this possibility, given the consistency of and the lack of major errors in the spelling of Oriental names.

55. Laurence Lockhart, *The Fall of the Safavī Dynasty and the Afghan Occupation of Persia* (Cambridge: Cambridge University Press, 1958), p. 210; Axworthy, *The Sword of Persia*, p. 67.

56. Von Hammer, *Geschichte des Osmanischen Reiches*, vol. VII, pp. 337–338 and 339; Lockhart, *The Fall of the Safavi Dynasty*, pp. 288–293.

57. Idem, *Nadir Shah*, pp. 27–28; Axworthy, *The Sword of Persia*, p. 72.

58. On Iese, cf. David Marshall Lang, "Ali-qoli Khan", in *Encyclopaedia Iranica*, vol. I, p. 874.

59. On Beneveni's mission, cf. at least V. G. Volovnikov, *Poslannik Petra I na Vostoke* (Moscow: Nauka, 1986); Nicola Di Cosmo, 'A Russian Envoy to Khiva: The Italian Diary of Florio Beneveni', in *Proceedings of the XXVIII Permanent International Altaistic Conference, Venice, 8–14 July 1985*, ed. Giovanni Stary (Wiesbaden: Otto Harrassowitz, 1989), pp. 73–114; Svetlana Gorshenina, *Explorateurs en Asie Centrale* (Geneva: Éditions Olizane, 2003), pp. 146–147. He came of course from Ragusa in Dalmatia (present-day Dubrovnik) and not from Ragusa in Sicily as stated in Di Cosmo, 'A Russian Envoy to Khiva', p. 73. I am indebted to Dr. Paolo Sartori both for his kindly putting Volovnikov's book at my disposal and for his translations from the Russian.

60. Volovnikov, *Poslannik Petra I*, pp. 36–39, 39–41, and 47–50.

61. Di Cosmo, 'A Russian Envoy to Khiva', pp. 73, 76, 91, 113.

62. Cf. the remarks in footnote 82, *infra*.

63. Volovnikov, *Poslannik Petra I*, p. 28.

64. The articles of the treaty were made public in Constantinople on 18 November 1727: cf. Krusinski, *The History of the Late Revolutions*, vol. II, p. 194; *Chronicle of the Carmelites*, vol. I, n. 2 p. 580 (based on Krusinski).

65. Volovnikov, *Poslannik Petra I*, p. 12.

66. Cf. *infra*, footnotes 87, 106, and 107.

67. Ibid., p. 24; cf. also Gorshenina, *Explorateurs en Asie Centrale*, pp. 146–147.

68. Volovnikov, *Poslannik Petra I*, p. 83.

69. Lockhart, *The Fall of the Safavi Dynasty*, p. 100; Noelle-Karimi, *The Pearl in Its Midst*, pp. 87–88.

70. Willem Floor, 'Who Were the Shamkhal and the Usmi?', *Zeitschrift der Deutschen Morgenländischen Gesellschaft*, 160 (2010): p. 360.

71. 'Breve giornale dell'anno corente 1725 dal Mese di Feuraro [. . .]', in A. Popov, *Snoshenija Rossii c" Khivoiu i Bukharoiu pri Petre Velikom'* (St Petersburg: Tipografija Imperatorskoj Akademii Nauk", 1853), pp. 160–188.

72. Ibid., pp. 165 (*Irat* and *Candehar*), 170, and *passim* (*Astrahan*), 179 and 185 (*Astrabat*).

73. Ibid., pp. 162 and *passim* (*sciah*), 178 (*Sciruan*), 186 (*Augani* and *Ispahan*). The author of *Varij ragionamenti* writes actually *avgani/avghani* and *Scirvan*, but in the Italian texts of the time /u/ often replaces what would be spelt today as /v/. Furthermore, our text is probably a copy.

74. Quotation marks will be used for translations from the original.

75. Here our author makes some curious mistakes: Mohammad was born at Mecca and died at Medina, and not the other way around as he states; also the last independent ruler of Egypt defeated by Selim I was of course Tumanbay (1516–1517) and not the Ayyubid Salahu'd-din (1169–1193).

76. A slightly later Dutch source put the population of Isfahan at 240,000 in 1727: cf. Willem Floor, *The Economy of Safavid Persia* (Wiesbaden: Reichert Verlag, 2000), p. 3.

77. An Ottoman ambassador visiting the Persian capital at the beginning of 1729 reported 'many people dying of starvation in the streets of Isfahan': cf. Lockhart, *The Fall of the Safavi Dynasty*, p. 294. Cf. also Axworthy, *The Sword of Persia*, pp. 89–90.

78. Kandahar was indeed ruled by Ashraf's cousin, Hoseyn, who stayed in power there until the city was captured by Nader Shah in 1738: cf. Lockhart, *Nadir Shah*, pp. 16, 120; idem, *The Fall of the Safavi Dynasty*, pp. 210, 279, 283; Axworthy, *The Sword of Persia*, p. 186.

79. Rumours, which later were to prove unfounded, spread indeed in the spring of 1729, according to which Hoseyn had left Kandahar and was marching against his cousin: cf. Lockhart, *Nadir Shah*, p. 35; idem, *The Fall of the Safavi Dynasty*, p. 329.

80. A Dutch source of the time confirms the figure of 40,000: cf. *The Afghan Occupation of Safavid Persia 1721–1729*, ed. and English trans. Willem Floor (Paris: Association pour l'Avancement des Études Iraniennes, 1998), p. 247. Lockhart, *The Fall of the Safavi Dynasty*, p. 288, and Axworthy, *The Sword of Persia*, p. 88, speak instead of 17,000 and 12,000 men, respectively.

81. Ibid., pp. 87–89.

82. Tahmasp had proclaimed himself Shah in Qazvin on 10 November 1722: cf. Lockhart, *The Fall of the Safavi Dynasty*, p. 193. After having to leave northwestern Persia in order to escape the invading Ottomans, he was defeated by the Afghans in December 1725 and again in May 1726 by Fath-Ali Khan Qajar, who was the one actually in control of Astarabad and, after this victory, the strongman behind the throne until the advent of Tahmaspqoli Khan: cf. ibid., pp. 278, 281, 304–305. Instead of attacking the Afghans as surmised by the anonymous author, Shah Tahmasp II and Fath-Ali Khan Qajar marched against Malek Mahmud Sistani, 'the weakest of Tahmasp's foes', in July 1726: cf. ibid., p. 306.

83. The only notable clash between Afghans and Russians took place near Langarud (Gilan) towards the end of 1727 and ended in a Russian victory: cf. ibid., p. 296.

84. Article 5 of the Treaty. This and the remaining articles are summarized in ibid., pp. 233–235.

85. 'By December 1725 the Turks were seriously thinking [...] of demanding the cession of Gilan from Russia': cf. ibid., p. 353. The Ottomans made an incursion into Gilan in 1726: cf. ibid., p. 358.

86. But not from those of the plague, which decimated Shah Tahmasp II's troops as well as the local population: cf. ibid., p. 279.

87. In 1722, an Indian trader informed the Russians that, before the Afghan invasion, Gilan used to export 5,000 bales of silk to Turkey every year, each bale weighing between 252 and 324 lbs.: cf. ibid., p. 238. However, the reality was different. Some 700 bales of silk were moved through Erzurum in 1719; 'little or no Iranian silk' reached Aleppo in 1725; less than 200 bales were sent to Astrakhan in 1726: cf. Rudi Matthee, *The Politics of Trade in Safavid Iran* (Cambridge: Cambridge University Press, 1999), pp. 226–227. Gilan virtually escaped both the Afghan and the Ottoman invasion, but its trade was ruined by the Russian occupation. On Persian silk exports during the last three decades of Safavid rule, cf. ibid., pp. 203–230, 244–245.

88. On the trade between Gilan and Russia cf. Floor, *The Economy of Safavid Persia*, pp. 238, 252–253, which does not mention saffron, fruits, and vegetables (but cf. also pp. 160–161, 251–252). *Memoirs of Peter Henry Bruce*, p. 318, lists silk, coffee, saffron, cotton, and fruits (grapes in particular) as the products of the provinces of Gilan, Mazandaran, and Astarabad.

89. *Tadhkirat al-Muluk*, English trans. Vladimir Minorsky (London: E. J. W. Gibb Memorial Trust, 1943), pp. 106–107, 174–175, puts the revenues from Gilan at slightly more than 69,115 *toman*.

90. While it is not correct that Russians and Ottomans 'were not supposed to share a border', it is true that the Treaty granted Ardabil to Shah Tahmasp II: cf. Lockhart, *The Fall of the Safavi Dynasty*, p. 234. The city was taken by the Ottomans in the summer of 1725: cf. ibid., p. 266.

91. The general attitude of intolerance towards all non-Shiites (including Sunnis) grew increasingly worse in Persia at least from the 1680s and is well outlined in Matthee, *Persia in Crisis*, pp. 219–222, 253–254. This state of things did not escape the attention of the Ottoman ambassador Dürri Ahmed Efendi, according to whom the Sunnis made up 30 per cent of the population of Safavid Persia and 'only waited for a ruler of their own religious convictions who would liberate them from their present oppressors': cf. Suraiya Faroqhi, 'An Ottoman Ambassador in Iran: Dürri Ahmed Efendi and the Collapse of the Safavid Empire in 1720–21', in eadem, *Another Mirror for Princes* (Istanbul: The ISIS Press, 2008), pp. 176–178 (quotation from p. 177). The possibility of Sunni uprisings was entirely real, of course, as the revolts of the Lezghis and of the Afghans (both starting in 1709) had showed: cf. *infra*, footnote 97. For the situation in the south, cf. Jean Aubin, 'Les sunnites du Larestan et la chute des Safavides', *Revue des Études Islamiques*, 33 (1965): pp. 151–171; Willem Floor, 'The Revolt of Shaikh Ahmad Madani in Laristan and the Garmsirat (1730–1733)', *Studia Iranica*, 12 (1983): pp. 63–93.
92. A reference probably to the loss of thirteen Russian supply ships during Peter the Great's expedition of 1722: cf. Lockhart, *The Fall of the Safavi Dynasty*, pp. 185–186.
93. This might be a reference to the anti-Ottoman uprising of Shanshe, *eristavi* of Ksani in northern Georgia, around 1726: cf. *Histoire de la Géorgie depuis l'Antiquité jusqu'au XIXe siècle*, French trans. M. Brosset, *IIe partie. Histoire moderne. Ire livraison* (St. Petersburg: Imprimerie de l'Académie Impériale des Sciences, 1856), p. 127. Shanshe also tried to convince Vakht'ang VI to resume the fight: cf. *Sakartvelos ist'oriis nark'vevebi*, ed. Mamia Dumbadze (Tbilisi: Sabch'ota Sakartvelo, 1973), p. 424.
94. The sentence in italics appears on the right margin of the page in the original text.
95. He was appointed governor of Tbilisi in 1724–1725: cf. Giampiero Bellingeri—Giovanni Curatola, 'Sul tarh-ı jedid, "art nouveau", dei Jaq'eli di Bayazid', in *Georgica II: Materiali sulla Georgia Occidentale*, ed. Luigi Magarotto and Gianroberto Scarcia (Bologna: Il cavaliere azzurro, 1988), p. 152.
96. A description of the fortress of Darband, confirming the detail of the seventy guns on the side of the fortress facing the sea, can be found in Evliya Chelebi, *Travels in Iran and the Caucasus, 1647 and 1654*, English trans. Hasan Javadi and Willem Floor (Washington, DC: Mage Publishers, 2010), pp. 93–94. *Memoirs of Peter Henry Bruce*, p. 282, speaks of one hundred sixty guns; 'Abbas Qoli Aqa Bakikhanov, *The Heavenly Rose-Garden: A History of Shirvan and Daghestan*, English trans. Willem Floor and Hasan Javadi (Washington, DC: Mage Publishers, 2009), p. 115, has twenty-three pieces of ordnance, whereas 'Abbasqoli Aqa Bakikhanuf, *Golestan-e Eram*, ed. 'Abdo'l-Karim Alizadeh (Tehran: Entesharat-e Qoqnus, 1383), p. 152, has two hundred three. For a description of the city and fortress of Darband, cf. *Memoirs of Peter Henry Bruce*, pp. 282–284. Below (fol. 92b) the anonymous author wrongly identifies Shirvan with ancient Hyrcania, on which cf. A. D. H. Bivar, 'Gorgān.V.Pre-Islamic History', in *Encyclopaedia Iranica*, vol. XI (New York: Encyclopaedia Iranica Foundation, 2003), pp. 151–153.
97. The Lezghis of Daghistan, ever difficult to subdue, were in a state of rebellion at least since 1709: cf. Clemens P. Sidorko, '"Kampf den ketzerischen Qızılbaš!" Die Revolte des Haggi Da'ud (1718–1728)', in *Caucasia Between the Ottoman Empire and Iran, 1555–1914*, ed. Raoul Motika and Michael Ursinus (Wiesbaden: Reichert Verlag, 2000), pp. 133–145; idem, *Dschihad im Kaukasus* (Wiesbaden: Reichert Verlag, 2007), pp. 57–70; Matthee, *Persia in Crisis*, pp. 223–226. Without underestimating the importance of other factors, Sidorko, *Dschihad im Kaukasus*, p. 69, acknowledges the significance of the religious element in what he calls 'Hajji Da'ud's jihad' against the Safavids.
98. A reference to the treacherous conquest of the capital of Alsace by the French in 1681. Other accounts of the conquest of Darband can be found in *Memoirs of Peter Henry Bruce*, pp. 281–282; Lockhart, *The Fall of the Safavi Dynasty*, pp. 184–185; Bakikhanuf, *Golestan-e Eram*, pp. 151–152; Bakikhanov, *The Heavenly Rose-Garden*, p. 115.
99. 3,000 according to *Memoirs of Peter Henry Bruce*, pp. 282, 290–291. Baku had a garrison of 4,000: cf. ibid., p. 321.
100. One wonders if the word *Chingi* is related to the Kangits, the 'eastern tribal group of the Kipchak-Cuman confederacy' that used to live in the desert north of the Caspian

Sea until they were expelled by the Mongols: cf. István Vásáry, *Cumans and Tatars* (Cambridge: Cambridge University Press, 2005), pp. 8–9. It could perhaps be a distorted form for Chingizid.

101. Again, the anonymous author is quite inaccurate when dealing with much earlier events. Friedrich II was Emperor between 1220 and 1250; Rudolf I of Habsburg was King of Germany between 1273 and 1291, whereas the first Emperor of the same House was Friedrich III (1452–1493). The Mongols invaded Poland and Hungary in 1241.

102. The *Shamkhal* of the Qumuq, 'Adel Girey, indeed a Persian vassal, had submitted to Peter the Great as early as 1717 or 1719, but he rose in revolt in 1725: Lockhart, *The Fall of the Safavi Dynasty*, pp. 176, 355–356; Sidorko, ' "Kampf den ketzerischen Qızılbaš!" ', pp. 140–141; idem, *Dschihad im Kaukasus*, pp. 67–69; Floor, 'Who Were the Shamkhal and the Usmi?', pp. 359–360. *Murtasà Bei* is probably Morteza-Ali, 'Adel Girey's older brother: see ibid., pp. 358–360. One wonders if *Andre Bei* is a corruption of *derebey*, a term which was often used in the Ottoman empire to indicate local chiefs. It might, however, simply mean 'the Lord of Enderey/Andreevo', the place in Qumuq territory where the appointed successor to the *Shamkhal* usually lived: see ibid., pp. 343–344, 347, 352, 356, 362, n. 91 p. 359. See also *Russian Embassies to the Georgian Kings (1589–1605)*, ed. W. E. D. Allen, 2 vols. (Cambridge: Cambridge University Press, 1970), vol. II, pp. 370, 450, 559.

103. The Russian fortress of Terki or "Terek-town," on the estuary of the Terek river, not to be confused with the capital of the *Shamkhal*, Tarku: cf. ibid., vol. I, pp. 20–23 and 36–47. On Terki in 1722, cf. *Memoirs of Peter Henry Bruce*, pp. 260, 263.

104. Cf. *supra*, footnotes 91 and 97. Alarmed by Russian war preparations against him, Hajji Daud submitted to the Ottoman Sultan as early as spring 1722, whereas Ganjeh fell to the Ottomans in August 1725: cf. Lockhart, *The Fall of the Safavi Dynasty*, pp. 216, 266; Sidorko, ' "Kampf den ketzerischen Qızılbaš!" ', p. 140; idem, *Dschihad im Kaukasus*, p. 64.

105. That is, *Sciamkal Bei, Andre Bei*, and *Murtasà Bei*.

106. The excessive figures given for the forces available to these local Caucasian chiefs as well as the absurd 'strategic plan' ascribed to the Tatars, which disregards geography (among other things) entirely and reminds closely of the plot of Jules Verne's *Michel Strogoff*, may perhaps be an echo of Russian propaganda and *dezinformacija*, as the praise of Russia's 'timely rescue' by Peter the Great seems to confirm.

107. Black Russia or Black Ruthenia, in the western part of present-day Belarus.

108. Strangely, the anonymous author does not mention the port of Baku.

109. Cf. *supra*, footnote 96.

110. Malek Mahmud Sistani had indeed led an army to Isfahan in 1722, but instead of relieving the besieged city, he had struck a deal with the besieging Afghans and obtained rule over Khorasan as the reward for his treason: cf. Lockhart, *The Fall of the Safavi Dynasty*, pp. 167, 279; Axworthy, *The Sword of Persia*, pp. 53–54. Of course, Khorasan and ancient Bactria did not exactly coincide: cf. P. Leriche, 'Bactria.I.Pre-Islamic Period', in *Encyclopaedia Iranica*, vol. III (London–New York: Routledge and Kegan Paul, 1989), pp. 339–343; Noelle-Karimi, *The Pearl in Its Midst*, p. 6.

111. Cf. *supra*, footnote 69.

112. These words, like others below, appear underlined in the original text.

113. The sentence in italics is written in the right margin of the page.

114. HHStA, *Staatenabteilungen ausserdeutsche Staaten, Persien*, Kart. 1 (Konv. 1691–1753), fols. 87a–93a.

12

Nader Shah, the Delhi Loot, and the 18th-Century Exotics of Empire

SUSSAN BABAIE

Kalat (fort or *qal'a*), the focus of this chapter, is a small town some 150 kilometers north of Mashhad as one drives toward the border of Iran and Turkmenistan. It stands inside a natural fortification in a remote location in Khurasan, hidden from view of travelers (Figure 12.1).[1] Kalat has had a long history predating its 18th-century fame as Kalat-e Naderi, Kalat of Nader Shah (r. 1736–1747), reaching back to a reference in the *Shahnama* as well as to the late 13th–early 14th century Mongol/Il-Khanid period.[2] The town's association with Nader Shah hinges on an enigmatic building at its center, popularly known as Qasr-e Khorshid, the "sun palace," or as Emarat-e Naderi (Figure 12.2). The building is an extraordinary hybrid of styles and materials, its assembly of volumes almost incomprehensible from an architectural point of view but fitting the particularities, as shall be the focus of this discussion, of Nader Shah's patronage in light of his ambitious imperial designs for India.

The building remains little-studied, in large part because of its remote location and the sensitivity of proximity to the border with Turkmenistan (almost beyond reach of scholars and archaeologists during the Soviet era). Its historical location however, is inextricably tied with Nader Shah's Indian campaign of 1739. The (in)famous plunder of Delhi by Nader Shah and his troops that followed the February 13, 1739 defeat of the Mughals at the battle of Karnal has left behind an important trail of visual and material-cultural evidence, ranging from coinage to architecture, from ceremonial armor to paintings (Figures 12.5 and 12.6). The loot, amassed during his "reign" in Hindustan from March 9 through May 5, 1739 and carted back to his homeland in Khurasan (northeastern Iran), left its impact on the building of Kalat. This deliberate form of hybridization informs significantly on the historical circumstances and representations of

Figure 12.1. Kalat-e Naderi, Iran, view from the pavilion of Nader toward the mosque, the town, and the mountains that form the fortification around the city. (Photo: @SBabaie, 1994.)

Figure 12.2. Nader Pavilion or Qasr-e Khorshid, Kalat-e Naderi, Iran, view from the "garden" level, looking up at the platform on top of which stands the octagonal two-story pavilion supporting a cylindrical tower. (Photo: @SBabaie, 1994.)

Nader's ambition as a world ruler, a *shahanshah*, especially charged since he came onto the scene as the protector of the lands of Iran and of the deposed Safavid (1501–1722) princes whose capital city Isfahan and its treasures were looted by the Afghan invasions of 1722. Yet Nader's patronage has only solicited statements in passing and of little art-historical significance. Surveys of the Naderi period in the history of Persian arts tend to be confined to lists of gems and jewels stolen, furniture dismantled, precious objects gifted away, and images and styles briefly discussed as poor extensions of a late-Safavid artistic production. Otherwise, Nader's patronage—and that of his dynasty of the Afshars (1736–1796)—is rarely addressed if not outright dismissed as an insignificant period of inaction before the rise of artistic, and political, vivacity in the "new" Qajar era (1785–1925).[3]

As Michael Axworthy suggests in this volume, and my brief account of art-historical disinterest indicates, an inherently hostile view toward Nader and his short-lived reign has prevailed, whereby the period of Nader's reign—a mere 11 years—and of his successors—another 49 years—is often discussed as a continuation of the downward spiral that was beset by late-Safavid economic and political deterioration, the ensuing Afghan invasion, and the collapse of the centralized system of rule in Iran.[4]

This chapter finds in Nader Shah's reign the deep imprint of some entirely different agendas in patronage of the arts. It suggests that the arts were not as neglected as has been imagined nor as degenerate or visually and technically unworthy of scholarly consideration as the neglect might imply. Instead, his world-conquering designs, which became the last to have risen from the Islamicate world before the 20th century, had necessitated the same expediency in deploying the power and charisma of the arts to represent authority and to persuade claims to legitimacy as with any ambitious conqueror. The artistic evidence, seemingly scattershot, is both numerous and impressive, albeit not aesthetically coherent, and it points to a rather concentrated burst of productivity in the midst of his tumultuous reign.

More importantly, I will argue that art and architecture made for Nader was intended to deliberately recall those carried out for Timur (1370–1405), the other conqueror of Delhi and northern India during his famous campaign of 1398–1399.[5] As was with Timur, Nader Shah's loot went beyond dazzling objects to also include materials and technologies. Nader Shah also brought back hundreds of Indian craftsmen and artisans who ended up working—presumably alongside locals—to make this spectacularly hybrid monument as the central piece of a projected urban center at Kalat-e Naderi. Nader Shah's building project, it is argued here, yields the visual traces of that Indian expedition as a signifier of a self-consciously historicized and imperial aestheticizing of the exotic.

The Kalat

A saucer-like platform, the Kalat measures 20 miles long (from west-northwest to east-southeast) and five to seven miles wide. The rim of limestone cliffs with dramatic jagged peaks rises some 700 to 1,100 feet before one's eyes when driving to the site on the Mashhad road. The natural fortress is impassable except for two (or three) narrow gorges. On the interior entranceway of one of those gorges, giving access into the fortified town, the visitor encounters—above and behind one's head—a large inscription carved into the rock, composed in four columns of couplets framed by a pointed-arch border design of floral motifs.[6] The inscription is a versified eulogy of Nader in a Turkic dialect peculiar to the Afshar court and it remains incomplete, presumably left so at the end of Nader's life in 1747.[7]

Kalat was Nader's showcase. His contemporary historians refer to it as the *dar al-sobat,* the abode of steadfastness, and the place on which he spent enormous sums.[8] Although Nader and his associates knew Kalat as the fortress site, the building campaigns were carried out after his return from India, between 1739 and his assassination. This was indeed a city, or intended to be so, as remains of a coordinated pair of buildings, a mosque, visible in Figure 12.1, and a pavilion (Figure 12.2) point toward an urban plan, albeit rudimentary and incomplete. Excavations around the base of the pavilion have revealed traces of water channels indicating a garden setting—or at least an intention to develop one.[9] The pavilion, in plan and in its two-story-high elevation, is designed on the nine-fold, octagonal *hasht-behesht* model. If indeed a garden with water channels (*juy*) and little gathering pools (*hauz*) were part of the composition, this would be a perfectly recognizable *hasht-behesht* (eight-paradises) type of building—a familiar arrangement of eight spaces articulated as either solid bases or voided rooms surrounding a central open space that rises the entire height of the two stories and often has a domical lantern at its crown. Such an architectural scheme would have been suitable for either a tomb or a garden pavilion and is widely found across the Persianate world.[10] The building, however, is most surprising for the additional tower-like feature above the *hasht-behesht* pavilion which crowns the central space. Internally, the central space reads as a domed two-story-high feature, again resonant of typical *hasht-behesht* building designs, minus the lantern source of light. Externally, however, the cylindrical tower of some 20 meters in height and 12 meters in diameter reads exactly as a tower and not a domical or lantern roof of the central space.

The distinction between the two volumes—that of the tower and the *hasht-behesht* pavilion—is further emphasized by the fact that the tower is encased in fluted ridges and clad in cream-colored stone, while the pavilion's external

Figure 12.3. Nader Pavilion or Qasr-e Khorshid, Kalat-e Naderi, Iran, detail from of one of the niches on the façade with stone carved vase of flowers atop a tray of fruits and other carved floral and vegetal patterns. (Photo: @SBabaie, 1994.)

surfaces alternate between flat niches and recessed *ayvan*s; the former faced with carved stone panels, the latter with paintings on whitewashed walls.[11] The interior of the tall central space, the only internal space to have been functional, is also whitewashed and covered in murals of floral/vegetal patterns and an epigraphic band, all of which survive only in fragments.[12] For the purposes

Figure 12.4. Nader Pavilion or Qasr-e Khorshid, Kalat-e Naderi, Iran, detail from one of border designs with naturalistic carving in stone of irises framing one of the niches on the façade. (Photo: @SBabaie, 1994.)

of this discussion, it suffices to underscore the disparity in forms and materials of construction between the two parts of the building as well as between the baked-brick fabric of the structure and its stone façade surfaces. Moreover, there is no evidence of how the tower would have been capped. Its shape— notwithstanding for the moment the strangeness of positioning it atop an octagonal pavilion—resembles tomb towers of which medieval examples in Iran abound: the so-called *mil* tomb towers in the Mazandaran region, which are usually capped with a domical crown, or the examples not far from Kalat, where the tomb towers in Bastam or Gurgan are capped with a conical crown.[13]

The building in general seems to have been left unfinished, as it is not only missing a cap but also as some niches on the exterior walls of the octagonal pavilion are fitted with fully carved stone panels while others are either half-carved or else left plain. In many ways then this is a puzzling building: the structure is of baked brick, but the exteriors are given a stone sheathing, a most uncommon material for buildings in the Khurasan region and in Iran in general; the lower section of a pavilion in a *hasht-behesht* design is topped by a disproportionately tall and wide tower, which is moreover fluted along its cylindrical shape and uncapped; and the building's exteriors are fitted with stone-sheet-clad niches, some with carved motifs of flowers and vases in extraordinary compositions and carving techniques given the construction date (Figures 12.3 and 12.4). These features make the building a concoction of the most incomprehensible features of Iranian architecture, some of which—as will be suggested here—are hybridized and adopted as exotic elements from an Indian context.

The Delhi Loot

Nader Shah's spectacularly successful military strategies and his rapid conquest of territories in Afghanistan and northern India have been extensively studied but more significantly were written up already in his lifetime in Iran, India, and Central Asia and in European languages.[14] Napoleon called him the Great Warrior of Persia; Eurocentric histories have even dubbed him the Napoleon of Persia! His fame as a conqueror rests mainly on his bold venture into India and his 1739 defeat of the Mughal troops of Mohammad Shah (1719–1748).

Following the humiliating conditions of the defeat of Mohammad Shah, whereby the latter was virtually held hostage at Nader's camp near Karnal, a rapid succession of events, beginning with his entry into Delhi, the proclamation of Nader as the sovereign from the *minbar* (pulpit) of the imperial congregational mosque, the preparation of the Mughal throne and the palace (Red Fort) to receive the newly minted *shahanshah* (king of kings), and two successive massacres—first of the Persians, then, in retaliation, of a larger number of Indians—concluded with Nader recrowning Mohammad Shah as the rightful emperor of Mughal Hindustan and vacating the throne in favor of the latter. All this, however, was negotiated as an exchange of the emperor's right to sovereignty for an enormous indemnity that included thousands of kilograms of silver, gold, jewels, clothing, and furniture. Among those were some of the best-known

Figure 12.5. Nader Shah at the sack of Delhi. Battle scene with Nader Shah on horseback, possibly by Muhammad Ali ibn Abd al-Bayg ibn Ali Quli Jabbadar, mid-18th century, Museum of Fine Arts, Boston, Francis Bartlett Donation of 1912 and Picture Fund. (© 2016 Museum of Fine Arts, Boston.)

and richest objects in the imperial *khazana* treasury of the Mughals: two giant diamonds including the famous Koh-e Nur, several bejeweled daggers, carved rubies and emeralds, masses of pearls, and, allegedly, folios from the illustrated manuscript of *Hamzanama*. Perhaps the most crucial item among the loot was the famed Peacock Throne, the throne of Mughal emperors since Shah Jahan and one upon which Nader Shah was depicted enthroned (Figure 12.6).[15]

The loot points to two particularly important facets of Nader's Indian campaign. One is the assumption of the posture of the king of kings, the *shahanshah*, and the conqueror of the world, comparable to Timur, with whom he also shared

Figure 12.6. Nader Shah on the Peacock Throne after his defeat of Mohammad Shah, c.1850, San Diego MOA. Opaque watercolor on paper Display Dimensions: 12 1/8 in. x 16 9/16 in. (30.8 cm x 42.1 cm). Credit line: Edwin Binney 3rd Collection Accession Number: 1990.407. (© San Diego Museum of Art, USA/Bridgeman Images.)

the conquest of Delhi. I will return to this point about the Nader–Timur axis below. The second facet is that many of those dazzling gems, jewels, and bejeweled ceremonial objects (daggers, swords, and the like) were incorporated into a new fashion for imperial regalia, much like the Mughals and unlike the Safavids, that also included the invention of a crown. Portraits of Nader Shah, which emanate mainly from a series of paintings and drawings made at the Mughal court or by Indian artists and their followers in Iran, show this new kind of imperial fashion (Figure 12.7).[16] Having abandoned the two centuries of the Safavid turban-*taj*, Nader is seen wearing a crown-hat, a *kolah-taj* of his own invention with four finials/corners on the top of the hat, which is further enwrapped with gem-studded bands and strings of pearls and jewels.[17] Compared to the increasingly thickly wrapped turbans of the late Safavid fashion—absurdly big on the head—or the strange flat-topped turban-hats with multiple plumes, Nader looks positively modern. Indeed, the regalia and the adoption of the crown in these renditions of Nader Shah underscore the significance of the Delhi encounter for him.[18] A comparison between Figures 12.6 and 12.7, one with Nader as an Indian emperor, the other as the Persian one, indicates the extent to which such pictorial

Figure 12.7. Portrait of Nader Shah Afshar, by Mohammad Reza Hindi, after 1739.
Oil on canvas, Victoria and Albert Museum, London. (© Victoria and Albert Museum,
London.) This is one of only two surviving portraits of Nader Shah in oil colors on
canvas. He is shown seated on a Mughal carpet and wearing bejeweled adornments—
armband, belt, strings of pearls—and with such accouterments of rule as gem-studded
dagger and sword. All including the object that resembles a candlestick in front (inkpot
or spittoon?) are encrusted with what appears to be the gems and jewels looted from the
Mughal treasury. He wears the unusual four-cornered crown-hat of his own design, which
is also adorned with pearls, gems, and jewels presumably of Mughal origin.

conventions adopted the seated pose, the crown, and the fullness of the ceremonial accoutrements as aspects of Nader Shah's imperial iconography.

Nader's plunder of Delhi treasures and the assumption of the Mughal
throne, even if temporarily, left their indelible marks on the trajectory of imperial imagery in Iran. Even though very little attention has been directed to this

episode of an Irano-Indian blending of forms and fashions, it is impossible to imagine the emergence of crowns and imperial regalia of the Zand and especially Qajar periods without Nader's adoption of things Indian.[19] In fact, the idea of crowning a king by another king rather than by a clergyman—an imperial ceremony long out of fashion in the Iranian world—is revived in Nader's time, or at least instigated by his example, when Nader Shah is depicted reinstating Mohammad Shah to the Mughal throne in one of the paintings that accompany the 1757 copy of the famous *(Tarikh-e) jahangosha-ye Naderi* (History of world-conquering Nader) written by Mirza Mehdi Khan Astarabadi, one of Nader's official historians.[20]

An oil-on-canvas painting now housed at the Museum of the Sa'adatabad Palace in Tehran is even more revealing of the Naderi manner of conferring kingship. The painting depicts Nader Shah wearing his distinctive four-corner crown-hat with the other famous Mughal diamond, Darya-ye Nur (Sea of Light) set at its center, placing a smaller version of the crown on the head of Reza Qoli Mirza (later blinded by Nader Shah) in the company of his other sons and a mulla (the religious authority who used to "crown" Safavid shahs), in a ceremony of investiture whereby his son was to become Crown Prince. The painting by Abolhassan is dated to 1774, confirming furthermore the longevity and appeal of Nader's Indian-inspired ceremonials and accoutrements of kingship well after his death and the loss of power by his successors.

The length limits of this chapter and its focus on Kalat-e Naderi do not allow deeper analyses of all the visual clues to the changing paradigm of kingship in this pivotal moment in Iranian history or to the semantics of rule as projected through the charisma of objects, ceremonials, and pictorial reiteration of imperial aspirations. Nor is there enough space here to discuss the purposeful dispatch of gifts by Nader to his rivals and especially to the Ottoman court.[21] Some of the most spectacular gem-studded objects and furnishings plundered from Delhi were sent as royal gifts to the Ottoman Sultan Mahmud I (1730–1754), are now housed in the Topkapı Treasury, and were dispatched to appease the Ottomans.

In connection with the Ottoman threats, Nader Shah had already declared the Ja'fari school of thought and jurisprudence, predicated on Ja'far al-Sadiq (702–765), the sixth Shi'i Imam, as a more Sunni-friendly substitution to Safavid Twelver/Imami Shi'ism, as it was bringing together the devotional practices of the two: the Sunni veneration of the first four caliphs with the Twelver/Imami Shi'i devotion to the direct descendants of the Prophet, the *ahl al-beit*—Muhammad, his daughter Fatima, and the Twelve Imams.[22] Nader's motivations were multifaceted, as Tucker has argued, and included a strong desire to benefit from the economic vitality of the Shi'i shrines in Iraq as well as from the holy pilgrimage sites and *hajj* income in Arabia, which were under

Ottoman rule. Visual and material-cultural reverberations of this important shift in religio-political terms have been little-studied, but research on a distinctive type of amulets shows the way toward greater potential for understanding the complexity of the cultural fabric of the Naderi period. Sheila Blair has studied such objects of personal devotion as the carved carnelian amulet in the Walters Art Museum, dated 1748, noting the distinctive epigraphic content and the density of carved inscriptions.[23] On the amulet, the fusion of the names of the Four Rightful Caliphs (Sunni) and the Fourteen Infallibles (Shi'i) is discussed at great length; however, it is considered an imitation of Ottoman arts, in part on the assumption that Nader and his dynasty represented a failed episode in Iranian history. The earliest talismanic amulet of this complexity to come from Iran is indeed this dated example from the Naderi period; its highly praised techno-artistic quality must also be considered as an indicator of the underlying motivations and complexity of the politico-religious calculations that instantiated its making.

What seems in need of emphasis is that the entire artistic production of this period and especially objects connected with Nader Shah himself should be reinterpreted in light of a deliberate strategy of inclusion, an ecumenical approach toward desirable and highly complex hybridizations that are not sought after because of the weakness of "local" talent or the ineptitude of patrons but because they bring the elements of an "empire" together, representing its diverse and exotic constituent parts. In this too, Timur is Nader's role model.

Kalat-e Naderi, Nader Shah, and Timur

Nader Shah's achievement remains principally tied up with his rapid and enormously successful military ventures—securing territories in the face of Ottoman and Russian incursions, installing himself as the sole authority in a post-Safavid chaos amidst inept contenders, and indeed skillfully carrying out the hugely important invasion of northern India. The Indian campaign had indeed all the hallmarks of a world-conquering ambition, albeit abandoned prematurely.[24] In a brilliant counterfactual writing of history, Sanjay Subrahmanyam has taken Nader's shattering of the Mughals and his puzzling withdrawal afterwards as scene-setting events leading up to conditions that ripened into the eventual rise of the British Raj as the colonizer par excellence of South Asia.[25] However, the point here is not whether an Indo-Persian empire was indeed possible under Nader Shah's authority but the fact that the historical run-up to and aftermath of the conquest of India and Delhi point to just such a vision. "Visions" are too difficult to grasp in the retrospective light of history, but their reverberations tend to be concretized in the physicality of material culture, art, and architecture.

Despite Nader's reputation as a warrior and not a builder, Kalat-e Naderi was not the only construction initiated by him. With the exception of Kalat, all that we know of his building patronage is through textual sources: he had several major works done in Mashhad; had built a domed structure in celebration of his birthplace near Darra Gaz in Khurasan, which was called Moludkhana (birth place); had ordered the foundation of the brand-new cities of Naderabad (city of Nader), outside Qandahar, after the old city was leveled, and Fathabad (city of victory) in Daghestan.[26] Most interesting, however, for its relevance to the Kalat project is Nader's order to remove and bring to him the dark-green jade cover of Timur's sarcophagus from his burial place at the Gur-e Amir in Samarqand; it was given in 1740, after Nader's return from Delhi. The stone was broken in half when it reached Nader in Mashhad, and it was soon returned to Samarqand. But the very demand for a physical "piece" from Timur is not simply a matter of vanity or madness. Rather, it serves as one among many such gestures toward Timur as the world-conqueror to whose rank Nader had aspired. As Ernest Tucker has suggested, the inscription on the rock-face inside one of the entrances into the Kalat fortress-city celebrates Nader as "associated with the hearth of Timur," a panegyric that further illustrates Nader's focus on the site and the invocation of the memory of Timur.[27]

Timur loomed especially large in relation to Kalat. The historian Marvi recounts an elaborate dreamlike encounter Nader experienced during a hunting expedition, when a fire-breathing dragon appeared guarding a pit where Nader was to find Timur's treasures along with a tablet upon which was inscribed "advice" from Timur to whoever finds his *ganjina*.[28] The significance of such dream sequences in constructing political authority and claims to legitimacy are not unique or surprising, but the fact that Nader's historian implies the link between Kalat, the hidden treasury, and the treasury of advice on rulership from Timur to Nader is extraordinary, especially since all this precedes the conquest of India and the building campaign in Kalat. As Axworthy has noted, the idea of Timur as the role model for Nader may have issued from the fact that Timur had in 1382 captured Kalat and had made it one of his own fortresses.[29]

In light of such connections drawn with Timur, could it be that Kalat was chosen for the construction of a city and especially a pavilion in order to host Nader's Indian loot as a treasury? On the one hand, the building's function as a mausoleum for Nader, as suggested by many, while reasonable, seems nevertheless to be limiting other possible functions—given that the evidence is not entirely convincing.[30] On the other hand, there is evidence of a great deal of dispersal of the Indian loot, including massive donations to the Shrine of Imam Reza in Mashhad, Nader's capital.[31] Regardless, the point here is not whether the building was intended as Nader's resting place, a pleasure pavilion, or a treasury. Rather, the strangeness of the structure calls for thinking more flexibly about Nader's patronage and his potential intentions and indeed allowing for all those functions to have been part of Nader's intention.

Turning to the awkward joining of two very distinct architectural volumes of differing conceptions of monumentality, the immediate verdict is that they are also mismatched in their scale, style, and architectural compositions and decorative strategies. As already noted in the description of the building above, the cylindrical tower is most striking. The only comparable building to my knowledge is in Delhi, the base of the unfinished 1316 minaret, known as the Alai Minaret, which stands as a "stump" in the second courtyard of the first congregational mosque of Delhi, the Quwwat al-Islam (Figure 12.8).[32]

It must be assumed that Nader had seen the Quwwat al-Islam, although no written evidence can support this. Notwithstanding the significant addition of an imperial Friday mosque by Shah Jahan in the 1630s, the Quwwat al-Islam stood for Delhi as a symbol of the victorious Ghurid conquest of northern India by Muslims and the defeat of the Rajput kings in the late 12th and early 13th centuries. The mosque's original layout and some of its signature features (stone screens, for example) further served as models for additions and expansions by succeeding Sultanate dynasties, of which the 14th-century unfinished minaret of Sultan Ala al-Din Khalji (1296–1316) attempted to surpass the gigantic

Figure 12.8. Delhi, India, Quwwat al-Islam Mosque, view of the Alai Minaret, left unfinished in 1316. (© dbimages/Alamy.)

Qutb Minaret of the mosque's original building phase. The shape and perhaps symbolic weight of that minaret—be it the original Qutb or the unfinished Alai one—suggest an implicit link, a desire to draw from earlier stamps of conquest on Delhi while also preserving and disseminating through a tangible and legible form the memory of Nader's sovereignty over the city. Although more can be said about such parallels drawn from revered monuments and sites—for instance the fluting of the dome on a tall cylindrical drum that crowns the burial chamber at the Gur-e Amir—the closest visual recall remains that of the Alai Minaret.

Kalat's formal and indeed monumental hybridity further signals not one but multiple parallels drawn through architecture between Nader and Timur, and it does so through the shared heritage of conquest—especially of Delhi. Timur's capture of Delhi in 1398, according to Sharaf al-Din Yazdi, Timur's historian, was followed by the transfer of some 400–480 marble columns from nearby quarries on the backs of 95 elephants.[33] These were to be used in the construction of the Great Mosque of Samarqand, which also celebrated in its very fabric the fruits of that victory. Timur's venture predated the arrival of the Mughals into Delhi and India by a century and half, but his name lent the Mughal dynasty its claim to legitimacy. By his conquest of Delhi, Nader in effect had ascended the same throne that had acquired its legitimacy through Timur. In other words, Nader, too, ascended the throne of Timur. Although this must have been a narrative largely invented by him and his historians, it is also worth noting that Indian pictorial representations of Nader, which are numerous and precede those made in Iran, also depict him as a member of the Mughal dynasty in the 18th century, if not central to the Mughal claim to authority.[34] The Indian adoption of Nader as king—surely a matter of great debate from the point of view of the Mughals—is nevertheless evidenced by the presence of at least one lavishly illustrated copy of Astarabadi's *(Tarikh-e) jahangosha-ye Naderi* that is made in northern India and bears the same date of 1171/1757–1758 as the one produced in Iran—both being the earliest illustrated copies of the text.[35]

To return to the Kalat monument once again, it is reported that the stone used for the sheathing of this building—itself an unusual method of surface treatment in the architecture of this region—was carted from the area of Maragha in northwestern Iran. While the material was thus sourced from another region of Iran, it must be clear that the intention was indeed to enwrap the building with the luxurious slabs of stone so distinctive of the Delhi monuments Nader must have seen. What Nader brought back from India, in addition to the 13,000 boxes of riches and the exotic and pack animals in the thousands, was a large number of craftsmen who could work that stone, and more. Nader's booty included hundreds of skilled people: one hundred and fifty scribes (*nevisanda*), two hundred steelworkers (*ahangar*), three hundred builders (*banna*), one hundred stone carvers (*sangtarash*), two hundred woodworkers (*najjar*).[36] Contemporary historians note that these people were set to work in various projects across his conquered territories. There is also a report, for instance, of Indian artisans having built a wooden pillared pavilion for Kalat from where the shah could enjoy the cool breezes!

The most compelling evidence for the presence of those Indian stone carvers in Kalat comes from the carved panels adorning some of the niches on the exterior of the pavilion (Figures 12.3 and 12.4). These panels evoke Mughal parallels in every respect: the subdivisions and juxtapositions of shallow niches, the general flavor of the carving style, with its display of a keen eye for observations of the natural phenomena, and a tendency to represent those motifs with a degree of realism and liveliness that is not encountered in Persian repertoire. These bring the stone cladding of the otherwise brick building in Kalat closer to the Mughal sources that Nader had encountered when he lodged himself at the Delhi Red Fort, albeit the carving may not be as high in skill and fluidity of conception as those of the Mughal palace.

Here then, Nader's capacity to command an imperial reach into India, where Timur had ventured centuries earlier, and his acquisition of the skills and riches of places he had conquered, as Timur had done before him; these concepts and postures of authority are foregrounded in the very fabric of the Kalat pavilion and in the display of the handiwork of the skilled Indian craftspeople. A final remark that must await full discussion in another place, is this: the remarkable carved stonework of Kalat introduces a novel idea for the early 18th century, when nothing like it had been seen in the arts in Iran for centuries. More importantly, the reappearance of stone relief in the 19th-century Qajar monuments, often attributed solely to the Qajar revivalist urge to look back at Sasanian symbols of kingship, seems seriously debatable in light of Nader's Kalat building campaign. One might suggest that while the themes of much Qajar relief carving aspired to Sasanian royal subjects, when decorative motifs were concerned—of which a large quantity can be found—Kalat's precedent and its skilled labor seem to be of greater significance than any other source. Reverberations of Naderi "style" are especially visible in the types of motifs and compositions—of vases, flowers, tabletops overloaded with fruit, and so forth—that have otherwise been called the Qajar Victoriana! Indeed, in rethinking Zand and Qajar repertoire of architectural decoration it can be said that they have more to do with India than with Europe, and Nader's Delhi loot is the key to this argument.[37]

Conclusion

Nader was the provocateur of a newly reformulated idea of warriorship, and this, I suggest, was modeled, conceptually, on the portrayal of an ancestral parallel deemed worthy of his ambitions. In that regard, India was indeed the strongest link through which Nader could align himself with the Mughal emperors and with the greatest of their ancestors, Timur. The portrait of Nader astride his horse in the pose of a warrior (Figure 12.5) is another of the pictorial evocations of a new posture of kingship. A king in a newly rescaled grandeur inspired by the conquered Mughals is entirely a product of that encounter and Mughal equestrian representations that properly fit into the category of portraiture are indeed the inspiration for those depicting Nader. As in the case of crowning and the new imperial regalia discussed above, this sort of visual alignment with India is not only suggested in Mughal images of Nader but, more importantly, in Nader's construction of a site worthy for displaying his lineage and his world-conquering ambitions.

Nader Shah's venture in India was cast here not as a madman's ambitious looting of rich treasures in a weak state but as part of an aspirational and deliberately programmatic imperial venture. His projects—buildings as much as motifs and styles of painting, carved panels, glazed tiles, strategies of gifting, ceremonial costumes, and practices—constituted the contours of a Naderi visual exoticism. I would also suggest that the agency of such visual strategies in the ideological formulations of empire, considered so central to the study of European colonial encounters, had in fact its precursor in this 18th-century Perso-Indian context. The articulation of the exotic in Nader Shah's building projects complicates the scholarly assumption that all non-West "mirrors" Europe in its rise to modernity, for which the 18th- to 19th-century rise of colonialisms is the benchmark. Aestheticized exoticism of colonial ventures, as understood since Napoleonic Egypt, have solicited little concern for, let alone scholarly attention to, any such enterprises outside the European ambit. Nader Shah's pre-Napoleonic encounters with an exotic "East" and his imperial expansionist designs have been ignored, and the possibility of any meaningful purchase for them in writing the history of 18th- and 19th-century arts of Iran, dismissed. A different and "empowered" understanding of the aesthetics of hybridization would articulate in Nader's patronage a visual representation of an imperial affront to the European, and especially English, expansion into Asia. This is material for further exploration but one hopes it will also challenge the history of the arts of post-Nader Iran to consider the deep imprint of Naderi "aesthetics."

Notes

1. I am grateful to Michael Axworthy for inviting me to contribute to this volume. The project from which this chapter derives began with a difficult journey I managed to arrange in the summer of 1994 with the kind support of the late Dr. Bagher Ayatollah-zadeh Shirazi, then the head of research at the Iranian Cultural Heritage Organization (ICHO). Two members of the Mashhad office of ICHO generously made this visit possible; I no longer have access to my notes from that trip to acknowledge them by name but remain most grateful to them. Conditions of a field trip in art historical research are rarely recounted, but here a brief is helpful, for it demonstrates the difficulty of access posed by Kalat even in our time. Despite it being in the summer, the journey took several hours and had to commence from Mashhad before dawn and be completed during the hours when the sun is up so that we could return from the Kalat before the roads were to freeze over. The then-still-unpaved surrounding of the building that I will discuss in this chapter was a thick rust-colored iron rich soil, which began to thaw into a sticky mud by late morning, a condition that made it difficult to walk on, as one's boots got stuck into its softened glue-like thickness. My memory of the day spent at Kalat, marked especially by the "sticky" ground that made looking at and photographing the pavilion so challenging, and by the kindness of the local keeper of the building, who invited me to his small room and offered me food and cups of tea, as well as the contrast between hardship of getting to Kalat and the respite experienced at the pavilion, bring to life the historical conditions that must have been as vivid as the building was in high noon on that day.
2. For the geographical location and historical references to Kalat prior to Nader Shah, see Xavier de Planhol, "Kalat-e Naderi," *Encyclopaedia Iranica*, accessed July 19, 2016, http://www.iranicaonline.org/articles/kalat-e-naderi.
3. The artistic and architectural landscape of the period of Nader Shah and his successors is not even mentioned in the volume of the *Cambridge History of Iran* devoted to the period from Nader Shah to the Islamic Republic of Iran, and not even in Jennifer Scarce's "The Arts of the Eighteenth to Twentieth Centuries" in Peter Avery, Gavin Hambly, and Charles Melville, eds., *Cambridge History of Iran*, volume 7, *From Nadir Shah to the Islamic Republic* (Cambridge: Cambridge University Press, 1991), 890–958. An equally problematic gap in the history of Iranian arts is found even in surveys purportedly more inclusive than any previously at hand; see chapter 12, "The Arts in Iran under the Safavids and Zands" and chapter 13, "Architecture in Iran under the Safavids and Zands," in Sheila S. Blair and Jonathan M. Bloom, *The Art and Architecture of Islam, 1250–1800* (New Haven and London: Yale University Press, 1994), 165–198. The exception is the work of Layla Diba, who has shed some light on painting of the Afshar period as a precursor, along with late-Safavid and Zand painting, for the main subject of her research, Qajar painting. See L. Diba with M. Ekhtiyar, eds., *Royal Persian Painting: The Qajar Epoch* (London: I. B. Tauris, 1998), 136–145.
4. I rely on the following two most important full-length studies on Nader Shah: Michael Axworthy, *The Sword of Persia: Nader Shah, from Tribal Warrior to Conquering Tyrant* (London: I. B. Tauris, 2006) and Ernst S. Tucker, *Nadir Shah's Quest for Legitimacy in Post-Safavid Iran* (Tallahassee: University Press of Florida, 2006). The assumption of Nader's madness and incompetent rule is summed up at the end of Rudi Matthee, *Persia in Crisis: Safavid Decline and the Fall of Isfahan* (London: I. B. Tauris, 2012), 255, where he notes that the long 18th-century chaos that unfurled after the Afghan invasion of the Safavid capital and the collapse of the dynasty was "exacerbated by the rapacious policies of Nadir Shah in the 1730s."
5. For Timur, see Beatrice F. Manz, *The Rise and Rule of Tamerlane* (Cambridge: Cambridge University Press, 1989).
6. Percy Molesworth Sykes, "A Fifth Journey in Persia (Continued)," *The Geographical Journal* 28/6, 1906, pp. 560–587.
7. For a description of the physical location of the Kalat and the inscription in full transcription, see Mohammad Reza Khusravi, *Kalat-i Nadiri*, in Persian (Mashhad: Mu'assasah-e chap-e Entesharat-e Astan-e Qods-e Razavi, 1988).
8. The most important historians of Nader Shah and the Afshars, also extensively studied by modern scholars, and especially relevant to this study are: Mohammad Kazem Marvi Yazdi,

Alam ara-ye Naderi, edited by Mohammad Amin Riyahi, 3 vols. (Tehran: Nashr-e Elm, 1369/1990), and Mirza Mohammad Mehdi Astarabadi, *Tarikh-e jahangoshay-e Naderi*; see footnote 20 below for the facsimile copy.

9. Giovanni Curatola, *Kalat-i Nadiri: Note sul "Barocco" indo-persiano* (Venice: Per l'Undici di Marzo, 1983). For Curatola's suggestion of an Indo-Persian Baroque, see the discussion below. See also Mohammad Reza Khusravi, *Kalat-i Nadiri*, and a picture book, Reza Nazar Ahari et al., *Pictorial Documents of Kalat-e Nadiri and Sarakhs: Asnad-e tasviri Kalat-e Naderi va Sarakhs*, in Persian (Tehran: The Foreign Ministry Publishing Department, 2013).

10. The literature on *hasht-behesht*-type buildings is vast. For the typology, see Michele Bernardini, "Hašt Behešt (2)," *Encyclopaedia Iranica*, accessed July 19, 2016, http://www.iranicaonline.org/articles/hast-behest-2. The building type has also lent its name to specific buildings, among which the most famous is the Safavid Hasht Behesht Palace in Isfahan; see Sussan Babaie, *Isfahan and Its Palaces: Statecraft, Shi'ism and the Architecture of Conviviality in Early Modern Iran* (Edinburgh: Edinburgh University Press, 2008), 31–34 for the pre- and early-Safavid examples and 198–206.

11. Old photographs show a much less "perfect" finish on the tower; the building has been restored at different times, including during my visit in 1994 when scaffoldings inside the building were raised in order to restore or secure the murals.

12. Detailed analyses of all the architectural and decorative features of the building will have to await another opportunity.

13. Melanie Michailidis, "In the Footsteps of the Sasanians: Funerary Architecture and Bavandid Legitimacy" in Sussan Babaie and Talinn Grigor, eds., *Persian Kingship and Architecture: Strategies of Power in Iran from the Achaemenids to the Pahlavis* (London: I. B. Tauris, 2015), 135–174.

14. Axworthy, *The Sword of Persia*, 212 among other places.

15. The famous enthroned portrait of Shah Jahan on the Peacock Throne is attributed to the great Mughal painter Govardhan and dated to *c*.1635; Harvard University Art Museums, Cambridge, MA.

16. For an Indian painting of Nader Shah wearing his crown and seated across from Mohammad Shah, now in Musée des Arts Asiatiques—Guimet, Paris, see William Dalrymple and Yuthika Sharma, eds., *Princes and Painters in Mughal Delhi, 1707–1857* (New Haven and London: Asia Society Museum and Yale University Press, 2012), 23, fig. 6. The painting, of tempera on paper, is dated to 1740, recording and reiterating the memory of Nader Shah on the Mughal throne. Nader's crown is much more elaborate in comparison to that worn by Mohammad Shah in this painting. See also the portrait by Bahram the painter, dated 1743–1744, now in the Hermitage; Adel Adamova, *Persian Manuscripts, Paintings and Drawings from the Hermitage Collection* (London: Azimuth Editions, 2012), 251, cat. 72.

17. The bejeweled turban of Shah Tahmasp in one of the murals at the Chehel Sotun Palace in Isfahan (mid-17th century) is the closest to the sort of extravagance seen in Nader's crown; see Sussan Babaie, *Isfahan and Its Palaces: Statecraft, Shi'ism and the Architecture of Conviviality in Early Modern Iran* (Edinburgh: Edinburgh University Press, 2008), especially plate 18. In contrast, see the large painting of Nader Shah (by Muhammad Sadiq, datable to the second half of the 18th century) shown astride a great horse leading his troops in battle and wearing his crown-hat; the painting is depicted on one of the central, large niches inside the audience hall of the Chehel Sotun Palace and occupies a space directly across the murals with Shah Tahmasp and Shah Abbas.

18. For some of these 18th–19th century images, see Hadi Seif, *Persian Painted Tile Work From the 18th and 19th Centuries: The Shiraz School* (Stuttgart, Arnoldsche Art Publishers, 2014).

19. See especially the important article by Layla Diba, "Images of Power and the Power of Images: Intention and Response in Early Qajar Painting (1785–1834)," in L. Diba with M. Ekhtiyar, eds., *Royal Persian Painting*, 30–49. The contrast between the Safavid habits and those of the Qajars is neither sufficiently underscored in scholarship nor really taken into consideration, with the Naderi period as key to the "gap."

20. For the facsimile copy of this illustrated history, see Mirzā Muhammad Mehdi Asterabadi, *Tarikh-e jahangoshay-e Naderi* (Tehran: Soroush Press and Negar Books, 1991).

234   CRISIS, COLLAPSE, MILITARISM AND CIVIL WAR

21. I thank Filiz Cakir Phillip for sharing with me information on the publication of the list of gifts in Selmin Kangal, ed., *Ten Thousand Years of Iranian Civilization: Two Thousand Years of Common Heritage*, Exhibition Catalogue, Topkapı Palace, 2009, 200–201, 304. Nader also sent Jewels to the Russian court, and some of these are still held in the Hermitage

22. Ernest Tucker, "Nadir Shah and the Ja'fari Madhhab Reconsidered," *Iranian Studies*, vol. 27, no. 1/4 (1994), 163–179. The significance of this hybrid creed and its political implications are discussed extensively in Tucker, *Nadir Shah's Quest for Legitimacy*, and in Axworthy, *The Sword of Persia*.

23. Sheila S. Blair, "An Amulet from Afsharid Iran," *The Journal of the Walters Art Museum*, vol. 59 (2001), 85–102.

24. For the invasion of Delhi and the puzzling retreat from the Mughal throne, see Axworthy, *The Sword of Persia*, esp. 175–215, and Tucker, *Nadir Shah's Quest for Legitimacy*, 59–77.

25. Sanjay Subrahmanyam, "*Un Grand Dérangement*: Dreaming of an Indo-Persian Empire in South Asia, 1740–1800," *Journal of Early Modern History* 4, 3–4 (2000), 337–378.

26. For the list of his constructions as culled from sources, see Axworthy, *The Sword of Persia*, 186, 227–228.

27. Tucker, *Nadir Shah's Quest for Legitimacy*, 70–71. The source is Marvi but the inscription may be dated after Nader's assassination in 1747.

28. Marvi, *Alam ara-ye Naderi*, 14–17.

29. Axworthy, *The Sword of Persia*, 57.

30. Most assuredly, this is discussed in Mohammad Hosein Qoddusi, *Nadernama* (Mashhad: Anjoman Asar Melli Khurasan, 1339/1960), 447–450. Axworthy also implies this as he discusses a "second mausoleum" in Mashhad. See also the German dissertation by Gita Ghassemi, *Das Bauwerk Kach-e Chorschid in Kalat-e Naderi (Nordost-Iran): Eine Studie zur Baugeschichte und die Beweisführung seiner ursprünglichen Nutzungsbestimmung als ein Mausoleum* (Berlin: Logos Verlag, 2007), which considers the building to be a mausoleum and not a palace or treasury.

31. Axworthy, *The Sword of Persia*, 228.

32. For an overview of the mosque and its parts, see Andreas Volwahsen and Henri Stierlin, eds., *Islamic India* (Cologne: Taschen Verlag, 1994), 13–19, 39–43; Catherine B. Asher, *Architecture of Mughal India* (Cambridge: Cambridge University Press, 1992), 2–9.

33. Discussions of Timur's building of the Great Mosque of Samarqand and the materials of construction brought back from India are found in Lisa Golombek and Donald Wilber, *The Timurid Architecture of Iran and Turan* (Princeton, NJ: Princeton University Press, 1988), especially 256–258.

34. The paintings have never been studied as a group and require further analysis. In addition to *Nader on the Peacock Throne* illustrated in Figure 6, see the painting in Musée des Arts Asiatiques—Guimet, noted in footnote 16 above, and the sensitively observed portrait of Nader Shah by a mid-18th-century Mughal artist in the Freer and Sackler Galleries of the Smithsonian Institution (F1907.256). An engraving with seven roundel portraits of Mughals includes the defeated Mohammad Shah and three of his successors surrounding Nader Shah at the center, evoking the images of the earlier Mughals who appear surrounding Timur. The sheet is a modern hand-colored steel engraving from the 1790s and on stylistic grounds is of northern Indian provenance. The image is found online, but unfortunately I have not been able to locate the source.

35. See footnote 20 above for the Iranian copy and Sotheby's, *Arts of the Islamic World*, London, April 20, 2016, 54–55, lot 57, for the Indian copy.

36. Jonas Hanway, *An Historical account of the British trade over the Caspian Sea*, 3rd edition (2 vols.) (London, 1762), vol. 2, 389.

37. Examples of motifs and styles of decoration in carved relief or tiles, for example, are found in the Narenjestan-e Qavam in Shiraz, datable to the second quarter of the 18th century and in the Madrasa of Ibrahim Khan in Kerman dated to 1824. Nader's legacy in architecture and decoration must have been more substantial had his other commissions—the mausoleum in Mashhad among them—survived.

INDEX

Page numbers followed by *t* or *f* indicate tables or figures. Numbers followed by n indicate notes.

242

INDEX

political system, 153, 155
relations with Russia, 164, 174–175
views from Central Europe of, 209n44
Zarinebaf-Shahr, Fariba, 39n43
Zoroastrians, 186

Zubov, V., 177
Zunuzi, ʿAbd Allah, 103n161
Zunuzi, Mirza Mohammad Hasan Hoseini,
78–79, 90